Diaspora Nationalism and Jewish Identity in Habsburg Galicia

The triumph of Zionism has clouded recollection of competing forms of Jewish nationalism vying for power a century ago. This study explores alternative ways to construct the modern Jewish nation. Jewish nationalism emerges from this book as a Diaspora phenomenon much broader than the Zionist movement. Like its non-Jewish counterparts, Jewish nationalism was first and foremost a movement to nationalize Jews, to construct a modern Jewish nation while simultaneously masking its very modernity. This book traces this process in Galicia, which was the second-largest Jewish community in Europe. The history of this vital but very much understudied community of Jews fills a critical gap in existing scholarship while revisiting the broader question of how Jewish nationalism – or indeed any modern nationalism – was born. Based on a wide variety of sources, many newly uncovered, this study challenges the still-dominant Zionist narrative by demonstrating that Jewish nationalism was a part of the rising nationalist movements in Europe.

Joshua Shanes is Associate Professor of Jewish Studies at the College of Charleston. His past awards include the Jacob Javits Fellowship, the Fulbright Fellowship, and awards from the National Foundation for Jewish Culture and the Memorial Foundation for Jewish Culture. He was also a Fellow at the Center for Advanced Judaic Studies at the University of Pennsylvania and a Fellow of the International Forum of Young Scholars on East European Jewry. He has published widely on Jewish cultural and political history in such journals as *Jewish Social Studies, Nations and Nationalism, Polin, Austrian History Yearbook,* and the *YIVO Encyclopedia of Jews in Eastern Europe.*

Diaspora Nationalism and Jewish Identity in Habsburg Galicia

JOSHUA SHANES

CAMBRIDGE UNIVERSITY PRESS

CAMBRIDGE UNIVERSITY PRESS
Cambridge, New York, Melbourne, Madrid, Cape Town,
Singapore, São Paulo, Delhi, Mexico City

Cambridge University Press
32 Avenue of the Americas, New York, NY 10013-2473, USA

www.cambridge.org
Information on this title: www.cambridge.org/9781107014244

First published 2012

Printed in the United States of America

A catalog record for this publication is available from the British Library.

Library of Congress Cataloging in Publication data
Shanes, Joshua, 1971–
    Diaspora nationalism and Jewish identity in Habsburg Galicia / Joshua
Shanes.
        p.   cm.
    Includes bibliographical references and index.
    ISBN 978-1-107-01424-4
    1. Jews – Galicia (Poland and Ukraine) – History – 18th century.   2. Jews –
Galicia (Poland and Ukraine) – History – 19th century.   3. Jews – Galicia (Poland
and Ukraine) – History – 20th century.   4. Zionism – Galicia (Poland and
Ukraine)   5. Nationalism – Galicia (Poland and Ukraine)   6. Galicia (Poland
and Ukraine) – Politics and government – 18th century.   7. Galicia (Poland and
Ukraine) – Politics and government – 19th century.   8. Galicia (Poland and Ukraine) –
Politics and government – 20th century.   9. Galicia (Poland and Ukraine) – Ethnic
relations.   I. Title.
    DS134.66.G35S53   2012
    305.892′40438609034–dc23   2011039451

ISBN 978-1-107-01424-4 Hardback

To my parents, with all of my love.

Come now, Joseph nudged himself, we are getting rather like the Irish – or the Welsh who deplore that all cities on the isles haven't got names with fifteen consonants on a string. But then, nationalism is only comic in others – like being seasick or in love.

Arthur Koestler, Thieves in the Night (New York, 1946)

Contents

List of Illustrations

Acknowledgments

Innumerable individuals and organizations have made this book possible. It is my great pleasure to thank them now.

Generous federal funding through the Jacob Javits, FLAS, and Fulbright fellowships made my initial research possible in Wisconsin and Vienna. The George L. Mosse Graduate Exchange Program at the University of Wisconsin provided funds for my subsequent research and writing in Israel. I would like particularly to thank John Tortorice for his support during that time. I also received generous support from the Memorial Foundation for Jewish Culture; the National Foundation for Jewish Culture; the Center for Advanced Judaic Studies at the University of Pennsylvania; and the School of Languages, Cultures and World Affairs at the College of Charleston, my current home. I am grateful to all of them.

Many colleagues and mentors have read all or part of this manuscript and made countless suggestions to improve it. David Sorkin served as a model dissertation advisor, and now cherished colleague, whose quick and detailed editing was the envy of my peers. Alison Frank and Rudy Koshar, the other members of my dissertation committee, greatly improved the text that became the core of this book. I am especially grateful to Professor Frank for her continued interest in my progress and her suggestions for the manuscript as it evolved into its present version. I would also like to thank Maria Kovac, whose course on Diaspora nationalism during my first year of graduate school piqued my interest in this phenomenon generally and in East Central Europe in particular. Marsha Rozenblit and Hugo Lane both read the entire manuscript during one of its early manifestations, and it greatly benefited from their comments. Yohanan Petrovsky-Shtern has likewise read the entire manuscript, made numerous contributions to it, and has been a cherished mentor, colleague, and friend over the past decade. Harald Binder, with whom I enjoyed countless hours in the basement of the Österreichische Nationalbibliothek, served as an encyclopedic resource on all things Galician. In Jerusalem, I benefited from conversations with Ezra Mendelsohn, the late Jonathan Frankel, Rachel Manekin, and Israel Bartal, whose own view of Jewish national construction parallels very much the argument presented here. Jeremy King offered theoretical suggestions on my introduction and generously shared a draft of an unpublished article. David Birnbaum, Nathan Birnbaum's grandson, shared a number of important artifacts from the Nathan and Solomon Birnbaum archives in Toronto, most importantly, the photograph that graces this book's cover. I thank him for his generosity. Paul Magocsi generously gave permission to reprint his map of Galicia. Lew Bateman and the anonymous readers and editors at Cambridge University Press shepherded my rough manuscript into its current form, for which I am extremely grateful. Earlier versions of some of these pages appeared in *Polin* 16 (2003): 167–87; *Austrian History Yearbook* 34 (2003): 191–213; *Studies in Jewish Civilization* 16 (2005): 285–96; and *Nationalism, Zionism, and Ethnic Mobilization of the Jews in 1900 and Beyond*, edited by Michael Berkowitz (Leiden: Brill, 2004): 153–78. I thank those publishers for their permission to include this material. Finally, my colleagues at the College of Charleston have provided a wonderful environment in which to teach and write. I particularly thank Adam Mendelsohn, who is always willing to lend a critical eye to any writing I share. Of course, any remaining faults are my responsibility alone.

A large portion of my life these last dozen years has been devoted to raising my three magnificent children: Brocha, Levi Yitzchak, and Rosa. Their humor, love, and accomplishments have been a tremendous source of blessing and joy for me. They are each blessed with unique talents and personalities, and I cherish every moment spent with them. I am so proud of all of you.

Finally, I dedicate this book to my parents. No words suffice to express the extent of my love and gratitude for all they have done for me. Certainly this book could never have been completed but for their sacrifice and support. They are model human beings who continuously demonstrate what it means to be givers and not takers, and model Jews whose joy in all things Jewish, and whose sacrifice to raise Jewish children and grandchildren, have taught me to take Jewishness seriously. You are my greatest role models. Thank you.

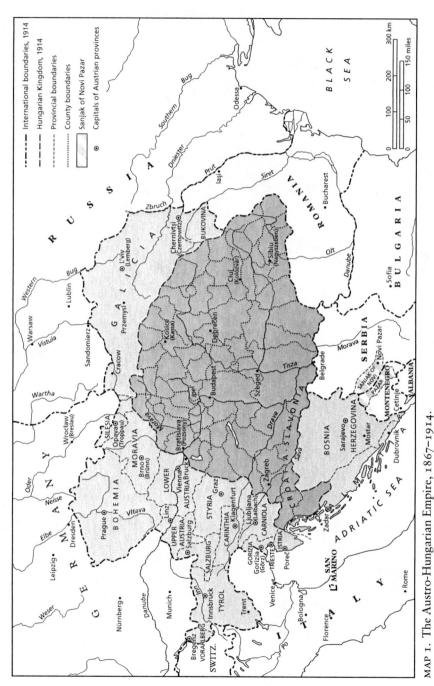

MAP I. The Austro-Hungarian Empire, 1867–1914.
Source: Paul Robert Magocsi, *Historical Atlas of East Central Europe* (Seattle: University of Washington Press, 1993), p. 81.

xiii

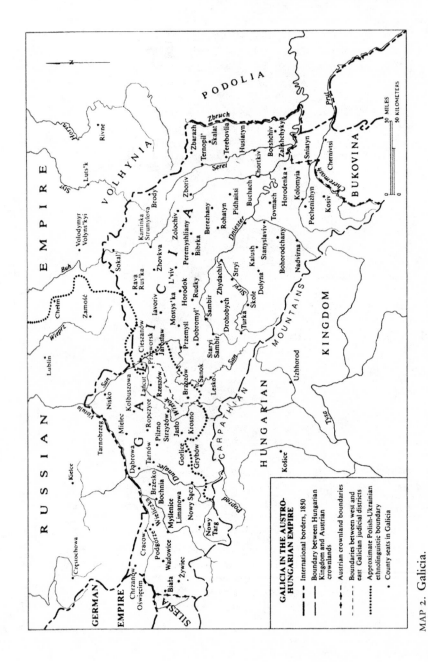

MAP 2. Galicia.

Source: Map prepared by Paul R. Magocsi. Reprinted with permission.

Introduction

This study explores the process by which nationhood became the key category of Jewish self-understanding in Galicia.[1] It sheds new light on the nature and development of Jewish nationalism beyond the Zionist movement by examining how a Diaspora Jewish nationalism came to dominate the entire spectrum of Jewish politics by the beginning of the twentieth century. Despite having been fully emancipated since 1867, most Jews in Galicia remained for years largely unpoliticized, unfamiliar – like many residents of East Central Europe – with notions of "assimilation" or "nationality."[2] By 1914, Galician Jews had grown considerably more aware of their political power and how to wield it, and most agreed that the Jews in fact constituted one of the nationalities of the Habsburg Empire that deserved national rights.

Zionism was a part of the rising nationalist movements in Europe and not simply a reaction to them. As nationalist assumptions increasingly shaped the terms of political discourse in Galicia, increasing numbers of Jews there absorbed these ideas, which guided their cultural and political choices. More and more Jews imagined themselves members of a Jewish national community. Other options were available. Notions of Jewish identity grounded in religion or ethnicity, identification with the Austrian state and/or with another nationality, persisted throughout this

---

[1] I use the term *self-understanding* rather than *identity* to avoid the problems of ambiguity and reification suggested by the latter. See Rogers Brubaker and Frederick Cooper, "Beyond Identity," in Brubaker, *Ethnicity without Groups* (Cambridge, Mass., 2004), 44–6. Later uses of the term *identity* should be read with this perspective in mind.

[2] Jeremy King, "The Nationalization of East Central Europe: Ethnicism, Ethnicity, and Beyond," in *Staging the Past* (West Lafayette, Indiana, 2001), 112.

period alongside multiple forms of Jewish national identity.[3] Nationalist intellectuals, aware of the wide variety of modern identities affecting their potential constituents, struggled to convert uncommitted souls to their camp. In the process, their definition of the nation itself – its symbols, membership, and political program – evolved. This mirrored similar developments among the Jews' Galician neighbors.[4] Indeed, Jewish, Polish, and Ukrainian nationalism developed not only parallel to one another but in constant conversation and cross-fertilization with each other.[5] All three communities similarly possessed potential national components but only late in the nineteenth century developed a widespread consciousness of nationhood. Jewish national identities were thus both modern and constructed; they did not represent the inevitable discovery of an existential truth, as Zionist historians have typically suggested.

A case study of the Jewish nationalist movement in Galicia offers numerous advantages. Galician Jewry constituted one of the largest Jewish communities in the world before the First World War, yet it has attracted very little scholarship.[6] The Kingdom of Galicia and Lodomeria

---

[3] Marsha Rozenblit has demonstrated the tendency of Habsburg Jewry to espouse a "tripartite" identity: Austrian politically, German (or Czech or Polish) culturally, and Jewish ethnically. This last part constituted a spectrum that ranged from religious ties to political nationalism, which she argued was held only by a minority of Jews. While this multilayered identity obtained in Galicia as well, by 1907 most Galician Jews – in contrast to those in other parts of Cisleithanian Austria – did embrace political nationalism and demanded their rights accordingly. Marsha Rozenblit, "Sustaining Austrian 'National' Identity in Crisis: The Dilemma of the Jews in Habsburg Austria, 1914–1919," in Pieter Judson and Marsha Rozenblit, eds., *Constructing Nationalities in East Central Europe* (New York, 2005), 178–80, and M. Rozenblit, *Reconstructing a National Identity: The Jews of Habsburg Austria during World War I* (Oxford, 2001).

[4] Keely Stauter-Halsted, *The Nation in the Village: The Genesis of Peasant National Identity in Austrian Poland, 1848–1914* (Ithaca, 2001), 4.

[5] Kai Struve, "Gentry, Jews, and Peasants: Jews as Others in the Formation of the Modern Polish Nation in Rural Galicia during the Second Half of the Nineteenth Century," in Nancy Wingfield, ed., *Creating the Other: Ethnic Conflict and Nationalism in Habsburg Central Europe* (New York, 2003), 103–26.

[6] For example, Marsha Rozenblit's 1992 review of literature on Habsburg Jewry skips over Galicia completely, a problem which she herself recognized. Marsha Rozenblit, "The Jews of the Dual Monarchy," *Austrian History Yearbook*, 23 (1992): 160–80. The lacuna is most obvious in William McCagg's *A History of Habsburg Jews, 1670–1918* (Bloomington, 1989); McCagg's entire thesis of Jewish national "self-denial" rests on labeling Galician Jews, two thirds of Cisleithanian Jewry, an exception to the rule. An important corrective to this gap is Israel Bartal and Antony Polonsky, eds., "Focusing on Galicia: Jews, Poles and Ukrainians 1772–1918," *Polin* 12 (1999), and particularly the recent work of Rachel Manekin. See also Piotr Wróbel, "The Jews of Galicia under Austrian-Polish Rule, 1869–1918," *Austrian History Yearbook*, 25 (1994): 97–138. Post-Habsburg Galician Jewry, especially in the period of the Holocaust, has received more

(a province of the Habsburg Empire, now part of Poland and Ukraine) was home to nearly 900,000 Jews by 1910, constituting about 11 percent of the area's total population.[7] Moreover, as a disproportionately urban population, Jews comprised over a quarter of the province's two major cities (Lemberg and Cracow) and formed either a majority or plurality in dozens of smaller towns and cities, particularly in the eastern half of the province.[8] Jews spoke their own language (Yiddish), practiced a different, largely endogamous religion (Judaism) whose rituals served as barriers to integration, and performed a unique economic role (overwhelmingly and disproportionately commercial) in a society in which language, religion, and occupation served as the key determinants of nationality. Jews also broadly shared a belief in several millennia of commonality, a bounded group favored by God. In short, although officially recognized only as a religious group by the Austrian authorities, Jews in Galicia in fact constituted a group economically and culturally distinct from their non-Jewish neighbors, much as they did in Russia.[9]

Unlike Jews in Tsarist Russia, however, Galician Jews since their emancipation in 1867 enjoyed wide-ranging civil and political rights more typical of Central and Western Europe.[10] Jews in Galicia, for example,

---

attention. See, for example, Shimon Redlich, *Together and Apart in Brzezany: Poles, Jews, and Ukrainians, 1919–1945* (Bloomington, 2002) and Omer Bartov, *Erased: Vanishing Traces of Jewish Galicia in Present-Day Ukraine* (Princeton, 2007) and the sources cited there.

[7] The remaining population was predominantly Polish (about 88%) west of the San River and Ruthenian (about 65%) east of the river, with a significant Polish minority (about 22%).

[8] In 1880, for example, Jews constituted 45.6 percent of the city residents and 48.1 percent of the town residents in Eastern Galicia. Max Rosenfeld, *Die polnische Judenfrage* (Vienna, 1918), 77.

[9] Stauter-Halsted, op. cit., 37. Jerzy Motylewicz emphasizes the foundations of *national* differentiation even before the nineteenth century, although his use of that term is anachronistic. "Jews, Poles, and Ruthenians formed the three basic national communities, each with its own religion, language, culture, and internal cohesion that defined the group's place in urban society.... The groups were partially segregated and sometimes concentrated in particular 'ethnic streets.' Their houses were also differentiated, both externally and internally, and this was linked closely to their occupational differentiation. The overall outcome of these manifold differences, above all religious and economic differences, was to provide a solid basis for the rivalries and antagonisms that manifested themselves with increasing vigor from the middle of the nineteenth century on." Jerzy Motylewicz, "Ethnic Communities of the Polish-Ukrainian Borderland," in *Galicia: A Multicultured Land* (Toronto, 2005), 48.

[10] In contrast to Western Europe, where emancipation was "marked more by continuity than by rupture," Jewish emancipation in the Habsburg Empire followed a Central European model, "comprehensive in scope and protracted in duration." David Sorkin, "Port Jews and the Three Regions of Emancipation," *Jewish Culture and History* 4.2 (Winter, 2001), 42. In the case of Galicia, the process lasted from 1789 until 1867. See Chapter 1.

enjoyed freedom of occupation, residence, and property ownership. In marked contrast to Russian Jewry, Galician Jews could publish relatively freely, vote and hold political office if their tax bracket allowed it, and hold public meetings in any language. Galician Jews, in fact, enjoyed a key legal advantage even over their Western counterparts. There existed the theoretical possibility of securing certain national rights, guaranteed to linguistic minorities in the Habsburg Empire after 1867. In practice, Jews were never recognized as constituting such a community.[11] Yet Jews still benefited from living in a multinational context in which, unlike in Western Europe, national pluralism was the norm and national minority movements flourished.

Galician Jews thus sat on the frontier between Eastern and Central Europe, religiously and economically similar to Russian Jewry, but legally more like their Western brethren.[12] As such, they present an ideal community in which to examine the process of nationalization. Polish, Ukrainian, and Jewish intellectuals attempted to mobilize their potential constituents behind competing political programs throughout divided Poland in the second half of the nineteenth century. Only in Galicia, however, were they relatively free to do so. The press operated without severe censorship, associational life expanded every year, and political enfranchisement provided opportunities for engagement and empowerment. Galicia's unique conditions led Paul Magocsi to locate the "roots of Ukrainian nationalism" in the province, dubbing it "Ukraine's Piedmont" in reference to the Italian province that led the unification of modern Italy. Keely Stauter-Halsted has argued the same regarding the development of

[11] See Gerald Stourzh, "Galten die Juden als Nationalität Altösterreichs?" *Studia Judaica Austriaca X* (1984): 73–98, and his larger work, *Die Gleichberechtigung der Nationalitäten in der Verfassung und Verwaltung Österreichs 1848–1918* (Vienna, 1985). See also Kurt Stillschweig's dated but important article, "Die nationalitätenrechtliche Stellung der Juden im alten Österreich," *Monatsschrift für Geschichte und Wissenschaft der Judentums* 81 (July–August 1937), 321–40.

[12] Israel Bartal perhaps overstates the case in writing that "Galician Jewry was no different from the rest of East European Jewry." Galician Jewry, for example, maintained a greater rural presence than in Russia or Posen. (36.6% of Galician Jews lived in small villages in 1897 compared to 18.1% of Russian Jews; Ben Zion Rubstein, *Galizia un ihr Bevölkerung* [Warsaw, 1923], 71.) Nevertheless, the basic point is correct. As Bartal notes, "The Jews of Galicia performed the same function in the ethnic and class structure of the surrounding society as did the Jews elsewhere in divided Poland. They constituted a distinct social class with their own religion and economic role in an environment in which every ethnic group possessed its own distinguishing economic features." Israel Bartal, "'The Heavenly City of Germany' and Absolutism a la Mode d'Autriche: The Rise of the Haskalah in Galicia," in Jacob Katz, ed., *Toward Modernity: The European Jewish Model* (New Brunswick, 1987), 34.

Polish nationalism.[13] Galicia served a similar function in the history of Jewish nationalism.

Yet Jewish historians have tended to overlook Galicia by focusing either on the numerically more significant Russian Jewry or on the other emancipated communities in Western and Central Europe. Most Zionist historiography has also under-emphasized the importance of this community, particularly in the pre-Herzlian period, by which time Galician Zionists could already boast a considerable degree of organizational infrastructure.[14] This neglect reflects the general historiographical trend overlooking this community but is also due to the unusual nature of Galician "Zionism." This was largely a Diaspora-oriented movement, directed primarily toward national cultural work in the Diaspora (i.e., building Jewish national consciousness) and the acquisition of national minority rights, long before Zionists in either Russia or the West had begun to engage in such activity.

Precisely because of its focus on "normal" nationalist activities such as the cultivation of Jewish national culture and the nationalization of Jewish identity, however, Galician Zionism offers an excellent opportunity for integrating the history of Jewish nationalism into its European context. A case study of Jewish nationalism in Galicia corrects past bias by scholars who, focusing primarily on Russia and Western Europe, have tended to emphasize the uniqueness of Zionism as a national movement. Jews, many point out, were not concentrated in a single territory, and Zionism ostensibly sought not the overthrow of foreign rule but rather the removal of its people to a foreign territory.[15] This view sees nationalism

---

[13] Paul Magocsi, *The Roots of Ukrainian Nationalism: Galicia as Ukraine's Piedmont* (Toronto, 2002); Stauter-Halsted, op. cit., 11–15.

[14] Characteristic of this trend is David Vital's *The Origins of Zionism* (Oxford, 1975), whose narrative moves geographically from Russia to the West, skipping over Galicia completely. Just two monographs have focused on Galician Zionism. Nathan Gelber's *Toldot ha-tenuah ha-tsiyonit be-Galitsyah, 1875–1918* (Jerusalem, 1958), although dated, remains the classic work on this subject. Gelber, born and raised in Galicia, is still that community's most important historian. However, his work is very affected by its Zionist agenda. One senses in it that Zionism is some hidden stream of history that Jews increasingly discovered, rather than a conscious choice that Jews increasingly made. Zionist chauvinism also leads him to focus primarily on the organizational history of the Zionist movement rather than understanding Jewish nationalism as constituting a range of ideas across the political spectrum. Adolf Gaisbauer's *Davidstern und Doppeladler* (Vienna, 1988), far more limited than Gelber due to its use of only German-language sources, similarly focuses on the organizational history of the movement and tends to ignore the critical issues of culture and identity that were at the heart of Zionist discourse.

[15] Arthur Hertzberg, for example, begins the introduction to his classic sourcebook as follows: "Zionism exists, and it has had important consequences, but historical theory

as essentially a state-seeking movement, an assumption which has of late been questioned.[16]

By seeing beyond the long-term territorial goals of Zionism and focusing instead on the processes that engendered and drove the movement, several scholars of Jewish nationalism have begun to integrate its history into broader models of nation formation, particularly those that consider the premodern roots of contemporary nations. Gideon Shimoni, for example, while recognizing the novelty of the Jewish nationalist movement, has resoundingly rejected postmodernist theory, with its emphasis on the "inventedness" of nations, at least as applied to the Jewish case.[17] Increasingly dissatisfied with, as Michael Stanislawski put it, "the school of thought whose Bible is Benedict Anderson's *Imagined Communities* and whose warring high priests have been Ernest Gellner and Eric Hobsbawm," many Jewish scholars prefer the model outlined by Anthony Smith. Smith acknowledges the role of modernization in sparking nationalist movements but stresses the importance of preexisting "*ethnie*" as the basic material out of which nations are formed.[18]

does not really know what to do with it.... The root cause of [the historians'] difficulty ... is that Zionism cannot be typed, and therefore easily explained, as a "normal" kind of national *risorgimento*. To mention only one important difference, all of the other nineteenth-century nationalisms based their struggle for political sovereignty on an already existing national land or language (generally, there were both). Zionism alone proposed to acquire both of these usual preconditions of national identity by the *élan* of its nationalist will. It is, therefore, a maverick in the history of modern nationalism." Arthur Hertzberg, *The Zionist Idea* (New York, 1959), 15. Jewish linguistic, cultural, and even religious disunity further undermined their claim to nationhood, although Eugen Weber and others have shown how such disunity plagued even the most "advanced" national cultures well into the nineteenth century. Eugen Weber, *Peasants into Frenchmen: The Modernization of Rural France 1870–1914* (London, 1979).

[16] Rogers Brubaker, "Myths and Misconceptions in the Study of Nationalism," in John Hall, ed., *The State of the Nation* (New York, 1998), 276–8. Brubaker indicates four examples of non-state-seeking nationalisms, including "the nationalism of national minorities," precisely the case here analyzed.

[17] Gideon Shimoni, *The Zionist Ideology* (Hanover, 1995), 4–51. Landmark works of the "postmodernist" perspective include Benedict Anderson, *Imagined Communities: Reflections on the Origin and Spread of Nationalism* (London, 1983); Eric Hobsbawm and Terence Ranger, *The Invention of Tradition* (Cambridge, 1983); and Eric Hobsbawm, *Nations and Nationalism since 1780* (Cambridge, 1990). For a thorough review and critique of modernist and postmodernist paradigms, see Anthony Smith, *Nationalism and Modernism: A Critical Survey of Recent Theories of Nations and Nationalism* (London, 1998), and A. Smith, *Myths and Memories of the Nation* (Oxford, 1999).

[18] See A. Smith, *Nationalism and Modernism*, 187–98, A. Smith, *The Nation in History: Historiographical Debates about Ethnicity and Nationalism* (Hanover, 2000), 52–77, and A. Smith, *The Ethnic Origins of Nations* (Oxford, 1986). To be sure, the so-called modernist scholars do not deny the cultural origins of modern nations. Ernest Gellner,

"Modern Jewish nationalism," concludes Stanislawski, "did not invent the Jewish nation, nor did the pre-nationalist notion of nationhood coincide with its later meaning."[19] Jewish nationalism, in other words, may have arisen out of a preexisting *ethnie*, but the transformation of Jewish "corporative" identity into Jewish nationalism was ultimately a function of the Jewish encounter with modernity and the "identity crisis" that this engendered.[20]

Shimoni especially emphasizes the role of the intelligentsia in affecting this transformation.[21] Estranged from past, primarily religious forms of Jewish identity, but unwilling or unable to integrate fully into non-Jewish national collectives, Jewish nationalism provided secular intellectuals with a solution to this existential angst. Intellectuals drew especially on deeply engrained, religious traditions of the Jewish *ethnie*. This reflects Anthony Smith's critique of the entire notion of "invented traditions." "The 'inventions' of modern nationalists," he writes, "must resonate with large numbers of the designated 'co-nationals,' otherwise the project will fail. If they are not perceived as 'authentic,' in the sense of having meaning

for example, followed his famous quip, "It is nationalism which engenders nations, and not the other way around," by noting that nationalism uses preexisting "cultural wealth." It would be a mistake to conclude, he writes, "that nationalism is a contingent, artificial, ideological invention, which might not have happened, if only those damned busy-body interfering European thinkers [had not imposed it upon us]." Gellner, op. cit., 55–6. The problem is not so much these scholars' denial of preexisting cultural building blocks but rather their explanation of their transformation. As Shimoni points out, they explain the emergence of national movements such as Zionism in terms of "economic displacement and social hostility (anti-Semitism)," but do not sufficiently consider the role of "collective ethnic consciousness" among Jews. Shimoni, op. cit., 8.

[19] Michael Stanislawski, *Zionism and the Fin de Siècle: Cosmopolitanism and Nationalism from Nordau to Jabotinsky* (Berkeley, 2001), xviii.

[20] Israel Bartal, *The Jews of Eastern Europe, 1772–1881* (Philadelphia, 2005), 13. On the role of identity crisis in the development of nationalist movements more generally, see Miroslav Hroch, *Social Preconditions of National Revival in Europe* (New York, 2000), xiv ff. For a critique of the notion of crises in Jewish history, see Benjamin Nathans, *Beyond the Pale* (Berkeley, 2002), 8–10.

[21] See also the now dated work of Miroslav Hroch, op. cit. Like Smith, Hroch emphasizes the necessity of "preconditions" for nationalist movements but is most interested in tracking the role of the intelligentsia in creating them. He delineates three phases of a successful national movement. First, intellectuals begin to explore the history and culture of their perceived nationality out of a purely "scholarly interest." This exploration then expands into a period of "patriotic agitation," which sometimes leads to the rise of a mass national movement. Hroch's study of the "smaller European nations" skips Jewish nationalism, despite his passing recognition that the Jews "only underwent assimilation in certain individual cases" (96). Elsewhere, however, Hroch argued against those who would exclude Zionism from comparative typologies. Hroch, "Zionismus als eine europäische Nationalbewegung," *Judentum und Christentum* 1 (2000): 33–40.

and resonance with 'the people' to whom they are addressed, they will fail
to mobilize them for political action."[22] Ironically, only by understanding
the unique building blocks that formed the Jewish nationalist movement
can one appreciate its similarities to other movements.[23]

To be sure, recent scholarship has questioned the distinction between
this "ethnicism" and outright "primordialism," the worldview – advocated
most of all by nationalists themselves – that assumes the premodern existence of nations. "Ethnicism," writes Jeremy King, "amounts to a more
subtle elaboration of primordialist errors," because it traces a direct line
between premodern ethnic groups and later nationalist manifestations.[24]
Even asserting the existence of bounded, ethnic groups before the rise of
nationalism is problematic, he argues, and reflects a teleological nationalist bias. "Ethnic groups are not national antecedents but national prod-
ucts," insists King. Rogers Brubaker has similarly criticized the tendency
of historians to reify nations and ethnic groups rather than viewing them
as contingent and shifting. "They are not things *in* the world, but perspectives *on* the world – not ontological but epistemological realities."[25]
Nevertheless, Jews in fact did manifest *groupness* (to use Brubaker's term)
in the prenational period. Pieter Judson, for example, emphasizes that Czech
nationalists focused on linguistic distinctiveness because "Czechs" and
"Germans" could not be differentiated by religion, class, or color.[26] Jews,
however, were distinguished by religion and class, as well as linguistically –
at least among the traditional masses. King himself – in the same passage
just cited – describes Bohemian Jews as having long constituted a "tightly
bounded community, its members ... defined consistently by multiple institutions and practices."[27] Keely Stauter-Halsted has likewise argued that

---

[22] Smith, *Nationalism and Modernism,* 198. Nationalists, he writes elsewhere, are more akin
to archaeologists selectively mining their nation's past for material than to chefs who are
inventing new dishes out of universal ingredients. Smith, "Gastronomy or Geology? The
Role of Nationalism in the Reconstruction of Nations," *Nations and Nationalism* 1, no. 1
(1995): 3–23. Hroch writes similarly, "Intellectuals can invent national communities only
if certain objective preconditions for the formation of a nation already exist." Hroch,
"From National Movements to the Fully-formed Nation: The Nation-building Process in
Europe," in Gopal Balakrishnan, ed., *Mapping the Nation* (London, 1996), 79.

[23] Smith makes this point specifically in regard to the Zionist case. See his "Zionism and
Diaspora Nationalism," *Israel Affairs* 2, no. 2 (Winter, 1995): 1–19. Brubaker also
acknowledges the benefit of "raw materials" in explaining the success of a nationalist
movement. Brubaker, *Ethnicity without Groups,* 14.

[24] Jeremy King, "The Nationalization of East Central Europe," 114.

[25] Brubaker, *Ethnicity without Groups,* 79.

[26] Pieter Judson, *Guardians of the Nation* (Cambridge, Mass., 2006), 21.

[27] Jeremy King, *Budweisers into Czechs and Germans* (Princeton, 2002), 7–8.

rural Polish Roman Catholics, Ukrainian Greek Catholics, and Jews living in close proximity to each other while sharing few cultural institutions, "encouraged the formation of group identity among co-religionists."[28]

This approach reflects the current direction of scholarship in Habsburg studies. In recent years, numerous scholars have analyzed the process by which nationalist intellectuals in the Habsburg Empire constructed their various communities, and not necessarily out of a single, clearly bounded ethnic group.[29] The popular paradigm of "construction," which implies that existing "materials" can be assembled in a variety of ways, suggests both the "ethnic origins of nations" as well as their modernity, belying nationalist teleologies that present nations as ontological realities, or at least as the inevitable product of history.

Unfortunately, little attempt has been made to consider the construction of a Jewish nationality.[30] Scholars still tend to understand Jewish nationalism as a reaction to anti-Semitism and the emergence of organic nationalist movements in Central and Eastern Europe rather than as parallel and coterminous with other nationalist movements as a result of the same forces. Shimoni and others, however, have successfully demonstrated how our understanding of Jewish nationalism can be broadened through the use of theoretical typologies, and equally, how these typologies can be enhanced through the study of Jewish nationalism.

[28] Stauter-Halsted, op. cit., 37. This Polish sense of Jewish "otherness," she writes, only grew toward the end of the century, as some Polish nationalist leaders used economic and cultural references to the Jews as foreigners to strengthen national identity among Polish peasants. Stauter-Halsted, op. cit., 42.

[29] See, for example, Jeremy King, *Budweisers into Czechs and Germans*; Keely Stauter-Halsted, op. cit.; John-Paul Himka, *Galician Villagers and the Ukrainian National Movement in the Nineteenth Century* (New York, 1988) and ibid, "The Construction of Nationality in Galician Rus': Icarian Flights in Almost All Directions," in Ronald Suny and Michael Kennedy, eds., *Intellectuals and the Articulation of the Nation* (Ann Arbor, 1999), 109–164; Pieter Judson, *Guardians of the Nation: Activists on the Language Frontiers of Imperial Austria* (Cambridge, Mass., 2006); Tara Zahra, *Kidnapped Souls: National Indifference and the Battle for Children in the Bohemian Lands, 1900–1948* (Ithaca, 2008). Recently, over a dozen of the empire's leading historians contributed to a volume entitled, *Constructing Nationalities in East Central Europe*. The theme of construction also runs through the essays in Nancy Wingfield, ed., *Creating the Other: Ethnic Conflict and Nationalism in Habsburg Central Europe*. Rashid Khalidi's classic study of Palestinian nationalism understands its subject in these terms as well. Rashid Khalidi, *Palestinian Identity: The Construction of Modern National Consciousness* (New York, 1997).

[30] Bartal's work, op. cit., is a critical exception. The original Hebrew title of his survey of East European Jewish history, *Me-umah le-leum* (From Corporation to Nation), emphasizes precisely this process. See also I. Bartal, "From Corporation to Nation: Jewish Autonomy in Eastern Europe, 1772–1881," *Jahrbuch des Simon-Dubnow-Instituts* 5 (2006): 17–31.

Like other nationalist movements, the "Zionist" movement in Galicia focused on nationalizing Jewish identity and securing national rights in the Diaspora. It provides an excellent example of how integrated into its European environment the Jewish nationalist movement truly was. It also addresses the problem of the Jews' anomalous demographic dispersion. Situated in the multinational Habsburg Empire, Galicia provides a context in which total territorial concentration was not a prerequisite for securing national rights. More important, it provides a context in which nationalist movements themselves did not necessarily demand full independence, that "the political and national unit should be congruent," but could be satisfied with a degree of national autonomy.[31]

In fact, by approaching Jewish nationalism as a cultural process rather than simply a political movement, one can incorporate even self-declared "assimilationists" into the narrative of Jewish national construction. One of the problems in dealing with Zionist sources, including Zionist historiography, is their tendency to dismiss opponents – many of whom subscribed to strong notions of Jewish collective identity – as assimilationist.[32] Part of the problem lies in the ambiguity of the terminology itself. Nineteenth-century Jewish activists who described themselves as assimilationist rarely meant that they advocated the total abandonment of their Jewish identity, what Todd Endelman has labeled "radical assimilation."[33] Most intended only the modernization of the Jews and their *integration* into non-Jewish society *as Jews*. Recent scholarship drawing on Milton Gordon's distinction between "acculturation," "integration," and "assimilation" is helpful in clarifying this misunderstanding.[34] As Jonathan Frankel put it, "the loss of linguistic and cultural distinctiveness is not seen [among modern scholars] as necessarily bringing with it a loss of collective identity."[35]

---

[31] Gellner, op. cit., 2. On Jewish Diaspora Nationalism in Austria, see David Rechter, "A Nationalism of Small Things: Jewish Autonomy in Late Habsburg Austria," *Leo Baeck Institute Yearbook* (2007): 87–109, and Gerald Stourzh, "Max Diamant and Jewish Diaspora Nationalism in the Bukovina," in *From Vienna to Chicago and Back* (Chicago, 2007), 190–203.

[32] Nathan Gelber, for example, consistently refers to the Zionists' integrationist opponents in this way.

[33] Todd Endelman, *Radical Assimilation in English Jewish History, 1656–1945* (Bloomington, 1990), 4.

[34] Stanislawski, op. cit., 7–9; Benjamin Nathans, *Beyond the Pale* (Berkeley, 2002), 11–12.

[35] Jonathan Frankel, "Assimilation and the Jews in Nineteenth-Century Europe: Towards a New Historiography?" in Jonathan Frankel and Steven Zipperstein, eds., *Assimilation and Community: The Jews in Nineteenth-Century Europe* (Cambridge, 1992), 22.

It is not simply that Jewish supporters of assimilation failed to achieve their goal. Rather, many so-called assimilationists openly supported the continuation of a Jewish identity. In fact, while many leading Zionists viewed the Jewish nationalist movement as a means by which to integrate Jews into secular European culture, many of their so-called assimilationist opponents were far more concerned with defending Jewish collective interests, economic and cultural, as they perceived them.[36] "Who is more assimilated," Vienna's Chief Rabbi Moritz Güdeman (1835–1918) reportedly asked, "the nationally minded Jew who ignores the Sabbath, or the observant Jew who feels himself to be a German?"[37]

This study takes issue with the conventional distinction between self-described "Zionists" and other Jewish nationalists.[38] Scholars typically define "Zionism" as representing one variety of Jewish nationalist vision, namely, a territorial solution in Palestine, in contrast to "Diaspora Nationalists" who sought national rights in Europe. While there is some truth to this division, in light of the focus of self-described Zionists in Galicia (and elsewhere) on raising Jewish national consciousness among Galician Jews, the distinction is problematic. In contrast, this analysis emphasizes the interconnectedness and fluidity of all Jewish ideologies and political movements.[39] Jewish nationalism must be seen as part of a broader political discourse, in which the question of Jewish nationhood assumed an increasingly important role. Beyond Zionism, the rubric of "Jewish nationalism" must be expanded to include non-Zionist nationalist ideologies, including socialist nationalism in its many varieties, as well as those which viewed Jews collectively but denied that the Jews constituted a modern nation. In short, Jewish nationalism was an umbrella term for a wide variety of cultural and political ideologies. At its core, it must be understood as a movement designed to strengthen Jewish ethnic pride and identity, and ultimately to organize Jews politically *as Jews*, self-conscious people of a modern nation. Consequently, this study considers the social and cultural history of Jewish nationalism in Galicia, rather than focusing exclusively on its organizational dimension.

[36] Stanislawski, op. cit., passim. Adolf Stand, one of the most important Zionist leaders in Galicia, similarly turned to Zionism as a means of transforming Polish romantic nationalism into a Jewish context. See Eugenia Prokop-Janiec, "Jewish *moderna* in Galicia," *Gal-Ed* 14 (1995): 27–38.

[37] Josef Fraenkel, "The Chief Rabbi and the Visionary," in *The Jews of Austria* (London, 1967), 114.

[38] This study uses the term *Zionist* to indicate members of a self-described Zionist organization, whatever that group's actual agenda.

[39] See Jonathan Frankel, *Prophecy and Politics: Socialism, Nationalism, and the Russian Jews, 1862–1917* (Cambridge, 1981).

This work is divided into five chapters. The first brings the reader into the Galician context, providing an overview of the period between the annexation (and thus creation) of Galicia by the Habsburg Empire in 1772 and the aftermath of Jewish emancipation achieved as part of the restructuring of the empire in 1867. During this period, Galician Jewry confronted a program of Germanization by the new ruling regime, which particularly affected members of the elite in certain major cities, especially Lemberg, Brody, and Tarnopol. The rise of middle-class associational life led to the formation of a Liberal Jewish society as well as politicized "Orthodox" leaders opposed to them.[40] Following their emancipation, both Liberal Jewish leaders and their Orthodox opponents launched political parties and organs to defend their respective interests. Signs of politicization among the traditional Jewish masses, however, were not yet widely manifest.

Chapter 2 describes the emergence and activities of the province's first Jewish nationalist associations. These groups differed from the better known Russian Chovevei Zion societies in relegating the dream of a national home in Palestine to the distant future and concentrating on Jewish life in the Diaspora. They emerged less as a result of anti-Semitism than out of a growing ethnic pride among integrated Jews, as well as the broader context of exploding associational life in the empire. Like their Ruthenian and Polish counterparts, they at first sponsored primarily cultural activities such as history lessons and holiday celebrations designed to nurture Jewish pride. Yet by building consciousness of national historical roots, by creating a new type of Jewish public sphere, these activities laid the foundation of a Jewish national movement.

Activists in this early period focused their efforts on recruiting the secular intelligentsia, by now largely Polonized. They attracted not only thoroughly Polonized Jews, however, but also Jewish elites raised in a religious milieu who were drawn to secular culture. Jewish nationalism provided what to them seemed an authentic identity at once Jewish and modern. These intellectuals played a critical role in transmitting Jewish nationalist ideas to the traditional masses by developing Yiddish-language propaganda saturated with religious symbolism appropriated for the nationalist movement.

Chapter 3, "Building a Nation of Readers," analyzes the first major effort at reaching out to traditional Jews through new media, a revolutionary series of Yiddish-language populist newspapers, virtually ignored

---

[40] Pieter Judson, *Exclusive Revolutionaries* (Ann Arbor, 1996), 18 ff.

by scholars, which Zionists and others began producing as early as 1890. These newspapers were designed to convince traditional Jews not only that the Jews constituted a nation but that they needed to become politically active to win the same rights as other nations in the empire. The papers were analogous to the Polish peasant press, which was developing at roughly the same time – using many of the same strategies – as part of the movement to nationalize Polish-speaking peasants. Jewish secular intellectuals had to refashion their nationalist rhetoric to fit it onto this new audience just as upper-class Polish nationalists negotiated new notions of the Polish nation as they brought their message to Polish-speaking peasants.[41] Like the Polish peasant press, the Yiddish papers claimed their authenticity not only linguistically but also religiously through the appropriation of religious norms which their readers shared. They expose the important distinction between "traditional" and "Orthodox" Jews, that is, self-conscious, politicized defenders of "Orthodoxy." While the latter generally rejected Zionism as heresy, many traditional Jews – though uncomfortable with outspoken attacks on the religious establishment – were willing to consider Jewish nationalist arguments based on religious rhetoric, particularly if focused on a domestic agenda.

Chapter 4 seeks to embed the Galician story in a larger Zionist narrative by tracking the history of the Jewish national movement during the short reign of Theodor Herzl. Galician Zionists largely flocked to his Zionist Organization at first, most of them briefly abandoning their previous preference for Diaspora work in favor of political Zionism. Although Zionism still remained a movement of the intelligentsia, at least as measured by its membership roles, it was during this period that Jewish nationalism began to penetrate into traditional communities throughout Galicia. Yiddish-language propaganda grew dominant, while synagogues and study houses emerged as important venues for Zionist events. This chapter recreates the environment in which Jewish national ideas spread among the masses based on a wide variety of sources including memoirs, newspapers (particularly letters to the editor), published speeches, and chapbooks. This activity was expanding rapidly by the turn of the century, precisely the moment in which scholars have identified the solidification of a sharply anti-Zionist position among the Orthodox, especially Hasidic leadership.[42] Critically, as Orthodox hostility toward

---

[41] Keely Stauter-Halsted, op. cit., 185–94, 3.

[42] Yosef Salmon, *Religion and Zionism: First Encounters* (Jerusalem, 2001), 306ff; Aviezer Ravitzky, *Messianism, Zionism, and Jewish Religious Radicalism* (Chicago, 1996), 14–19ff.

Zionism mounted, traditional Jews grew increasingly influenced by the Jewish national idea.

The final chapter focuses on the 1907 parliamentary elections, the first in Austria based upon universal manhood suffrage, which both completed and exposed the nationalization of Galician Jewry. Galician Zionists quickly returned to their Diaspora-oriented program of 1893 and entered the parliamentary election campaign full force. They even forged an electoral alliance with the major Ukrainian political faction, an episode of profound importance in the history of Ukrainian-Jewish relations which highlights the interactive development of Jewish and Ukrainian nationalisms. Jewish nationalists succeeded in electing four members to the Austrian Parliament, including one from Bukowina, forming the first Jewish faction in modern history. More important, the general atmosphere of mass mobilization provided an unprecedented opportunity for Zionists – and their opponents – to penetrate into the traditional, and often still politically immobilized Jewish masses. Extensive newspaper coverage, police reports, campaign materials, parliamentary speeches, memoirs, and even fictional literature based on that year testify to the intense political activity of those months and the widespread participation of Galician Jewry in the campaigns. The election highlighted how Jewish nationalism had come to redefine the entire spectrum of Jewish political discourse. By 1907, no candidate or party could approach the Jewish electorate without some program of collective rights, usually presented as *national* rights.

This study presents the development of the Jewish national idea across the political and cultural spectrum. It reframes the history of Jewish nationalism in Galicia as first and foremost a movement responding to widespread social dislocation among Galician Jews in the last decades of the nineteenth century.[43] Galician Jews, like their Ukrainian and Polish counterparts, experienced the collapse of extant forms of self-identification and sought to reestablish themselves as members of a broader community. In late nineteenth-century Europe, particularly in the Habsburg Empire, this increasingly meant a "national community." Although Zionists could claim few party members before 1914, by that

---

[43] Stephen Poppel makes the same argument about German Zionism. "Here, then, lay the real personal significance of Zionism for its adherents in Germany – not as the vehicle for fund raising, charitable work for the *Ostjuden*, or the promotion of *aliyah*, but as the source of a coherent, integrated, and compelling world view; in short, as the source of a viable and supportive identity." Stephen Poppel, *Zionism in Germany 1897–1933: The Shaping of a Jewish Identity* (Philadelphia, 1977), 92.

time most Jews in the province had come to accept a nationalist definition of their community and demanded political rights accordingly. This
is the story of how that happened.

A NOTE ON TRANSLATION

Any study of the Habsburg Empire must come to terms with the difficulty
that most cities are known, or have been known, by as many as four different names. In order to achieve some modicum of consistency, this study
employs the German names in nearly all cases. This is less in deference
to government sources than to the Jews themselves, whose Yiddish place
names usually resemble the German once transliterated into Latin characters. Thus we refer to the capital of Galicia as it was known by both
Yiddish- and German-speaking Jews, Lemberg, and not Lwów (Polish)
or L'viv (Ukrainian). The only exceptions will be those place names with
well-known English equivalents: Vienna, Cracow, and Galicia itself. The
spelling of the Orthodox party Machsike Hadas follows the masthead of
that group's newspaper.

This study follows John-Paul Himka and others in referring to the
Ukrainian-speaking residents of the empire as *Ruthenian*, a term to which
they themselves did not object in the nineteenth century.[44] Only in the
early twentieth century was the term gradually replaced by the preferred
Ukrainian, while use of the term *Ruthenian* grew to be a political statement that denied the connection between Ukrainian speakers on the two
sides of the Austrian-Russian border.[45] Although the Viennese *Ruthenische
Revue* was renamed the *Ukrainische Rundschau* in 1906, government
documents, Jewish sources, and Ukrainian-speakers themselves continued to use the former term throughout the period of this study.

All translations, unless otherwise noted, are my own.

---

[44] John-Paul Himka, *Religion and Nationality in Western Ukraine* (Montreal, 1999), 8–9.
[45] Alison Frank, *Oil Empire* (Cambridge, Mass., 2005), xvi.

Galician Jewry under Habsburg Rule

The First Century, 1772–1883

Galician Jews lived under Habsburg rule for more than a century before the emergence of an organized Jewish nationalist movement. During much of this period, Galician Jewry confronted a program of Germanization by the ruling regime, which particularly affected members of the elite in several major cities. The simultaneous rise of the Hasidic movement, among other factors, limited its impact on the Jewish masses. The revolutionary crises starting in 1846 contributed significantly to the politicization of Galician Jewry, particularly among members of the Liberal elite but also among a subset of traditional Jews as well. Neither element, however, saw their struggle in terms of "national" rights as did some of their Polish and Ruthenian counterparts. Following their emancipation in 1867, both Liberal Jewish leaders and their Orthodox opponents launched political parties and organs to defend their respective interests. The former initially supported German Liberalism, uniting with its supporters in a short-lived 1873 political alliance. With the growing Polonization of the province, however, Jewish elites were increasingly drawn to the Polish national camp. Signs of politicization among the traditional Jewish masses were not yet widely manifest.

GALICIAN JEWS CONFRONT HABSBURG GERMANIZATION

In 1772, Austria, Russia, and Prussia carried out the first of three partitions of Polish territory that would eventually lead, in 1795, to the total dissolution of the Polish state. Austria's portion, renamed the Kingdom of Galicia and Lodomeria, remained under Habsburg rule for nearly a century and a half, until the empire's disintegration in 1918. Galicia was the largest of the empire's Crownlands, or provinces. It extended over 31,600 square miles, constituting about one quarter of the Austrian part of the empire after the latter's division in 1867. Its population, despite the exodus of more than 2 million people in the twenty-five years before the First World War, grew from roughly 2.5 million at the time of the partitions to more than 8 million by 1914.[1] The province's inhabitants were divided (at least legally) mainly between three ethnolinguistic groups – Poles, Ruthenians, and Jews – although the first two are somewhat problematic terms.

Ruthenians were residents of the Habsburg Empire who spoke the language we would now call Ukrainian. They were defined not only by language but also by religion, being mostly adherents of the Greek Catholic, or Uniate Church (which practiced the Eastern Orthodox ritual but recognized the Roman Pope as its spiritual leader) as well as by occupation, constituting by-and-large a poor peasantry. *Poles* is also a problematic term, for the Polish nation historically referred only to the Polish nobility, less than 10 percent of the population of the old Polish-Lithuanian Commonwealth. Only in the mid-nineteenth century did the term increasingly denote an ethnolinguistic group and thus embrace the Polish-speaking peasants as well.[2]

Demographically, the province was divided between its eastern and western regions. In the area west of the San River, Poles (including Polish-speaking peasants who may not have considered themselves *Polish*) formed an overwhelming majority of the population and the Jews a significant minority, about 8 or 9 percent. East of the San, Polish elites constituted the political masters of the region, but not the numerical majority, which was Ruthenian (again, according to the census, not necessarily by self-identification). Galician Jews also settled disproportionately in the east, where about three quarters of them lived, constituting about 13 percent of the population. (See Table 1.1.) Jews were especially visible in the urban centers. Jews made up over a quarter of Galicia's two largest cities, Lemberg and Cracow, and formed either a majority or a plurality in many other Galician cities and towns, especially in the east. In 1880, for example, Jews constituted 45.6 percent of the city residents and 48.1 percent of the town residents in the eastern half of the province.[3] Nearly four

---

[1] Norman Davies, *God's Playground: A History of Poland* (New York, 1982), 147.

[2] Frank, *Oil Empire* (Cambridge, Mass., 2005), 40–3, and Stauter-Halsted, *The Nation in the Village: The Genesis of Peasant National Identity in Austrian Poland, 1848–1914* (Ithaca, 2001).

[3] Due to faster urbanization and lower rates of emigration among both Ruthenians and Poles, by 1910 these numbers had dropped to 38.5 percent and 42 percent, respectively.

TABLE I.I. *Jewish Population of Galicia 1869–1910*

	1880	1890	1900	1910
West Galicia	169,545	183,311	192,382	213,269
	(8.02%)	(7.96%)	(7.69%)	(7.92%)
East Galicia	517,051	585,534	618,801	659,706
	(13.44%)	(13.60%)	(12.85%)	(12.36%)
TOTAL	686,596	768,845	811,183	872,975
	(11.52%)	(11.63%)	(11.09%)	(10.86%)

Source: From Teresa Andlauer, *Die jüdische Bevölkerung im Modernisierungsprozess Galiziens (1867–1914)* (Frankfurt am Main, 2001), 39. The percentage of total population is from Max Rosenfeld, *Die polnische Judenfrage*, 72–80.

out of every five residents of Brody were Jewish, while six other cities saw absolute Jewish majorities (Buczacz, Zolkiew, Stanislau, Tarnopol, Kolomea, and Drohobycz). In the west the numbers were lower but still impressive, with Jews constituting about 34 percent of the city dwellers and 32.2 percent of the town dwellers in 1880.[4]

In addition to their urban concentration, the Jews' economic profile also continued to distinguish them from their non-Jewish neighbors throughout the Habsburg period. In 1900, for example, 86.3 percent of Christian workers labored in agriculture versus 17.7 percent of Jews. In contrast, 1 percent of employed Christians worked in commerce and transportation versus 29.4 percent of Jews, and 4.2 percent worked in industry versus 26.4 percent of Jews (the latter overwhelmingly in foodstuffs and textiles, which they dominated). Put differently, in 1900 Jews still constituted 69.1 percent of workers in commerce and transportation (despite growing competition from Poles and Ruthenians) but only 1.5 percent of those in agriculture.[5]

Max Rosenfeld, *Die polnische Judenfrage* (Vienna, 1918) 72–80. Some other studies give lower numbers. See Richard Engelmann, "Die konfessionellen und sprachlichen Verschie bungen in den städtischen Wohnplätzen," *Statistiche Monatshefte* 40 (1914): 473–507, and Tomasz Gasowski, "Jewish Communities in Autonomous Galicia: Their Size and Distribution," in Andrzej Paluch, ed., *The Jews in Poland* (Cracow, 1992), 205–22.

4 Here the numbers did not drop significantly in later years. In 1910, Jews still constituted 31.2 percent of the city population and 30.6 percent of the town population in western Galicia. Rosenfeld, op. cit., 75–7; Thon, op. cit., 20. In western Galicia, only Rzeszow had a majority Jewish population in 1880 (52.1 percent), but it dropped to 37.1 percent by 1910. Ben-Zion Rubstein, *Galizia un ihr Bevölkerung* (Warsaw, 1923), 109. Nearly one-third of Jews remained in rural villages throughout this period (versus 80–90 percent of non-Jews), while urban Jews increasingly lived in cities of over 5,000 inhabitants. Slawomir Tokarski, *Ethnic Conflict and Economic Development: Jews in Galician Agriculture 1868–1914* (Warsaw, 2003), 72–73.

5 Thon, op. cit., 124.

At the time of the first partition, Galician Jewry still largely lived as an autonomous community, self-governed and in many ways separated from their non-Jewish neighbors.[6] To be sure, recent scholarship has increasingly emphasized the myriad levels of interaction between the groups, particularly commercial ties (which also fostered a degree of social integration) but also at the level of popular culture, such as common beliefs about the occult.[7] Nevertheless, most scholars still agree that the communities, in accordance with the corporate structure of premodern European society, did live in separate, if not "entirely separate" social spheres.[8]

In short, although Jews did interact with non-Jewish society on multiple levels, they still remained in the eighteenth century a people distinct from those around them. They spoke a different language (Yiddish),[9] possessed their own elite culture (produced in Hebrew), married endogenously, and practiced a different religion whose calendar, regulations, and values informed their lives at the daily and weekly levels. They also filled a unique economic function, virtually dominating the commercial sector with disproportionately low numbers in the agricultural and (later) industrial sectors, in a setting "in which every ethnic group possessed its own distinguishing economic features."[10] Thus while one cannot speak of any Jewish nationalist movement before the late nineteenth century, Jews

---

[6] On the autonomous community, see Jacob Katz, *Tradition and Crisis: Jewish Society at the End of the Middle Ages* (New York, 1993). Jewish autonomy was under increasing attack from the Polish magnates throughout the eighteenth century, but it was still functioning at the time of the first partition in 1772, at least at the community level. (Polish Jewry's supra-communal "Council of the Four Lands" was dissolved in 1764.) Moshe Rosman, *The Lords' Jews: Magnate-Jewish Relations in the Polish-Lithuanian Commonwealth during the Eighteenth Century* (Cambridge, Mass., 1990), 185–205.

[7] Moshe Rosman, *Founder of Hasidism: A Quest for the Historical Ba'al Shem Tov* (Berkeley, 1996), 56–8; Adam Teller, "The Shtetl as an Arena for Polish-Jewish Integration in the Eighteenth Century," *Polin* 17 (2004): 26–40. See also the important collection of essays edited by Glenn Dynner, *Holy Dissent* (Detroit, 2011).

[8] Gershon Hundert, *The Jews in a Polish Private Town* (Baltimore, 1992), 36–45; Teller, op. cit., 37; Stauter-Halsted, op. cit., 37. Hundert emphasizes that both Jewish and church regulations attempted to limit interaction between the communities, although the latter also "simultaneously enhanced the degree of Jewish integration into the economy of the state." Hundert, *Jews in Poland-Lithuania in the Eighteenth Century* (Berkeley, 2004), 77.

[9] Although many Jews could roughly communicate in Polish, only a small elite could write or speak Polish well, much less Ukrainian. Rosman, *The Lords' Jews*, 174–83, and Daniel Stone, "Knowledge of Foreign Languages among Eighteenth-Century Polish Jews," *Polin* 10 (1997): 200–18.

[10] Israel Bartal, "'The Heavenly City of Germany' and Absolutism a la Mode d'Autriche: The Rise of the Haskalah in Galicia" in Jacob Katz, ed., *Toward Modernity: The European Jewish Model* (New Brunswick, 1987), 34.

did constitute an ethnoreligious group.[11] How was this identity affected by efforts at political integration by the centralizing state on the one hand and Jewish elements themselves promoting integration into non-Jewish society on the other?

With the annexation of Galicia in 1772, Austria's Jewish population doubled to some 400,000, about half of whom lived in the former Polish territory, constituting about 10 percent of the Galician population.[12] Suddenly confronted with such a huge Jewish population, Austria's first legislation aimed to curb its growth while supporting those Jews (particularly wealthy merchants) whose economic activity was seen as beneficial. Empress Maria Theresa (reigned 1740–80), a devout Catholic and severe anti-Semite, was torn between her personal anti-Jewish animus and mercantilist logic which demanded the Jews' exploitation.[13] Thus in 1773, she imposed draconian restrictions on the right to marry and ordered the deportation of all Jewish "vagrants," a category that included any adult, male Jew who failed to pay the "poll tax" for himself and his family for three consecutive years.[14] These and other decrees proved difficult to enforce, however, and the Court soon began the process of developing a more comprehensive policy toward Galician Jewry.[15]

[11] Hundert writes of "an incipient Jewish national consciousness" in eighteenth-century East Central Europe, parallel to the intertwining of Catholicism and early Polish nationalism, but this rings of anachronism. Hundert, *Jews in Poland-Lithuania in the Eighteenth Century*, 78.

[12] Samuel Myovich, *Josephism at Its Boundaries: Nobles, Peasants, Priests, and Jews in Galicia, 1772–1790* (unpublished dissertation, Indiana University, 1994), 206–8. A contemporary scholar suggested fewer Jews in the province, 178,072 in 1789, up to 217,985 in 1821, and 246,147 by 1827. Michael Stöger, *Darstellung der gesetztlichen Verfassung der galizischen Judenschaft* (Lemberg, 1833), 60. In contrast, Stanislaw Grodziski recently suggested about 1 million Jews in the empire by the end of the century, half of them in Galicia. S. Grodziski, "The Jewish Question in Galicia: The Reforms of Maria Theresa and Joseph II, 1772–1790," *Polin* 12 (1999): 61–72. Population figures for this period were based on conscription records, which many Jews attempted to avoid. Thus the first census not related to conscription in 1851 shows the Jewish population at 448,973, or 9.69 percent of the province, up from 333,451 (7.32%) in 1846, an increase of 35 percent in just five years! M. Rosenfeld, "Die jüdische Bevölkerung Galiziens von 1772–1867," *Zeitschrift für Demographie und Statistik der Juden*, 9/10 (1914), 142.

[13] Robert Wistrich, *The Jews of Vienna in the Age of Franz Joseph* (Oxford, 1989), 15.

[14] Myovich, op. cit., 224–9. Jews were forbidden to marry without special permission of the Galician provincial administration, which was awarded only upon payment of a special marriage tax. Although in practice this was often avoided through unreported religious ceremonies, the ever-present risk of informants (rewarded with the violators' property) hung over those who married surreptitiously. A number of other direct and indirect taxes were imposed on Jews as well. Raphael Mahler, *A History of Modern Jewry: 1780–1815* (New York, 1971), 323–4.

[15] Myovich, op. cit., 231.

As an absolutist, Maria Theresa was guided above all by her desire to subordinate the Jewish community to state control, similar to her approach toward other local privileges.[16] To this end, on July 16, 1776, the empress issued a Jewish Ordinance (*Judenordnung*) for Galicia. The ordinance left the structures of internal Jewish administration (*kahals*) largely intact but dramatically increased state supervision through new agencies. It consolidated the number of *kahals*, dissolving the most debt-ridden, and divided Galician Jewry according to the province's recently established six regional districts. It created a General Directory of the Jews, charged with supervising the communities' financial transactions, and a provincial Chief Rabbi with authority over the directory. This rabbi, in addition to his administrative functions, supervised all religious and educational matters within the communities. The ordinance also reduced the jurisdiction of rabbinical courts and consolidated various forms of communal funds into the hands of district elders. Increased taxes on meat, candles, marriage, and "toleration," as well as a myriad of other special taxes applied only to Jews, led to considerable financial hardship. Jewish separateness was reinforced in direct contradiction to the goals of enlightened reform, that is, legal unity and economic integration.[17]

Following the death of his mother, Joseph II (reigned 1780–90) began a decade of independent rule during which he attempted to implement his vision of a centralized and efficient state, one more informed by Enlightenment thought than his mother's. Notions of religious tolerance and the common good were noticeably more influential. Like his mother, Joseph sought to promote the maximum economic development of the empire and its subjects, particularly through industry and commerce. As an absolutist, he sought to break down social castes. Members of the nobility were brought increasingly under the jurisdiction of the state, the authority of the state was enhanced vis-à-vis the church, and the legal status of the peasants was upgraded.[18]

Joseph's overarching goal of integrating Galicia and its population into the Habsburg state guided his policy toward the Jews as well. Influenced by contemporary rhetoric, which demanded Jewish "productivization," the emperor introduced a series of reforms – the first in 1781 for the

[16] Sinkoff, *Out of the Shtetl: Making Jews Modern in the Polish Borderlands* (Providence, 2004), 212–13.

[17] Myovich, op. cit., 231–46; Sinkoff, op.cit., 212–3; Mahler, *A History of Modern Jewry*, 324.

[18] Stefan Kieniewicz, *The Emancipation of the Polish Peasantry* (Chicago and London, 1969), 35–40.

Jews of Bohemia – designed to "improve" the Jews' social and economic behavior and to integrate them into civil society. This meant not only the subordination of Jewish law under civil law but also occupational change (away from commerce in favor of agriculture and artisan crafts) and educational reform, particularly the introduction of secular subjects and German-language instruction into the Jewish curriculum.[19] Reforms such as the removal of most restrictions on Jewish economic activity and the expansion of Jewish educational opportunities placed the emperor at the cutting edge of Jewish emancipation. In Galicia, these efforts reflected both the influence of Enlightenment ideas that sought to ease Jewish restrictions, as well as the state's view of the Jews as important Germanizing agents in an overwhelmingly Slavic province.[20] The new legislation did not seek maliciously to assimilate the Jews, as often suggested by older scholarship, but rather viewed Germanization as a means of incorporating Galicia into the Empire.[21]

Toward this end, in 1785 Joseph proclaimed a new edict (*Judensystem*) for Galician Jewry, which rescinded many aspects of Jewish communal autonomy while expanding the sphere of economic activities permitted to Jews.[22] The decree liquidated the General Directory as well as the office of the Chief Rabbi and abolished the judicial autonomy of the communities, which were limited to religious and charitable affairs. Individual Jews were now subject to state courts, which had jurisdiction even over disputes about marriage contracts and divorce proceedings. Moreover, even these emasculated corporations were not left to internal Jewish control alone. After a six-year transition period, only those with a command of the German language would be eligible for election as community

---

[19] Sinkoff, op. cit., 214. Non-Jewish schools underwent a similar process of Germanization. Peter Wandycz, "The Poles in the Habsburg Monarchy," in Andrei Markovits and Frank Sysyn, eds., *Nationbuilding and the Politics of Nationalism: Essays on Austrian Galicia* (Cambridge, Mass., 1982), 74.

[20] Myovich, op. cit., 248, and Josef Karniel, *Die Toleranzpolitik Kaiser Josephs II* (Gerlingen, 1986), 450–8. They were especially concerned that acculturating Jews be drawn to German rather than Polish. Grodziski, op. cit., 65. Joseph's 1781 legislation in Bohemia similarly promoted "the cultural integration of Jews into the German language sphere of the monarchy." Myovich, op. cit., 250–1.

[21] For examples of the older view, see Mahler, *A History of Modern Jewry*, 330–3 and Artur Eisenbach, *The Emancipation of the Jews in Poland 1780–1870* (Oxford, 1991), 55–7. For a recent revision, see Nancy Sinkoff, op. cit., 202–25.

[22] On the 1785 legislation, see Myovich, op. cit., 262–78 and Sinkoff, op. cit., 215 ff. It also rescinded an earlier attempt at promoting occupational change, the ban on Jewish leaseholding which caused widespread destitution, and dramatically reduced other tax burdens.

leaders. Hebrew and Yiddish, including German written in Hebrew characters, were banned in Jewish public and commercial records; henceforth, all community records (e.g., birth, marriage, and death registers) were required to be kept in German.[23] In 1787, Galician Jews were forced to adopt German surnames while in 1788 all distinctive Jewish clothing was banned as of 1791 (although this was later rescinded).

In 1787 the emperor also obligated Jewish children to attend German-language schools, a decree enforced indirectly by requiring proof of such attendance to obtain a marriage license or to serve as a community rabbi. Although these were Jewish schools staffed with Jewish teachers (each community was required to establish and fund such a school), their pedagogical methodology and textbooks all had to be approved by state-appointed administrators. This mirrored similar schools established for other religious minorities, which were also designed to homogenize educational standards and spread the use of the German language throughout the Empire.[24] To run the new school system, Austria imported a German *maskil* (supporter of the Jewish Enlightenment, or Haskalah) from Bohemia named Herz Homberg (1749–1841).[25] By 1792, a hundred such schools had been founded in Galicia, eventually enrolling about 4,000 students before being closed down in 1806 due to lack of attendance.[26]

Perhaps most important, in 1788 Jews became liable for military service. The conscription of Jews symbolized everywhere their acceptance as "fellow-citizens," whether of the state or later of the nation.[27] Indeed, despite the empire's growing need for recruits during the 1770s and 1780s, the decision to enlist Jews was made not by the Austrian War Council, which

[23] Polish was allowed temporarily as well. Sinkoff, op. cit., 216.

[24] Rachel Manekin, "Rules for the Behavior of Jewish Teachers in the Schools of Galicia and Ludomeria" (Hebrew), *Gal Ed* 20 (2006): 113–24. Manekin reprints the instructions, which she argues were designed to reassure Jewish parents that the schools did not intend to sever its students from Jewish tradition.

[25] On Homberg, see Mayer Balaban, "Herz Homberg in Galizien," *Jahrbuch für jüdische Geschichte und Literatur* 19 (1916): 189–221 and Manekin, op. cit., 113–24.

[26] Sinkoff, op. cit., 224 and Eisenbach, op. cit., 246. Mahler blames the closures on an agreement between the emperor and the Catholic Church restoring the administration of Austria's schools to the clergy, adding that Homberg was himself suspected of revolutionary activities that year. Raphael Mahler, *Hasidism and the Jewish Enlightenment: Their Confrontation in Galicia and Poland in the First Half of the Nineteenth Century* (Philadelphia, 1985), 70.

[27] Michael Silber, "From Tolerated Aliens to Citizen-Soldiers: Jewish Military Service in the Era of Joseph II," in Pieter Judson and M. Rozenblit, eds., *Constructing Nationalities in East Central Europe* (New York, 2005), 19–20.

opposed Jewish conscription, but by the emperor himself, who viewed it as central to the integration of Jews as "fellow-citizens" of Austria.[28] The Austrians did not use the military in a targeted campaign to convert Jews to Christianity, as Nicholas I did in Russia in the 1820s. In fact, in order to minimize disruption of their religious life, Joseph kept Jews together in transport units where he permitted them to establish separate *Kameradschaften* (fellowships) to cook kosher food.[29] This also served to limit the possibility of career advancement in the military.[30] Despite these religious considerations, traditional Jews nearly uniformly opposed the draft, fearing that military life, whatever the dispensations for Jewish religious needs, inevitably severed Jewish soldiers from communal life and religious observance. Even if Jewish law allowed for these violations under the exceptional conditions of military life, religious authorities correctly predicted that the soldiers were likely to remain aloof of these strictures after their release.[31]

This entire series of decrees received official ratification in May 1789 in the form of a *Judenordnung* issued for Galician Jewry.[32] In many ways, the edict was extraordinarily liberating and progressive. Its purpose, wrote the Austrian monarch, was "to annul the differences which legislation has so far maintained between Christian and Jewish subjects, and to grant the Jews living in Galicia all the benefits and rights which our other subjects enjoy."[33] The edict appeared almost simultaneously with the elimination of the peasant's compulsory labor tax (Robot) and was designed to "unite Jews with all other Galician residents under a single system of law and administration."[34] It guaranteed free exercise of religion, raised the age of consent to baptism from eight to eighteen and stiffened penalties for violators, ended the marriage tax (but not the requirement for a German school certificate), ended the expulsion of vagabond Jews as well as all major restrictions on migration, and ended most remaining occupational

---

[28] Erwin Schmidl, "Jews in the Habsburg Armed Forces," *Studia Judaica Austriaca* 11 (1989): 98–103; M. Silber, op. cit., 24–6.

[29] Silber, op. cit., 24–5. Silber points out, however, that this was not always feasible, particularly during wartime, and that Joseph was adamant in requiring Jews to work on Saturdays just as Christians did on Sundays.

[30] Myovich, op. cit., 285–6.

[31] Silber, op. cit., 28–9.

[32] Similar ordinances had been issued for Jews in other areas of the empire since 1781 but were titled instead Edicts of Toleration (*Toleranzpatent*). For a detailed discussion and copy of the Galician ordinance, see Josef Karniel, "Das Toleranzpatent Kaiser Josephs II. für die Juden Galiziens und Lodomeriens," *Tel-Aviv Jahrbuch* 11 (1982), 55–89. See also Myovich, op. cit., 278–92.

[33] Karniel, op. cit., 75.

[34] Myovich, op. cit., 206.

restrictions. It also established Jewish equality in criminal courts. Jews could even enter production guilds and serve in city government.[35]

Despite such grand promises, the effects of the edict were more limited. For example, it left the decision to grant municipal citizenship and civil rights to local municipal authorities, which universally refused to award them. Moreover, it retained various special taxes on Jews, such as the kosher meat tax and even the degrading toleration tax. Worse, despite lofty language opening up nearly all vocations to Jews heretofore forbidden to them, it maintained the ban on Jewish settlement in villages, except by those engaged in agriculture or handicrafts. Jews were still forbidden to hold leases or to distill or sell liquor, occupations that had once been central to their economic activity.[36] Previous decrees designed to foster Germanization were reaffirmed, such as the ban on Jewish dress (except religious officials) and the requirement of *kahal* records and deliberations to be conducted in German.[37]

The period following Joseph's death in 1790 rolled back many of the progressive reforms of the various Edicts of Toleration but left untouched most of their more oppressive aspects.[38] In particular, the new regime continued to support the Germanization of Galician Jewry, pursuing this with even less benevolent means than its predecessor. Following the closure of the German-Jewish schools in 1806, the Austrians reinforced their Germanization efforts with a new series of legislative acts.[39] In 1806, all officials of the larger Jewish communities were required to have a command of German. In 1810, German literacy was made a requirement even to vote in community (*kehilla*) elections. An 1814 edict invalidated Hebrew and Yiddish documents as evidence in courts or in government bureaus.[40] In order to marry, Jewish couples were even required to pass

---

[35] Myovich, op. cit., 277–82, 295.

[36] Myovich, op. cit., 282–6. Close to one third of the Jewish population had lost its livelihood as a result of the restrictions. S. Grodziski, op. cit., 66.

[37] Myovich, op. cit., 288–90. Here Myovich describes Joseph's efforts to "assimilate" Jews, although he seems to have meant this in the sense of bringing them into the German cultural sphere. Earlier Myovich stakes his position as opposed to earlier scholarship that "views the 1789 patent as an assault on the institutions of Galician Jewish communal autonomy and its very cultural identity." Myovich, op. cit., 204.

[38] Indeed, a particularly odious tax was added in 1797, the candle tax, which forced every married Jewish woman to pay a weekly tax for Sabbath candles, whether or not she could even afford to buy the candles.

[39] Filip Friedman, *Die galizischen Juden im Kampfe um ihre gleichberechtigung (1848–1868)* (Frankfurt am Main, 1929), 105–15.

[40] Reconfirmed by the Constitution of 1849, the law was challenged in Parliament by Adolf Mahler, a member of the Jewish Club (parliamentary faction), in 1908.

a German-language examination on a catechism written by Homberg, although most avoided this as before by undergoing a religious ceremony alone. Finally, in 1820, an imperial decree directed all synagogues to conduct their services either in German or in the local language.

Decades of such efforts clearly made an impression on Galician Jewry's cultural makeup, although it was at best a qualified success, limited until mid-century to a small elite of wealthy *maskilim* in the major commercial cities, especially Lemberg, Tarnopol, and Brody (as well as Cracow, then an independent city-state).[41] These consisted mainly of wealthy merchants, but also included lessees of Jewish taxes (i.e., the meat and candle tax), as well as members of the professional intelligentsia such as physicians, teachers from the German schools, and a large number of independent intellectuals supported by wealthy patrons.[42] Vienna's Germanization agenda fed naturally into the growth of the Haskalah, which in Galicia, as in Russia, looked to Berlin for inspiration and guidance.[43]

Haskalah (Jewish Enlightenment) is a much-contested term, among historians today as well as among its nineteenth-century adherents.[44] Broadly speaking, the Haskalah was an intellectual movement that sought to integrate Jews into European society *as Jews*, without denying their constituting a particular group. It was a relatively conservative and moderate form of modernization in that it sought to transform and rejuvenate Judaism and Jewish society through its embrace of European culture and Enlightenment values.[45] It argued for a rationalistic and historical interpretation of Judaism and promoted a positive Jewish identity based on a romantic revitalization of biblical Hebrew and a scholarly encounter with Jewish history.[46] In short, it sought "some sort of golden modernizing

---

[41] Jerzy Holzer, "Enlightenment, Assimilation, and Modern Identity: The Jewish Elite in Galicia," *Polin* 12 (1999): 79–85; Israel Bartal, "'The Heavenly City of Germany' and Absolutism a la Mode d'Autriche," 33–42. Mahler notes that these three commercial cities were "virtually the exclusive centers of the *Haskalah* movement in Galicia." Mahler, *Hasidism and the Jewish Enlightenment*, 32.

[42] Mahler, *Hasidism and the Jewish Enlightenment*, 34–36.

[43] Bartal, op. cit. as well as ibid., "The Image of Germany and German Jewry in East European Jewish Society during the 19th Century," in Isadore Twersky, ed., *Danzig, between East and West: Aspects of Modern Jewish History* (Cambridge, 1985).

[44] See Shmuel Feiner, "Towards a Historical Definition of the Haskalah," in Shmuel Feiner and David Sorkin, eds., *New Perspectives on the Haskalah* (London, 2001), 184–219.

[45] Ibid., 218–19.

[46] Immanuel Etkes, "Immanent Factors and External Influences in the Development of the Haskalah Movement in Russia," in Jacob Katz, ed., *Toward Modernity*, 14–15. On the *Haskalah* in Eastern Europe, see Immanuel Etkes, ed., *Hadat vehaHayim: Tenuat haHaskalah ha-Yehudit beMizrah Europa* (Jerusalem, 1993). On the *Haskalah* in Galicia,

mean" between tradition and assimilation.[47] Finally, although generally associated with its program for educational and social reform, the
Haskalah also promoted a new set of political assumptions. Above all,
maskilim venerated the absolutist state as the highest authority to which
Jews owed their allegiance, and they opposed all forms of Jewish political
autonomy, which symbolized to them the supposedly inferior status of
the Jews in medieval Europe.[48]

The *maskilim*'s favorable predisposition toward the ruling regime,
and its general tendency to oppose clerical power within the *kehilla*,
obviously meshed well with Vienna's efforts to bring Galician Jewry into
the German cultural sphere. That this endeavor enjoyed only limited success was partially a result of the rise of Hasidism, whose rapid expansion
coincided with government efforts at Germanization.[49] Jewish communal
autonomy, suffering from declining authority, was increasingly replaced
by voluntary submission to charismatic Hasidic leaders who adamantly
opposed government and *maskilic* attempts at Germanization.[50] At
times such opposition straddled the border between religious vigilance
and outright ethnicism. Menachem Mendel of Rymanow (d.1815), for
example, opposed acculturation based on the same rabbinic tradition
popular with religious nationalists in the modern period, that the biblical Israelites were redeemed from Egypt only by virtue of not having
changed their names, language, or dress, the critical signatures of cultural uniqueness.[51] Another leader decried the prohibition of Hebrew-
language legal documents and the supplanting of Yiddish by German.
"Keep your children as much as possible from foreign tongues and God

---

see Sinkoff, op. cit.; Shmuel Feiner, *Haskalah and History: The Emergence of a Modern Jewish Historical Consciousness* (Oxford, 2002), 71–156; R. Mahler, *Hasidism and the Jewish Enlightenment*, 33–67.

[47] Feiner, "Towards a Historical Definition of the Haskalah," 219.

[48] David Biale, *Power and Powerlessness in Jewish History* (New York, 1986), 103–117.

[49] Most historians agree that Hasidism had captured a significant percentage of Galician Jewry by the beginning of the nineteenth century. However, the critical archival work necessary to prove this assumption has yet to be done. For examples of such work in Congress Poland, see Glenn Dynner, *Men of Silk: The Hasidic Conquest of Polish Jewish Society* (Oxford, 2006) and Marcin Wodzinski, *Haskalah and Hasidism in the Kingdom of Poland: A History of Conflict* (London, 2005). While these two authors disagree on the timing of the Hasidic "conquest" in Congress Poland, both agree that the movement had long since spread throughout Galicia.

[50] Bartal, op. cit., 36.

[51] On the confluence of ultra-Orthodox anti-modernism and modern nationalism, see Michael Silber, "The Beating Jewish Heart in a Foreign Land," (Hebrew) *Cathedra* (1995), 84–105.

will bring his nation to speedy deliverance in our day as He did for our forefathers in Egypt."[52]

Other factors limited the progress of Germanization as well. Following the demise of Joseph II, and particularly during the reactionary period following Napoleon's defeat, Austrian bureaucrats had become skeptical of Enlightenment ideas and sought not to reform Jewish society as the *maskilim* hoped, but merely to placate it.[53] Most important, Galician Jewry's socioeconomic composition, which naturally resembled other areas of Poland far more than Central Europe, was simply not conducive to Germanization. Unlike elsewhere in Central Europe, no German middle-class existed in Galicia into which the Jews might integrate, other than the government bureaucracy, which remained largely out of reach. As a result, Israel Bartal concludes, "In such a city as Brody the Jewish community was no more Germanized than many communities on the other side of the Russian border. In both cases the *maskilim* among the Jewish elite were immersed in German culture while large sectors of traditional society saw German influence as destructive and disruptive."[54]

Still, the secular intelligentsia at least was thoroughly Germanized by mid-century. As Rachel Manekin has noted, they had become *deitschn* (Germans), not in the national sense of the term but rather in their cultural modernization. They cut their sidelocks and wore short jackets rather than long caftans, for example, and they adopted the German language and pursued a classical education.[55] This change is visible in their construction of modern synagogues known as "Temples" in Tarnopol and Lemberg bearing German names and offering German-language sermons.[56] (The progressive Temple in Cracow, completed in 1861,

---

[52] Rafael Mahler, *Hasidism and the Jewish Enlightenment*, 14. Mahler, following Zionist historiographical tradition, emphasizes that it was the "national trait" of Hasidism that evoked such intense opposition by the government, concluding, "The attachment of the Hasidim to Yiddish and to the Jewish national and religious tradition was the greatest obstacle to the success of the government's policy of Germanizing Galician Jewry." Ibid., 70.

[53] Bartal, op. cit., 36–7.

[54] Bartal, op. cit., 40.

[55] Rachel Manekin, "'*Deitschn*,' 'Poles' or 'Austrians'?" (Hebrew), *Zion* 68 (2003): 225. "Polish" Jews, by contrast, continued to wear long caftans, speak Yiddish, and reject any formal non-Jewish education.

[56] Eisenbach, op. cit., 246. The modern synagogue filled an important role in the *maskilim*'s broader project of modernization. Religious reform in Eastern Europe did not directly model itself on the German Reform movement, however, but rather followed the "Vienna Rite." It carefully integrated those aspects of the Reform Temple that reflected modern aesthetic sensibilities, such as a vernacular sermon, beautiful music, and an orderly,

had a Polish orientation from the start.)[57] The progressive synagogue erected in Lemberg in 1846, for example, was known as the Deutsch-Israelitisches Bethaus (German-Israelite House of Prayer). It continued to offer German-language sermons into the twentieth century, decades after the city had become overwhelmingly Polonized.[58]

To be sure, Germanization had partially taken root among the Jewish masses as well. Jews did, after all, obediently adopt German surnames, and Jewish knowledge of the German language (eased by its similarity to Yiddish) grew over the course of the century. Homberg's short-lived German-Jewish schools certainly contributed to this, and other German-Jewish schools were opened during the *Vormärz* (pre-1848) period as well, the first in Tarnopol by the *maskilic* opponent of Hasidism, Joseph Perl (1774–1839).[59] By mid-century, over fourteen towns in Galicia offered such schools, with a total enrollment of about 3,000 students.[60] All of the schools were run by prominent *maskilim* with curricula reflecting their philosophy. As a result, Orthodox opponents rallied against them, often preferring when forced to send their children to Christian schools, which at least did not desanctify Jewish tradition through secular analysis of holy texts. The schools were thoroughly German. Officially known as German-Israelite Teaching Institutions, they taught in German "as the mother language of Galician Israelites."[61] Ultimately, with no significant German middle class available to absorb Galician Jews, the major effect of these efforts was not to transform the Jews into German

decorous service, while maintaining the traditional liturgy in Hebrew and rejecting antinomian practices such as an organ on Shabbat. See Michael Meyer, "The German Model of Religious Reform and Russian Jewry," in Isadore Twersky, ed., *Danzig, between East and West: Aspects of Modern Jewish History*, 67–91. Despite the modesty of this reform, a Hasidic extremist – apparently backed by the Orthodox establishment – murdered the Lemberg Temple's first rabbi, Abraham Kohn, and his infant daughter in 1848. See Michael Stanislawski, *A Murder in Lemberg* (Princeton, 2007).

[57] Hanna Kozińska-Witt, "The Association of Progressive Jews in Kraków, 1864–1874," *Polin* 23 (2010): 121.

[58] Although the city had become largely Polonized by the 1880s, only at the end of the century did the Temple change its name to the Gminna Synagoga Postępowa. The rabbi gave his sermons in German until 1903, when the synagogue board hired an assistant rabbi (a Zionist!) able to offer Polish-language sermons on alternate weeks. For a history of the Lemberg Temple, see Julian J. Bussgang, "The Progressive Synagogue in Lwów," *Polin* 11 (1998): 127–53 and Majer Balaban, *Historia Lwowskiej Synagogi Postępowej* (Lwow, 1937).

[59] On Perl, see Mahler, *Hasidism and the Jewish Enlightenment*, 121–70, and N. Sinkoff, op. cit., 225–75.

[60] Eisenbach, op. cit., 246. On these schools, see also Sinkoff, op. cit., 225–37, and Friedman, op.cit., 29–33.

[61] Friedman, op. cit., 33.

Israelites but rather to widen the cultural gap between these Jews and their Slavic neighbors.[62]

THE STRUGGLE FOR EMANCIPATION

During the period before 1848, Galician Jews – particularly among the Hasidim – displayed a considerable degree of passive resistance to the various discriminatory restrictions and taxes placed upon them. Most avoided the marriage tax, for example, by undergoing a religious cere-mony alone, while they skirted the tax and permit requirement on orga-nized prayer services by meeting secretly in small, private synagogues (*shtiblekh*).[63] Because of their large numbers and absolute allegiance to their respective leaders, the Hasidim constituted an important factor in Galician politics. Overall, however, they acted more as an instrument of the ruling authorities, albeit in exchange for certain concessions, than as an independent political force. "The Jewish masses remained for the most part indifferent to political struggles," concluded Filip Friedman, except during the crises in 1848, 1861, and 1866–68. Lacking any "active poli-tics," Jews relied heavily on individual efforts at government intervention by religious and economic leaders.[64]

Galician *maskilim* did establish the first Jewish secular associations during this period, in Lemberg in 1831 and Cracow in 1843. These were part of the emerging network of middle-class associational life in late eighteenth- and early nineteenth-century Austria. These groups – osten-sibly social, cultural, philanthropic, or professional – played a vital role in developing civic society and a sense of groupness within the middle class, and thus had critical political consequences.[65] These first Jewish groups were originally approved by the authorities as cultural socie-ties established to promote secular education and occupational reform (particularly toward handcrafts) among Galician Jews. Increasingly, however, the groups attempted to persuade the monarch to remove

---

[62] Grodziski, op. cit., 71.

[63] Mahler, *Hasidism and the Jewish Enlightenment*, 20–3.

[64] Friedman, op. cit., 43–4, 208–11. On those critical years, see discussion later in the chapter. On the role of "crisis" as a catalyst for transforming Jewish politics, see Jonathan Frankel, "Crisis as a Factor in Modern Jewish Politics, 1840 and 1881–82" in Jehuda Reinharz, ed., *Living with Antisemitism* (Hanover, 1987). For a critique of this para-digm, see Benjamin Nathans, "A 'Hebrew Drama': Lilienblum, Dubnow, and the Idea of 'Crisis' in East European Jewish History," *Simon Dubnow Institute Yearbook* 5 (2006): 211–27.

[65] Pieter Judson, *Exclusive Revolutionaries*, 18 ff.

the special taxes paid by Jews in Galicia and to grant them municipal citizenship and access to government posts.[66] Although all of these
efforts proved unsuccessful, they point to the beginnings of politicization among Galician Jewry's emerging secular elite. These societies,
like their non-Jewish counterparts, would eventually become centers of
Jewish political life.[67]

Political consciousness began to emerge during the revolutionary crises of 1846 and 1848 when Galician Jews first tasted complete emancipation, only to lose it when the revolutions collapsed. In 1846 a revolution
broke out in Cracow.[68] The insurgents called not only for the liberation and reunification of Poland but also for the abolition of serfdom
and the full emancipation of Polish Jews.[69] Unfortunately, the Liberal
revolutionaries' assumption of national unity between Polish-speaking
peasants and gentry proved to be fatally flawed. The peasants, distrust-
ing the sincerity of the revolutionaries and encouraged by promises of
emancipation by the Austrian authorities, turned on the local gentry in
a violent *jacquerie*, killing more than two thousand noblemen before the
Austrians could restore order.[70] The insurrection quickly collapsed and
ended ignominiously with the incorporation of Cracow into Galicia. The
inclusion of Jews as fellow Poles by the insurgents, however, sparked
widespread support for the revolution among Cracow Jews.[71] Not only
the secular elite but also many traditional Jews rushed to support the
revolution, most prominently Rabbi Berush (Ber) Meisels (1798–1870),
an ardent Polish patriot who later served as a delegate to the Austrian
Constituent Assembly (Reichstag).[72]

No attempt was made in Galicia to overthrow Austrian rule during the
European-wide revolts of 1848 known as the "Springtime of Nations."[73]

---

[66] Eisenbach, op. cit., 205–6.
[67] Eisenbach, op. cit., 353. Judson, op. cit., 29 ff.
[68] On the role of the Jews in the 1846 revolution, see Eisenbach, op. cit., 325–31, and N. M.
Gelber, "Die Juden und die polnische Revolution im Jahre 1846," in Gelber, *Aus zwei
Jahrhunderten* (Vienna, 1924), 261–5. Gelber's short chapter railed against Polish scholarship at the time, which had falsely posited that Jews opposed the revolution.
[69] Łukasz Tomasz Sroka, "Changes in the Jewish Community of Kraków in Autonomous
Galicia," *Polin* 23 (2010): 73.
[70] Norman Davies, op. cit., 147–8.
[71] Łukasz Tomasz Sroka, op. cit., 73–4.
[72] On Meisels, see Salo Baron, "The Revolution of 1848 and Jewish Scholarship, II,"
American Academy for Jewish Research Annual 20 (1951): 65–9, and Moshe Kamelhar,
Rabi Dov Ber Maizlish: gadol ba-Torah medinai ve-lohem (Jerusalem, 1970).
[73] On 1848 in Galicia, see Eisenbach, op. cit., 343–73, Friedman, op. cit., 52–78, and Baron,
op. cit., 62–82.

However, when the revolutions broke out, Polish and Ruthenian groups both sent petitions to the emperor demanding national rights and socio-political reforms. In April, in order to secure their support for the crown, the governor of Galicia, Franz Stadion, unilaterally freed all serfs, who became the owners of the land they worked.[74] A week later the emperor issued a new constitution, a short-lived document that abolished religious discrimination in civil and political rights and guaranteed the freedom of association. It also decreed the leveling of the tax burden among all citizens, suggesting the abolition of all special Jewish taxes, one of the most pressing Jewish concerns in Galicia. Thanks to the intervention of Stadion, these were specifically abolished by the Reichstag on October 5, with the approval of the emperor on October 20. Stadion, who feared a looming Polish-Jewish rapprochement in Galicia, sought to secure Jewish support for the Crown by preempting Polish outreach toward the Jews and proposing the abolition of these taxes before the Polish revolutionaries could achieve it.[75]

Although imperial forces had regained the upper hand by winter, the March Constitution issued by the emperor in 1849 reconfirmed most of these rights. Unfortunately, these proved to be ephemeral. Local municipal opposition often thwarted implementation, as it had during past attempts at Jewish emancipation from above. Moreover, an imperial edict issued in December 1851 rolled back the vast majority of reforms of the revolutionary years – with the important exception of serf emancipation – and the Jews' legal status returned largely to its pre-1848 position.[76]

The most lasting effect of the revolutionary upheaval for Jews was thus not the securing of civil rights but the sudden, if short-lived, political activism, especially of secular elements but also, to a lesser extent, of traditional ones. At first, this political activism expressed itself as Polish patriotism, for the Poles had deliberately included Jewish emancipation among their demands in 1848 hoping to win Jewish support for their cause. Liberal Jews were virtually compelled to join the wave of Polish nationalism. Ironically, it was the "German" Jews who principally joined

---

[74] Landowners were compensated, however, with generous government payments that were converted into taxes, which disproportionately burdened peasants, who thus paid for their land for decades. Kieniewicz, op. cit., 133–9.

[75] Manekin, "'*Deitschn*,' 'Poles' or 'Austrians'?" 251. Stadion similarly won over many Ruthenian peasants, and undermined the authority of the Polish National Council, by supporting the establishment of the conservative clerical Ruthenian National Council. Peter Wandycz, "The Poles in the Habsburg Monarchy," 79–81.

[76] Eisenbach, op. cit., 346, 380–3.

the revolution, not the "Polish" (i.e., traditional) ones.[77] While Jews generally displayed extreme Polish nationalism only in Cracow and Lemberg, Jews throughout the province participated in Polish national councils and even joined divisions of national guards.[78] *Kehilla* representatives from all over Galicia assembled in Lemberg and demanded that the new Parliament grant Jews full emancipation.[79] Yiddish political propaganda even began to appear during this period.[80] Early in 1848, for example, a *maskilic* writer named Abraham Mendel Mohr published a Yiddish pamphlet explaining contemporary events, which he claimed sold 5,000 copies within a month. He then launched a Yiddish weekly in Lemberg called the *Zeitung*, which lasted about eighteen months, despite enjoying only 200 subscribers. In 1849, frustrated at the lack of enthusiasm for emancipation among the Jewish masses, he published an inexpensive Yiddish translation of the March Constitution, with an introduction exclaiming its great promise for the Jews.[81]

Events did not only push the secular elite to action; they also encouraged the Orthodox. Aided by their recently won freedom of speech, Orthodox leaders in Lemberg began to stage mass demonstrations to retake control of the *kahal*, which secular *maskilim* ruled through government support. They also emerged as an important factor at the polls, allegedly undermining the election of liberal Jewish candidates in Lemberg to the Austrian Constituent Assembly in favor of Polish candidates whom they pressed for religious autonomy. In Brody, they even ran one of their own members, Mayer Kallir, previously a delegate to the abortive Galician Diet, although he was soundly defeated by the liberal majority.[82]

Critically, Jewish activists framed their demands in terms of *natural* and not *national* rights. They demanded the removal of personal legal disabilities but not national rights as Polish and Ruthenian leaders had.

---

[77] Manekin, "'*Deitschn*,' 'Poles' or 'Austrians'?" 233.

[78] Baron, op. cit., 71.

[79] Eisenbach, op. cit., 354.

[80] Manekin, "'*Deitschn*,' 'Poles' or 'Austrians'?" 234–50. For an analysis of Polish leaflets printed for Jewish consumption, and Jewish leaflets printed for Polish consumption, see Manekin, "Taking It to the Streets: Polish-Jewish Print Discourse in 1848 Lemberg," *Simon Dubnow Institute Yearbook* 7 (2008): 215–27.

[81] Baron, op. cit., 74–6. The *Zeitung*, although printed in Hebrew characters, was less Yiddish than Judeo-German. Gershom Bader described it as a "mishmash of a German-Yiddish jargon, mixed with Hebrew words." See his biography of Mohr in the unpublished manuscript of his "Galician Jewish Celebrities." Gershon Bader Papers, YIVO Institute for Jewish Research.

[82] Baron, op. cit., 71, 79. Kallir again won a seat on the Galician Diet in 1861.

As the historian Artur Eisenbach noted, "The 1848 revolution was for many ethnic groups in Europe, in particular Central Europe, an incentive to deepen their national consciousness; as far as the Jews were concerned, the most dominant feature was the deepening of their political consciousness." They were still too focused on winning civil emancipation, he argues, to concern themselves with national emancipation.[83]

Eisenbach's observation presupposes that the Jews ontologically constituted a modern nation, albeit not yet awakened. This is certainly a problematic assumption in view of the contemporary view of nations as modern constructions. In any case, only in the last years of the nineteenth century, after the doctrine of national self-determination had progressed sufficiently to become for some a prerequisite for self-respect, would Jews begin to turn to Jewish nationalism in order to achieve "personal dignity" and overcome their sense of "humiliation." After 1851, those modern Jews who sought any form of broader identity at all certainly chose the "Austrian option," as Manekin put it. They had become for the first time "Austrian Jews," but this was a political, not a national identity.[84]

EMANCIPATION AND ITS LIMITATIONS: POLONIZATION, NATIONAL RIGHTS, AND JEWISH EXCLUSION

Following a decade of conservative reaction, a new period of liberalization opened in the early 1860s.[85] A series of laws and decrees removed many of the most onerous abuses of Jewish civil rights, ending most restrictions on marriage, occupation, residence, and the right to employ Christian servants.[86] The early 1860s also witnessed a unique period of Polish-Jewish cooperation that climaxed, and abruptly ended, during the failed January Uprising in Russian Poland in 1863.[87] In 1861, members of the Jewish intelligentsia joined the Polish Election Committee for the Galician Diet and issued a call in German for Jewish electors to support the Polish National Party. Three Jews were elected that year, joined by one more during the subsequent elections in 1867. These Jews were elected as individuals and did not represent the Jewish community. Their

---

[83] Eisenbach, op. cit., 354, 358.

[84] Manekin, "'*Deitschn*,' 'Poles' or 'Austrians'?" 254–62.

[85] Defeated by Piedmont and France in 1859, the emperor hoped through liberalization to avoid further military confrontation with his constituent nationalities.

[86] Eisenbach, op. cit., 405–6.

[87] See Magdalena Opalski and Israel Bartal, *Poles and Jews: A Failed Brotherhood* (Hanover, 1992).

political sympathies lay not with Jewish emancipation per se, but with the liberal wing of the Polish National Party. They had no clear political program to win Jewish rights, although they supported this cause when they could.[88]

Complete Jewish emancipation was finally achieved only as part of the reconstruction of the Habsburg Empire in 1867. Under pressure after his crushing defeat by the Prussians in 1866, the young Austrian Emperor Franz Joseph II (reigned 1848–1916) was forced to conclude a compromise with the Hungarians, the largest and most threatening of the monarchy's non-German nationalities.[89] The agreement created the dualist Austro-Hungarian Empire, whereby Hungary enjoyed complete independence in its domestic rule. It also advanced a more federalist approach to Galicia, in favor of the Poles, as discussed below. On December 21, Franz Joseph issued a series of "Fundamental Laws," which although not technically a "constitution," essentially established a constitutional monarchy. It called for the formation of a parliament, or Reichsrat, whose delegates would be elected by the provincial diets.[90] Most important, the constitution not only guaranteed the equal rights of all of its citizens, including the freedom of religion, but also the equal treatment of all nationalities. Article 19 read as follows:

1. All ethnic Peoples (*Volksstämme*) of the state have equal rights, and each has the inalienable right to defend and nurture its nationality (*Nationalität*) and language.
2. The state recognizes the equal rights of all customary (*landesüblichen*) languages in schools, government offices and public life.
3. In those areas in which several Peoples reside, public education institutions are to be so founded that each People, without compelling the learning of a second language, receives the necessary means for education in its own language.[91]

---

[88] F. Friedman, "Die Judenfrage im galizischen Landtag 1861–1868," *Monatsschrift für Geschichte und Wissenschaft des Judentums* (1928), 384. A conservative, anti-Jewish coalition of Polish conservatives, Ruthenians, and Polish farmers prevented any move toward Jewish emancipation during this period.

[89] On the nationality conflict in the Habsburg Empire, see C. A. Macartney, *The Habsburg Empire, 1790–1918* (New York, 1969) and Robert Kann, *The Multinational Empire: Nationalism and National Reform in the Habsburg Monarchy 1848–1918* (New York, 1950).

[90] This changed in 1873, at which time *Reichsrat* delegates became directly elected, albeit via a severely restricted suffrage system.

[91] Gerald Stourzh, *Die Gleichberechtigung der Nationalitäten in der Verfassung und Verwaltung Österreichs 1848–1918* (Vienna, 19:5), 56.

Note that the language of Article 19 did not recognize nations but rather *Volkstämme*, ethnic peoples. One's *Volkstamm* was determined by linguistic criteria, based on *Umgangssprache*, or language of daily use.[92] The government set a list of nine languages from which to choose: German, Bohemian-Moravian-Slovakian, Polish, Ruthenian, Slovenian, Serbo-Croatian, Italian, Romanian, and Magyar. Yiddish, the mother tongue and often the only language of the vast majority of Galician Jews, was deliberately not recognized and thus was not guaranteed the protection afforded to the approved languages. These included the right of public education in Yiddish, the requirement of government publications and signs to be issued in Yiddish in areas in which it was in widespread use, the right to use Yiddish in courts and state offices and to petition the same in Yiddish, and so on. Yiddish contracts were not even legally binding. In fact, Yiddish and Hebrew, unlike other unapproved *Umgangssprachen* such as Slovakian, had been specifically forbidden in two separate royal edicts in 1814 and 1849, a legacy of Vienna's long history of Germanization of its Jewish subjects. Jewish intellectuals themselves regarded the Jewish "jargon" to be a corrupted form of German, which they considered to be the Jews' true language. In short, the general consensus of the period held that the Jewish "jargon" was simply a peculiar dialect of German, and one to be disdained at that.

The census, designed to placate national strife by granting national minority rights, ironically tended to exacerbate tensions. "By asking the language question," Eric Hobsbawm notes, "censuses for the first time *forced* everyone to choose not only a nationality, but a linguistic nationality."[93] Jews, like others, for the first time had to declare themselves officially members of one of the approved nationalities. They could no longer simply be "Austrian," at least legally. Politically and culturally, of course, the census did not necessarily create any sense of nationality or "bounded groupness," Polish or otherwise.[94] On the contrary, as we shall see, most Jews remained apathetic toward the census until after they had already become convinced of Jewish nationhood.

[92] For a detailed discussion of the issue of *Umgangssprachen* in Austrian censuses see Emil Brix, *Die Umgangssprachen in Altösterreich zwischen Agitation und Assimilation* (Vienna, 1982).

[93] E. J. Hobsbawm, *Nations and Nationalism since 1780* (Cambridge, 1990), 110. See also Brix, op. cit., 114. On the impact of forced ethnic attribution in Moravia, see G. Stourzh, "Ethnic Attribution in Late Imperial Austria: Good Intentions, Evil Consequences," reprinted in *From Vienna to Chicago* (Cambridge, Mass., 2004), 157–76.

[94] Brubaker, *Ethnicity without Groups*, 53–4.

Ultimately, it was not the Germans but the Poles who would most benefit from the exclusion of Jews from national designation. In exchange for their support of the Crown, Franz Joseph granted the Poles in Galicia virtual autonomy in a series of decrees between 1867 and 1871.[95] Galician provincial administration passed quickly from German to Polish control, while the ruling Poles engaged in an intensive Polonization campaign.[96] As a result, Galician Jews, overwhelmingly Yiddish-speaking, were usually registered as Polish, increasingly so as Polish autonomy entrenched itself. While in 1869 Jews were still generally recorded as German, with the Polonization of the state bureaucracy, Galicia's "German" population (according to the census) steadily declined in favor of the Polish, as Jews were increasingly counted among the Polish ranks. By 1880, 60.4 percent of Galician Jews were "Polish"; these numbers rose to 74.6 percent in 1890, 76.5 percent in 1900, and more than 92 percent in 1910. By then, the number of "German" Jews had dropped from 138,000 to just 25,631, and of the 40,475 Jews who answered "Ruthenian" in 1900, just half that number did so in 1910.[97]

While the Poles enjoyed near autonomy, others – Ruthenians, who constituted the majority in the eastern part of the province, and Jews, who

[95] Besides the power of the Polish-controlled diet, buttressed by the Polish gentry's political domination at the district level, in 1867, Galicia's formerly German-oriented schools were Polonized through the formation of a Polish-dominated school board; in 1869, an imperial decree made Polish the language of the bureaucracy and courts in Galicia; and in 1870–1, Polish became the official language of instruction for Galicia's two universities in Cracow and Lemberg. In 1871 a permanent cabinet ministry without portfolio was created to oversee Galician affairs, a post held continuously in Polish hands. See James Shedel, "Austria and Its Polish Subjects, 1866–1914: A Relationship of Interests," *Austrian History Yearbook*, 19–20, Part 2 (1983–4): 23–42.

[96] Not only was municipal and provincial government (as well as middle-class associational life and higher education) now conducted in Polish, but the urban landscape itself was transformed as well. Lemberg, for example, was quickly transformed into Polish "Lwów" through the replacement of German and even bi-lingual street and square names with purely Polish ones, the use of all major public buildings designated "to project Polish national pride and Polish cultural and political achievement," and the frequent organization of Polish national festivals in public streets and arenas. Harald Binder, "Making and Defending a Polish Town: "Lwów" (Lemberg), 1848–1914," *Austrian History Yearbook* 34 (2003): 57–81.

[97] Max Rosenfeld, *Die polnische Judenfrage*, 147. For a more recent analysis of census politics in Galicia, see Brix, op. cit., 353–83. These results were indicative of Polish power and not of Jewish Polonization, per se. As late as 1931, by which time Polish Jewry had undergone a substantial degree of Polonization since the prewar period, still only a quarter of Galician Jews declared Polish to be their "mother tongue." Still, this was more than double the national average of 12.2 percent, a legacy of the success of prewar Polonization in Galicia. Jacob Lestchinsky, "The Mother-Tongue of the Jews in Independent Poland" (Yiddish), *YIVO Bleter* 12 (November–December 1943), 156.

remained roughly 11 percent – fared worse. In theory, national groups (defined by language) were guaranteed certain "inalienable" national rights by Austrian law. In practice, Ruthenian and Jewish nationalists (the latter for lack of classification as a nationality) faced Herculean opposition in their struggle to realize these rights. The curial suffrage system combined with electoral corruption to ensure Polish domination both in the provincial diet and, consequently, in the Galician delegation to the national Parliament, or Reichsrat, itself selected by the diet.[98] As Jeremy King notes of Polish territorial autonomy, "self-rule by one 'nationality' came at the expense of self-rule by others."[99]

While few Jews before the end of the nineteenth century considered themselves a national minority due national rights, national consciousness among Ruthenians grew apace in these years, as did their frustration at their lack of proportional political representation and the gross disparity between the Ruthenian- and Polish-language educational infrastructure.[100] As nationalist tensions between the economically and politically subordinate Ruthenians and the dominant Poles sharpened, the Jews grew increasingly unable to avoid the conflict. The question of Jewish nationhood had critical repercussions for the Ruthenians; in fact, many Ruthenian nationalist leaders eventually came to support Jewish nationalist aspirations as a counter-measure against Polish domination.[101] They were especially interested in the Jews winning recognition as an official nationality in the state census. By counting the Jews, Galicia's Poles could claim numerical superiority over the Ruthenians; without them, the Poles and Ruthenians were roughly equal.[102] Galician Jewry

[98] On the curial system, see later in the chapter. The Reichsrat was directly elected after 1873, but it continued to be dominated by the ruling Poles due to voting restrictions and electoral manipulation.

[99] Jeremy King, "Which Equality? Separate but Equal in Imperial Austria," unpublished paper draft. My thanks to Jeremy King for sharing this with me.

[100] Ann Sirka, *The Nationality Question in Austrian Education: The Case of Ukrainians in Galicia 1867–1914* (Frankfurt-am-Main, 1980).

[101] Initially, however, the growth of Ruthenian nationalism deepened Ruthenian-Jewish enmity by politicizing the traditional economic conflict between the two groups, particularly the role of the Jews as agents of the Polish nobility. See John-Paul Himka, "Ukrainian-Jewish Antagonism in the Galician Countryside during the Late Nineteenth Century," in Howard Aster and Peter J. Potichnyj, eds., *Ukrainian-Jewish Relations in Historical Perspective* (Alberta, 1988). This began to change only toward the end of the century.

[102] In 1890, for example, Poles constituted 53.3 percent of the Galician population by *Umgangssprache*, Ruthenians 43.1 percent, and Germans 3.4 percent. By religion, Jews constituted 11.66 percent of the population in that year. Had Yiddish been accepted as an *Umgangssprache*, the Poles would actually have numbered about 44 percent,

thus played a powerful but potentially dangerous role, holding the demographic balance between two equal-sized nationalities. Such a situation often proved especially conducive to the establishment of a robust Jewish nationalist movement throughout Eastern Europe.[103] Jewish nationalists would draw considerable inspiration from their Ruthenian counterparts and frequently made reference to their political successes. The difficult position of the Jews caught between Poles and Ruthenians also provided Jewish nationalists with a powerful message in favor of their position. Jewish nationalism enabled Jews to avoid allying themselves with either side in the Polish-Ruthenian conflict, an especially appealing benefit as Ruthenian nationalism grew increasingly militant. A Jew from eastern Galicia, for example, described his frustration in this 1904 letter to the short-lived non-Zionist Yiddish weekly, *Der Emes'r Yid*:

A hired Jew traveling through our town asked his foreman something in Polish in the middle of the City Square. A Ruthenian peasant who happened to be standing nearby fell on the Jew murderously and shouted, "Cursed Jew; you live on Ruthenian land, you eat Ruthenian bread and you speak Polish!" He began to beat the Jew with a big stick and he [the Jew] was barely able to get away from him. The Jews just don't know what to do; however they speak, it all [turns out] bad. The Poles scream that they are German, because they speak Yiddish, which is similar to German. If they speak Polish, the Ruthenians are angry. Whatever they do, it's not right.[104]

Since the annexation of the province by Vienna, the political and cultural orientation of Galician Jewry, particularly among the secular intelligentsia, had grown gradually more German. With the Polonization of both the state apparatus and the public schools, however, Germanness (*Deutschtum*) became an increasingly impractical self-identification in Galicia. Many discovered their Polish roots in this period and joined those Jews who had already staked their future with the Polish nation. Others

roughly the same as the Ruthenians. See Thon, op. cit., 110; Heinrich Rauchenberg, *Die Bevölkerung Österreichs* (Vienna, 1895), and Wolfdieter Bihl, "Die Juden," in Adam Wandruszka and Peter Urbanitsch, eds., *Die Habsburgermonarchie 1848–1918*, Volume 3/2 (Vienna, 1980), 880–948.

[103] Ezra Mendelsohn, *The Jews of East Central Europe between the World Wars* (Bloomington, 1983), 19. Mendelsohn compares the situation in eastern Galicia to that of Transylvania, Slovakia, and Bohemia. See also Mendelsohn, *On Modern Jewish Politics* (Oxford, 1993), 38. On the crisis of Bohemian Jewry, sandwiched between Germans and Czechs, and its effect on Jewish nationalism, see Hillel Kieval, *The Making of Czech Jewry: National Conflict and Jewish Society in Bohemia, 1870–1918* (New York and Oxford, 1988).

[104] *Der Emes'r Yid*, March 4, 1904. On the history and orientation of this paper, see Chapter 4.

were unwilling or, due to rising anti-Semitism, felt unable to find a place
for themselves among Polish nationalists, particularly in the east, where
the Poles constituted only a minority.[105] It is in this context that the Jewish
nationalist movement emerged in the last decades of the Habsburg Empire,
as portions of the secular Jewish intelligentsia – despite their own personal
linguistic acculturation – began to perceive themselves as constituting a distinct Jewish nation, deserving the same national rights as everyone else.[106]

It was not only Polish power that undermined decades of Germanization
among Galician Jews. As German nationalism itself grew progressively
more *völkisch* during the 1870s and 1880s, it increasingly excluded the
Jews from its ranks. In 1880, for example, the city council of Brody,
an overwhelmingly Jewish city, sued the Galician Board of Education
over its intention to erect only Polish elementary schools.[107] The council
demanded German as the language of instruction, insisting that under
Article 19 the Jews' rights as Germans had been violated. The Viennese
Education Ministry rejected their claim, stating that the Jews "have no
right to declare themselves as belonging to the German nationality and
the German language as their language."[108] The Jews appealed to the
Reichsgericht in Vienna, the higher court that dealt with violations of
constitutional rights. It ruled that Brody's Jews could demand German
instruction as Austrian citizens, German being an official language of the
land, but it upheld the Education Ministry's position that the Jews could
not claim to belong to the German nation. The inability of Galician Jewry
to register as a *Volksstamm*, coupled with their increasing rejection by
those nationalities from which they had to choose to identify (at least
for census purposes), highlights the challenges faced by Jews in forging a
modern Jewish identity in this period.

---

[105] On the transformation of Polish nationalism and the growth of anti-Semitism, see Brian
Porter, *When Nationalism Began to Hate: Imagining Modern Politics in Nineteenth-
Century Poland* (New York and Oxford, 2000).

[106] There was no assimilationist movement toward Ruthenians. With their generally uned-
ucated, often anti-Semitic peasant population and largely clerical intelligentsia, itself
struggling to overcome Polish domination, they did not present an appealing option
for most Jews. As John-Paul Himka put it, "For the Jews to hitch their wagon to the
politically marginalized, oppressed, and plebian Ukrainians would have made no sense."
John-Paul Himka, "Dimensions of a Triangle: Polish-Ukrainian-Jewish Relations in
Austrian Galicia," *Polin* 12 (1999): 35.

[107] On this incident, see Gerald Stourzh, "Galten die Juden als Nationalität Altösterreichs?"
Studia Judaica Austriaca 10 (1984): 73–98, and Kurt Stillschweig, "Die nationalitäten-
rechtliche Stellung der Juden im alten Österreich," *Monatsschrift für Geschichte und
Wissenschaft des Judentums*, July/August 1937: 321–40.

[108] Stillschweig, op. cit., 336.

SHOMER ISRAEL AND THE EMERGENCE OF "JEWISH" POLITICS

Elite Jews began to assert an independent political agenda almost immediately after their emancipation, before the process of Polonization had uprooted their predominantly German cultural identity. Already in 1868, leading members of the lay Jewish elite in Lemberg, led by Reuven Bierer (1837–1931), Philip Mansch, and Joseph Kohn, established one of the community's first semi-political societies, Shomer Israel (Guardian of Israel). Initially more cultural than political, it sought to modernize Galician Jewry by spreading western (i.e., German) culture among the Jewish masses, to teach them to understand their new social and political obligations, and to build allegiance to the Habsburg monarchy in general and German Liberalism in particular. In other words, it promoted the values of the moderate Haskalah. It also reflected the general flourishing of bourgeois associational life – particularly political clubs – in the aftermath of the 1867 constitution.[109] Shomer Israel hosted lectures and a library, and beginning in 1869 it published a German-language paper, *Der Israelit*, at first in Hebrew characters but from 1873 in standard, Gothic script.[110]

Despite its initially cultural orientation, Shomer Israel – again like its non-Jewish counterparts – quickly evolved into a more political association, largely as a result of an important political opportunity. In 1873, just a few years after its adoption, Austria's electoral system was amended; the national Parliament (Reichsrat) was to be directly elected rather than appointed by the provincial diets.[111] Suffrage in parliamentary elections would be based upon the same criteria as in elections for the provincial diets, namely, the so-called curial system, a four- (later five-) class system based on domicile and income.[112] While all great landowners and

---

[109] Judson, op. cit., 143–64.

[110] The paper survived, with brief interruptions, until 1914. On the orientation and history of the paper, see Jacob Toury, *Die jüdische Press im Österreichischen Kaiserreich* (Tübingen, 1983), 59.

[111] The amendment was designed to thwart the obstructionist tactics of the Czechs, who had attempted to undermine the *Reichsrat* by directing their diet-appointed delegates not to take their seats. See William Jenks, *The Austrian Electoral Reform of 1907* (New York, 1950), 14–16.

[112] In 1896 a fifth curia was added, open to all adult men. Its importance was limited, however, as it only elected about a fifth of the Parliament and was open even to those privileged to vote in another curia, men who were thus given a second vote. See Jenks, op. cit., 22–6.

members of the chamber of commerce were permitted to vote, members of the general rural and urban curia had to pay at least ten guilder in annual taxes.[113] This was a very high sum and the vast majority of peasants and workers were thereby excluded from the voting franchise. In 1873, just 6.7 percent of the urban population and 8.9 percent of the rural population could vote. Further, although these two groups represented the vast majority of the Galician population, they elected only two thirds of its Reichsrat delegates. Less than 2,000 large landowners and literally a few dozen members of the chambers of commerce elected the remaining third. In practical terms, this meant that each urban delegate represented 29,373 people and each rural delegate represented 186,456 residents, but just 93 large landowners elected each of their delegates and in 1879 just 25 members of the chambers of commerce could send one of theirs![114]

Despite the severely unequal voting franchise, the 1873 amendment dealt a significant blow to Galicia's Polish majority, which lost its ability to select almost single-handedly Galicia's delegation to the Reichsrat through its control of the Galician diet. Polish domination of the diet had meant that Poles could easily limit the representation of Jews and Ruthenians in the Reichsrat; now those minorities would be able to elect their delegates directly. Of course, in addition to the financial influence of the Polish nobility, Polish bureaucrats were still in charge of conducting the elections and could manipulate the results with nearly total impunity.[115] Thus Galicia's Ruthenian and Jewish minorities would need to organize politically in order to take advantage of their new rights.[116]

In May 1873, Jewish intellectuals in Lemberg, mostly members of the pro-German Shomer Israel society, founded the first Jewish Election

---

[113] The minimum tax was lowered to five gulden in 1882. See Jenks, op. cit., 17–19. Great landowners had to pay at least fifty gulden in annual taxes to vote, but few would have been unable to meet this requirement.

[114] Calculations based on statistics in G. A. Schimmer, *Die Reichsraths-Wahlen vom Jahre 1879 in Oesterreich* (Stuttgart, 1880), 70.

[115] Electoral manipulation was relatively easy as the Polish gentry maintained power through its domination of the *Bezirkshauptmannschaften*, the county prefects who conducted the elections and confirmed their results. Moreover, the peasant curia, already limited in its percentage of parliamentary seats, elected their representatives indirectly, so that ultimately only a small number of peasant electors had to be bribed or threatened to vote as the Polish gentry wished. John-Paul Himka, "Dimensions of a Triangle," 35.

[116] Rachel Manekin, "Politics, Religion, and National Identity: The Galician Jewish Vote in the 1873 Parliamentary Elections," *Polin* 12 (1999): 104.

Committee, which quickly formed branches throughout Galicia.[117] The Committee supported the German Liberals' centralist policies and strongly opposed Polish autonomism, which threatened to undermine the rights of the province's minorities. Aside from their German cultural orientation, the Jews' position reflected their recognition of German Liberalism as the source of their freedom. It was, after all, the Habsburg Liberal constitution that had emancipated Galician Jewry and guaranteed religious and civil equality, whereas Polish leaders in Galicia sought the complete Polonization of the province. Just five years earlier the Polish-dominated diet had debated whether even to confirm Jewish emancipation, as guaranteed by Austrian law. It did so ultimately only under the influence of Franz Smolka, president of the Assembly, who assumed that Jews would reciprocate by integrating into the Polish nation and joining the Polish national struggle. This argument eventually convinced a sound majority of the diet.[118]

The common interest of Ruthenians and Jews in Galicia to overcome Polish domination ultimately led to a semi-secret alliance between the Jewish Election Committee and the Rada Ruska, the Ruthenian Council.[119] The former agreed to support Ruthenian candidates in rural districts, where Jewish candidates would stand no chance of election, while the Ruthenian Council promised to support certain Jewish urban candidates.[120] They successfully elected Jewish deputies in three districts (Brody, Kolomea, and Drohobycz), all of whom joined the Liberal faction rather than the dominant Polish electoral block known as the "Polish Club"[121] (see Appendix A).

---

[117] Manekin, "Politics, Religion, and National Identity," 105 ff. Most activity was concentrated in the East. Liberal Jews in Western Galicia, especially in Cracow itself, tended more often to be Polish patriots and rejected the Shomer Israelites' anti-Polish stance.

[118] See *Die Debatten über die Judenfrage in desr Session der galizischen Landtages von J. 1868* (Lemberg, 1868). Smolka even used the legendary story of the "Jewish king Abraham" as proof of Jewish rootedness in Poland.

[119] The committee initially sought an agreement with the Polish Central Election Committee, whereby Jews would support the Poles in exchange for six guaranteed seats (Lemberg, Brody, Kolomea, Stanislau, Przemysl, and Drohobycz), as well as the nomination of liberal, anti-federalist candidates in districts with significant Jewish minorities. Only after the Poles refused did the Jewish Committee approach the Ruthenians. Filip Friedman, op. cit., 186. This tends to support John-Paul Himka's assertion that the two sides were each allied with the German centralists in the election rather than with each other. John-Paul Himka, "Dimensions of a Triangle," 34.

[120] Manekin, "Politics, Religion, and National Identity," 111 ff.

[121] A fourth Jew, Albert Mendelburz, elected by the Cracow Chamber of Commerce curia, joined the Polish Club.

By 1879, however, Polish political hegemony in Galicia and the threat
of Polish economic retribution was strong enough to prevent nearly any
candidate from winning election without Polish approval. *Der Israelit*
remained almost completely silent about the 1879 parliamentary elections, dispassionately endorsing the Polish Club, which had promised
to include four Jewish candidates.[122] Moreover, in 1878 Orthodox
Jewish leaders had formed their own political organization, Machsike
Hadas (Defenders of the Faith), in opposition to Shomer Israel. The new
Orthodox party specifically endorsed the Polish Catholic candidates over
the Jewish, anti-clerical Liberals. It did so despite generally believing that
districts with a Jewish majority ought to have a Jewish representative.
(In four districts, however, the group nominated its own candidates and
called on supporters to unite behind these "warriors for God.")[123] The
president of Machsike Hadas, Rabbi Simon Sofer (Schreiber), who won
election to Parliament in the Kolomea-Buczacz-Sniatyn district, described
his support for the Polish Club as natural. When asked what faction he
would join, Sofer responded, "I have no choice but to join the Polish
party. The Poles are religious people who fulfill the precepts of their religion, and I also have only one goal – to strengthen religion."[124] Just three
Jews won election from Galicia in 1879. Two, including Sofer, joined
the Polish Club, while one maverick who managed to win despite Polish
opposition, Nathan Kallir of Brody, joined the Liberal Club instead.[125]

Does this first attempt at Jewish politicization qualify as nationalist?
Manekin has justly noted that in 1873, "the Jews in the various communities did organize as Jews and that alone gave the [Jewish electoral]
organization a distinctly nationalist flavour."[126] Letters she found to the
Central Jewish Election Committee concerned about defending Jewish

[122] Rachel Manekin, "The New Covenant: Orthodox Jews and Polish Catholics in Galicia
(1879–1883)" (Hebrew), *Zion* 64 (1999): 163.

[123] The party's new newspaper, which was quickly becoming a fully Hebrew-language publication, printed the directives to support the Polish conservatives as well as its own
party's four candidates in both Yiddish and Hebrew just before the election. *Machsike
Hadas*, June 11, 1879; June 25, 1895. The paper subsequently celebrated God's hand in
electing Sofer. See especially *Machsike Hadas*, July 23, 1879, 3.

[124] Quoted in Manekin, "Politics, Religion, and Nationality," 118. True to his word,
Sofer voted consistently with the Polish Club and never once even raised his voice in a
debate. On the early history of Machsike Hadas, see Rachel Manekin, *The Growth and
Development of Jewish Orthodoxy in Galicia: The "Machsike Hadas" Society 1867–
1883* (Hebrew), (unpublished dissertation, Hebrew University, 2000).

[125] This was the son of Mayer Kallir, the Orthodox delegate to the Sejm, who had passed
away in 1875.

[126] Manekin, "Politics, Religion, and National Identity," 109.

pride and even Jewish "nationalist interests" certainly belie Saul Landau's smug dismissal of the Shomer Israelites as being devoid of "any Jewish platform."[127] They were not merely a "Galician replica of the Viennese [Liberal] Constitutional Party," as Landau charged but were in fact attempting to create a Jewish politics, oriented toward Liberalism to be sure, but independently so. Their alliance with the Ruthenians certainly demonstrates independent political organization. Indeed, Shomer Israel's entire agenda of Jewish politicization, raising Jewish political awareness and motivating Jews toward political activity, anticipates the same project by many Jewish nationalists half a generation later.

At the same time, however, Landau's characterization of these Jewish leaders as "Jewish notables" is not entirely inaccurate. They may have been attempting to rally Jewish support for their respective candidates, but they were not trying to forge a mass movement. Suffrage itself was severely restricted, after all, and Liberalism did not favor universal suffrage or the formation of mass political parties. More important, these Jewish leaders did not view the Jews as a national group but rather as a religious and political community. Insofar as they were seeking to defend Jewish rights, they had in mind only civil, not national rights. Manekin rightly quotes *Der Israelit* as representative of Shomer Israel's national position in 1873: "The nationality of the Jews is humanity in its entirety; its fatherland the globe."[128] Only a decade later would some Jews begin to think otherwise.

---

[127] Ibid., 109; Saul Raphael Landau, *Der Polenklub und seine Hausjuden* (Vienna, 1907), 7.
[128] Manekin, "Politics, Religion, and National Identity," 109.

2

Neither Germans nor Poles

Jewish Nationalism in Galicia before Herzl, 1883–1896

The real birth of Jewish nationalism in Galicia, as in the rest of Europe, would come only in the 1880s.[1] The critical catalyst traditionally credited with sparking the Jewish nationalist movement is the series of pogroms in Russia in 1881–2, whose psychological and political impact reached well beyond the borders of the Tsarist Empire. It had an especially direct impact on Galicia, where scores of thousands of Russian Jewish refugees fled for safety, particularly to the border town of Brody and the capital Lemberg. The pogroms, one of which took place in Warsaw in 1882, allegedly undermined the confidence of many Galician intellectuals in the possibility of Jewish integration into the Polish nation. Many Zionist historians point to previously isolated and ephemeral incidents of individuals promoting settlement of the land of Israel, or cultural projects such as the revival of the Hebrew language, and note how these "proto-Zionist" models began to bear fruit after 1881.[2]

To a certain extent, this model, typically applied to Russian Jewry, holds true in Galicia as well. The Galician Zionist leader Gershom Bader (1868–1954), for example, writing just a decade after the pogroms,

---

[1] This dating of its origins has been the subject of recent scholarly reevaluation sparked by Eli Lederhendler's critical study of pre-1881 Russian Jewish politics and communal life. Lederhendler charts the emergence – already in the 1860s and 1870s – of the principle of the "people's will" as the basis for a new type of "political community." "The call for Jewish autoemancipation," he concludes, "grew out of the political crisis of Russian Jewry before 1881." Eli Lederhendler, *The Road to Modern Jewish Politics* (New York, 1989), 155.

[2] See, e.g., David Vital, *The Origins of Zionism* (Oxford, 1975), 65ff. The most important of these "proto-Zionist" groups described by Gelber was the Przemysl Society for Settling the Land of Israel, established in 1875. Gelber, *Toldot ha-tenuah ha-tsiyonit be-Galitsyah* (Jerusalem,1958), 65–7.

credited the flood of refugees to Galicia with igniting the initial spark of Jewish nationalist activity in the province. The importance of the pogroms for Bader, however, lay not in their undermining of Jewish hopes for integration, but rather in the material repercussions of the crisis itself. Bader described how the severity of the crisis led Galician Jews to establish a network of associations and charity funds designed to aid the fleeing Jews. Although these groups initially lacked any nationalist orientation, the indifference of "assimilationists" to the plight of the refugees, he wrote, lent the aid societies a certain nationalist character.[3] Thus, Bader's point serves to mitigate the actual role of the 1881 crisis (in terms of its discrediting of integrationist optimism) in sparking the Jewish nationalist movement, and credits instead a more gradual process by which Jewish relief activity assumed a nationalist character.

In fact, Bader's article directly challenges the applicability in Galicia of the traditional Russian Zionist paradigm, which sees the 1881 crisis replacing Jewish hopes of emancipation with the principle of "auto-emancipation."[4] Bader's description of 1881 sparking Jewish associational life focused on work in the Diaspora rather than the sort of Palestine-centered activities more common further east. This highlights a critical difference between the Galician and Russian responses to the crisis. To be sure, Jewish intellectuals emerged on both sides of the Russian-Austrian border who questioned the possibility of Jewish integration into non-Jewish society. Many of these formed the first Jewish nationalist societies in the 1880s. In Russia, however, where the Tsarist regime was perceived as having had at best tolerated the violence and at worst induced it, this disappointment led to the emergence of a decidedly Palestine-centered Zionist ideology. Jewish nationalists at the time generally agreed that only through emigration could Jews fully emancipate themselves.[5] In Galicia, by contrast, Jews rarely experienced pogroms or civic repression. On the

---

[3] G. Bader, "The National Movement among Our Jewish Brothers in Galicia" (Hebrew), *Achi'asaf*, 1894/95, 172. On the paradigmatic, if counterfactual Zionist claim of "assimilationist indifference" to Jewish suffering, see later in the chapter.

[4] See Vital, op. cit., 49–186, and Jonathan Frankel, *Prophecy and Politics: Socialism, Nationalism, and the Russian Jews, 1862–1917* (Cambridge, 1981), 49–133. "Autoemancipation" was the title of Leon Pinsker's landmark 1882 booklet. As noted, recent scholarship has suggested that this trend began already in the 1870s and was merely accelerated in 1881. See Lederhendler, op. cit., and John Klier, *Imperial Russia's Jewish Question, 1855–1881* (Cambridge, 1995), esp. 358–63, which emphasizes the impact of a major pogrom in Odessa in 1871.

[5] Gideon Shimoni, *The Zionist Ideology* (Hanover, 1995), 32. Only at the turn of the century would a Diaspora-oriented Jewish nationalism take root in Russia. Its most

contrary, a Liberal constitution protected their civil rights and even guaranteed limited national rights to recognized linguistic minorities. Jewish nationalists in Galicia thus felt more confident that they might achieve national rights without having to emigrate. This factor – the possibility of realizing national minority rights in Europe – would distinguish Galician Zionism from its Russian and Western counterparts for most of this period.[6]

Of course, the events of 1881–2 did not impact all sectors of Jewish society equally. Whereas "radical assimilationists" continued to advocate the total elimination of a distinct Jewish identity, some "integrationists" who had always supported the persistence of such an identity, albeit hyphenated, now began to despair of such a possibility.[7] Beyond the problem of intractable anti-Semitism, there remained a deeper issue facing European Jews in the late nineteenth century. In a society in which one's nation increasingly demanded primary or even exclusive allegiance, a hyphenated Jewish identity seemed increasingly untenable to some. Even in the Habsburg Empire, where the dynastic foundation of the state had enabled Jews to assert an ethnic identity without it questioning their "national" allegiance, dynastic loyalty grew progressively less able to protect them from the hyper-nationalist atmosphere of the late nineteenth century.[8] Modernizing Jews felt pressured to define themselves nationally, by their cultural and linguistic choices as much as by state law, and the available options increasingly demanded assimilation as the price

important advocate was the Jewish socialist party known as the Bund, which by 1901 had begun calling for Jewish national-cultural autonomy, although the ideology was most famously formulated by the anti-socialist Jewish historian Simon Dubnow in a series of articles beginning in 1897. See Koppel Pinson, ed. *Nationalism and History: Essays on Old and New Judaism by Simon Dubnow* (Philadelphia, 1958). Following the 1905 Russian Revolution, Russian Zionists themselves also adopted a resolution to pursue national rights in Russia.

[6] Viennese Zionists, who obviously also enjoyed the benefits of the Habsburg constitution, nevertheless also generally remained focused on Palestine in this period. A Diaspora nationalist party, the Jüdische Volkspartei, was founded in Vienna only in 1902. Austrian Zionists began agitating for national minority rights on the eve of universal manhood suffrage in 1906. See Chapter 5, and Marsha Rozenblit, *The Jews of Vienna 1867–1914: Assimilation and Identity* (Albany, 1983), 161–93. Rozenblit's division of Jewish nationalists into "Diaspora nationalist" and "Zionist" camps, albeit with overlapping membership and activities, emerges in Galicia as well, although there the distinction is less clear because those who called themselves Zionists adopted an ideology closer to Rozenblit's Diaspora nationalism.

[7] Shimoni, op. cit., 49.

[8] Recall Marsha Rozenblit's notion of the Jews' "tripartite" identity: "Austrian by political loyalty, German (or Czech or Polish) by cultural affiliation, and Jewish in an ethnic sense." Marsha Rozenblit, *Reconstructing a National Identity* (New York, 2001).

of their inclusion, or else simply defined Jews as inherently foreign to the Polish (or Ukrainian) nation.[9]

Jewish nationalism, however, was less a retreat from integration in response to anti-Semitism than it was an expression of an internal momentum within Jewry itself. The progenitors of Jewish nationalism included not only disillusioned integrationists, drawn to Jewish nationalism as an outlet for their European values (whether of the Enlightenment or of romantic nationalism), but also "ethnicists" who came to Zionism from within traditional Jewish society in order to revitalize Jewish culture through the integration of secular knowledge.[10] In Galicia, as in Russia, this camp consisted of Jews raised in a traditional milieu but, exposed to secular values and learning, turned to Jewish nationalism as a means of uniting these identities. In short, like all nationalist movements, Jewish nationalism, above and beyond its political platforms, responded to the needs of individuals facing the crises common to all traditional societies coping with the social, economic, and political transformations wrought by modernization.[11] For Jews, it provided a means to integrate into the modern world without abandoning their sense of authentic Jewishness. Thus Jewish nationalism drew support from two disparate groups: acculturated integrationists, propelled to Zionism by an inhospitable Gentile world, and modernizing ethnicists seeking a secular, Jewish identity able to compete with rival national ideologies.

The Jewish nationalist movement in Galicia, especially in the period before the appearance of Theodor Herzl, provided a framework to include both of these groups through its strong and early support for Diaspora nationalist activity. On the one hand, Jewish nationalists focused on revitalizing Jewish culture in a secular, European framework obviously applauded efforts to win Jewish national autonomy in Galicia. The establishment of state-funded Jewish schools with a Jewish curriculum taught in Yiddish or Hebrew, for example, constituted a central goal of such nationalists. At the same time, "disillusioned" acculturated Jews who joined the Zionist movement to express nationalist feelings ignited but

---

[9] Keely Stauter-Halsted, *The Nation in the Village* (Ithaca, 2001), 38–42, 133–41. Stauter-Halsted emphasizes the economic basis of this antagonism, which encouraged Polish nationalists to use anti-Semitism to forge a sense of shared national feeling between Polish-speaking gentry and peasants.

[10] For an explication of this dichotomy, see Shimoni, op. cit., 46–51.

[11] M. Hroch, "The Social Interpretation of Linguistic Demands in European National Movements" (San Domenico: European University Institute Working Papers 94/1, 1994), 25.

also denied to them by Polish nationalism, those who turned to Zionism to regain their self-respect in a hyper-nationalist era and to protect Jewish political interests, would naturally want to win Jewish national rights in Galicia as well. After all, this was precisely what the other nationalities struggled to achieve.

Jewish nationalism in Galicia before 1897 remained a small, minority movement of a few thousand Jewish intellectuals. In this critical period, Jewish nationalists largely worked to convince members of the secular intelligentsia, a tiny minority of Galician Jewry, that the key to full Jewish emancipation and equality was the recognition of the Jews as a nationality.[12] Their program, although always maintaining the acquisition of a national home in Palestine as a long-term goal, focused almost entirely on objectives similar to those of the other nationalist movements in the empire: the transformation of Jewish identity from a "community of faith" into a national community, and the acquisition of national minority rights.

Although Jewish ethnicists formed a critical foundation of the early movement's leadership, early activists focused most of their efforts on reaching out to disillusioned integrationists, especially students at the gymnasia and universities. Only toward the end of this period did the movement begin to gain ground among the broader populace. The critical transition into a mass movement was facilitated within the intelligentsia itself, when nationalists began to expand their outreach to this growing class of young students raised in a religious milieu but increasingly attracted to European culture and the modern world. It was this class of Jews, still deeply connected with traditional Jewish life, who would ultimately prove so important in the nationalization of traditional Jews.

In sum, Jewish nationalism was not primarily a reaction to anti-Semitic violence. Rather, it resulted from the ability of isolated nationalist arguments and distant pogroms to become part of the realm of experience of large numbers of people in an age of rapid communication and transportation. Urbanization, railroads, rapid mail delivery, and the proliferation of news media meant the penetration of new ideas into heretofore isolated groups, as well as a growing sense of community based on this shared discourse. To be sure, these ideas took many years to evolve. We are not dealing here with two opposing camps, assimilationists and nationalists.

---

[12] This roughly corresponds to Hroch's second phase of small nation formation, that is, the beginning of "patriotic agitation" among intellectuals.

Rather, there existed a dizzying array of political and cultural visions which Galician Jews combined in countless permutations. Many figures adopted different approaches over the course of their own lives, often tolerating tremendous inconsistencies at various moments. Jewish nationalists, for example, railed against Poles and Polonization – in Polish – while Orthodox leaders who could not speak Polish insisted on supporting Polish Conservatives. Self-described assimilationists encouraged young Jews to study Hebrew and express Jewish pride while Zionists held rallies in Polish insisting that the Jews constituted a nation based on Hebrew, which they could not speak. And despite Austria's defining nationality in terms of "language of daily use," Jewish nationalists for years refused to ground their claim to nationhood on the Jews' actual unique language of daily use, Yiddish, or even to use that medium in their speeches and publications.

MIKRA KODESH AND ITS OPPONENTS

As in Russia, Jewish students dominated the first nationalist societies in Austria, which began to appear in Vienna as early as 1882. That May, Reuven Bierer (1837–1931), originally a founding member of Shomer Israel in Lemberg but now at age forty-five a medical student at the University of Vienna, brought together Peretz Smolenskin (1842–85), the Russian-Zionist publicist then living in Vienna, and the Orthodox Rabbi Salomon Spitzer (1825–93), to form a Palestine-colonization association called Ahavath Zion (Love of Zion).[13] This was a part of the broader Lovers of Zion (Hibbat Zion) movement, based in Russia. The society was a direct response to the Russian pogroms and the ensuing refugee crisis, Bierer later recalled, and had the stated purpose of resettling the fleeing Jews in the "Holy Land."[14] As a result of a conflict between its Orthodox and secular leadership, however, the group collapsed within a short time.[15] Bierer's second attempt at establishing a Jewish-nationalist society proved more enduring. In late 1882, he joined with two other students,

---

[13] Bierer was one of the architects of the Liberal Jewish election committee in 1873, as well as of the 1878 Galician "Community Day," but later left Shomer Israel over its pro-Polish transformation. Gelber, "*Mikra Kodesh* and the First Zionist Circles in Galicia (1881–1890)" (Yiddish) in *Galizianer Yovel-buch* (Buenos Aires, 1966), 156.

[14] *Drohobyczer Zeitung*, May 2, 1902, 3.

[15] The group's president, Rabbi Spitzer, simply refused to work with Smolenskin. For Bierer's account, see *Drohobyczer Zeitung*, May 9, 1902, 2 and *Neue National-Zeitung*, April 9, 1909, 4–5.

Moritz Schnirer (1860–1942) and Nathan Birnbaum (1864–1937),[16] to form a Jewish-nationalist academic association at the university. A few weeks later, with a small coterie of other students and the support of Smolenskin, Kadimah (Forward or Eastward) was born.[17]

Officially, in order to ensure approval by the authorities, the new fraternity's statutes were carefully drafted to preclude any political tendency. The group limited itself to promoting the "cultivation of Jewish literature and scholarship." This also brought the benefit of attracting support from groups like Shomer Israel, which strongly endorsed efforts at Jewish education but opposed the more radical nationalist agenda of rebuilding the Jewish nation in Palestine. In fact, in July 1883 *Der Israelit* published Kadimah's nearly column-length appeal for material and moral support, particularly library donations. The article, whose call to *Stammesgenossen* seems to have been heard by the gentlemen of Shomer Israel, describes the group's purpose as reconnecting Jewish students to their history and literature and building their love for the Jewish people (Volk). It avoids any discussion of Palestine or the rebuilding of a Jewish state, although it does ask for donations toward the "regeneration of the Jewish nation."[18]

[16] Birnbaum, who was also a member of Ahavath Zion, soon became the most important and influential Zionist leader in Austria, although he later abandoned his strict Palestine-centric Zionism in favor of the movement for Jewish national autonomy based on Yiddish language and culture. Eventually he abandoned this movement as well and, having become a devoutly religious Jew, was elected general secretary of the ultra-Orthodox party Agudat Yisrael. On Birnbaum, see Jess Olson, *Nation, Peoplehood and Religion in the Life and Thought of Nathan Birnbaum* (Ph.D. dissertation, Stanford University, 2006); Robert Wistrich, "The Clash of Ideologies in Jewish Vienna (1880–1918): The Strange Odyssey of Nathan Birnbaum," *Leo Baeck Institute Yearbook* 33 (1988): 201–30; and Joshua Fishman, *Ideology, Society, and Language: The Odyssey of Nathan Birnbaum* (Ann Arbor, 1987).

[17] Bierer claimed to be the driving force behind the establishment of the society and even hosted its first meeting in his apartment. The students later brought in Smolenskin for name recognition. *Neue National-Zeitung*, April 9, 1909, 8–9 and *Die Welt*, August 13, 1897, 6. Schnirer gives more credit to Smolenskin, particularly emphasizing that it was he who chose the name. *Jüdische Zeitung*, January 31, 1908, 2–3. For a history of the society, see Julius H. Schoeps, "Modern Heirs of the Maccabees – The Beginnings of the Vienna Kadimah, 1882–1897," *Leo Baeck Institute Yearbook* 27 (1982), 155–70, and Olson, op. cit., 19–37. Olson argues that the impact of Smolenskin was far more profound than Bierer (and his son) suggest.

[18] *Der Israelit*, July 27, 1883, 6. They may not have had to be so careful in wording their appeal. The following year, the paper printed a plea for support by Ahavath Zion to help settle Romanian- and Russian-Jewish refugees in Palestine. The paper printed this despite the appeal's submission by Joseph Bloch, the Galician rabbi who had just trounced the president of Shomer Israel in a bitterly contested parliamentary election. *Der Israelit*, August 15, 1884, 6.

Unofficially, each member of Kadimah pledged himself in writing to "combat assimilation, seal his commitment to the Jewish nation, and support the colonization of Palestine."[19] Nevertheless, on March 23, 1883, the authorities approved the foundation of Austrian Zionism's most important association of this period, the academic fraternity Kadimah. Over a dozen years before the publication of *Der Judenstaat*, Kadimah laid the foundation for Theodor Herzl's movement, providing a positive, secular Jewish identity for Jewish students disillusioned with the prospects of integration or assimilation.[20]

The Jewish national idea found even more fertile ground in Galicia, which had provided the majority of the founding members of Kadimah.[21] Organized Jewish nationalist activity in the province dates at least to the foundation of the Jewish cultural association Mikra Kodesh (Holy Assembly), established in Lemberg in the summer of 1883. The new association, founded by (President) Joseph Kobak (1828–1913) and (Vice-president) Reuven Bierer, now back in Lemberg, was not explicitly nationalist in theory, but in practice its activities clearly advanced Jewish nationalist objectives. Ideologically, it rested firmly in the tradition of the Jewish Enlightenment, or Haskalah. In other words, Mikra Kodesh was not a response to anti-Semitism but rather reflected the Haskalah's traditional championing of Jewish culture in a modern framework.

As an association dedicated to the ideals of the Haskalah, Mikra Kodesh was perfectly compatible with Shomer Israel. Indeed, Kobak, a Lemberg-born but German-educated rabbi, was an active member of the latter society while Bierer was one of its founding members. Kobak also taught religion at a Lemberg gymnasium and served as religious educator for the Lemberg Temple, the religious home to members of Shomer Israel. Kobak even served as the unofficial replacement for the Temple's aged and frail preacher, Bernhard Löwenstein, from 1883 until the rabbi's death in 1889.[22] Moreover, the editors of *Der Israelit* seemed to have

---

[19] Schoeps, op. cit., 156. See also Rozenblit, *The Jews of Vienna 1867–1914*, 161 ff.

[20] Although its founding members consisted overwhelmingly of self-conscious Jews raised in decisively Jewish milieus, the group's propaganda and activities (like those of the first nationalist associations in Galicia) targeted Jews from strongly acculturated backgrounds. By the mid-1890s, the association was dominated by "assimilated" Jews returning to the Jewish fold. See Gaisbauer, *Davidstern and Doppeladler* (Vienna, 1988), 51.

[21] Over two thirds of Kadimah's fifty-four founding members were Galician. Gelber, *Toldot HaTenuah HaZionut B'Galitsia*, 138 ff.

[22] Julian J. Bussgang, "The Progressive Synagogue in Lwów," *Polin* 11 (1998), 145. According to Julian Hirshaut, the Temple board refused to hire him as Löwenstein's replacement, either because of his Zionist leanings or possibly because of his wife's "scandalous" indiscretions. When they hired a former member of Mikra Kodesh (Samuel Gutman) to serve

gladly printed Kobak's "important" (*beherzigenswerthen*) call for membership and financial support on the occasion of his receiving government approval for the new organization in 1885.

> Every sincere Jew feels and knows how neglected the youth has become for several decades regarding religion, biblical knowledge, Hebrew language and Jewish science. To redress this daily and ever-expanding disease, an association has been founded here under the name "Mikra Kodesh" ... where free daily instruction will be offered by experts in the above fields to any Jew from 13-years old (Bar Mitzvah). Therefore, we ask our honorable colleagues, those who have a refined, warm-feeling heart for Jewish sciences, to join our association.[23]

In fact, many members of Shomer Israel and even of the pro-Polonization group Agudas Achim did attend the new group's first meetings, before the society's more overtly nationalist orientation grew dominant. Shomer Israel even sponsored some of the group's early events.[24]

Mikra Kodesh did not simply constitute an academic branch of Shomer Israel. Rather, it represented something more akin to what Shmuel Feiner has labeled the "national *Haskalah*." This was an emerging movement, led most vocally by Peretz Smolenskin in Vienna, which rejected the moderate Haskalah's campaign against the "benighted" religious masses and concerned itself far more with what it perceived as a growing assimilationist trend within the Haskalah itself.[25] Whereas Shomer Israel had defined its purpose in terms of bringing enlightenment to the Jewish masses, Mikra Kodesh focused on acculturated Jews who had lost contact with their Jewish heritage. Kobak in particular emphasized the religious need for his group, which would teach the "holy Torah" to ensure that Jewish children remained "true Jews."[26] Mikra Kodesh had no interest in projects to promote the settlement of Palestine but rather defined itself as a cultural and religious society, offering Hebrew language courses, biblical classes, history lessons, and holiday celebrations. In December of 1883, Mikra Kodesh organized the province's first Maccabee festival, the annual celebration that became the central propaganda event of the Zionist movement. Like Kadimah, Mikra Kodesh was constituted as an academic

---

as assistant rabbi in 1903, Kobak left Lemberg for several years to assume a rabbinical post in Innsbruck. Hirshaut, *In Gang Fun Der Geshichte* (Tel-Aviv, 1984), 247.

[23] *Der Israelit*, May 29, 1885, 3. The paper had printed appeals from Kadimah in 1883 and Ahavath Zion in 1884.

[24] Jacob Toury, *Die Jüdische Presse im Österreichischen Kaiserreich* (Tübingen, 1983), 66.

[25] Shmuel Feiner, *Haskalah and History* (Oxford, 2002), 317–40.

[26] Kobak's call for support in the *Drohobyczer Zeitung* was far more religiously framed than in *Der Israelit*. See his January 12 letter in *Drohobyczer Zeitung*, Nr. 2, 1885. 4–5.

association, although at the gymnasium rather than the university level. The society attracted two distinct groups of members. Despite its charter purpose of reaching out to Jews disconnected from their Jewish heritage, the association initially focused more on religious students beginning their secular education. It worked to ease their transition into secular studies, for example by offering help with German, while maintaining their ties to Judaism with Jewish studies classes taught through the lens of the Haskalah (e.g., biblical studies with modern philological commentaries, Hebrew language and Jewish history). Young yeshiva students like Mordechai (Markus) Ehrenpreis (1869–1951), Yehoshua (Osias) Thon (1870–1936), and Mordechai (Markus) Braude (1869–1950) were attracted to the new fraternity not as a result of despair following the 1881 pogroms but simply in order to get help preparing for their entrance examinations at the local gymnasium.

Very quickly, however, these traditional *bochurs* were joined by gymnasium students from Polonized backgrounds who, having suffered various experiences of anti-Semitism, sought to express their nationalist feelings in a Jewish context.[27] For these students, the sense of rising anti-Semitism among Galician Poles was of critical importance in their joining the new fraternity. Isaac Feld, who like many such students first came to Mikra Kodesh as a volunteer to tutor the new initiates in secular studies, praised Bierer (who was moving to Belgrade) for saving the Jewish secular youth from "aimless wandering" in search of an identity.

Before you appeared in our midst, a chaos of ideas ruled in the local academic community. The greater portion thereof, who have only materialism [*Magenfrage*] in mind, sought their salvation in the denial of their heritage [*Abstammung*] and endeavored to cling to foreign elements, even with contemptuous forwardness. The smaller portion of them, on the other hand, who were moved to remain true to their ancient flag, were suspended in terror as a result of the terrorism of the blinded [*verblendeten*] majority.... You, honorable doctor, awakened us out of this lethargy. You have through [your] wise advice, and no less through your admirable and model example, shaken up the minority to action and saved them from the errors of the majority. You caused the Jewish spark, which glows in our hearts, to grow into a mighty flame.[28]

[27] See the memoirs of two of the society's most important members, Braude and Ehrenpreis, both of whom came from traditional backgrounds, as well as those of Adolf Stand, who came from a thoroughly "assimilated" background. M. Braude, "Memoirs of Rabbi Dr. Mordechai Ze'ev Braude (1870–1908)," (Hebrew) in Dov Sadan, ed., *Zikhron Mordechai Ze'ev Braude* (Jerusalem, 1960), 80, 95; M. Ehrenpreis, *Bein Mizrach L'Maarav* (Tel Aviv, 1986), 25–6; Adolf Stand, *Kitvei Stand* (Tel-Aviv, 1943), 69–76.

[28] *Selbst-Emanzipation*, April 3, 1885, 5.

To be sure, the turn to Jewish nationalism was not the necessary conclusion of rising anti-Semitism among Polish nationalists. On the contrary, in Galicia, more so than in Russia, Jewish hopes for social equality through integration remained strong among the secular intelligentsia.[29] In fact, a year before the formation of Mikra Kodesh, Lemberg also saw the foundation of the group's decade-long rival, Agudas Achim (Union of Brothers, or Przymierze Braci), which blamed Jewish intransigence for anti-Semitism and promoted the integration of the Jews into the Polish nation.[30] Note, however, that it sought their integration but generally not their total assimilation. The group's advocacy of "assimilation" was in the nineteenth-century sense of the term. It also drew inspiration from the Haskalah, although it tended to emphasize the later Haskalah's program of modernization and less the earlier movement's championing of Jewish culture. Still, their official organ *Ojczyzna* (Fatherland) was published opposite a more traditional *maskilic* Hebrew sister-paper, *HaMazkir*, until 1886.[31] *HaMazkir*, whose editors Moses Landau and Isaac Bernfeld (1854–1930) later joined Mikra Kodesh, praised Hebrew language and literature and sought to spread awareness of it among Jews, although it too called for Polish-Jewish integration. For its emblem the paper chose the Polish eagle with a Star of David across its breast.[32]

The rivalry between the two groups was extremely fierce, for the two sides competed for the same constituency, namely, the secular Jewish intelligentsia, particularly the gymnasium students. Born in the 1860s, these students were raised in a Polonized province and school system and they rejected both their parents' liberal Germanism and any traditional religious worldview. This was the pool of initial recruits for the fledgling Jewish nationalist movement, and the increasingly anti-Semitic and

---

[29] Recent scholarship has begun to question the extent to which this disillusionment held true even in Russia. See Benjamin Nathans, *Beyond the Pale* (Berkeley, 2002).

[30] On Agudas Achim and one of its most important advocates see Ezra Mendelsohn, "Jewish Assimilation in L'viv: The Case of Wilhelm Feldman" in Andrei Markovits and Frank Sysyn, eds., *Nationbuilding and the Politics of Nationalism: Essays on Austrian Galicia* (Cambridge, Mass., 1982), 94–110, and Rachel Manekin, "The Debate over Assimilation in Nineteenth-Century Lwów," in Richard Cohen, Jonathan Frankel and Stefani Hoffman, eds., *Insiders and Outsiders: Dilemmas of East European Jewry* (Oxford, 2010), 120–30.

[31] The full name of the supplement was *HaMazkir ahavah le'erets moladeto* (The Reminder of Love for the Homeland). According to Gershom Bader, Bernfeld ended the supplement because he took a job as a religious teacher in Stryj. G. Bader, *Medinah va-ḥakhameha* (New York, 1934), 53.

[32] Manekin, "The Debate over Assimilation in Nineteenth-Century Lwów," 121ff.

exclusivist nature of Polish nationalism made such Jews choice targets for Zionist propaganda.[33]

The defection of any "Agudianer" to the Jewish nationalist camp was heralded by the latter as evidence of the steady decline of assimilationism. An 1885 correspondence to the Jewish nationalist paper *Selbst-Emanzipation*, for example, celebrated the spread of the Jewish national idea among former assimilationists. The author reported that at a recent conference of Agudas Achim and Shomer Israel, which by 1885 had become an advocate of Polonization rather than Germanization, members held a discussion on the question, "Are the Jews a nationality?" The debate was led by Philip Mansch, one of the founders of Shomer Israel and the editor of *Der Israelit*, who had printed a series of articles in that paper against the Jews constituting a nationality but now argued that they did constitute a nation. (Mansch had actually felt that the Jews were a nation since his student days in the 1860s, yet another sign of the counterfactual nature of Zionist accusations against the assimilationist founders of Shomer Israel. A surviving letter from Ludwig Gumplowicz to Mansch in 1861 responds to Mansch's assertion that "Jews are a nationality.")[34] Similarly in favor was Bernhard Löwenstein (1821–89), the preacher at the Lemberg reform Temple, who just the previous Yom Kippur had allegedly called from the pulpit that "the Jews have no more fatherland; they are not a nation, they are merely a community of faith." Opposing them were the major figures of Shomer Israel and Agudas Achim, Emil Byk and Bernard Goldman.[35]

The defection of Alfred Nossig (1864–1943), a founder of Agudas Achim and its Polish-language organ *Ojczyzna*, was a celebrated victory.[36] Nossig exemplified his generation's search for identity. Born in 1864, Nossig rejected his father's Germanism at an early age and became an

[33] Mendelsohn, op. cit., 108. On the growing anti-Semitic tendencies in Polish nationalism, see Brian Porter, *When Nationalism Began to Hate* (New York, 2000). On the growth of Zionism among former integrationists due to the 1898 anti-Semitic riots in Galicia, see Daniel Unowsky, "Peasant Political Mobilization and the 1898 anti-Jewish Riots in Western Galicia," *European History Quarterly* (July 2010): 412–35.

[34] An English translation appears in Werner J. Cahnman, "Scholar and Visionary: The Correspondence between Herzl and Ludwig Gumplowicz," in Raphael Patai, ed., *Herzl Year Book*, Vol. 1 (New York, 1958), 167. Cahnman calls Mansch, "one of the earliest proponents of Jewish nationalism in Galicia."

[35] *Selbst-Emanzipation*, January 1, 1886, 5.

[36] See Ezra Mendelsohn, "From Assimilation to Zionism in Lvov: The Case of Alfred Nossig," *Slavonic and East European Review* 49 (1971): 521–34, and "Wilhelm Feldman and Alfred Nossig: Assimilation and Zionism in Lvov" (Hebrew), *Gal Ed* 9 (1975): 89–111.

important leader and intellectual within the Polish-assimilationist movement, founding *Ojczyzna* when he was just sixteen years old. As Polish
nationalism turned increasingly anti-Semitic, however, he came to reject
all hopes of Jewish-Gentile co-existence and joined Mikra Kodesh, for
which he likewise became an important spokesman.[37] The Jewish nationalists recognized the significance of his transformation immediately:

> The "Agudianer" have suffered a great setback. The founder of their association,
> the founder of their organ *Ojczyzna*, the student Alfred Nossig, one of the most
> talented and intelligent young men of our city, who was the "hottest" Pole, the
> first and also the only Jew who wore the Polish national costume as his daily
> garment ... has not long ago left the Agudianer and has gone over – to the enemy
> camp, to the camp of the National Jews.[38]

Nossig's conversion is a striking example of how Feld's notion of a
"chaos of ideas" truly presented the pressures Jewish students faced. As
the ideologies of the various Jewish factions crystallized in the 1880s and
1890s, it was not at all unusual for Jews to pass from one party to another.
Nossig himself published a book of Polish romantic poetry as late as
1888 and would later abandon Zionism in favor of territorialism, that is,
Jewish national resettlement outside of Palestine.[39] Echoing Feld's words,
Yehoshua Thon's daughter described the conversions as reflecting "the
ideological chaos which prevailed in the Jewish juvenile movements. The
ideological situation became by and by clearer in the years towards the end
of the century, but the road to this enlightenment was long and painful."[40]

Moreover, despite Zionist insinuations, the stream of conversions
flowed in both directions. Perhaps the most dramatic example of the
latter phenomenon is Herman Diamand (1860–1931), an early member of Mikra Kodesh and one-time president of its successor, Zion, who
soon thereafter became a leading force in the Polish socialist party and its

---

[37] Nossig's attraction to Polish romanticism led him to study sculpture in the 1890s, with a
preference for Jewish heroic characters. Nossig was also a pioneer in Jewish demography,
establishing the Zionist-oriented Society for Jewish Statistics in 1904. He remained a maverick in the Zionist movement, ultimately alienating himself from many of its most important leaders. He died accused of treason at the hands of the Jewish Fighting Organization
on the eve of the Warsaw Ghetto Uprising in 1943. See Shmuel Almog, "Alfred Nossig: A
Reappraisal," *Studies in Zionism* 7 (Spring 1983): 1–29, and Ela Bauer, "Alfred Nossig"
in the *YIVO Encyclopedia of Jews in Eastern Europe* (New Haven, 2008), 1274.

[38] *Selbst-Emanzipation*, August 3, 1885. See Nathan Gelber's copies of Nossig's correspondences with Nathan Birnbaum, which begin in the spring of 1885! (N.M. Gelber Papers,
Central Archives for the History of the Jewish People, Jerusalem)

[39] Bauer, op. cit., 1274.

[40] Nella Rost Hollander, *Jehoshua Thon: Preacher, Thinker, Politician* (Montevideo,
Uruguay, 1966), 12.

biggest advocate of Jewish assimilation. So strong was his initial inclination toward Zionism that his peers in that group praised him at the time as a true "National Jew," a "Kadimahner with his body and soul."[41]

Nossig's conversion also exposed a basic division within Mikra Kodesh and its successor group, Zion. The association, originally visited by students raised in a traditional environment, was increasingly filled by secular students coming from a largely Polonized background. Whereas the first group came to Jewish nationalism as a secular expression of their already deep-seated Jewish identities, the latter (exemplified by Nossig) had been committed Polish nationalists who only "discovered" their Jewishness after having experienced rejection by their Polish brethren. Naturally, the two sides understood the meaning of Jewish nationalism in discordant ways. While the original members focused on Jewish culture and the Hebrew language, Nossig was a political Zionist interested in settling Palestine.[42] This conflict anticipated the later dispute between political and cultural Zionists, and in fact Ehrenpreis and Thon later became leaders of the culutral camp.

Nossig's first lecture to the association, on Moses, shocked Braude and other religious students who felt that it reflected a non-Jewish psychological analysis, so much so, wrote Braude, that "we felt that there was no connection between him and us." The more Polonized students, however, applauded Nossig's scientific research. "We came to sharp disagreements," Braude noted, "which highlighted the great distance between our group, which came to Zionism from within Judaism itself, and those who lacked an original connection to Judaism and arrived at their nationalism only out of a rejection of assimilationism." This conflict would be settled after the association's transformation in 1888, but for the time being the first group held the upper hand and Nossig was not invited to speak again.[43]

Lacking their own party organ, Jewish nationalists in Galicia relied on the paper of the entire Austrian movement, namely Nathan Birnbaum's *Selbst-Emanzipation*.[44] Birnbaum devoted an extraordinary degree of

[41] *Selbst-Emanzipation*, June 2, 1886, 5. Diamand was elected to the board of Mikra Kodesh at the group's second annual convention in 1885, at which he offered a resolution to thank J. S. Bloch for his efforts in rescuing Rachel Stieglitz. *Selbst-Emanzipation*, April 17, 1885, 5. More on Diamand later in this chapter, in Chapter 5, and in Henryk Piasecki, "Herman Diamand w Latach 1890–1918," *Biuletyn Żydowskiego Instytutu Historycznego* 106 (1978): 33–49.

[42] Mendelsohn, "From Assimilation to Zionism in Lvov," 533.

[43] M. Braude, op. cit., 98.

[44] *Selbst-Emanzipation*, founded and closely edited by Birnbaum in 1885, appeared regularly until mid-1886, when it was discontinued, and then it appeared regularly from 1890

coverage to Galicia, particularly negative coverage of Agudas Achim, whom the paper frequently referred to as "Agudas Akum," a slight shift which changed the meaning of the name from "Union of Brothers" to "Union of Pagans." The paper continuously attacked assimilationists as unimportant and devoid of any real support, an obsession which suggests that just the opposite was the case. For example, although it claimed that only eighteen to twenty guests assembled at the seventeenth annual meeting of Shomer Israel, the paper has two articles – over three columns of text combined – that discussed just how unimportant the meeting was.⁴⁵ Another article later that year noted that Agudas Achim membership had fallen from five hundred to under fifty ("One could not complain for lack of space" at their fund-raiser), while an 1886 article put the number at about twenty members.⁴⁶

Nationalists mocked assimilationists for so quickly abandoning German for Polish, arguing that they were pathetic sycophants who sought simply to join those in power. The nationalists' "eternal contra-candidate," Emil Byk (1845–1906), the one-time president of Shomer Israel, was an especially popular victim of this argument.⁴⁷ Byk was an architect of the 1873 Jewish Central Election Committee and served as its secretary, but by 1883 he had become an ardent Polish nationalist. As a leader of the assimilationist movement, whose impassioned German liberalism seemed suddenly replaced by Polish patriotism, he became an obvious target for Jewish nationalists. Joseph Bloch recalled of Byk, for example, "The association *Schomer Israel* [sic] as well as Byk and the preacher Löwenstein had once in their unregenerate days gone in for anti-Polish, German-centralist politics, together with the Ruthenians; they were now super-patriots and sang 'Jescie Polska'[sic]."⁴⁸

---

to 1893. On the history of this paper, see G. Kressel, *"Selbst-Emanzipation"* (Hebrew), *Shivat Zion* 4 (1956): 55–99, and Olson, op. cit., 47–71.

⁴⁵ *Selbst-Emanzipation*, February 2, 1885.

⁴⁶ *Selbst-Emanzipation*, May 3, 1885, and March 17, 1886.

⁴⁷ The quote, from a May 3, 1885, *Selbst-Emanzipation* article about Byk's opposition to the reelection of the outspokenly Jewish candidate Joseph Bloch, proved prophetic; he remained a leading opponent of Jewish nationalism until his death in 1906. He opposed Bloch in parliamentary elections no less than four times (1883, 1885, 1891, and 1897). S. Y. Agnon, in one of his semi-autobiographical stories, even refers to the time as the period of Bloch-Byk. S. Y. Agnon, "Bi-na'arenu u-vi-zqenenu," in *Kol sipurav shel Shmuel Yosef Agnon*, Vol. 3 (Tel-Aviv, 1960), 283. The Bloch-Byk elections are discussed later in this chapter and in Chapter 3.

⁴⁸ J. S. Bloch, *My Reminiscences* (New York, 1923), 78. ("Jeszcze Polska" are the first words of the Polish national anthem.) Saul Landau wrongly dates Byk's conversion to 1891, recalling in his memoirs that Shomer Israelites dropped their pro-German orientation at

Many of the new polonophiles, Jewish nationalists gleefully pointed out, could not yet even speak fluent Polish. An article in *Selbst-Emanzipation* about a political rally staged at the Lemberg Temple, for example, focused on how many of the new Polish nationalists still had not even mastered the language.

One heard a lot about assimilation, the Polish fatherland, blending in, introducing the Polish language, and the like. Suddenly – - - shot [from] out of this Jewish, Polish-national mouth of the Herr President – God stand by us! – unadulterated German words! What would the gentlemen of *Agudas Achim* like to say to that![49]

Similarly, several years later, during a discussion following an academic lecture on "present currents in Judaism," a Zionist student questioned why Agudas Achim promoted Polonization and not Ruthenianization in Eastern Galicia, where Ruthenians were clearly the demographically dominant nationality. A member of Agudas Achim responded that the assimilationist party "has not yet considered that." *Selbst-Emanzipation* seized on the gaffe: "These words characterize at best the assimilationists, who continuously go hand in hand with those in power, in order to get themselves some imaginary profit."[50]

Of course, if one views Jewish nationalism not as an existential truth but as a cultural and political choice, than the turn toward Zionism by former Polonizing Jews may be viewed as an equally capricious conversion. Bloch himself, the cause célèbre of early Jewish nationalists until his increasing opposition to Zionism became too much for them to bear, railed against the "sham Poles" who opposed his reelection in 1891 on account of his "anti-Polish tendencies" only to become "national Jews" and oppose him later on account of his assimilationism.

The former contributors of the *Ojcyzna* (sic) turned into fervent Zionists, and then they once more fought against me pretending that I was an "assimilator." Formerly they had accused me of hindering assimilation and now they discovered

that time to become "House Jews of the Polish Club" in exchange for a parliamentary mandate in Brody. S. R. Landau, *Sturm und Drang im Zionismus* (Vienna, 1937), 32. In fact Byk, as president of Shomer Israel, announced the society's switch in early 1885, as reported in their paper *Der Israelit* on February 6, 1885.

[49] *Selbst-Emanzipation*, November 17, 1885.

[50] *Selbst-Emanzipation*, July 1, 1890. The president of the Ruthenian Academic Association notably responded by supporting the Jewish-national position. "If the Jews do not constitute a nation, than to what is there assimilation? Should, however, such an occurrence be possible [i.e., the assimilation of a Jewish national entity into the Polish national entity] ... it follows that a Jewish nation, with its own independent goals, must be recognized."

that I was a true bacillus of assimilation. The swampy ground of Lemberg is a hot-bed of curious Jewish patriotism.[51]

Mikra Kodesh, for its part, attempted to maintain its cultural focus, although its members grew increasingly aware of the political consequences of their cultural activities. The society offered free Hebrew language courses, lessons in Jewish history and related subjects, and weekly Saturday afternoon lectures on various Jewish topics. The latter in particular, according to one correspondent, attracted very large audiences, presumably because Jews were free from work to attend. Indeed, for centuries Sabbath afternoon had been the accepted time for religious sermons; now this function was being overtaken by associations outside of the religious sphere. Speakers took advantage of other religious occasions as well. During the summer of 1885, for example, the Russian Hebraist Reuben Broides (then living in Lemberg and a leading member of Mikra Kodesh) spoke twice about the Jewish nationality and the destruction of Jerusalem. On the eve of Tisha B'av, the solemn summer holiday commemorating the destruction of the Jerusalem Temples, Kobak himself spoke to a crowd of one hundred people.[52] By the early 1890s, the group was sponsoring over one hundred lectures each year, mostly in Polish or German, but occasionally in Yiddish and even Hebrew. This is in addition to periodic festivals such as an annual memorial on the anniversary of Peretz Smolenskin's passing, memorial celebrations of Adolf Cremieux (1883) and Moses Montefiore (1884), a celebration in honor of the German-Jewish historian Heinrich Graetz in 1887, and many others.[53]

The group's central event was certainly its annual Maccabee festival, first held in 1883, the same year as Kadimah's original festival in Vienna.[54] The Zionist celebration of Hanukah spread far beyond the borders of Austria-Hungary, eventually establishing itself as one of the movement's most important symbols.[55] This development needs some explanation. Hanukah commemorates the rededication of the Second Temple in Jerusalem in 164 BCE after its defilement by the Seleucid king

---

[51] Bloch, op. cit., 270. On Bloch's election campaigns, see later in this chapter and Chapter 3.

[52] *Selbst-Emanzipation*, August 3, 1885.

[53] Gelber, op. cit., 110–12.

[54] Although organized by Mikra Kodesh, the event was first hosted by Shomer Israel and only gradually assumed the more stridently Zionist orientation described here, a process completed by 1888.

[55] Francois Guesnet, "Hanuka and Its Function in the Invention of a Jewish-Heroic Tradition in Early Zionism, 1880–1900," in Michael Berkowitz, ed., *Nationalism, Zionism, and Ethnic Mobilisation* (Brill, 2004), 227–46.

Antiochus IV Epiphanes and recapture by the forces led by the Hasmonean family, known as the Maccabees. The eight-day holiday has two traditional components. On the one hand, the holiday liturgy gives thanks for the Maccabean military victory, against overwhelming odds, over the Seleucid Greeks and their Jewish sympathizers.[56] The primary commandment of the holiday, however, is the lighting of the Hanukah Menorah, which celebrates the legend of a single flask of pure oil found in the Temple that was sufficient for just one day, but miraculously burned for eight. As a rabbinically ordained holiday, it enjoys a relatively minor status compared to the central biblical festivals of Passover, Shavuoth and Sukkoth. Unlike those holidays, for example, work is permitted on Hanukah, except while the candles of the Menorah are actually burning.

All religious holidays were appropriated by Jewish nationalists, as they were by other political movements as well.[57] Passover, for example, provided Zionists with a narrative of national liberation from exile, while Tisha B'av recalled Jewish hopes for a return to Jerusalem. Hanukah, however, was not merely appropriated by Jewish nationalists; it was totally transformed from a relatively minor holiday into the central annual celebration of the movement.[58] Moreover, while the miracle of the oil defined traditional celebrations of the holiday, it was specifically the military victory of the Hasmoneans that defined Zionist celebrations. This story was tailor-made for the fledgling nationalist movement for it gave a historical example of Jewish heroes who successfully fought with might against the forces of assimilation.[59] The attraction of many Jews toward Hellenist culture, particularly among the upper classes, and their support of the Assyrians against the Maccabees, made the story even riper

[56] On the revolt, see Shaye Cohen, *From the Maccabees to the Mishnah* (Philadelphia, 1987), 30–1.

[57] On the use of holiday festivals in other national movements, see Maria Bucur and Nancy Winfield, eds., *Staging the Past* (Lafayette, 2001), and Stauter-Halsted, op. cit., 208–15. On the use of celebrations to bolster an imperial identity, see Daniel Unowsky, *The Pomp and Politics of Patriotism: Imperial Celebrations in Habsburg Austria, 1848–1916* (Lafayette, 2005).

[58] Guesnet, op. cit., 230–1. In 1895, the *Jüdisches Wochenblatt* (the short-lived Yiddish-language "Organ of the Zionist Party in Galicia") prefaced its survey of that year's festivals with the following: "The Maccabee festivals have grown so strong together with the Zionist idea, and so closely united, that it is simply impossible to think of one without the other." *Jüdisches Wochenblatt*, January 24, 1895, 2.

[59] This transformation of the Maccabees into modern heroes of national liberation had already been prepared for Jewish nationalists by the great nineteenth-century historian Heinrich Graetz, whose contribution to Jewish historical consciousness was critical to the later emergence of a full-fledged Jewish nationalism. See Shlomo Avineri, *The Making of Modern Zionism: The Intellectual Origins of the Jewish State* (New York, 1981), 32.

for appropriation. Jewish nationalists explicitly described themselves as modern-day Maccabees fighting modern-day Hellenists. A report from Lemberg's 1895 festival, for example, declared:

Filled with feeling and excitement was the speech of Mr. David Schreiber, who compared today's "assimilationists" with the former Hellenists, and the "Lovers of Zion" with the Maccabees, and expressed the hope that the Zionist idea will in the end be victorious and the assimilationists will be defeated just as the former Hellenists. The speech was greatly applauded.[60]

The festivals also connected the movement to Jewish religious observance, thereby appealing to traditional groups without alienating its secular core. Thus the lighting of the Hanukah candles, the central religious commandment of the holiday, continued to constitute a climactic moment of the evening. Braude recalls triumphantly how he succeeded in getting the city's aged preacher, Bernhard Löwenstein, to speak at Zion's first Maccabee festival in 1888, despite the latter's opposition to Zionism. According to Braude, Löwenstein had no idea about the society's nationalist program and was only too happy to find Jewish youth interested in Judaism.[61]

Typically, aside from speeches decrying the assimilationists and calling upon Jews to join the nationalist movement, the festivals also featured a series of cultural presentations such as poetry readings and musical performances. These attracted listeners to the more important lectures, but also contributed to a broader nationalist agenda of providing a positive Jewish identity for the secular intelligentsia, the primary audience of these Zionist productions. The Maccabee celebrations mirrored similar festivals in the surrounding bourgeois culture, but in a Jewish national context.[62] Zionist historians who describe the festivals as "uniting all layers of the Jewish population" are repeating a misleading mantra.[63] The celebrations, at least during their first years, did not unite all layers of the Jewish population but rather specifically targeted the secular bourgeoisie.

Contemporary Zionist descriptions of the festivals admitted this strategy openly. In his report of the group's second festival held in December 1884, for example, Mordechai Ehrenpreis (at just fifteen years old already

---

[60] *Ha'am-Dos Folk*, January 10, 1896. Zionist opponents who dismissed the festivals as unimportant celebrations of a foreign people (i.e., ancient Israel) naturally made the comparison even easier. *Ojczyzna*, for example, once wrote of the festivals: "What are the Maccabees to us, they who lived 2,000 years ago in Asia Minor, while we are Poles and have no part in them." Gelber, op. cit., 110.

[61] Braude, op. cit., 98.

[62] Guesnet, op. cit., 233–4.

[63] Gelber, op. cit., 109.

an important spokesman for the society) made it absolutely clear that the festival he helped organize specifically targeted acculturated Jews. Ehrenpreis, himself a product of a traditional religious education, noted that the event's two hundred guests consisted overwhelmingly of students. Kobak's opening lecture, ending with the lighting of the Menorah, was followed by a variety of Polish and French songs, including a tribute to the great Polish nationalist poet Adam Mickiewicz (1798–1855), whose embrace of Jews as fellow Poles "of the Mosaic Confession" made him especially dear to integrationist Jews. The remaining lectures were held mainly in Polish.[64]

The fact that the festival was conducted largely in Polish and included a tribute to Mickiewicz drew no special explanation from Ehrenpreis and highlights the extent to which the early Zionist movement focused its appeal on the secular intelligentsia. It also again underscores the fluidity of Jewish ideologies during the 1880s, when the lines between national-ists and assimilationists were not yet clearly drawn. Shomer Israel, for example, consistently reiterated its dedication to the goal of assimilation but defined this as the integration of Jews into the Polish nation with their Jewish identity strongly intact.[65] In 1884, the cover editorial of *Der Israelit* asked, "What danger poses the greatest threat to Jewry," to which it answered "not anti-Semitism … but indifference," the indifference of the younger generation to the history and religion of the Jewish people.

We wish nothing more ardently than the assimilation of the Jews among the various peoples in whose midst they live. This assimilation, however, should not and must not occur with the surrender of [our] innermost religious nature. The nature of Judaism is based on the knowledge of its 4000 year-old literature [*Schriftthums*] and on the care of its religious customs, which rest on historical foundations through meaningful symbolism that bring the most exalted ideas to poetic expression.[66]

It is thus not at all difficult to understand why Shomer Israel, an out-spokenly assimilationist organization, had been so keen on supporting

---

[64] *Hamagid*, January 1, 1885, 4. On Mickiewicz and his relationship to the Jewish ques-tion see Magdalena Opalski and Israel Bartal, *Poles and Jews: A Failed Brotherhood* (Hanover, 1992).

[65] See, e.g., *Der Israelit*, February 16, 1883, 3, where the paper objects to *Ojczyzna*'s mock-ing of Shomer Israel's recent adoption of a pro-Polish position. The paper characterizes the 1873 alliance with the Ruthenians and German Liberals as a decision "dictated by an assembly of notables, of whom three quarters had never belonged to our association." "From the first days of our existence," it writes, "without interruption, we have reso-lutely stood up for the nationalization and assimilation of the Jews."

[66] *Der Israelit*, January 18, 1884, 1.

Kobak's new fraternity designed to inspire Jewish ethnic pride. In fact, so close was the relationship between the two groups in these early years that Shomer Israel actually sponsored the first Maccabee festival in 1883, hosting the event at its own quarters! Its paper praised the festival's successful strengthening of the students' knowledge of Jewish history and of their feelings toward Judaism, although it also sharply criticized the contingent of young "dreamers" whose "backward vision" of Jewish national rebirth displayed a total ignorance of "irreversible historical facts." "The present [situation] sets the justifiable demand on Jews," concluded the paper, "to feel themselves one with the nation under which they have lived for centuries, to work for the benefit of the land in which they live, and to promote actively the national and economic interests of this land, to the extent of their ability."[67]

Two weeks later, in response to an apparent smear campaign by *Ojczyzna* against the festival, its principal organizers (particularly Joseph Kobak) and the entire Shomer Israel association, *Der Israelit* reiterated its support for the "worthy" event, although it suggested now that their permission to stage the "harmless Hanukah celebration" in their facilities was granted despite Shomer Israel personally remaining distant from the event itself. The paper reiterated its opposition to the ideology of the young Jewish nationalists, but noted that the young upstarts did not speak on the festival program, and it defended them against false accusations by *Ojczyzna* such as their having spoken hostile words against the Polish nation. Clearly enraged by the personal attack on Kobak's character, the editors added that they understood "assimilation" to mean the absorption of the best Christian mores into Jewish culture, while the editors of *Ojczyzna* must believe it to mean the adoption of even the basest, crudest traits such as libel, characteristic of the Polish anti-Semitic press.[68]

Similar sentiment was expressed at the second annual festival, held in 1884. A local gymnasium student concluded the event's keynote lecture about the history of the Maccabees and the reasons that "no trace of Hellenist influence remained in the spirit of the Jewish People," on a "fitting" final sentence, "that we Jews living in Galicia have found a fatherland in Poland, which we have the obligation to love with true devotion and self-sacrifice."[69] In short, the Maccabee festivals began not

---

[67] *Der Israelit*, January 4, 1884, 3.

[68] *Der Israelit*, January 18, 1884, 6.

[69] *Der Israelit*, December 23, 1884, 4. His denial of Hellenist influence on later Judaism and Jewish history is grossly erroneous.

as a nationalist revolt against those who denied Jewish nationhood, but as a deeply felt expression of the integrationist vision of Jewish national assimilation coupled with Jewish pride and consciousness.

Nevertheless, this would be the last Maccabee festival under the co-auspices of the self-proclaimed assimilationist organization. By 1885, the lines between the two groups had grown more distinct. Rhetoric praising Poland as the Jews' fatherland disappeared as the young "dreamers" took increasing control of Mikra Kodesh and its activities. Virtually all memory of the event's original co-sponsors disappeared as the Hanukah festival emerged as the Zionists' most identifiable annual event. Neither Nathan Gelber, their historian, nor the memoirs of any of the members of Mikra Kodesh admitted the involvement of Shomer Israel in these early festivals. Their stark anti-assimilationist rhetoric, a rhetoric that emerged only later in the decade, does not seem to have room for the murky days of the early 1880s. The ultimate irony occurred in 1890, when Zionists blasted the assimilationists for hosting a celebration of Mickiewicz at the reform Temple during Hanukah, either forgetting or ignoring their own celebration just six years earlier.[70]

Beginning in 1885, but especially after the transformation of Mikra Kodesh into Zion in 1888, the celebrations displayed increasing signs of their new Zionist hosts. For example, Braude recalled how at the 1888 Hanukah festival the younger members finally felt free to "remove the holiday from its narrow framework of the Hanukah miracle [of the oil lasting eight days] and to highlight the story of the Hasmoneans as a historical phenomenon of national uprising and military might."[71] This was a revolt against the Haskalah as much as against Judaism, for *maskilim* had traditionally emphasized the spiritual, rather than national military aspects of Hanukah. "More than we recall the physical valor of the Maccabees" wrote the lead editorial of *Hamagid* in 1857, "we understand the war as a struggle for spiritual deliverance from Greek culture."[72]

The festivals also increasingly included Hebrew lectures and poetry readings, largely symbolic since few participants would have understood them. Already in 1885, by which time organizers could boast that the

---

[70] "We cannot blame the Poles when they exuberantly celebrate their greatest poet at every opportunity. But we Jews, have we no other pains and worries? Are the conditions of today's Jewish community in such marvelous shape? Is the poverty here so brilliantly organized, that these gentlemen out of sheer arrogance can present an alien Messiah in our house of God?" *Selbst-Emanzipation*, December 14, 1890.

[71] Braude, op. cit., 98.

[72] Feiner, *Haskalah and History*, 213.

"house was packed" an hour before the festival even started, the event opened with a Hebrew speech and closed with a Hanukah poem read in both Hebrew and Yiddish. Most of the evening was again conducted in Polish, although President Kobak probably spoke in German. After denouncing the assimilationists and their "pernicious effects on the development of the Jewish spirit," Kobak lit the Hanukah menorah and student member Adolf Stand (1870–1919) read telegram greetings from various Jewish notables and other nationalist associations.[73]

Early Zionists were surely frustrated at their inability to conduct the festivals in Hebrew. The president of the Commerce and Bookkeeping Society in Stanislau, for example, opened that association's first Maccabee festival in 1885 by emphasizing that the event should be held in Hebrew, but because so few would be able to understand it, he preferred Polish, the "language of the land." Unfortunately, he continued, as only a small portion of the audience understood Polish, he was forced to revert to German. The audience clearly included members of the older secular elite, fluent in German but not Polish, and possibly some Yiddish speakers able to follow the German. The speaker emphasized the importance of Jewish self-awareness (*Selbstbewusstsein*), and called upon the audience to hold fast to the national tradition and excitedly to call out, "*Ivri Anochi, Ich bin ein Jude!* (I am a Hebrew, I am a Jew!)"[74]

In a land in which language largely defined national identity, the organizers' choice had deep political consequences. Hebrew, officially the national language of the Jewish people, was hopeless, exposing its somewhat artificial status. But organizers were not willing to hold the festivals in Yiddish; following traditional *maskilic* bias, they still did not regard Yiddish as a language – certainly not as a national language – but rather as a corrupted form of High German.[75] Thus overall, while the Maccabee festivals proved to be a popular and effective tool to generate a positive Jewish identity among acculturated Jews, they also revealed the artificiality of Jewish national identity among those same Jews. Other nationalists could use such festivals to strengthen the national identity of

---

[73] *Selbst-Emanzipation*, December 17, 1885.

[74] *Selbst-Emanzipation*, December 17, 1885, 6. The festival was held on December 9, 1885.

[75] On the question of Yiddish as Jewish national language, see later in the chapter. Gelber writes that Laibel Taubes and David Hirsch Tieger, later both editors of nationalist Yiddish papers, delivered Yiddish speeches at a Maccabee celebration outside Lemberg. However, it is unclear which celebration he means. His Hebrew date corresponds to 1881, which he falsely converts to 1882, both of which precede the founding of Mikra Kodesh. No other source mentions these Yiddish speeches. Gelber, op. cit., 109.

their participants simply by holding these events in the folk language. In contrast, early Zionists awkwardly claimed Hebrew as the Jews' eternal, living language in Polish- and German-language speeches, while (until 1886) their assimilationist opponents promoted Polish nationalism in a Hebrew-language journal!

THE NATIONALISTS' FIRST CAMPAIGN: J. S. BLOCH VERSUS EMIL BYK

The cultural work of Mikra Kodesh laid a crucial foundation for the Jewish nationalist movement. The tenacious Zionist claim of direct continuity between the "glorious" past of ancient Israel and contemporary Jews – a connection which the history and Hebrew classes, as well as the Maccabee festivals, essentially sought to strengthen – would ultimately form an important basis of Jewish claims to nationhood.[76] This reliance on ancient history was especially pronounced in the Habsburg Empire, where Jews could point to other "non-historical" peoples who had won recognition as nationalities and argue that their claim was at least as sound. "The national awakening in the nineteenth century," writes Shmuel Almog,

introduced the distinction between "historical" and "non-historical" nations, on the premise that only peoples that had lost their independence, such as the Greeks or the Poles, were entitled to political autonomy. Nevertheless, the so-called non-historical peoples – the Slovaks, Serbs, and the like – cited evidence to the effect that they, too, were national entities with historical roots.... In broad strokes, then, the past was not only a source for satisfying the craving for dignity but also a basis for substantiating the claim to nationhood.[77]

In other words, these so-called cultural activities had serious political consequences.

Moreover, despite Mikra Kodesh's primarily cultural mandate, it quickly began to assume an openly political role. For example, in 1885 its vice-president Jacob Stroh was elected head of the finance division of the Jewish Community Council on a platform of tax relief.[78] In October,

---

[76] See Anthony Smith, "The 'Golden Age' and National Renewal," in Geoffrey Hosking and George Schöpflin, eds., *Myths and Nationhood* (New York, 1997), 36–59.

[77] Shmuel Almog, *Zionism and History: The Rise of a New Jewish Consciousness* (Jerusalem, 1987), 32.

[78] *Selbst-Emanzipation*, January 1, 1886. The paper does not mention Stroh's also being a member of Shomer Israel, again highlighting the continuing connections between these two groups. Joseph Bloch endorsed Stroh and a slew of other Jewish nationalist

the society's future president, Carl Stand (1860–1939), spoke about the need to support the Jews just expelled from Prussia "in the name of the association," despite the group's actual mandate to advance knowledge of the Hebrew language and preserve Jewish ethnic consciousness (*Stammesbewusstsein*). He demanded that funds be mobilized in the city. The speech was very warmly received, and President Kobak promised to dedicate his Saturday lecture to the subject.[79]

By far the group's greatest political effort was mobilized behind the popular champion of Jewish rights, Rabbi Joseph Samuel Bloch (1850–1923). Bloch, a native of Galicia serving as a rabbi in the Floridsdorf suburb of Vienna, had soared to popularity among Austrian Jews as a result of his successful refutation of August Röhling, an anti-Semitic pseudo-Talmudist. In 1883, he won a special parliamentary election to replace the deceased president of Machsike Hadas, Rabbi Simon Sofer, in the heavily Jewish Kolomea-Buczacz-Sniatyn urban district. (Bloch defeated the president of Shomer Israel, Emil Byk, for the first of several times, with two thirds of the vote.) A Jewish industrialist in Kolomea, impressed by one of Bloch's lectures, had persuaded the local electoral committee to nominate Bloch – sight unseen – as a worthy successor to Sofer.[80] Sofer had been a loyal member of the Polish Club, which he viewed as a far more natural ally than the anti-clerical German Liberal Party. Bloch similarly agreed to join the Polish Club, as demanded by the hastily convened Jewish electoral committees of the three towns who had invited him to run in the first place.[81]

Unlike Sofer, Bloch did not sit silently in Parliament.[82] The thirty-three-year-old Bloch became an outspoken champion of Jewish rights and

candidates as "men of patriotic mind and Jewish hearts." *Österreichische Wochenschrift*, Nr. 39, 1885, 6.

[79] *Selbst-Emanzipation*, October 1, 1885.

[80] Chaim Bloch, "Dr. Joseph Samuel Bloch: Dem ruhmreichen Verteidiger des Judentums – ein Blatt des Gedenkens," in Joseph Bloch, ed., *Erinnerungen aus meinem Leben*, Vol. 3 (Vienna, 1933), 305. My thanks to Ian Reifowitz for providing me with a copy of this work.

[81] Like their assimilationist opponents, the members of these committees "were obliged" (as Bloch put it) to insist on this promise, "as it was in the interest of the Jews that their deputies should act jointly with their Christian colleagues in all affairs concerning the country." This admission, made decades after the election, certainly undermines the nationalists' smug dismissal of Byk's pro-Polish orientation. Bloch, op. cit., 77–8. Bloch similarly defended his decision to join the Polish Club in a 1907 election bid speech reprinted in the third volume of his memoirs. Bloch, *Erinnerungen aus meinem Leben*, Vol. 3, 171.

[82] Sofer voted consistently with the Polish Club and never once raised his voice in a debate. One Friday night the Polish Club arranged a minyan for him at the Reichsrat so that he

opponent of anti-Semitism in the Reichsrat, as well as a leading spokes-man in the fight against *Mädchenraub*, the kidnapping of young Jewish women by the Catholic Church in Galicia.[83] His reelection in 1885, again opposed by Emil Byk, was given high priority by Mikra Kodesh and *Selbst-Emanzipation*, which viewed his ultimate victory as proof of the ascendancy of the Jewish national idea.[84] The paper called on Jews to elect their own candidate, who would represent Jewish interests and not sit as a stooge of the Polish Club.

> Do we want, then, to send a Jew to Parliament, in order to play himself a lackey of the Poles, the typical "Aryan Moszko"? Beware!!! We want to see an inde-pendent Jew elected, who considers it his first and highest task to work for his own Jewish People, with all of his patriotism and by all of his love to the People, among whom he lives.... He [Bloch] proclaimed that it would be his mandate to defend Jewish interests.... Every Jew, to whom his People is beloved and valued, will joyfully reach out his hand to Dr. Bloch.[85]

Recognizing that few Galician Jews read or even cared about the Viennese *Selbst-Emanzipation,* Jewish nationalists in a then radical move also distributed a Yiddish-language leaflet in Bloch's district with the

would not have to leave before the votes were collected. Bloch, *My Reminiscences,* 77. Bloch claimed that Sofer knew too little German to speak in Parliament, a story repeated by Nathan Gelber. However, Joseph Margoshes – who enjoyed extended visits with Sofer over the course of several years – insisted that the Hungarian-born rabbi spoke German well but was simply uncomfortable using it in public. J. Margoshes, *A World Apart: A Memoir of Jewish Life in Nineteenth Century Galicia* (Boston, 2008), 24. Likewise, the editor of the Polish nationalist paper *Gazeta Narodowa* visited Sofer and commented on his impressive command of German. Manekin, "Orthodox Jewry in Kraków at the Turn of the Twentieth Century," *Polin* 23 (2010), 177.

[83] The case of Rachel Stieglitz became a particularly celebrated cause, reported simply as the "Stieglitz Affair" throughout the press, which earned Bloch letters of support from a wide range of Jewish organizations, including Kadimah and Mikra Kodesh. See Bloch, *My Reminiscences,* 202–8.

[84] Jewish nationalists were not alone in seizing on Bloch's election as evidence of Jews asserting their national rights. The Polish *Gazeta Narodowa* wrote of the election that the Jews "through the election of Dr. Bloch ... showed that they consider themselves as a separate nation within a nation, and therefore do not think about assimilation with the population!" Quoted in Jacob Toury, "Josef Samuel Bloch und die jüdische Identität im Österreichischen Kaiserreich," in Walter Grab, ed., *Jüdische Integration und Identität in Deutschland und Österreich 1848–1918* (Tel Aviv, 1983), 47.

[85] *Selbst-Emanzipation,* June 2, 1885, 2. "Moszko," Polish for Moses, is the slang pejora-tive with which nationalists dismissed assimilationists. Poles regularly called all Jews Moszek or Moszko much as Americans used to call all African-Americans "Rufus." (My thanks to Michael Steinlauf for that point.) Zionists conveniently overlooked the fact that Bloch pledged, if elected, to join the Polish Club, which he dutifully did, cost-ing him his previous support among German-Jewish liberals in Vienna. See Bloch, *My Reminiscences,* 78–9.

same message: Jews are in danger and only electing Bloch will save them. "Jewish brothers! Yikes [*Gewalt*]! Jews, a fire is burning. Consider brothers and reflect – if it doesn't happen now, it will never happen again. All Jewry is in danger and we have the power to save all Israel [*klal Yisrael*], namely by electing Dr. J. S. Bloch."[86]

Above all, Bloch portrayed himself as the people's candidate, his own poverty and lack of means starkly contrasted with the wealth of his opposition (see Figure 2.1).[87] He delighted in one supporter's observation in Sniatyn that Jewish campaign posters were printed on plain white paper in contrast to the Polish and Ruthenian signs printed over their national colors. The Jews are so impoverished, he laughed, that they can't even afford their own national colors.[88] Bloch's reception in the electoral district at the end of his first term, he wrote, "was like a triumphant entry in a fairy tale."

Horsemen in colored costumes on gaily decorated mounts fetched me in solemn procession and I was led through the streets to the town hall whilst enormous masses of people rejoiced aloud; their enthusiastic speeches were addressed to me and I made my first political speech. Every word I said was acclaimed and they did not tire of saying that the electoral district was proud of having sent me to the Austrian Parliament.[89]

Bloch's 1885 campaign anticipated a type of politics that Jewish nationalists in Galicia had not yet broadly embraced. At a time when their movement was in its infancy, and still largely focused on the Jewish intelligentsia, Bloch led a populist revolt against the Jewish establishment. "It was a struggle not between individuals," he wrote after his victory, "but rather between holy principles, a struggle of Right against Might, a struggle of honesty against shameless corruption."[90] His memoirs detail at great length the extraordinary wealth and corruption of Jewish political elites and the moral perseverance of common Jews who refused to be

---

[86] *Drohobyczer Zeitung*, May 8, 1885, 1–2.
[87] Recounting his first election in 1883, for example, Bloch described how he had no plans for a campaign tour, lacking the funds to finance it. In contrast, "About a fortnight before the elections came off an assembly of so-called Jewish 'Notables' met in Lemberg to protest solemnly against my candidature.... Dr. Emil Byk, a childless wealthy lawyer, President of the [Reform] Congregation and of the association Shomer Israel, wishing to stand in my place, had engineered this assembly." Bloch, *My Reminiscences*, 78.
[88] Chaim Bloch, op. cit., 305. The comment was made by Laibel Taubes, who recalled the incident decades later. Revealingly, Bloch responded that the "pure, white [glattweisse] basis of the Jewish electoral call is the Jewish color. Our Torah was also written in black fire on white fire!"
[89] Bloch, *My Reminiscences*, 202.
[90] *Österreichische Wochenschrift*, June 26, 1885, 2.

FIGURE 2.1. Emil Byk and Joseph Bloch (as an older man).

intimidated or bought.[91] (Of course, most such Jews were excluded from voting for Bloch as suffrage was then still restricted.)[92] Bloch broke new ground by conducting political rallies in Yiddish rather than Polish or German, "to show that the 800,000 Jews in Galicia had a right to confer about politics with each other in their own mother-tongue," a practice which brought the scorn of the town's Jewish elites.[93]

Bloch, who enjoyed unique legitimacy as a pulpit rabbi well known for his Talmudic erudition, also held numerous rallies in synagogues, including on the Sabbath. On the Monday preceding the election, Buczacz's 450 Jewish electors (who had protested outside city hall for three straight days to obtain their voter cards) assembled in the synagogue to swear "before God and the community to vote for the candidate of Judaism, Doctor Bloch." Rumors even spread that Byk's election would result in the criminalization of circumcision![94] Bloch appropriated the Torah itself to prove his righteousness, noting at a rally just before Election Day, for example, that the weekly Torah portion, *Va'yeshev*, contained in its letters the "strict admonition," *wählt Yosef Shmuel Bloch* (elect Joseph Samuel Bloch).[95]

Despite his appeal to Torah and pulpit in the campaign, Bloch did not have the support of the organization whose seat he filled in 1883, Machsike Hadas. Bloch, whose secular education and penchant for biblical criticism already undermined his standing with the Orthodox party, refused to submit himself to its leadership. As a result, that party's spiritual

[91] For a detailed account of the 1885 campaign, see Bloch, *My Reminiscences*, 209–26. Even granting his narcissistic tendency to aggrandize his own popularity, the memoirs – when read with other contemporary sources – are quite useful. Bloch details egregious acts of electoral corruption, including the use of dead electors, single electors given multiple votes, and the simple purchase of votes from those willing to sell. He repeatedly portrays his opponent, Emil Byk, as lacking any popular base of support, a party of "officers without an army." See also the reports in Bloch's organ, the *Österreichische Wochenschrift*, from which Bloch lifted text verbatim for his memoirs. *Österreichische Wochenschrift*, May 15, 1885, 5–7; May 22, 1885, 1–2; May 29, 1885, 1–2; June 16, 1885, 1–3; June 26, 1885, 1–5.

[92] In 1879, only 3,373 of the district's 36,540 residents (less than 10 percent) were enfranchised. G. A. Schimmer, *Die Reichsrath-Wahlen vom Jahre 1879 in Oesterreich* (Stuttgart, 1880), 61.

[93] Bloch, *My Reminiscences*, 216.

[94] S. Bickel, ed., *Pinkas Kolomey*, 84.

[95] The story, recalled by Bloch in his memoirs, also appears in Joseph Auerbach, "Miscellanea" in Israel Cohen, ed., *Sefer Buczacz* (Tel Aviv, 1956), 204. Bloch recalls a second such argument against Byk, that the Bible specifically forbids supporting him, for it says clearly, "Thou shall not *Byk*," Byk meaning "bow down" in Yiddish. Bloch, op. cit., 215.

mentor, the rebbe of Belz (Yehoshua Rokeach), directed his *hasidim* in that first election to support the Christian candidate, Baron Romaszka.[96] Gershom Bader, who incorrectly remembered the rebbe instructing his supporters not to take part in the election, claimed that Rokeach stated, "If the choice is to support such a Jew as Bloch, it would be better to have a *goy!*"[97]

That Bloch could still harness broad popular support and successfully portray himself as *the* candidate of traditional Jews and traditional Judaism highlights the extent to which historians must beware of conflating the interests and identity of the "Orthodox" Jewish leadership with the religiously observant Jewish masses. In fact, *Der Israelit*'s front page report of the 1883 election results focused entirely on the failure of the rebbe to influence the Jewish electorate of the three towns, who voted not only for a progressive Jew, but for a progressive rabbi. "Thus insofar as the election of Dr. Bloch is a sign that the influence of such a harmful party for the interests of Galician Jewry as Machsike Hadas is declining, we can be happy with the election results in the Kolomea electoral district."[98]

Bloch's populist crusade did not only oppose Machsike Hadas and Shomer Israel. In fact, the "conference of notables" that Bloch recalled Byk engineering just before the 1883 elections included a far broader segment of the population than he remembered. Shomer Israel did host a self-described conference of Lemberg notables, but its participants were not at all limited to Shomer Israelites, whose support for Byk would have been virtually automatic. Invited guests included not only several Orthodox figures, but also Joseph Kobak and Salomon Buber (1827–1907), a powerful man in the Lemberg Jewish community and a key supporter of the Zionist cause from its earliest days in Galicia.[99] Although neither of their contributions to the debate was reprinted in *Der Israelit*, the paper clearly noted that the resolution opposing Bloch's nomination passed unanimously. The speakers all restated their great respect for

---

[96] *Machsike Hadas*, June 4, 1885, 1. Rokeach repudiated an endorsement that was circulating which claimed he favored Byk, writing that "neither [Bloch nor Byk] acted according to Torah" and so he preferred to elect a non-Jew, "a straight man who loves all humanity." Rokeach's endorsement of the Christian candidate was noted in multiple issues of *Der Israelit*.

[97] A. L. Shussheim, "Jewish Politics and Jewish Parties in Galicia" (Yiddish) in *Pinkas Galizia* (Buenos Aires, 1945), 44.

[98] *Der Israelit*, June 3, 1883, 1.

[99] On Buber, see later in the chapter and Chapter 3. By 1891, Buber had become one of Bloch's most vociferous supporters.

Bloch for his brilliant refutation of August Röhling, but insisted that this did not qualify him to represent the Galician district in the Reichsrat. Typical comments stressed that Galician Jews needed a representative able to defend local Jewish interests, both in terms of his political experience and in terms of his intimate knowledge of the land.[100]

Despite Bloch's memories of a grassroots campaign, Bloch did not rely merely on popular support in the election but engaged in a great deal of realpolitik as well. Soon after he arrived in Kolomea to launch his 1885 reelection campaign, a "Bloch party" was founded under the name "The Good Fellows" and joined by Jacob Bretler (1820–1905), head of an influential family in the city.[101] Besides securing the support of the venerated Polish leader Franz Smolka, Bloch entered into an electoral alliance with a member of the city council named Wisniowski. In exchange for a guarantee of support for Wisniowski's list in the upcoming municipal elections, the Polish politician agreed to back Bloch's reelection bid. In fact, he and his friend Stephan Ritter von Szczepanowski ran Bloch's reelection campaign, although the Central Polish Election Committee supported Byk. Despite the allegedly violent campaign conducted against Bloch (Jews threatened with a pogrom in the event of Bloch's election, propaganda among non-Jewish voters that Bloch hated Christians, etc.),[102] Bloch's Polish allies ultimately led his campaign to victory in an extremely tight race: 1,671 votes to Byk's 1,656.[103] Jewish nationalists may have seen Byk's loss to Bloch in 1885 as a sign of assimilationism's defeat, but it was far more a result of practical politics.

Bloch, in the end, did not join the Zionist movement. After briefly flirting with Zionism, he eventually preached an identity of Jewish ethnic pride combined with Austrian patriotism. Jews should become Austrians sans phrase, he wrote, the only true Austrian citizens in an era of hypernationalism.[104] Thus Bloch seems to represent an "anti-anti-Semitic pressure group" and not a nationalist platform.[105] But this is beside the point.

---

[100] Der Israelit, May 4, 1883, 1–3.

[101] An obituary of Jacob Bretler appears in Hamicpe, March 31, 1905, 5. In 1898, Bretler ("one of the province's few millionaires") donated 40,000 kroner to the Jewish National Fund, which he earmarked for an old-age home and other similar projects.

[102] The Polish anti-Semitic politician Jan Dobrzanski threatened at a voter rally in Kolomea, "If you elect Dr. Bloch, it will go badly for you, not only in this city, but rather every single voter will have opportunity to feel the anger of this land." Österreichische Wochenschrift, June 26, 1885, 2. (Further details of corruption are documented there.) See also Bloch, Erinnerungen aus meinem Leben, Vol. 3, 171.

[103] Drohobyczer Handels-Zeitung, June 12, 1885, 1.

[104] See Joseph Bloch, Der Nationale Zwist und die Juden in Österreich (Vienna, 1886), 41.

[105] Toury, op. cit., 49.

Bloch's election and reelections invigorated those circles that saw him as a nationalist candidate and not in his district alone. Bloch's memory of his campaign dominating Galician Jewish political discourse is certainly reflected in the contemporary press, which covered the election very closely. When news of his reelection reached Lemberg, hundreds of Jews celebrated in the streets on their way to the train station to welcome him (by mistake, welcoming Byk's men instead).[106] "Never did Israel have days as great as those, in which the weak were made strong," wrote S.Y. Agnon (1888–1970) of Bloch's victory over Byk. Agnon describes one *Hasid* actually grabbing a woman in the market and dancing with her, out of joy for Bloch's reelection.[107] This may well have been a comical exaggeration on Agnon's part, but even so it highlights the powerful memory of Bloch's victory among a generation of Galician Jews born after the event. Zvi Heller, recalling decades later Bloch's elections in Buczacz, described him as the editor of the "*Jüdisches Wochenblatt*," a revealing misnomer of Bloch's actual paper, the *Österreichische Wochenschrift*.[108] Another Buczacz native, Joseph Auerbach, similarly recalled Bloch's ascending to Parliament "to fight God's war against the enemies of Israel." When he won his first reelection, wrote Auerbach, the Jews donned their Sabbath *shtreimelekh* and celebrated like it was Purim – "*V'ha'ir Buczacz Tzahala v'semeicha.*"[109]

The Jewish nationalist societies were ecstatic as well. Mikra Kodesh immediately telegrammed its congratulations to Bloch, while a number of academics and merchants sent letters of appreciation to Wisniowski and Szczepanowski.[110] *Selbst-Emanzipation* was so enraptured that it even predicted that he would soon join the nationalist camp.[111] After all, he was close to both Kadimah and its predecessor Ahavath Zion, even serving briefly as the president of the latter.[112] And as late as 1885 he accepted in person an honorary membership in Mikra Kodesh, praising the society's activities, which he frequently covered in the widely read Viennese-Jewish

---

[106] Bloch, *My Reminiscences*, 222–3.

[107] S. Y. Agnon, op. cit., 283.

[108] Zvi Heller, "From My Memories" (Hebrew), in Israel Cohen, ed., *Sefer Buczacz* (Tel Aviv, 1956), 142.

[109] Joseph Auerbach, op. cit., 204. Auerbach is playing on a famous verse from the Book of Esther, "And the city of Shushan celebrated joyfully."

[110] *Selbst-Emanzipation*, June 17, 1885, 3.

[111] *Selbst-Emanzipation*, May 1, 1885.

[112] On Bloch's leadership of Ahavath Zion, see Bloch, *Erinnerungen aus meinem Leben*, Vol. 3, 299. The group's appeal for help published in *Der Israelit* is co-signed by Bloch as president, noting his status as parliamentary representative and listing his home address to which donations could be sent. *Der Israelit*, August 15, 1884, 6.

weekly which he edited, the *Österreichische Wochenschrift*.[113] That he ultimately split from the Zionists did not undermine the significant charge his elections gave to the nationalist movement. Indeed, even after his anti-Zionist position emerged, nationalists continued to devote a great deal of energy to his reelection campaigns, although according to Bloch they turned on him following his final reelection in 1891.[114]

Moreover, despite Bloch's outspoken opposition to Jewish nationalism, if we understand nationalism not simply as a movement to win recognition for Jews as a nationality to whom national rights are due but rather (as many Galician Zionists themselves did) as a movement designed to organize Jews politically *as Jews* and to strengthen Jewish ethnic pride and self-consciousness, then Bloch in fact did represent a nationalist platform. After all, fostering *Stammesbewusstsein* was the primary goal of Mikra Kodesh. Similarly, throughout his long career, Bloch continuously chastised Jews who considered themselves members of "foreign" nationalities, whether German, Polish, or Czech, and he insisted that while Jews were politically Austrian they remained nonetheless members of the Jewish people. Bloch's election, then, serves as a prime example of the diffusion of nationalist sentiment beyond the so-called Jewish nationalist movement.

In fact, by broadening our understanding of Jewish nationalism to include such sentiment, we are in a better position to question the Zionist trope about the assimilationist movement itself. Zionist denouncements of Byk and his assimilationist backers deliberately ignored the fact that Byk and his supporters also pledged themselves to work for the betterment of the Jewish community. *Der Israelit*, despite its sharp rejection of the notion that Jews' constituted a "nationality," continued to describe the Jews as a people (*Volk*) and ethnicity (*Stamm*), and it repeatedly

---

[113] On the history of this paper, see Toury, *Die Jüdische Presse im Österreichischen Kaiserreich*, 74–82.

[114] Bloch, op. cit., 270–1. On the 1891 election, see Chapter 3. In that campaign, *Selbst-Emanzipation* did endorse him, despite acknowledging that Bloch was not a Jewish nationalist. It encouraged Jewish nationalists in Kolomea to support Bloch's candidature actively and hoped thereby to draw Bloch back into the nationalist camp. *Selbst-Emanzipation*, February 16, 1891, 3. Bloch was successfully reelected in 1891 but was pressured by the Polish Club to resign his seat in 1895 and lost his reelection bid that year. In 1897, he ran again against Byk, this time in Brody, who finally defeated him in a landslide. In 1907, he ran briefly in the overwhelmingly Jewish second District of Vienna (Leopoldstadt), opposed this time by the head of the Austrian Zionist Party, Isidor Schalit. Bloch withdrew from that race and instead ran in the urban Galician district based in Zolkiew and Rawaruska. On his later, unsuccessful bids for Parliament, see Chapter 5.

endorsed Byk in language very similar to that of the Zionists.[115] In 1883, for example, the paper applauded a growing recognition among all sides, including the Poles, that Rabbi Sofer's replacement must be a Jew. It opposed Bloch (a natural choice considering Byk's presidency of Shomer Israel) not because it opposed the idea of Jewish collective representation but because it supported such representation and feared that Bloch would not be able to deliver. Bloch was an outsider, wrote the paper, who despite his pledge to sit on the Polish Club could not really advance the Jewish cause because he allegedly did not speak "one word of Polish."[116] In 1885, the paper similarly demanded a Jewish representative to defend and advance Jewish emancipation, still incomplete, it wrote, because of continued discrimination in many sectors of society. The paper demanded that the Polish Central Election Committee nominate Jewish candidates at least in those districts with Jewish majorities.[117]

In 1885, Byk received the endorsement of nearly every Jewish and Polish paper, including *Ivri Anochi* (a *maskilic* Hebrew-language paper published in Brody), and even the Zionist-leaning *Drohobyczer Zeitung*, an independent German-language Jewish newspaper, printed in Hebrew characters, which appeared from 1883 until 1913.[118] Despite that paper's growing Zionist tendencies, and despite its previous endorsement of Bloch against Byk in 1883, its editors now argued that the best means of defending Jewish collective interests was not by highlighting Jewish separatism but rather by demonstrating "at every opportunity" that the Jews are "in every respect true children of the land." Jews needed a representative with close connections to the national and local governments, wrote the paper, who would work "tirelessly and objectively as a representative and defender of true Jewish interests." Like *Der Israelit*, the

---

[115] See, for example, the paper's long series of front-page articles, "The Nationality of the Jews," a highly apologetic work presented as a response to an anti-Semitic journalist who "falsely" claimed that Jews, as a foreign nationality, were incapable of national assimilation. The author referred to the Jews as a people (*Volk*) and ethnicity (*Stamm*), but defined nationality in terms of state, territory, and language and thus insisted that the category did not apply to the Jews. *Der Israelit*, December 23, 1884, 1–3; January 9, 1885, 1–3; February 20, 1885, 1–3; May 1, 1885, 2–3.

[116] *Der Israelit*, May 4, 1883, 1. I have not seen any evidence substantiating this charge, which seems rather unlikely. Aside from Bloch's frequent citation of Polish-language publications in his memoirs, the issue certainly would have played a prominent role in future opposition to his reelection, yet the charge does not ever resurface.

[117] *Der Israelit*, May 15, 1885, 1.

[118] *Ivri Anochi*, June 5, 1885, 1–2. For a list of other endorsements, see *Drohobyczer Handelszeitung*, June 12, 1885, 1. *Hamagid*, however, backed Bloch. *Hamagid*, June 11, 1885, 3.

Drohobyczer Zeitung concluded that only Emil Byk was qualified for the job. Bloch had proven unable to work with the aristocrats in Parliament and especially with the Poles themselves, who now wanted nothing to do with him. Byk, by contrast, had a track record of defending Jewish interests throughout Galicia, for example, by securing public support for numerous Jewish charities. Although Byk belonged to the "progressive party," the paper admitted, nevertheless Hasidim and progressives alike could rally behind him for his concerted efforts on behalf of all Jews. The paper patronizingly encouraged Bloch to resume his post as a pulpit rabbi, where he could best serve Jewish interests.[119]

These papers endorsed Byk according to the same criteria by which the nationalists supported Bloch. They called for a "true" Jewish representative to defend "true Jewish interests," for all Jews. While the Zionist press denied Byk's right to serve as such a representative because of its perception of an irreconcilable conflict between Polish and Jewish interests, Byk's supporters argued that more could be accomplished by an experienced politician working from within the Polish Club than by a relative newcomer who was disliked by the ruling Poles. In other words, the dispute was more tactical than ideological. All of these endorsements were based on the candidate's defense of Jewish collective interests, and thus in recognition of the Jews constituting a unique collectivity.[120]

Moreover, Byk's endorsements were not simply election propaganda; they represent the true rhetoric of the so-called assimilationist camp at that time. Despite contemporary and latter-day Zionist accusations to the contrary, neither Byk nor Shomer Israel sought the total assimilation of the Jews, in the modern sense of the term. Byk's oft-cited 1885 speech at

---

[119] *Drohobyczer Zeitung*, May 8, 1885, 1–2. As election day neared, the paper's criticism of Bloch's candidacy grew even sharper. Quoting the Bloch campaign's Yiddish-language leaflet cited earlier, the article attacked its composers sharply, criticizing the group as fanatics akin to Sabbateans. "What sort of danger threatens us? Don't we live freely with our co-citizens, Poles and Ruthenians of Galicia?" Jews constitute the majority of the district, admitted the paper, but this did not mean that they had to threaten the minority with a candidate like Bloch, who by his aggressive anti-Polish politics represented the true danger to Galician Jewry. *Drohobyczer Handels-Zeitung*, May 29, 1885, 1.

[120] In 1891, apparently impressed by Bloch's performance (or possibly reflecting the paper's more crystallized Zionist orientation), the *Drohobyczer Zeitung* praised both candidates as dedicated and able, but this time decided to endorse Bloch. The paper expressed its wish that Byk withdraw his candidacy in order to avoid a divisive campaign in the Jewish community but that he find a different district in which to run. Ultimately, this is exactly what transpired. See Chapter 3. *Drohobyczer Zeitung*, February 13, 1891, 1. For a celebratory description of both candidates' victories, see *Drohobyczer Handels-Zeitung*, March 6, 1891, 1.

the seventeenth annual conference of Shomer Israel, for example, during which he called for the association to work toward the Polonization of Galician Jewry, clearly assumed that Jews would continue to thrive as an ethnic group (*Stamm*) in the province.

We must have no other political aspirations than fraternization with the Poles among whom we live. Their aspirations and interests, their rights and obligations must become ours, totally and fully. There remains always enough room for the upholding of our beliefs, our great past and our religious and ethnic [*stammlichen*] togetherness.[121]

More tellingly, in a rhetorical style virtually indistinguishable from his nationalist opponents, Byk demanded that the group work to elect Jewish candidates for both Parliament and local municipal offices in order to combat anti-Semitism in those bodies and to defend Jewish rights at the Reichsrat in Vienna. In contrast to nationalist accusations that he represented blind support of the dominant Poles, Byk called for a "genuine" and independent Jewish leadership.

When I say, finally, that **Jews** must be elected in the upcoming Lemberg City Council elections this year, this is no "lapsus lingua," for I mean by it men with genuine Jewish hearts, who in this position will not simply see a highly desirable honorary position from which connections and protection can be won here and there, but rather a mandate that is obligated to activity for the public good.[122]

In short, the Zionists' portrayal of Byk as a stooge of the Polish Club is simply unfair. While Byk clearly did advocate the cause of Polonization, he did so on tactical grounds. Like the moderate *maskilim* who founded Shomer Israel in the first place, Byk argued that the Jews' best chance to realize equal rights was through acculturation and integration, by joining the Poles rather than fighting them. "Our unshakable goal is the realization of equal rights," he declared at that famous speech.

We want our equal place at the table of political rights and we want social equality. How can this succeed without our mastering the language and writing of the surrounding population? How could this be possible for us without a living world language? If we therefore strive for the education and progress of our co-religionists, so we agree with all good sons of Israel in our ultimate goals.[123]

That both Byk and his opponents should carry on such a debate in German- and Polish-language speeches and articles highlights the extent

---

[121] *Der Israelit*, February 6, 1885, 2. See also *Drohobyczer Handels-Zeitung*, February 14, 1885, 1.

[122] *Der Israelit*, February 6, 1885, 2. Bold in original.

[123] *Der Israelit*, February 6, 1885, 2.

to which Byk may have been more of a realist than his Zionist detractors acknowledged.

To be sure, Jewish nationalist denunciations of the so-called assimilationists may not have been disingenuous. Many young activists failed to grasp the true nature of their assimilationist opponents, expressing bewilderment at the latter's efforts to defend specifically Jewish interests and at the "failure" of everyone else to see through this "ruse." In 1885, for example, Mikra Kodesh reported that it would not be organizing relief aid for the Jewish refugees from Germany because the local assimilationists had already established a committee for the same purpose. "So degenerates," concluded the correspondent, "purely national undertakings in *Assimilantnisse*."[124] In December, *Selbst-Emanzipation* described how Agudas Achim found a means to "throw sand in the eyes of the people by erecting everywhere schools for Hebrew and general education," schools funded entirely by "rich assimilated Jews." "But it baffles us," the author concludes, "that there are people, who despite [their] anti-assimilationist thought, do not want to recognize that the association Agudas Achim has more to do with Polonization than with the spread of education."[125] This last statement may have been true, but this did not mean that the group could not support Jewish education as well.

MIKRA KODESH BECOMES ZION

Soon after Bloch's first reelection in 1885, Mikra Kodesh ceased to exist and was transformed into the province's first explicitly Jewish nationalist organization, Zion. Already in 1885, Birnbaum's newly launched *Selbst-Emanzipation* started referring to the group as the "Jewish-national association *Mikra Kodesh*," and during the following three years the organization split between two factions. One, headed by its president and founder, Kobak, focused on Jewish education and hoped to nurture a strong sense of Jewish ethnicity among its student members. A second faction of younger members, however, mostly students in their teens, pushed for a more open declaration of Jewish nationhood and a corresponding increase in political activities supporting both Jewish national life in Galicia and, ultimately, the settlement of Palestine.[126] Whereas the former group represented the traditions of the Jewish Enlightenment,

---

[124] *Selbst-Emanzipation*, October 16, 1885.
[125] *Selbst-Emanzipation*, December 2, 1885.
[126] See the memoirs of Braude, Ehrenpreis, and Stand, op. cit.

which comfortably combined Habsburg patriotism with Jewish ethnic pride, the latter came of age in an atmosphere in which one's national identity increasingly demanded prime and even exclusive allegiance from its members. As such, those Jews who sought to maintain their Jewish identity, albeit in a secular framework, needed a more authentic (that is, in their eyes, more nationalist) foundation for it. A leading member of the group, Yehoshua Thon, later recalled how the young men moved from traditional Judaism through the Haskalah to Jewish nationalism.

Something began to grow in us at that time, which prepared us to climb up onto the stage itself, not merely as observers but really as actors. An idea had matured in our hearts that the redemption of Israel would not come, as it was then held, from the old or the new "tent of Torah," and not from the "Haskalah" and "knowledge" of *Mikra Kodesh*, but rather with the vision and brilliance of "Zion."[127]

Mordechai Ehrenpreis recalled being similarly disillusioned with the program of the Haskalah.

So we, the younger [members], took the matter into our own hands. Out of an acute awareness of the call of our times, we were pursuing new ideas to which we could adhere, ideas which would reward us much more than the Haskalah alone. The [new] Jewish generation was being released into a new era, one possible meaning of which was – a Jewish renaissance. The gate to western culture was already opened before us. However this was not sufficient cause that the door behind us to the Jewish cultural tradition should be closed at a stroke. True, we received civil rights and took upon ourselves the yoke of civil obligations; however in no way did we renounce our right to live as Jews.... It was clear to us that the meaning of history could not be the liberation of the Jews, as individuals, from the oppression of the ghetto, in order for Judaism, as a whole, to sink into the abyss of oblivion.

Such an ideology, however, one which affirmed their commitment to both Western and Jewish culture, was not yet available. So they had to create one for themselves. "Galician Jewry was divided into three separate camps," Ehrenpreis wrote, "ultra-Orthodox *Hasidim*, Liberals who favored Austria-Germany, and assimilationists in Polish culture."

Our group was seeking for itself an independent way of its own, above this complex atmosphere of external and internal division. We were struggling over a distinct Jewish type that would suit both our civil position as well as our connection to Western culture. Religious observance was, in our opinion, a personal matter.[128]

---

[127] Yehoshua Thon, "Dimuyot MeLvov" in Yisrael Cohen and Dov Sadan, eds., *Pirkei Galitsye* (Tel Aviv, 1957), 369.

[128] Mordechai Ehrenpreis, op. cit., 26.

Heading the young group of "rebels" were key future leaders of Galician Zionism, including students from both traditional and acculturated backgrounds. The latter group included Adolf Korkis (1869–1922) and Isaac Feld, the former was led by Ehrenpreis, Thon, and Braude.[129] Ehrenpreis, Thon and Braude were childhood friends who together jumped from yeshiva to gymnasium,[130] who all discovered Jewish nationalism through Mikra Kodesh and who all continued their secular studies in Berlin, eventually receiving rabbinical ordination (see Figure 2.2). Thon and Braude received appointments at the Cracow and Stanislau Temples, respectively, while Ehrenpreis was hired in Croatia and later became Chief Rabbi in Bulgaria and eventually Sweden. These three typified the modernizing "ethnicist" for whom Jewish nationalism provided a modern identity firmly rooted in Jewish tradition, even in the continued observance of Jewish law. Their pursuit of rabbinical careers was fundamentally tied to their Jewish national identities. Thon's daughter, Nella Rost Hollander, later described her father's circle as blazing a new path in Jewish existence. "In Berlin the fate of the three friends was the same," wrote Hollander.

The three of them pursued the same end, which they expressed in the same manner. "We three shall be the first to create a new type of rabbi and we three shall be Princes of the spiritual aristocracy." ... My father thought that in the first place it was necessary to obtain a general science and a Jewish knowledge as a first class weapon against all the attacks and all arguments on the Jewish National ideals.

But questions still lingered, she wrote, above all, "[What] would be the position of this new modern Zionist rabbi?" The answer, they insisted, was that he would be not just a spiritual leader, but a political one, using his pulpit to "preach the revolution of the contemporary generation."[131]

Under pressure from these younger forces, Kobak agreed to step down in early 1888. On his recommendation, the association elected as president

---

[129] An electoral struggle between the religious and secular students broke out almost immediately after the society's transformation, ending with the victory of the former group. Many secular students left the association at that time, although several remained and emerged as important leaders for the movement including Korkis, Feld (Ehrenpreis's German tutor), and David Heschcles. See Braude, op. cit., 102.

[130] There were various influences in each of their lives that drew them to modern learning, although the influence of Ehrenpreis's father, a traditional Jew increasingly attracted to Haskalah literature through his work running a Hebrew printing house, was especially pronounced. Ehrenpreis, op. cit., 14–20. Braude recalls that Thon and Ehrenpreis joined Mikra Kodesh before he did and drew him to it. Braude, op. cit., 80.

[131] Nella Rost Hollander, op. cit., 14. On the leadership of Uniate priests in the Ruthenian national movement see Himka, *Religion and Nationality in Western Ukraine* (Montreal, 1999), esp. 158–62.

FIGURE 2.2. Ehrenpreis (from left), Braude, and Thon in 1887. From A. Holzman, ed., *Le'an?: masot sifrutiyot* (Jerusalem, 1998).

the Lemberg lawyer Wilhelm Holzer (1834–1910), whom Braude praised as honorable but lacking deep political insight or any sense of the younger members' opinions and aspirations.[132] According to Thon, Holzer was forced out when he "naively" recommended the merger of Zion with

[132] Braude, op. cit., 96. Bierer had left Lemberg for a medical post in Belgrade in 1885.

Agudas Achim because, he argued, both groups sought what was best for Jews.[133] Of course, Holzer's suggestion only seemed naïve as Thon considered it many years later. At the time, it reflected values that both groups genuinely shared, despite critical differences.

Finally, in October 1888, Mikra Kodesh officially became Zion, with Adolf Korkis elected to serve as its new president. Unlike its predecessor, which charged itself primarily with nurturing the Jewish cultural heritage, Zion specifically intended to develop a Jewish national identity among Galician Jews and to prepare the ground for the Jewish return to Palestine.[134] In effect, however, Mikra Kodesh had already been doing this and Zion's methods did not vary tremendously from Kobak's. Despite the coup, Zion remained firmly committed to the cultural objectives of its predecessor. Statute 2 of its new bylaws, published in 1888, stated: "The purpose of this association is to promote and spread Jewish-national awareness, without, however, any political orientation." Its means were, the "revival of the Hebrew language, celebration of historic memorial days, formation of libraries and reading halls, etc."[135] Zion continued to offer lectures and discussion evenings designed to strengthen the Jewish national identity of their participants, although they now felt free to preach the Zionist program itself, despite Ehrenpreis's disclaimer. Lecture topics such as "The task of the Jewish intelligentsia," "The position of the Jews vis-à-vis the non-Jewish fellow citizens," and "The solution of the Jewish question through the colonization of Palestine" appeared frequently. History lessons continued to focus on heroic periods in Jewish history such as the Maccabean and Bar-Kochba revolts against the Assyrians and Romans, respectively, as well as on great Jewish thinkers such as Judah Halevi and Maimonides. Zion also hosted so-called discussion evenings, with similar topics designed to attract Jewish intellectuals into the Jewish national camp: "Anti-Semitism," "The nationality concept in general and

[133] Thon, op. cit., 374. Adolf Stand recalled Holzer much more fondly, describing him as the heart of the movement due to his extensive charity and profound love for his fellow Jews. Holzer grew up totally estranged from traditional Judaism, unable to read the Hebrew alphabet. At the time he joined Mikra Kodesh, he taught himself fluent Hebrew and became a strictly observant Jew. A. Stand, op. cit., 71.

[134] See the announcement of the association's transformation in *Hamagid*, October 11, 1888, 307.

[135] Markus Ehrenpreis, "Vor Herzl und Mit Herzl" in Tulo Nussenblatt, ed., *Theodor Herzl Jahrbuch* (Vienna, 1937), 183. See also Ehrenpreis, "Zionist Movement in Galicia" (Hebrew), *Hamagid*, November/December 1894. Note that the announcement of Zion's foundation in *Hamagid* (October 11, 1888, 307–8) did not mention Palestine at all.

the Jewish national concept in particular," "Assimilation," and "Nation and confession."[136]

Shmuel Almog's emphasis on Zionism being, above all, a solution to the Jews' existential problem of self-respect and dignity in a hyper-nationalist age applies perhaps most of all to Galicia.[137] At a time in Habsburg history when national affiliation seemed increasingly imperative, Zionism gave "integrationist" and "ethnicist" Jews alike a positive identity to compete with rival national ideologies. Thus it is not surprising to find Ehrenpreis, in an 1895 restatement of the Zionist platform, focusing not on the insolubility of Jewish life in the Diaspora but rather on the need to reclaim Jewish life in the Diaspora. Beginning with a discussion of the problem of worldwide Jewish suffering (poverty, expulsions, etc.), he glided into a critique of national cultural suffering as well.

We see how our children grow up in foreign cultures and in foreign languages, without their own national ideals, without recognition of their own People's history and their own heroes and poets, who have struggled and suffered for them. Our youth lacks the moral light which raises man and dignifies him.

The cause of this, he wrote, was that Jews lacked any influence on the administration and legislature, and overcoming this disability lay at the center of the Zionists' program. "We want to make all of this better. We want to do what is in our power to decrease our misery, to raise our income, to multiply and increase our political rights, to improve the education of our children, to further the education and vocational training [*Ausbildung*] of our people [*Volksmassen*]."[138]

Still, Jewish nationalists could not ignore Palestine either. These two tendencies of colonization rhetoric and Diaspora-oriented nationalist activity were not necessarily contradictory. The conflict was solved in Galicia by the development of its so-called double program. In theory, this meant working simultaneously toward building a national home in Palestine while defending the sociopolitical needs of Jews in Galicia.

---

[136] *Selbst-Emanzipation*, January 2, 1891; December 19, 1892; February 10, 1893. Most amusing are lecture titles that suggest an open-minded discussion but would certainly not be so even-handed. On January 14, 1893, for example, Osias Schauer held a lecture in Cracow entitled, "What Do We Call a Nation and to Which Nation do the Jews belong?" "The concept nation was discussed with such expertise," wrote the paper, "and it was finally proved that we can still count ourselves to the Hebrew Nation; the Messianic idea is the hope of national rebirth." This he "proved" with a Talmudic statement that in the messianic age Jews will be again independent.

[137] Almog, *Zionism and History: The Rise of a New Jewish Consciousness*, 23–9.

[138] Ehrenpreis, "Our Aim" (Yiddish), *Jüdischer Volkskalender* (Lemberg, 1895), 1.

In practice, it tended to mean paying lip service to settlement of the land of Israel as a long-term dream while actually focusing primarily on cultural and political work in the Diaspora. So wrote Ehrenpreis, one of Zion's most prolific spokesmen:

This is what we want. On the one hand, we want to work with those who want the Jewish people freed from exile, who want to acquire our own home in the land of Israel for our poor emigrants. On the other hand, we want to work with all our powers to improve our position here in this country. We believe in the success of the colonization work in *Erez Israel* and we support the colonies, but we know that the liberation from exile must last many more years, and in the meantime, we cannot totally neglect the tasks here in this country. We want to worry about the future and the present, we want to work for tomorrow and for today. This is our double program.[139]

Note that the acquisition of a Jewish homeland was specifically designated for "our poor emigrants." In this regard, their ideology seems closer to Western Zionism, which viewed Palestine as a refuge for Russian and Romanian Jewry but prescribed local patriotism for themselves as emancipated Jews.[140] Indeed, Ehrenpreis elsewhere admitted quite candidly, "For the time being, colonization constitutes the first priority for the Russian and Romanian refugees and for those in our land [i.e., Galicia] forced to leave their homeland due to a lack of livelihood." In any case, he added, the land of Israel could hardly support the mass migration of all Jews immediately, which would devastate its current inhabitants. In the meantime, there remained nationalist work in the Diaspora. "We are not strangers in Galicia, and we are not leaving today and not tomorrow to the land of Israel, we will yet be here many more years and," quoting the famous passage from Jeremiah, "we will yet build houses and plant vineyards until the great *shofar* is blown to announce our freedom."[141]

Still, Galician Zionists did charge themselves with both objectives and credited themselves with the unique achievement of their effective synthesis. Reflecting many years later, Ehrenpreis felt justified in writing: "This double program distinguished Galician Zionism from the Western and Russian *Lovers of Zion*. Here Zionism is not only [about the] colonization of Palestine, but also [about] Jewish domestic politics [*Landespolitik*]. This is totally new in the program of Galician Zionists."[142] Gershom Bader,

---

[139] Ehrenpreis, "Our Aim" (Yiddish), *Jüdischer Volkskalender* (Lemberg, 1895), 3.

[140] Shmuel Almog, *Zionism and History*, 184.

[141] Ehrenpreis, "Zionist Movement in Galicia" (Hebrew), *Hamagid*, November 29, 1894, 369.

[142] Ehrenpreis, "Vor Herzl und mit Herzl," 185.

another young Zionist activist just beginning a long career as a Hebrew and Yiddish publicist, similarly focused on the uniqueness of Galician Zionism in his 1894 summary of the movement. Like Ehrenpreis, he emphasized that Zionists elsewhere took no interest in domestic issues whatsoever, focusing only on settling Palestine.[143] In fact, this "double program" was something then unique to Galician Zionism. Eventually, other Zionist groups adopted similar resolutions, including the Austrian Zionists, who decided to run candidates in parliamentary elections in 1907, as well as Russian Zionists at their Helsingfors conference in 1906. This union of *Gegenwartsarbeit* or "work in the present," together with efforts to achieve a state in Palestine, became known as "synthetic Zionism."[144]

Zion, like its predecessor, continued to target primarily the secular intelligentsia, although it issued its first publication in Yiddish in 1890, titled *Der Kantschik oder Kinos nach Tischa b'Av* (The Whip, or Lamentations for the Ninth of *Av*).[145] Although advertised as a popular work written for the "people," the booklet's intended audience was more likely the growing, but still small class of young students who had been raised in a religious milieu but were increasingly drawn toward the modern world.[146] That is, it addressed that same stratum from which the religious students at Zion themselves came. Zion's leadership wanted to ensure that these secularizing *bochers* would ultimately settle in the Jewish national camp.

The booklet, divided into three sections, begins with a warning against assimilation and an attack on Jewish "do-gooders" who were encouraging Jews to abandon their language in favor of Polish. (Whether this meant Yiddish or Hebrew was left deliberately vague, but it seems to be referring to the latter, despite the implications of the text itself being printed in Yiddish.) Assimilation, it explains, is both undesirable and impossible because it denied the Jew his essential identity.

Is it possible, my dear Jews, that one fine day, one of you will think to yourself that you are unhappy with your father, your mother and your brothers and

---

[143] G. Bader, op. cit., 171.

[144] See Shmuel Almog, *Zionism and History: The Rise of a New Jewish Consciousness*, 177–237.

[145] The booklet is printed anonymously; however, Braude identifies the author as Ehrenpreis. Braude, op. cit., 117. The booklet is about thirty pages in length and is small enough to fit inside one's hand.

[146] For a review of the book, see *Selbst-Emanzipation*, October 3, 1890. According to Ehrenpreis, Zion issued the manifest in Yiddish in order to counteract the spread of assimilationism among the Jewish urban masses, but it was principally the student youth who were attracted to Polonization, not the traditional masses. Ehrenpreis, "Zionist Movement in Galicia" (Hebrew), *Hamagid*, November 15, 1894, 353.

sisters, and you will get up and go to the market to find a new father, a new mother, and new sisters and brothers? You laugh – it is really comical. And yet it is just the same when a person wants to become a Pole. What is born with you, you cannot later change.[147]

Here Jews do not merely constitute a nation, but an ethnic nation. Assuming a Polish identity thus becomes a biological impossibility rather than an immoral cultural choice. Such rhetoric clearly speaks to Jews already experiencing Polonization, not to traditional Jews not yet so tempted. In fact, as the work progresses, it evinces an outspoken contempt for religious Jews by mocking them for their insincere *tisha b'av* prayers for the return to Jerusalem. (Notably, this section constitutes the only discussion of Palestine at all.)

But you, real Jews, how dare you come yet into the synagogue to complain over the destruction of Jerusalem? How are you not ashamed before God to say such lies? ... You can't [do anything about it]? You have then no money? For rendez-vous in Carlsbad and Franzensbad you can spend thousands, but have you yet once given something for the land of Israel? Maybe you throw here and there a penny in the *Erets Yisrael* charity can for old Jews who go there to die and make a cemetery out of the land of Israel. Why don't they go to live there? Why don't you send young, healthy people with strong hands to work the land, for which you pray morning and night? Your prayers are chatter without heart and feeling.[148]

Again we see a program designed to appeal to readers already dissatisfied with the religious establishment and searching for a new identity. Indeed, it argues that Zionism is the most authentic interpretation of Judaism and that those who oppose it are hypocritical, even irreligious. The book closes with a discussion of Zion's domestic political agenda, particularly the establishment of modern Jewish schools (an explicitly anti-religious program based on the Haskalah's campaign against the traditional *heder*), the elections, and the need for a Yiddish-language journal ("for the people") to defend Jewish interests.

One year later, Zion published a sequel to *Der Kantchik* entitled *Der Wecker* (The Alarm Clock).[149] Like its predecessor, *Der Wecker* reflects an

---

[147] *Der Kantchik*, 7.
[148] Ibid., 17.
[149] Samuel Gutman, *Der Wecker* (Lemberg, 1891). Zion did not initially intend to publish a sequel, but did so only because *Der Kantchik* sold poorly and, according to Gershom Bader, because Zion's attempt at a Yiddish newspaper (the *Jüdische Volkszeitung*) had folded. Although *Der Wecker* calls itself numbers two and three in Zion's "*Volksbibliothek*," *Der Kantchik* did not indicate it is a part of any series. G. Bader, op. cit., 175. The booklet is printed anonymously by the association Zion, but *Hamagid*'s review (July 9, 1891, 215) indicates the author.

agenda designed to influence traditional Jews seeking Enlightenment, and likely to offend those who opposed it. Its author, Samuel Gutman (1864–1935), came from a strictly religious and extremely poor family. Married at a very young age, Gutman was pressured by his in-laws to divorce his wife after his discovery of Haskalah literature led to a growing interest in secular learning. He soon discovered Mikra Kodesh and with its help succeeded in entering gymnasium and eventually in earning a doctorate in philosophy, as well as rabbinic ordination, in Vienna. He then returned to Lemberg, remarried, and in 1903 was appointed assistant rabbi in the Lemberg Temple, ironically due to his ability to deliver Polish-language sermons, which the senior rabbi (Ezekiel Caro) found too difficult.[150]

Der Wecker certainly reflects many of its author's own life experiences. It tells the story of a brilliant Talmudic student, Moshe, who through exposure to a Hebrew translation of Graetz's *History of the Jews* is awakened to the hypocrisy and close-mindedness of the religious world, in which neither Hebrew language nor Jewish history are valued at all, and begins a search for a more authentic Jewish identity. When a German book is found in his possession, his community stipend is cut and he is forced to seek menial labor to support himself.[151] This experience awakens him to the bitter poverty most Jews suffered, a situation of which the religious elite was totally unaware and unsympathetic.[152] After his father writes from Argentina of the miserable lot of immigrant Jews there, he and a relative resolve to move to Palestine together. For good measure, the booklet interweaves a second story of a Jewish assimilationist in Galicia who, despite his university education, could not secure any employment as a result of increased anti-Semitism. Devastated, his sister teaches him Hebrew and he finds a position as a teacher in the Jewish school. The entire story is framed in appeals by Zion to support the Russian refugees

---

[150] Braude, op. cit., 88–9 and Bussgang, op. cit., 144–5. Gutman was later named rabbi of the Temple.

[151] Notably, the story has the religious establishment blame Moshe's "heresy" on Machsike Hadas because of the rotten influence of their "newspaper," published (heretically) in Hebrew. The accusation was not merely that the Hasidic youth were being exposed to worldly knowledge, but that they were being exposed to the Hebrew language itself, which they had no business studying (i.e., as a modern language). Gutman, *Der Wecker*, 21.

[152] A prospective match for him had been threatened when the bride's father discovered that Moshe's father was a simple worker. This awakened a deep animosity in Moshe for the haughty contempt of the religious elite for manual labor; even the *heder* teacher, whose social position ranked very low in traditional Jewish society, scorned his father "because he is a manual laborer who earns his tiny piece of bread honestly, with his own hands." Gutman, *Der Wecker*, 22.

by contributing to the Zionist project in Palestine and to join and support the Galician Zionist movement.

The innovation of cloaking nationalist propaganda in a fictional story, narrated in a simple Yiddish style that closely resembled traditional storybooks, is clearly an important development both in Galician Zionism and in the history of Yiddish literature.[153] Moreover, the story justifies the Zionist ideology through the appropriation of religious imperatives: How can one pray properly without understanding Hebrew? What does "Next Year in Jerusalem" mean if not supporting those who actually try to move to the land of Israel?[154] In others words, it frames the demands of the Zionist movement as natural conclusions of religious Judaism. In this regard, the work resembles the populist Yiddish press just emerging in the provincial Southeast, discussed in Chapter 3. Unlike those papers, however, *Der Wecker* does not pretend to be a defender of Orthodoxy. On the contrary, its content clearly betrays the author's sharp anti-clerical, even anti-religious sentiment. It ridicules the religious establishment as both religiously hypocritical and socially insensitive, and argues that Zionism constitutes a more authentic Jewish ideology. In short, like *Der Kantchik*, it sought to influence the secularizing religious youth, who shared many of these criticisms, in favor of Zionism and the Jewish Enlightenment.

Zion's later publications tended to be in Polish, the language of the Jewish intelligentsia and secular elite.[155] In 1892, Zion published its first program statement, in Polish, titled, "What should be the program of the Jewish youth?"[156] Again, the brochure focused principally on the national needs of the Jews in Galicia (its "inner program"), but it also included a general affirmation of the ultimate goal of an independent state in

---

[153] According to its review in *Hamagid*, *Der Wecker* was deliberately written in a more colloquial Yiddish than its predecessor in order to be better understood "by the masses," while Bader adds that it "emphasized its Zionism more than their first brochure." *Hamagid*, July 9, 1891, 215, and G. Bader, op. cit., 175.

[154] This is the final sentence read at the Passover feast, a prayer for the coming of the Messiah and the ingathering of all Jews to the land of Israel. Despite its appropriation by the Zionists, the prayer did not demand that Jews move to Jerusalem, or support those that do. As Eli Lederhendler put it, "'Next year in Jerusalem' is not a statement of geographic intent, but of spiritual aspiration." Lederhendler, *Jewish Responses to Modernity* (New York, 1994), 26.

[155] Gershon Bader wrote that the group deliberately turned away from Yiddish in favor of Polish because Yiddish-language literature could influence only the religious masses and they intended to attract the intelligentsia. Bader, op. cit., 175. Zion twice attempted to publish a Yiddish weekly, *Der Carmel* in 1893 and the *Jüdisches Wochenblatt* in 1895, but both proved short-lived and fell apart within a year.

[156] *Jakim być powinien program młodzieży żydowskiej* (Lemberg, 1892).

Palestine (its "outer program"). "We want to work with full strength," the brochure declared, "that the Jewish people should develop a healthy and harmonious life. Our solution is: Bread, education, self-awareness and equal rights."[157] As its composers surely realized, such language recalled the original program of Shomer Israel and was likely to attract much of the same constituency.[158] Moreover, in attacking assimilationism, the brochure carefully differentiates between "civic" and "ethnic" assimilation and thereby subtly commends the activity of Shomer Israel and its members while portraying it as belonging to a bygone age.

At the beginning of the 60s, many of our brothers thought to improve our position through assimilation. But these first assimilationists wanted only civic [*Staats*] and not ethnic [*Stammes*] assimilation. The first assimilationists wanted us to go arm and arm with the Poles and to work together in building the state and thereby to improve our situation as well. The Poles saw this and genuinely celebrated ... until the hand of the Poles was raised over every facet of life in the province and they no longer needed the help of the Jews. They began to push them away with the right hand while drawing them in with the left, all according to what they needed. Then there arose new assimilationists in place of the old who taught that we have no choice but to assimilate among the Poles with complete assimilation, religious and ethnic, in order to erase the name Israel from under the heavens.[159]

Zionists printed eight hundred copies of the brochure, enough to attract the attention of *Der Israelit* and, according to Bader, every other paper in the province.[160]

Finally, in October 1892, the first issue of the Galician Zionists' official organ, *Przyszłość* (The Future), appeared in Polish, edited by Korkis,

[157] Quoted in Ehrenpreis, op. cit., 184. For a German translation of the "inner" program, see *Selbst-Emanzipation*, June 21, 1892, 117. For a Hebrew translation of the text's program, see Gelber, op. cit., 170–3.

[158] Obviously its "outer" program of settling Palestine, however, radically opposed Shomer Israel's entire agenda. In fact, *Der Israelit* printed a scathing review of the brochure, arguing that it worked against the achievement of equal rights for Galician Jewry. The paper particularly lamented the young age of the Zionists, who seemed to ignore their more experienced elders telling them that their "utopian" program had "no chance of any success." "The program of the Zionists," *Der Israelit*, June 15, 1892, 1. The article continued on June 30, 1892, 1–2.

[159] Quoted in Bader, op. cit., 176. For a German translation of this same passage, see Moses Landau, *Geschichte des Zionismus in Oesterreich und Ungarn* (unpublished dissertation, University of Vienna, 1925), 45. Note the subtle reference to Exodus 1:8, "A new king arose over Egypt ..."

[160] Abraham Khomet, "The Zionist Movement in Tarnow" (Yiddish) in A. Khomet, ed., *Torne: kiem un khurbn fun a Yidisher shtat* (Tel-Aviv, 1954), 356, and Bader, op. cit., 175.

Ehrenpreis, and Ehrenpreis's brother-in-law David Malz (1862–1936).[161] Its publication virtually coincided with the dissolution of Agudas Achim and its organ *Ojczyzna*, a fact that Galician Zionists never tired of pointing out. Indeed, *Przyszłość* literally took over *Ojczyzna*'s offices and its contents.[162] They clearly saw that failure as the deathblow to the assimilationist movement. "Assimilationism has just played itself out in Galicia," wrote *Selbst-Emanzipation*.[163] *Ojczyzna*'s final article, "Ostatnie Slowo" (Last word), Ehrenpreis wrote, "was a declaration of bankruptcy of the assimilationist idea," and he reprinted its closing words with obvious pleasure.

Filled with beautiful hopes, we began our work. We hoped that the Poles would accept us as brothers.... Only now we see that they accepted us [only] so long as they needed us, and when we demanded the wage for our cooperation, they pushed us away. Now we see ourselves forced to lay down our arms and step down from the stage.[164]

Ehrenpreis did not seem to catch the irony that Zionists celebrated their "victory" over Agudas Achim in a Polish-language party organ. The ideological battle between these groups was far more subtle than the Zionists were willing to admit.

CENTRALIZATION

Selbst-Emanzipation's obituary for the assimilationist movement was certainly premature. Agudas Achim may have disbanded, but Zionism still remained a minority movement on the fringe of Jewish society, while even most of the secular elite continued to subscribe to the maskilic vision of integration together with Jewish continuity. Still, by the early 1890s, Jewish nationalism had achieved something of a foothold in the province. Zion, the oldest and most important Jewish nationalist association in Galicia, was increasingly supported by parallel associations in other

[161] In 1890, Shomer Israel had invited Zion to participate in *Der Israelit*, and Zion even established an editorial board for this purpose. But it came to nothing, as Zion had already decided to establish its own Polish-language organ. *Selbst-Emanzipation*, November 2, 1890.

[162] Manekin, "The Debate over Assimilation," 130.

[163] *Selbst-Emanzipation*, June 12, 1892. Ezra Mendelsohn similarly described the dissolution of Agudas Achim as symbolic of the victory of Zionism over assimilationism. Ezra Mendelsohn, "Jewish Assimilation in L'viv," 110.

[164] Quoted in Ehrenpreis, op. cit., 185. Malz wrote the "obituary" for *Selbst-Emanzipation*, "Assimilationism's Last Word," on July 26, 1892 (published August 5, 1892, 156). The launch of *Przyszłość* was announced in *Selbst-Emanzipation*, September 19, 1892.

major Galician cities. Many of these were founded by Galician members of Kadimah in Vienna who continued their nationalist agitation while home from the university. Like their Polish counterparts, young educated Jews returning home served as key leaders in forging a provincial nationalist movement.[165] The West Galician city of Tarnow, for example, was transformed into a Zionist stronghold almost single-handedly by its three vacationing Kadimahners: Abraham Salz (1866–1942), Sigmund Bromberg, and Edward Schwager. By January 1, 1884, the three had succeeded in adding eight Jewish newspapers, plus the Hebrew annual *Hameasef*, to the shelves of the local Jewish reading hall, despite that body's assimilationist librarian. (The librarian was probably far less apprehensive about the periodicals than Zionist chronicles suggest.) Although the city's first Zionist association (established in 1884) dissolved almost immediately, Salz, Bromberg, and Schwager successfully converted the local youth group into a Zionist society and its clubhouse into a nationalist reading hall.[166] This proved far more enduring, and in December 1887 the organization sponsored Tarnow's first Maccabee celebration. Salz soon thereafter established the Hatechiya society, which sponsored lectures and discussion evenings at its locale.[167]

Jewish nationalists frequently joined existing associations and converted them into nationalist societies, which often proved to be the most stable. Among the most important early nationalist groups, for example, was the Commerce and Bookkeeping Society in Stanislau, a long dormant society reactivated in 1885 by Jewish nationalists.[168] Already that December, they

---

[165] Keely Stauter-Halsted, op. cit., 176–8. In her memoirs, Gusta Wurman from Tlumacz specifically credited students returning home with the spread of modern ideas such as Zionism. "The Jewish villagers in the province tried to send their children to school in the towns, and the wealthier ones sent them on to the university.... While attending school in town, the Jewish students took active part in public life. They served in the army, joined youth movements, broadened their horizons. When visiting their native village, they would gather the young Jews from neighboring villages for dances and get-togethers. In time, the rural, country-type of young Jew all but disappeared. The Zionist movement had its impress on the young people, as did the periodicals, in Yiddish and Hebrew, which reached the village and the youth movements in general." Shlomo Blond, *Tlumacz: Sefer Edut V'zikaron* (Tel-Aviv, 1976), xxxviii.

[166] The Association of Young Jewish Merchants [*Handelsjugend*], a formerly assimilationist organization, now became the Reading Hall of the Young Jewish Merchants.

[167] Abraham Khomet, "The Zionist Movement in Tarnow," 354–5. Khomet exaggerated the importance of Tarnow, claiming that its 1887 Maccabee festival was the first in Galicia and inspired the Lemberg Zion society to host its own festival the following year. In fact, Lemberg's first Maccabee festival preceded Tarnow's by four years.

[168] The society had previously existed under entirely different statutes but was now reestablished as a Jewish national association with the task of providing Jewish history

organized the city's first Maccabee festival, reportedly with great success.[169] Most of the other groups proved ephemeral, although two grew to be particularly important: Schochrei Toschia (from 1890 Haleum, [The Nation]) in Stryj, and Haivri (The Hebrew) in Drohobycz. Like the Stanislau association, both of these groups had specifically Diaspora-oriented programs, solidified in both cases after brief crises that ended with the victory of the Diasporist camp.[170] All of these groups catered either exclusively or primarily to Jewish students and members of the intelligentsia.[171]

The movement had begun to spread, but it still remained relatively fragmented. As early as 1891, Jewish nationalists in Galicia began calling for a single, unified organization to oversee nationalist work throughout the entire province.[172] The leading advocate of this unification was undoubtedly Abraham Salz, who actually changed the statutes of the Tarnow Zionist society Hatechiya so that they corresponded to those of Zion.[173] On March 26, leading members of Zion met to discuss an initiative of Salz, then president of Ahavath Zion in Tarnow, to form a single Galician federation of Jewish nationalist associations, which would provide autonomy for individual groups but would forge a unified strategy.[174] The initiative was approved and the group established a committee with members from Zionist associations throughout Galicia to organize a conference for the purpose of forming such a federation.[175] Two months later,

---

lessons in order to implant a foundation of national feeling among Jewish youth. *Selbst-Emanzipation*, September 2, 1885. Numbering 120 members at the outset, by December the group had grown to 150. *Selbst-Emanzipation*, December 2, 1885.

[169] For a report, see *Selbst-Emanzipation*, December 17, 1885.

[170] In 1890, Schochrei Toschia changed its name to Haleum by oral vote, and its second statute was amended to read: "The purpose of the association is principally the raising and spreading of Jewish national awareness among the Jews." *Selbst-Emanzipation*, December 1, 1890. (A separate group, Admath Israel, was quickly founded in Stryj for the purpose of collecting money to support settlement activity.) Haivri, founded in Drohobycz in 1889, was the successor of the association Einigkeit [Unity], founded in 1887. In this case, Haivri represented the continuation, not transformation, of its predecessor. Einigkeit's goals had already been the spreading of the Jewish national idea and Hebrew knowledge among the youth. See Gelber, op. cit., 140.

[171] Gelber, op. cit., 139–40.

[172] See, for example, the April 1, 1891 lead editorial in *Der Folksfreund*, a nationalist, but independent Yiddish-language newspaper published in Kolomea. (On this paper, see Chapter 3)

[173] Khomet, op. cit., 355.

[174] Founded by Salz in 1891, *Ahavath Zion* was the first Palestine-oriented Zionist organization in Galicia. Salz later became an important leader in the Theodor Herzl's Zionist Organization. On Salz and *Ahavath Zion*, see Chapter 4.

[175] The committee consisted of Carl Stand (President of Zion), Ludwig Mansch (Zion), Adolf Korkis (Zion), Abraham Salz (Ahavath Zion, Tarnow), Moses Pachtmann

on July 15, Zion announced an upcoming conference to form the "Jewish National Party of Galicia."

To the Jewish national associations and private individuals of Galicia!

It is known to each and every one how necessary "unity" is, and [yet] every undertaking by us Jews lacks only unity; this is the main cause why the Jewish national idea has so very few supporters among us in Galicia. Why have the few associations and corporations that exist not found the means to do what they see as necessary? Because unity is lacking, everyone goes his own way, everyone does what feels good to him alone, the worst [part] of this being that everyone likes something different.

But something must be done!

We see every day more and more how unsure and dangerous our position is made in all lands, how necessary the national unity of all Jews is, how necessary it is to work for our Galician Jews, especially the education of our children [which] is either totally *goyish*, or wildly fanatic and unpractical. The leaders of our People are corrupted, foolish and shameful, our political situation is miserable. We have plenty of duties! Rights? Very few! But all of this is possible to improve; this is the task of the Jewish National Party in Galicia.[176]

Tellingly, the advertisement focuses primarily on Diaspora issues: the need for Jewish but non-Orthodox education, the absence of full political equality, the problem of poor Jewish communal leadership, and above all the call to forge "national unity." There is no mention of colonization whatsoever. The very name of the proposed federation avoided the term *Zionist* altogether, although the term had already come into popular usage.[177]

To a large extent, the conference was an important assertion of leadership and autonomy by Galician Jewish nationalists, who were just beginning to break away from Vienna. The launch of *Przyszłość* in October 1892, which heralded the end of the Viennese *Selbst-Emanzipation* as the province's principal nationalist organ, is perhaps its best symbol. At that time, Zion also revised its statutes to include the obligation of founding other Zion branches throughout Galicia, again indicating the new leadership role that Lemberg nationalists were assuming.[178] Galician Zionists

---

(President of Haivri, Drohobycz), and Gershon Zipper (Admath Israel, Stryj). *Selbst-Emanzipation*, April 15, 1891

[176] *Der Folksfreund*, July 15, 1891. News of the Zion meeting was reported in *Selbst-Emanzipation*, April 15, 1891, while the announcement was officially published there in July 16, 1891.

[177] Alex Bein, "The origin of the term and concept "Zionism," *Herzl Yearbook* 2 (1959), 1–27.

[178] *Selbst-Emanzipation*, October 9, 1892. Its growth in membership also led it to acquire a larger headquarters in 1892, which probably contributed to the group's growing self-confidence. Gelber, op. cit., 133.

increasingly resented attempts at Viennese centralization, arguing that
conditions in Galicia were sufficiently different to warrant its own organization. Aside from vast cultural and linguistic differences separating
the Galician and Viennese communities, many Galician Zionists emphasized that widespread impoverishment in Galicia meant that domestic social programs in the province had to precede colonization work.
"They don't grasp that here in Galicia the matter lies differently than
elsewhere," wrote one correspondent to *Selbst-Emanzipation*, "that for
us social reform ... must be set as the first plan, that we cannot give our
proletariat any phrases in place of bread and that we ... could have no
better weapon than enlightenment and science."[179]

For this very reason, Nathan Birnbaum,[180] editor of *Selbst-
Emanzipation* and among the most important Viennese Zionist leaders,
opposed the idea of the Galician conference from the beginning, arguing
that the Zionist movement required centralization, namely in Vienna.[181]
He had always been especially concerned about Galicia's Diaspora-
oriented nationalism and correctly predicted that the conference would
merely solidify such tendencies.[182] Although he modified his views
toward Diaspora work in late 1891, acknowledging the importance of

---

[179] *Selbst-Emanzipation*, June 21, 1892.

[180] Birnbaum was staunchly Palestine-oriented in this phase of his life and could not tolerate
any deviation from this ideology, ironically-so considering he would eventually abandon
Zionism in pursuit of Jewish national autonomy in Austria. In 1886 he wrote: "A true
national Jew will always be a friend of Zion [i.e. the land of Israel]. And all of the weak
attempts, which are being made from many sides, to form an abstract Jewish nationalism without the Zionist idea, are pathetic, because they only lead to the obscuring of the
party program and to the division of [its] strength ... Without the Palestine-idea ... the
national idea is a useless and unsuccessful doctrinal past time." *Selbst-Emanzipation*,
February 16, 1886.

[181] See Gaisbauer, op. cit., 70–8 and *Selbst-Emanzipation*, June 1, 1891, 5. In 1892, Birnbaum
wrote about the "unusual" decision of Galician Zionists to form a provincial party before
a general federation had been constituted. He again called for the formation of such a federation, based in Vienna, which would provide central direction but would offer autonomy
to its branch organizations on local issues. *Selbst-Emanzipation*, June 21, 1892, 116.

[182] As to Galician Zionism's division between its "inner" and "outer" programs, Birnbaum
was careful to clarify that the resettlement of Jews in Palestine must be the starting
point, and not merely the final goal, of the Zionist movement. Any nationalist ideology
that denies the essential need for a territory, he wrote, was of "fleeting worth." "There
is for Israel no other 'social reform' than the colonization of Palestine. Therefore Jewish
nationalism and Zionism are identical concepts." *Selbst-Emanzipation*, June 21, 1892,
116. This was a clear response to the subsequent article in that issue in which Ephraim
Frisch (1873–1942), originally from Stryj but then studying at the German Gymnasium
in Brody, reprinted the "inner" program of *Zion's* program brochure and charged that
Zionists cannot begin with colonization "as the last consequence of the idea" without
first achieving a "fundamental progressive reform of the Jewish communities."

"agitation and propaganda," Birnbaum continued to insist on Viennese centralization and even made a failed attempt at forming a world Zionist union that summer.[183]

The conference, finally held in Lemberg on April 23–25, 1893,[184] attracted nearly every leading Zionist in Galicia.[185] Several Viennese Zionists attended as well, including Birnbaum, who rather than boycotting the conference, tried to steer it toward colonization rather than Diaspora work. His influence was certainly felt. On the one hand, discussion largely skirted the issue of colonization, focusing instead on organizational issues, the party press, "jargon" (i.e., Yiddish) literature and its reform, and other cultural questions. However, one very heated debate centered on whether colonization should even be considered a long-term objective of the new federation. Isaac Feld led the faction that answered in the negative, while Birnbaum supported those who insisted it must remain the party's long-term goal.

But it was a long-term goal. To be sure, the first statute of the platform committed the organization to Jewish colonization in Palestine. "The Jewish National Party in Galicia, as a part of the [general] Jewish National Party, strives for the rebirth of the Jewish People with the end goal being the reestablishment of a Jewish-national body in Palestine." But this was a distant dream; the means to this goal were entirely cultural, "to awaken and nurture Jewish national awareness," especially through a series of projects designed to revitalize the Hebrew language. In other words, the platform did not call for any activities actually to support the colonization of Palestine.[186] Moreover, its second statute focused exclusively on local issues: "The Jewish-National Party in Galicia recognizes

[183] Bein, op. cit., 12–13 and Khomet, op. cit., 356.

[184] The forum was delayed a full year as a result of very light response to Zion's initial 1891 call; just two groups had accepted the invitation, the Viennese Kadimah and Salz's Tarnow association itself. In the interim period Zion put out its program brochure and began publication of *Przyszłość*, which generated a wider response to the conference.

[185] Speakers included Ehrenpreis, Malz, and Korkis (the editors of *Przyszłość*), as well as Adolf Stand, Isaac Feld, Z. Bromberg, M. Sprecher and Abraham Salz, the initiator of the event. *Selbst-Emanzipation*, May 18, 1893. With the exception of Salz, party leadership rested exclusively with Lemberg Zionists.

[186] In 1892, the "outer" program of building a home in Palestine had at least been oriented towards that goal: to facilitate emigration of Jews from Russia and Romania to Palestine, to found agricultural settlements in Palestine, to awaken the national feelings of Jews already there and to replace their spoken Yiddish with Hebrew, to found agricultural schools, and to found associations in Europe to collect money for the settlements. Gelber, op. cit., 172. In 1893, other than its Hebrew-language initiatives, only the support of colonization societies made it into the platform (and only on the initiative of Birnbaum himself), but even here the job was passed to a different federation.

the necessity to defend the political, social, and economic interests of the Jews in the land, and considers it therefore its duty to pursue an independent Jewish politics in Galicia." Its goals here included winning majority control of Jewish community councils, supporting Jewish economic associations, and founding Jewish *Volk* associations to raise the spiritual and moral level of the masses.[187]

As to colonization work, all colonization associations in Galicia were invited to join an altogether different umbrella organization, the Vienna-based "Zion Union of Austrian Associations for the Colonization of Palestine and Syria." This federation was established in 1892 by the Viennese colonization association Admath Jeschurun, established in 1886, which was under Birnbaum's leadership. In the summer of 1892, Birnbaum led an "agitation trip" through Eastern Galicia to promote the foundation of branch organizations to Zion (not to be confused with the Lemberg society). Birnbaum's trip proved extraordinarily effective, leading to the foundation of over a dozen such groups, often in the same towns that had "Diaspora-nationalist" groups associated with the Jewish National Party.[188]

To a certain extent, tensions flared between the two sides. Adolf Gaisbauer's portrayal of the period as divided between two movements, a "Jewish nationalist" and a "Zionist," clearly reflects the rhetoric used by nationalists at that time.[189] Diaspora nationalists may have applauded the formation of colonization societies in Galicia, but they still insisted on the establishment of a "Jewish nationalist" association alongside it. Thus in late 1893, the new president of Kadimah in Vienna, Jacob Kohn, led his own agitation trip throughout Galicia to found specifically Diaspora-oriented nationalist groups, an endeavor that proved as successful as Birnbaum's trip the year before.[190] In many cases, Kohn's trip complemented local agitation for such groups. In Kolomea, for example, Birnbaum rallied sixty Jews at his 1892 lecture to elect on the spot a constituting committee to form a branch organization of Zion. In response, the local Jewish nationalist leader Laibel Taubes (1863–1933),

---

[187] *Selbst-Emanzipation*, May 18, 1893.

[188] He visited a total of 13 cities in Galicia and Bukowina: Cracow, Tarnow, Rzeszow, Jaroslau, Przemysl, Lemberg, Sambor, Drohobycz, Stryj, Stanislau, Kolomea, Czernowitz, and Radautz. *Selbst-Emanzipation*, August 3, 1892. The most important of *Zion's* branches was Ahavath Zion, first founded in 1891, but now reconstituted as a branch of the Viennese federation.

[189] Gaisbauer, op. cit., 66. On the history of these terms, largely coined by Birnbaum, see Bein, op. cit.

[190] Gaisbauer, op. cit., 66–7.

an important Zionist speaker and publisher of numerous Yiddish news-papers, immediately led a propaganda campaign to organize a "Jewish national" society. His efforts were crowned with success with the found-ing of Beis Yisroel (House of Israel) in 1894.[191]

In a similar vein, "Zionist" activists may have supported the founda-tion of Diaspora-oriented societies. But these certainly could not satisfy their need to organize Zion branches throughout the province as well, and to prevent the transformation of colonization societies into cultural nationalist associations. For example, when the Rzeszow Chovevei Zion association reconstituted itself in 1893 after a period of dormancy, its new board (made up largely of "younger strengths") expanded the organiza-tion's purpose. "Besides supporting colonization, the association's goals are now also the raising of Jewish national self-consciousness and the nurturing and spreading of the Hebrew language and Jewish sciences." This elicited a threat by Birnbaum that if the group added these other goals, they jeopardized their membership in the Zion federation. *Selbst-Emanzipation* recommended setting up a separate association for these other objectives.[192]

Still, the overall situation was less one of competition than com-promise between Birnbaum and the Galician nationalist leadership. As noted, the Jewish National Party had itself called for the formation of Zion branches in Galicia, and even unanimously named Birnbaum the convention's honorary chairman.[193] Moreover, the second annual meeting of the Zion colonization federation (August 30–31, 1894) was hosted at the headquarters of the Lemberg Zion association. It was scheduled to fall immediately before the second annual conference of the Jewish National Party (September 2–4, 1894) at the same location, presumably to enable delegates to participate in both conferences.[194]

[191] Its goals were (1) to spread Jewish national self-awareness, (2) to spread knowledge of Jewish history and literature, (3) to cultivate the Hebrew language, and (4) to support Jewish colonies in Palestine. Headed by Dr. Zipser, Taubes served as Vice-president. *Österreichische Wochenschrift*, June 22, 1894, 493.

[192] *Selbst-Emanzipation*, July 1, 1893.

[193] They also undertook to support *Selbst-Emanzipation*, alongside their own *Przyszłość*, as the party's official organ.

[194] In one of the only items on the agenda addressing Palestine at the Jewish National Party conference, Birnbaum was scheduled to speak on "the current position of the Zionist movement." *Österreichische Wochenschrift*, August 31, 1894, 680. Since by this time "Zionism," a term Birnbaum coined just a few years earlier, had generally come to mean the movement to establish a Jewish homeland in Palestine, this lecture seems to be a report to the "Jewish nationalists" about the separate movement of colonization societies. See Alex Bein, op. cit., 14 ff.

By this time, even Birnbaum himself had begun to consider the idea
of a broader Jewish national party, centered on Zionism but willing
in the short term to advocate the immediate Jewish interests in the
Diaspora.[195] Thus, while Jewish nationalism in Galicia was dominated
by non-Zionists, in Birnbaum's sense of the word, Jewish nationalist
leaders certainly supported the minority who continued to focus on
Palestine, most of whom ultimately joined the Viennese colonization
federation.

MEETING THE SOCIALIST CHALLENGE

By the mid-1890s, Jewish nationalism in Galicia had by and large
become a Diaspora-oriented movement, dominated by Jews committed to national-cultural development in Galicia, with a secondary, long-
term goal of settlement of Palestine. The largest of these groups, Zion in
Lemberg, formed the Jewish National Party of Galicia in 1893, which by
its second conference a year later represented thirty organizations. Those
nationalists who remained focused primarily on the colonization of
Palestine had by this time largely joined the Austrian federation Zion. By
1895, Zion included nineteen Galician colonization associations, often in
the same cities as Diaspora-nationalist groups.[196]

    By this time, the Jewish nationalist movement, which claimed 4,000
members throughout the province, had achieved a strong foothold among
the secular intelligentsia in Galicia.[197] It could hardly claim to represent
the hundreds of thousands of traditional Jews in the province, however.
Zionists occasionally discussed reaching out to these Jews, but the focus
of Zionist efforts continued to be the Jewish intelligentsia. Zionist publications, for example, in both language and content continued to reflect
a secular readership. Most Jews, after all, could read neither Polish nor
German and would have been alienated by the Zionist publications'
largely secular orientation. More fundamentally, the entire project of
Jewish nationalists to provide secular and secularizing Jews with a positive Jewish identity able to compete with Polish or German nationalism

---

[195] Nathan Birnbaum, "Ein jüdisches Volkspartei," *Neue Zeitung*, 1894, cited in Jess Olson,
"A Tale of Two Photographs" in Kalman Weiser and Joshua Fogel, eds., *Czernowitz at
100* (Lanham, 2010), 28. Birnbaum even considered running Jewish nationalist candidates in government elections, as well as an alliance with other oppressed people, a
harbinger of his growing alliance with Ruthenian nationalists.
[196] Gaisbauer, op. cit., 67–8.
[197] Ehrenpreis, "Vor Herzl und mit Herzl," 185.

was simply not appropriate for the traditional masses, most of whom did not yet suffer from such modernist angst.

Early indications of the movement's expansion beyond the intellectual elite did begin to appear even during this period, however. Zionist concern with Jewish impoverishment in Galicia, for example, certainly reflected a growing interest in attracting broader segments of the population to the movement. It was not simply the urgency of Jewish poverty that pressured Jewish nationalists to focus on local, material issues. In 1890, encouraged by the founding of the Austrian Social Democratic Party the previous year, two socialist parties were founded on Galician soil. Left-wing Ruthenian intellectuals managed to unite behind the Ruthenian-Ukrainian Radical Party, while a cadre of ten "Polish" intellectuals (including two Jewish students – Herman Diamand and Joachim Fraenkel) formed the Worker's Party, renamed the Galician Social Democratic Party in 1892.[198] The latter party constituted an important source of competition for Jewish nationalists as it expanded beyond the intelligentsia, for it too hoped to attract Jewish workers. In fact, Jewish socialists formed the first Jewish Workers Party in Galicia already in 1892. The group briefly published a Yiddish-language party organ, *Di Arbeter Shtime* (The Workers' Voice), which advocated the recognition of the Jews as a nationality and (anticipating later Austro-Marxist doctrine) the establishment of a federation of autonomous socialist parties in the empire along national lines.[199] Although this early attempt petered out quickly, the Galician socialist party launched its own Yiddish-language weekly in 1893, *Der Arbeter* (after 1896, the *Yidishe Folkstsaytung*), and managed to organize a number of rallies for Jewish workers.

[198] John-Paul Himka, *Socialism in Galicia: The Emergence of Polish Social Democracy and Ukrainian Radicalism (1860–1890)* (Cambridge, 1983), 165–72. In 1897, the party changed its name to the Polish Social Democratic Party of Galicia and Silesia (PPSD).

[199] On the Jewish Workers' Party and its paper, as well as the subsequent history of the Jewish socialist movement in Galicia, see Jacob Bross, "Towards a history of the J.S.D.P. in Galicia" (Yiddish) in *Royter pinkes; tsu der geshikhte fun der Yidisher arbeter-bavegung un sotsyalistishe shtremungen bay Yidn* (Warsaw, 1921), 26; ibid, "The Beginning of the Jewish Labor Movement in Galicia" (Yiddish) in F. Kursky [and others] ed., *Di Yidishe sotsyalistishe bavegung biz der grindung fun "Bund"* (Vilna, 1939), 491 (an abbreviated English version is available in *YIVO Annual*, 1950: 55–84); Henryk Grossman, *Der Bundizm in Galizien* (Cracow, 1907), 16–17; and Joseph Kisman, "The Jewish Social-Democratic Movement in Galicia and Bukowina" (Yiddish) in G. Aronson, ed., *Di Geshikhte fun Bund* (New York, 1960), v.3, 348. On the socialist movement among Galician Jewry in general, see Robert Wistrich, "Austrian Social Democracy and the Problem of Galician Jewry 1890–1914," *Leo Baeck Institute Yearbook* XXVI (1981): 89–124.

Although they opposed the establishment of an independent Jewish Workers Party,[200] Polish socialists in their first years fervently fought the rising anti-Semitic tide and even seemed to defend Jewish national rights. Hardly an issue of their organ *Naprzód* failed to condemn anti-Semitism, and the party's leader Ignacy Daszyński (1866–1936) even sat in jail at one point for his opposition to anti-Semitic reactionaries. Daszyński and his party enjoyed the support of the newly formed Party of Independent Jews and its leader, Adolf Gross (1862–1936), a close personal friend of Daszyński who invested heavily in *Naprzód*.[201] As a result, Daszyński's first election to Parliament in 1897 was made possible in large part by the overwhelming support of Cracow's Jews, including traditional Jews who in study houses and synagogues the previous Sabbath – at the time of the reading of the Torah – called on everyone to vote "for the beloved Jewish supporter" (Ohev Yisroel) Daszyński.[202] (Daszyński had other Jewish connections. He apparently sired an illegitimate son with Alfred Nossig's sister Felicja, and later took a different Jewish mistress whom he married in 1935 after his wife passed away.)[203]

Socialists also led Jewish workers to a number of strikes in the early 1890s, the most important of which was the 1892 walkout of the Jewish tallis (prayer shawl) weavers in Kolomea. Hundreds of local Hasidic Jews slaved fifteen to sixteen hours a day for subsistence wages (1–3 gulden per week) at the factory, and on July 24, 1892, they voted to strike. Austrian socialists rallied to their cause. Their Viennese organ, the *Arbeiter Zeitung*, reported on the strike almost weekly. The strike fund it launched collected money from throughout Galicia and Austria, ultimately amassing almost 1,000 gulden, its most successful fund during this period.[204] Aside from the urgent need for this material support, socialists claimed that the contributions also strengthened these Jewish

---

[200] The Austrian socialist organ, the *Arbeiter Zeitung*, initially welcomed the launching of the *Arbeter Shtime* and wished it luck. The following week, however, the paper printed a much longer attack on the paper's founders and withdrew its previous approbation. *Arbeiter Zeitung*, July 22, 1892, 4 and July 29, 1892, 4.

[201] Andrzej Żbikowski, "The Impact of New Ideologies: The Transformation of Kraków Jewry between 1895 and 1914," *Polin* 23 (2010), 142–4.

[202] Karol Einäugler, "The First Yiddish May-Call in Galicia and the May Issue of "Arbeter" (1894)" (Yiddish) in F. Kursky, ed., *Di Yidishe sotsyalistishe bavegung biz der grindung fun "Bund,"* 526. Daszyński later became a sharp proponent of Jewish assimilation, a move that Zionists blamed for his electoral downfall in 1907. See below, Chapter 5.

[203] Walentyna Najdus, *Ignacy Daszyński, 1866–1936* (Warsaw, 1988)

[204] The strike was first reported on August 5, 1892. The strike fund, just one of many advertised in that issue, is already the largest such collection by the following week. By October they collected over 800 gulden, occasionally even outpacing the party's all-important general agitation fund.

workers' class consciousness, their sense that they did not stand alone but rather together with all working people.[205] The signature attached to one donation, "because Rabbi Bloch represents Kolomea and he has not contributed," speaks legions about the workers' apparent preference for workers' rights over Jewish solidarity.[206]

It was not simply the plight of the weavers that captured socialists' attention. As the contemporary press never tired of pointing out, the strike's great significance rested in the socialists' seemingly successful penetration into a solidly Hasidic workforce. In particular, socialists claimed credit for having turned those workers against a similarly Hasidic employer, who as one socialist historian later commented, "traveled to the same rebbes as his workers."[207] The Polish socialist organ *Naprzód*, celebrating the eruption of class conflict between Jews, wrote in an oft-quoted passage, "The religious, Orthodox [workers] were compelled to strike against their no-less religious exploiters."[208]

Zionists were deeply alarmed by the socialists' success in mobilizing the workers to fight for their class rather than for their national interests. The strike was instigated by a Jewish socialist activist named Max Zetterbaum, then still a student but already a leading member of the Polish socialist party, which he helped found.[209] Zetterbaum, the son of an impoverished Jewish family who later studied law at the University of L'viv before returning to his native Kolomea, managed to get a job at the factory and quickly rallied the workers to strike for better conditions. Assembled at the synagogue with the rabbi present for the big vote, the workers pledged to punish violently anyone who crossed the picket line. In order to guarantee that pledge they then brought out the Torah scroll and each worker swore an oath on the holy Torah itself that they would

[205] *Arbeiter Zeitung*, September 9, 1892, 5.

[206] *Arbeiter Zeitung*, August 26, 1892, 5 and September 2, 1892, 6. A rally by the striking workers in early September, in which Bloch is specifically denounced as a tool of the Jewish capitalists and in no way the representative of those assembled, also declared that differences in religion and race are meaningless. The only real division in society, their resolution stated, is between the exploiters and the exploited. *Arbeiter Zeitung*, September 9, 1892, 5.

[207] Joseph Kisman, "The Jewish Social-Democratic Movement in Galicia and Bukowina" (Yiddish), 353.

[208] *Naprzód*, August 15, 1892. For a full Yiddish translation of the often-quoted *Naprzód* correspondences, see Bross, "The Beginning of the Jewish Labor Movement in Galicia" (Yiddish), 493.

[209] On Zetterbaum, see Timothy Snyder, "Kazimierz Kelles-Krauz, 1872–1905: A Polish Socialist for Jewish Nationality," *Polin* 12 (1999), esp. 263–6. From 1896–9, Zetterbaum served as editor of the socialist party's Yiddish-language paper, the *Yidishe Folkszeitung* (formerly *Der Arbeter*).

not cross the picket line even if it meant months in jail. The rabbi himself administered the oath, threatening a curse on anyone who returned to work before all their demands were met.[210]

Jewish nationalists viewed these events with consternation. Not only had socialists rallied traditional Jews to their cause but they had proven just as effective at appropriating Jewish religious rhetoric and symbols as their Zionist detractors. Watching these developments from Vienna, Nathan Birnbaum chastised local Zionists for allowing the socialists such great success. For Birnbaum, it was a zero-sum game. "Every single Jew whom they win and make into an exclusive fighter for their cause," he wrote, "is for us an irreplaceable loss." Socialism threatened to turn Galician Jewry into "a horde of barbarians, repulsive, common, crude, [and] nasty."[211] Despite his Herculean efforts during these same months to reign in the Diaspora-nationalist orientation of Galician activists, Birnbaum was moved by the strike to call on Zionists to reach out to Galician Jewish workers with Yiddish-language propaganda and a clear dedication to their socioeconomic needs. "The true national Jew must not tolerate the exploitation of the Jews; whoever holds differently is no national Jew, but rather a pest, who wants to plant the chauvinism of the European nations, this social weed, on our pure Jewish ground."[212] He called on Zionists to "gather our strengths" and he reminded them of the inherent advantages they enjoyed over their socialist competitors. "The people who swore their rebellion on the Torah stand closer to us than to the socialists. We are committing a crime against our great idea if we do not soon exploit this advantage.... What the socialists possess by the Jews, we can too; in fact we can have more, because we stand within Judaism [*Judentum*]."[213]

Equally confident of the Zionists' ultimate advantage over the socialists was David Silberbusch (1854–1936), one of Kolomea's leading Zionist activists and at the time of the strike publisher of the Hebrew paper *Ha'am*.[214] Silberbusch assumed that Birnbaum's critique specifically targeted him and his paper, charging them with failing to capture the tallis

---

[210] This was not the rebbe who refused to support either side. For a first-person memoir of the strike, see Abraham Locks, "Sloboda and Kolomea" (Yiddish) in Nehemia Zucker, ed., *Pinkes Galitsye* (Buenos Aires, 1945), 452–8.

[211] "Die Tallisweber von Kolomea," *Selbst-Emanzipation*, August 29, 1892, 167.

[212] "Aus dem Lager der Socialdemokratie," *Selbst-Emanzipation*, September 19, 1892, 179.

[213] "Die Tallisweber von Kolomea," *Selbst-Emanzipation*, August 29, 1892, 167.

[214] Silberbusch had previously put out the province's first Yiddish newspaper, the *Yidishe folkstsaytung*. See Chapter 3.

workers for Zionism before the socialists could penetrate their ranks. In response, he reiterated Birnbaum's optimism regarding the Zionists' ability to attract Jewish workers to their cause because of Zionism's essential connection to Judaism and traditional Jewish culture.

> Our "socialists" [i.e., the striking workers] have not stopped praying three times a day the blessing "may our eyes behold your return to Zion" [in the daily prayer service] nor the blessing "And rebuild Jerusalem" after each meal. There are even among them those who perform *chatzos* [the daily midnight service mourning the destruction of the Jerusalem Temple]. Socialism has not touched even one hair of their Judaism. But for their work they want more than simply a crumb of bread for themselves and for their wives and children.... They cannot make even a pair of shoes for their children from their love of Zion and Jerusalem.[215]

Silberbusch thus viewed the strike as an aberration caused by the workers' overwhelming economic misery and in no way feared that the anti-religious socialist ideology had made any headway among the striking workers. Despite the strike, Silberbusch suggested, the workers naturally identified not with the socialists but with their Hasidic employer. In his memoirs, Silberbusch describes the deep mutual affection between the factory owner and his employees, writing that they always behaved "Jewishly" one with the other. Every afternoon, the factory broke to pray with the owner himself often leading the service while the workers "derived proud pleasure [*nakhes*] from their boss's pious gestures." When a worker was inspired to share a Hasidic story or a word of Torah, the owner himself stopped working to listen intently. On the anniversary of their rebbe's passing, he brought refreshments for the whole factory, and on Purim he invited everyone to his home for the holiday feast.[216]

Birnbaum may not have been aware of this apparently affectionate relationship between the factory owner and his workers, but he clearly

---

[215] Silberbusch, *Menschen und Geschehenisse*, 53–6. Silberbusch proposed that the Zionists collect money to build a new *tallis* factory where the workers would all be partners and could divide the profits among themselves. According to Silberbusch, this article "exploded" in Kolomea and led the factory owner to approach him, explaining that he lacked the funds even to meet his dowry obligations for his daughter. Silberbusch supposedly told him that this hardly excused paying workers starvation wages and he managed to negotiate a settlement to end the strike. I am not aware of a single other source which credits Silberbusch with this accomplishment. Other accounts rely on the socialist correspondent who blamed ten workers with large, starving families for crossing the picket-line and sinking the strike. Loks, however, recalled the workers preventing Russian Jewish weavers from taking their jobs and said the owners simply outsourced some factories to Bohemia, and replaced other workers with non-Jews, ending Kolomea's famed *tallis* industry. Loks, op. cit., 456–8.

[216] David Silberbusch, op. cit., 49–50.

appreciated the significance of the strikers' decision to swear their allegiance to each other on a Torah scroll. He tried to emphasize the advantage Zionists enjoyed in their ability to tap into Jewish religious rhetoric
in a way that the anti-clerical socialists could not. Hasidic Jews would
hardly be attracted, for example, to the socialists' proudly defiant report
of the rebbe of Boyan (son of the Sadagora rebbe) coming out against the
striking workers, whom the rebbe described as "wicked."[217] Their Yiddish-
language publications were no more appealing. In fact, the Polish socialists'
so-called Yiddish newspaper *Der Arbeter* was actually written and edited
by assimilated (and even assimilationist) Jews, most of whom did not know
Yiddish. They relied on the publisher to translate their German articles,
often leaving them in an almost purely German language, Hebrew characters notwithstanding.[218] Moreover, the articles themselves often consisted of
exact translations of Polish material which made little sense in a Jewish cultural context. The paper thus proved, as a future founder of Jewish socialism put it, "unable to connect to the soul of the Jewish worker."[219]

The socialists' inability to publish a truly Yiddish paper able "to connect to the soul of the Jewish worker" contrasts starkly to the nationalists' simultaneous success at this very same endeavor. Beginning in 1890,
Jewish nationalists in Galicia began publishing a revolutionary series
of short-lived Yiddish-language papers. Written in a very folkish style,
often in a heavy Galician dialect, these papers appropriated traditional
Jewish themes such as Jewish unity and attachment to the land of Israel
in their efforts to convince traditional Jews to view themselves as a modern nation and to organize politically to secure national minority rights.
These papers represented the first sustained effort at Zionist outreach
beyond the intelligentsia, and it is to them that we now turn.

---

[217] The German-language paper mockingly transliterates the Jewish term "*Rashaim*."
Arbeiter Zeitung, October 28, 1892, 5. Note also Zetterbaum's virulent attack in Karl
Kautsky's *Die Neue Zeit* on Hasidism and the influence of the Talmud as "the root-
cause of Jewish poverty and corruption in Galicia." R. Wistrich, *Socialism and the Jews*
(Littman Library, 1982), 312–3.

[218] Karol Einäugler, op. cit., 512–19.

[219] Bross and Einäugler, both leading members of the breakaway Jewish Social Democratic
Party of Galicia, had reason to mock the ability of Polish socialists to reach Jewish workers.
Nevertheless, their assessment should not simply be dismissed as party propaganda. Bross
notes, for example, that the paper printed just 600 copies, many of which did not even
circulate, while other party resolutions to publish materials in Yiddish never materialized.
Jacob Bross, "Towards a history of the J.S.D.P. in Galicia" (Yiddish), 28–30. Bross later
wrote more generously about *Der Arbeter*, reprinting long passages from the paper and
suggesting that it did make an important contribution towards Jewish politicization. See
Bross, "The Beginning of the Jewish Labor Movement in Galicia" (Yiddish), 497–509.

3

Building a Nation of Readers

The Emergence of a Yiddish Populist Press

Jewish nationalism in Galicia, like its Viennese counterpart, remained through the end of the nineteenth century a movement largely of the secular intelligentsia, especially students. Raised in a Polish cultural and educational milieu, Jewish students tended initially to identify strongly with Polish nationalist aspirations. The increasing rejection many experienced from Polish nationalists, among whom anti-Semitism was sharply rising, made them choice targets for Zionist propaganda. Galician Zionists attacked their assimilationist rivals ferociously and tried to inspire Galician Jews to support the rebirth of a Jewish national culture instead. At first they relied on the German-language Viennese organ *Selbst-Emanzipation*, but by 1892 they had begun to publish their own Polish-language literature, including a party organ, *Przyszłość*. Their choice of a Polish-language organ reflected the early movement's agenda, which was still principally concerned with recruiting the secular intelligentsia. Most Jews could read neither Polish nor German and would have been alienated by the Zionist publications' largely secular orientation.[1]

Partially as a result of this political vacuum, a revolutionary literature emerged in Galicia in the early 1890s: a populist nationalist press published in the Yiddish language.[2] These papers, published and edited

---

[1] Neither could most read literary Hebrew. Thus although a number of Hebrew language journals appeared in the 1880s, many Zionist oriented, their readership remained Jews already committed to the Haskalah and not the more traditional "masses."

[2] These papers have been virtually ignored until now. This author found most of them still uncut at the National Library in Vienna, unread since their deposit over a century ago. For a short discussion of some of these papers, see Jacob Toury, *Die Jüdische Presse*

by Zionists and often supported by Zionist associations, represented an early, major effort of outreach beyond the secular intelligentsia. They constituted a revolutionary advance for the Jewish nationalist movement. Anticipating the eventual dominance of the Yiddish-language press in Galicia a decade later, they helped to lay the foundation for popular acceptance of Yiddish as a modern language worthy of its own press.[3] More important, they made a critical contribution to the transformation of Jewish self-consciousness from an essentially religious to a national orientation through the appropriation of religious norms that their readers shared. Papers such as *Dos Folk, Der folksfraynd*, the *Yidishe folkstsaytung,* and the *Yidishes folksblat* often survived just one or two years. Yet collectively, they provided a vernacular-language forum for nationalists to convince traditional Jews not only that the Jews constituted a nation – indeed that their nationalist ideology was a natural extension of traditional Judaism – but critically that they needed to become politically active to win the same rights as other nations. The ideas first promulgated to traditional Jews by these papers would become accepted truths by the end of the next decade.

THE TURN TO YIDDISH

Despite the fact that the vast majority of Galician Jewry read only Yiddish, the decision to publish in that language did not come naturally to Jewish nationalists. Until the 1880s at the earliest, Jewish intellectuals – including the founders of Yiddish literature itself – generally viewed Yiddish as ugly and inappropriate for literary purposes. Hebrew, on the other hand, was revered as aesthetically perfect, even divine.[4] This had much to do

---

im Österreichischen Kaiserreich, 131–8. The following papers published before 1897 are analyzed in this chapter: *Yidishe folkstsaytung* (*Jüdische Volkszeitung*), ed. David Silberbusch and Laibel Taubes (Kolomea, 1890–1); *Izraelitishes folksblat* (*Izraelitisches Volksblatt*), ed. Efraim Laufer (Kolomea, 1890–1); *Der folksfraynd* (*Der Volksfreund*), ed. Alter Teicher and Laibel Taubes (Kolomea, 1891–2); *Yidishes familienblatt* (*Jüdisches Familienblatt*), ed. Shevach Knöbel (Tysmienica, 1893–4); *Yidishes folksblat* (*Jüdisches Volksblatt*), ed. Shevach Knöbel (Tysmienica, 1894); and *Ha'Am-Dos Folk*, ed. Laibel Taubes (Kolomea, 1895–7). The last of these papers appeared originally as separate Hebrew and Yiddish publications, beginning in 1892. From 1895 the Yiddish paper was published alone under the combined name.

3 The percentage of Jewish papers in Galicia published in Yiddish continued to rise over the next two decades so that by the First World War, the vast majority of Jewish papers were in Yiddish. See Toury, op. cit., 138.

4 Dan Miron, *A Traveler Disguised* (New York, 1973), 47 ff. An important exception was the early Galician *maskil* Mendel Lefin of Satanow (1749–1826), who believed strongly

with the legacy of the Haskalah, which since its inception in the 1780s had promoted the abandonment of Yiddish in favor of a "cultured" European language (at first German, later Russian or Polish), as well as the rejuvenation of biblical Hebrew as the focus of a renewed Jewish ethnic identity.[5] Only with the rise of Jewish national ideologies in the 1870s and 1880s could Jewish intellectuals begin to approach Yiddish not as a regrettable means with which to influence the masses, but as a cultural heritage in itself.[6]

Jewish intellectuals in Galicia exhibited no greater affinity for Yiddish than their Russian counterparts.[7] Thus the Jewish press in Galicia through the 1880s included papers in German, Hebrew, and Polish, but Yiddish papers were conspicuously absent.[8] German papers included the

in the need for Yiddish publications in order to reach traditional Jews who knew no other languages. Lefin put out Yiddish scientific publications and even translated the Bible into Yiddish, earning him the scorn of other *maskilim*. N. M. Gelber, "Mendel Satanower, der Verbreiter der Haskala in Polen und Galizien," in Gelber, *Aus zwei Jahrhunderten* (Vienna, 1924), 39–57. For a critique of scholars who portray Lefin as a populist, see Nancy Sinkoff, "Strategy and Ruse in the Haskalah of Mendel Lefin of Satanow" in Shmuel Feiner and David Sorkin, eds., *New Perspectives on the Haskalah* (London, 2001), 86–102 and Sinkoff, *Out of the Shtetl* (Providence, 2004), 168–202. Several Russian *maskilim* also attempted to influence the masses, especially women, through Yiddish-language history books in the 1860s and 1870s. See Feiner, *Haskalah and History* (Oxford, 2002), 241–7.

[5] Israel Bartal, "From Traditional Bilingualism to National Monolingualism," in Lewis Glinert, ed., *Hebrew in Ashkenaz* (Oxford, 1993), 141–50.

[6] The most important agent in this transformation was Sholem Aleichem, who (along with several other key figures) essentially fabricated a literary history for the Yiddish language through the articles in his short-lived literary journal *Di yidishe folks-bibliotek* (1888–9); see Miron, op. cit., 27–33. Two other Yiddish journals appeared in the 1880s in Russia: the *Yidishes folksblat* (1881–90), ed. A. Zederbaum, and *Der Hoiz-freund* (1888–9, 1894–6), ed. M. Spector. Spector had edited the pioneering Yiddish-language supplement *Kol Mevasser* (1862–72) in which S. Y. Abramovitsh (Mendele Moycher-Sforim), as well as many others, made his Yiddish-language debut.

[7] As in Russia, Yiddish authors in nineteenth-century Galicia nearly all published their works anonymously. See Gershom Bader's short biography of the *maskilic* playwright Shlomo Ettinger (1803–55) in the unpublished manuscript of his "Galician Jewish Celebrities," op. cit., Yivo Institute for Jewish Research.

[8] For a detailed history of the Jewish press in Galicia since 1848, see Jacob Toury, op. cit., 25–35, 58–69, 122–38. Filip Friedman refers to several Yiddish papers appearing sporadically before this time; however, some of these might have been German-language papers published in Hebrew script, albeit at times with a discernible Yiddish influence. He includes the short-lived Lemberg *Zeitung*, for example, a Judeo-German paper published in Hebrew script in 1848. Friedman, *Die galizischen Juden im Kampfe um ihre Gleichrechtigung (1848–1868)* (Frankfurt am Main, 1929), 47–8. See also Gershom Bader's unpublished manuscript of "Galician Jewish Celebrities," which mentions a Viennese paper published by a Jewish emigrant from Przemysl in "simple German and printed with Jewish letters" that was widely read by Galician Jews both in Vienna and

Viennese *Selbst-Emanzipation*, the principal organ of Jewish nationalists in Galicia through the 1880s, as well as *Der Israelit*, which Jewish liberals continued to publish in German even after Shomer Israel's defection to the Polish camp. Besides these party organs, the *Drohobyczer Zeitung*, officially a *maskilic* paper of general Jewish interest but with strong Zionist leanings, appeared in German with Hebrew characters from 1883 until 1914. In addition, a few journals appeared in Hebrew, including *Ivri Anochi-Haivri* in Brody (1865–90) and *Hacharshu-Hashemesh* in Stanislau (1888–9).[9] Finally, both the assimilationist Agudas Achim as well as the nationalist Zion published their party organs, *Ojczyzna* and *Przyszłość*, in Polish. Ironically, while Polish integrationists in the aftermath of the 1848 revolution had to publish their papers in German, Jewish nationalists at the end of the century had to call for the rebirth of Hebrew in Polish.[10]

The emergence of these Yiddish papers in the 1890s demonstrated the independent and still radical view that Yiddish-language propaganda was needed to reach the traditional masses.[11] These were not merely isolated attempts at such outreach but rather represented a coordinated effort by a small number of educated, dedicated nationalists. Some of the papers were associated with mainstream Zionist associations. The first two to appear, the *Yidishe folkstsaytung* and the *Izraelitishes folksblat*, said so explicitly in their program statements. Both were available for sale at the offices of the three major Zionist groups then in existence, and both printed news of those groups' activities.[12] Moreover, papers often

in Galicia itself. The paper printed news of Jewish communities throughout the world, and beginning in 1881 included a lead editorial by the paper's second editor, Moshe Dornbusch, heavily influenced by Jewish nationalist ideas.

[9] The first was purely *maskilic* in content, and under pressure from its conservative patrons (community leaders in Vienna and elsewhere) supported the directing of refugees to America. The later was nationalist in content. It was edited by Hirsch Gottlieb, later an agent for the *Yidishe folkstsaytung* (see note 13 below). G. Bader, "The National Movement among Our Jewish Brothers in Galicia" (Hebrew), *Achi'asaf*, 1894–5, 173. Bader writes that none of the Hebrew journals achieved significant circulation in Galicia.

[10] Toury, op. cit., 66–8. The Jewish National Party made two short-lived attempts to publish a party organ in Yiddish, *Der Carmel-Der Wecker* in 1893 and the *Jüdisches Wochenblatt* in 1895, but neither approached the importance of *Przyszłość*.

[11] Recall that the incipient Galician socialist movement, also hoping to reach traditional Jews, launched a "Yiddish-language" organ in 1893 called *Der Arbeter*, replaced in 1896 by its own *Yidishes folksblat*, which survived until 1899. As noted, however, these were essentially German-language papers published in Hebrew characters by assimilated Jews who did not know Yiddish and lacked the cultural background to connect with traditional Jews.

[12] The three major Zionist groups were Zion (Lemberg), Schochrei Toschia (Stryj), and Haivri (Drohobycz). Zion later renounced its association with the *Yidishe folkstsaytung*

joined together in united subscription campaigns. Subscribers to either one of those papers, for example, automatically received its partner "so they should have a paper [to read] every Sabbath," as the *Folksblat* banner explained.[13] The *Yidishes familienblat* and the *Yidishes folksblat* were both edited by the same man, Shevach Knöbel, who did not offer the two papers for the price of one but did cross-advertise subscriptions between them. Laibel Taubes, whose agitation for Yiddish propaganda led to the birth of this press in the first place, launched at least three papers and even recycled material among them.[14]

Nevertheless, these papers were not a part of the Zionist movement per se; they were not the organs of any Zionist association.[15] The most obvious sign of their ideological independence was their attitude toward the Yiddish language. Generally speaking, the Zionist movement, even in Galicia, clearly considered Hebrew to be *the* Jewish national language. Zionist associations, from the beginning, invested a great deal in Hebrew language courses and generally regarded "jargon" to be a gutter dialect of High German. An article in *Selbst-Emanzipation* in 1885, for example, reporting on the formation of a new Jewish trade union, commented, "The language of the group is, of course, jargon, since the young men are unfortunately not yet at the level of the intelligentsia and able to make use of a modern language."[16] In 1891 the paper recommended to those wanting to protest the census, whose rubric did not include Jewish

when the paper suddenly endorsed the "assimilationist" candidate Emil Byk over Joseph Bloch in the 1891 parliamentary elections. The paper's editor, Laibel Taubes, had left town one week and his substitute (Ephraim Laufer) allegedly accepted a bribe to print the endorsement. Although Taubes immediately issued a correction and continued to endorse Bloch in future issues, Zion did not back down and the paper folded soon thereafter. This election campaign is discussed later in the chapter.

13 This relationship eventually went sour when the *Folksblat* discovered that Hirsch Gottlieb, the Hebrew publicist and now agent for the *Yidishe folkstsaytung*, had absconded with their subscription money; see *Izraelitishes folksblat*, August 23, 1891. On the heels of the Byk endorsement fiasco, the *Yidishe folkstsaytung* simply folded and Taubes (with Alter Teicher) launched his second paper, *Der folksfraynd*, which became the *Folksblat's* new partner; see *Der folksfraynd*, September 1, 1891. Taubes does not even mention the *Izraelitishes folksblat* in his brief memoirs, *Zikhrones fun Laibel Taubes* (n.p., 1920).

14 For example, *Ha'am* (January 20, 1896) reprinted a *feuilleton* from Reuvan Asher Brods, "Oyf dem Glitsh" from an old issue of the *folksfraynd* (Nr. 4, 1891). The editors justified this by explaining that at the time of original publication the elections were in full swing and so few people had bothered to read it.

15 The *Yidishe folkstsaytung* did at first receive support from Zion in Lemberg, but it was edited independently. The party organ of Galician Zionists remained *Przyszłość*. The Yiddish papers discussed here were published not in the capital cities but in the provincial southeast (see note 2).

16 *Selbst-Emanzipation*, February 2, 1885.

languages, that they should at least declare Hebrew rather than Yiddish as their language of everyday use.[17]

The position of the Yiddish press on the language question was more ambiguous. On the one hand, the papers officially championed Hebrew as *the* language of the Jewish people. Within the Yiddish press itself all references to "our holy language" self-evidently referred to Hebrew. *Der folksfraynd*, for example, in a piece entitled "On our National Language," argued this point at length, insisting that Hebrew was neither dead nor impossible to revitalize as a modern language in daily use.[18] More fundamentally, the article exclaimed, Hebrew embodied the Jewish spirit, which it alone has protected from assimilation in exile.

[Many nations] have lost the rights to their fatherland but they preserve their language with body and soul. They found linguistic associations to cultivate their language and its science, and they hold lectures in order to hold their language upright ... but why among us Jews is our language [so neglected]; our holy language, the first codified language with which the world was created, why have we neglected it so? Why do our young people study all foreign languages day and night, and not look at our language once??[19]

At the same time, these papers were deliberately and unapologetically Yiddish organs, "genuine" Jewish papers written "for the people" in the "language of the people." It is in these terms that they justified their existence. *Der folksfraynd*, the same paper quoted above praising

---

[17] *Selbst-Emanzipation*, January 2, 1891, 8. The census is discussed later in the chapter. In general, *Selbst-Emanzipation* did not assign great importance to the census campaign. When the *Izraelitishes folksblat* incorrectly reported that Nathan Birnbaum had set off on an agitation trip in Galicia on behalf of the census campaign, *Selbst-Emanzipation* printed an angry correction that his trip was on behalf of Palestine and had nothing to do with the census. *Izraelitishes folksblat*, December 8, 1890, and *Selbst-Emanzipation*, January 2, 1891, 8.

[18] The position that Hebrew could become a spoken language was no less radical than the view that Yiddish could be employed as a literary language. Only thirteen years earlier, Ben-Yehuda had written the first article arguing that Hebrew could become a spoken language "if only we wish." Chaim Rabin, "The National Idea and the Revival of Hebrew," in Jehuda Reinharz and Anita Shapira, eds., *Essential Papers on Zionism* (New York, 1996), 750. Zionists inherited this distaste for Yiddish, as well as their exaltation of Hebrew, from the Haskalah. Their program to revitalize Hebrew as the single spoken tongue of the Jews, however, constituted a revolutionary break from the Haskalah, which supported traditional diglossia, Yiddish being replaced not by Hebrew but by German, Russian, or Polish. Bartal, op. cit., 144–7.

[19] *Der folksfraynd*, November 15, 1891. The article responded to criticism that Hebrew lacked a modern vocabulary by noting that no language was born with such words; linguists would create them in Hebrew as they had done in every other language. As to Hebrew being dead and an embarrassment, it pointed out that the whole world revered Hebrew, even holding Hebrew-language conferences.

Hebrew as the Jews' "national language," had emphatically rejected it as an appropriate medium for a Jewish newspaper just as it rejected Polish and German.

Just as we certainly do not intend to speak and write to our people in Polish or German, so we do not attempt to speak and write only Hebrew. Our People, by which we mean the ordinary public, the majority of the people ... don't understand Polish, don't understand German and don't understand Hebrew. With these people one must speak simple Yiddish, just as we are used to speaking from childhood on, and just as we speak in our neighborhoods and in business, plainly and simply and without over-intellectualization [*on khokhmes*].[20]

It was not merely pragmatism that dictated the decision to use Yiddish. Most of the papers, including *Der folksfraynd* and the others more closely affiliated with the Zionists, regularly described Yiddish as the Jews' "national language" as well. Such a stance was a natural result of the papers' populist orientation, but it also reflected an important campaign, which they initiated, for Jews to declare Yiddish their *Umgangssprache* on the government census. Austrian law defined nationality (*Volkstamm*) by linguistic criteria but did not accept Yiddish as a legitimate language. As a result, Jews were not counted as a nationality in the Austrian census and did not qualify for national rights. Galician Jews, overwhelmingly Yiddish-speaking, were usually registered instead as Polish. Jewish nationalists thus had a tremendous stake in asserting Yiddish to be the Jewish national language, for in a system in which the existence of a nationality was determined by a unique "language of daily use," Hebrew could not possibly achieve legitimacy.

The real importance of Hebrew, then, seems to have been as a nationalist icon on which to ground a national identity among the Jewish masses. Indeed, Yiddish itself was also a symbol, albeit one laden with practical ramifications (i.e., inclusion on the census), and the papers freely fluctuated between the two depending upon the context. Joshua Fishman's observation that vernacular literature "provided the masses with the emotionalized link between language and nationalism that exists for elites at the level of ideological program" rings true for Galician Jewry.[21] However, in this case, whereas the innovation of Yiddish as a medium of print communication was vital, Yiddish as a symbol of Jewish nationhood did not supplant Hebrew but complemented it. By publishing in

---

[20] *Der folksfraynd*, January 1, 1891.
[21] Joshua Fishman, *Language and Nationalism: Two Integrative Essays* (Rowley, Mass., 1972), 52.

Yiddish the papers could simultaneously venerate Hebrew as the Jews' national language while visibly proving that Yiddish was also the (or a) Jewish national language. The very existence of the press, whatever its actual content, testified to the reality of the Yiddish language and by extension of a Jewish nation.

This same ambiguity vis-à-vis mainstream Zionism is echoed by the papers' treatment of the land of Israel (Erets Yisroel). To a certain extent, the papers' attitude toward Palestine did reflect the official program of Galician Zionists as formulated in their 1893 party platform. The Jewish National Party of Galicia then adopted its so-called double program that viewed the rebuilding of a Jewish homeland in Palestine as a long-term goal but directed its current activities toward the nurturing of "Jewish national consciousness" and the securing of Jewish national rights in Galicia.

The Yiddish press of the early 1890s, particularly those papers more directly affiliated with the Zionist associations, repeatedly described Palestine as the Jewish "fatherland" and called for its resettlement, especially through the support of the colonization association Admath Israel in Stryj. Such support, however, never entailed negating the Diaspora. On the contrary, the papers' Zionist agenda seems closer to the Western model of Palestine as a refuge for Russian and Romanian Jewry alongside local patriotism for themselves as emancipated Jews.[22] Consequently, the same papers that proclaimed Palestine to be the Jewish "fatherland" could simultaneously refer to Galicia as the Jewish "motherland" in defense of their domestic political agenda. Indeed, the papers' Diaspora orientation allowed them to formulate arguments of Polish patriotism framed in Jewish national terms. To those Jews who feared Polish reprisals for the assertion of Jewish national rights, for example, the *Yidishe folkstsaytung* argued that Jewish nationalism offered the best framework within which Galician Jews could work for the betterment of their shared homeland (i.e., Galicia) for "all" of its inhabitants. Here the paper describes Yiddish as the language of the Jews even as it celebrates Jews cultivating Polish language and literature and developing their "beloved motherland," Galicia.

---

[22] Shmuel Almog, *Zionism and History* (Jerusalem, 1987), 184. The papers characteristically expressed extreme reverence for the Austrian emperor, Franz Joseph, whom they credited with Jewish emancipation and whom they exonerated of any fault in the Austrian political system. This was surely somewhat tactical, catering to Habsburg Jewry's adoration of Franz Joseph, however it was likely quite sincere as well.

For can we not live with our Polish brothers in a truly brotherly [fashion] even if we should speak out the truth that we know we are of the People Israel? For can we not foster our Polish language as the language of the land and of our cherished Polish literature, even if we say that our own language is Yiddish? Yes, even those Jews who speak out the truth that they are a special nation, [they] can still be perfectly good Polish patriots; they can love the land of Galicia as their motherland and the Polish nation as [their] sister nation. We have one interest in common with our Polish brothers: their good is our good and we can work together for the betterment of the land, "for the good of our beloved motherland." We can and should respect and love the language of the land, the language of our sister nation. Of course, the Poles should also reciprocate as brothers, as brothers from one mother, and [treat] our nation as a sister nation.[23]

Note the total absence of reference to the Ruthenians, either linguistically or politically, despite the paper's publication in Kolomea on the far eastern side of the province. Clearly it feared appearing unpatriotic to the ruling Poles rather than to the subordinate Ruthenians.

As with its reverence for Hebrew, the purpose of invoking "the land of Israel" was a symbolic means to generate a national identity among Galician Jewry by drawing on the legitimacy and religious attachments latent in such vocabulary. As Eli Lederhendler has noted, Jewish nationalists frequently "brandished certain evocative words ... that they knew were central to religious meaning in Judaism.... Previously the sign and scepter of rabbinic dominance, the invocation of such consecrated words was intended to carry political weight in Jewish society."[24] This tendency was especially pronounced in Yiddish-language propaganda. The very nature of the Yiddish language, with its easy integration of religious rhetoric and biblical verse, enabled Zionists to take advantage of such rhetoric and its religious connotations on behalf of an argument that was certainly untraditional.

Erets Yisroel thus served as a natural focus for early Jewish nationalists. Like Hebrew, it appealed to religious sensibilities (devout Jews prayed daily for the ingathering of the exiles to the land of Israel), while simultaneously answering secular critics who argued that the Jews' territorial dispersion meant that they no longer constituted a nation.[25] The papers

---

[23] *Yidishe folkstsaytung*, December 1, 1890.

[24] Eli Lederhendler, *Jewish Responses to Modernity: New Voices in America and Eastern Europe* (New York, 1994), 30.

[25] But this did not necessarily imply a specific political program, even the resettlement of Palestine. As John Klier has noted, "The 'love of Zion' possessed a mythic quality for East European Jews, but was devoid of any practical implications." The "myth of Zion" was above all an efficacious symbol of Jewish unity. John Klier, "The Myth of Zion

often contrasted Palestine with America or Argentina (popular alterna-
tives to migrating Jews), which they argued were foreign, while in Erets
Yisroel Jews enjoyed both spiritual and even physical familiarity.

> Our only place of refuge is the land of Israel. This land is not foreign to us, thank
> God.... In this land every Jew feels at home, every corner, every stone is known to
> him, instills in him holy feelings, every mountain and every river speaks to him in
> brotherly language, reveals to him beautiful, elevated secrets and gives him greet-
> ings from his fathers, from his prophets, his kings and his heroes.[26]

Ha'am-Dos Folk, Laibel Taubes's third and most successful Yiddish
paper, highlights the loose relationship most of these papers shared with
the Zionist movement, particularly over the issue of Erets Yisroel. Taubes
was not only a dedicated Zionist but also one of the movement's best
orators.[27] Like nearly all Galician Zionists, Taubes was deeply moved
by the appearance of *Der Judenstaat* in 1896 and he became one of the
first Galicians to support Herzl's Zionist Organization. The paper immediately published a glowing review of the book, while Taubes wrote to
Herzl as early as March 7 for permission to publish it in Yiddish as soon
as possible, a request Herzl quickly approved despite receiving a negative report about Taubes from Nathan Birnbaum.[28] By fall, Taubes had

---

among East European Jewry," in Geoffrey Hosking and George Schöpflin, eds., *Myths
and Nationhood* (New York, 1997), 174, 181.

[26] *Yidishe folkstsaytung*, January 1, 1891. The myth of Jewish intimacy with the land of
Israel played a critical role in the Zionist movement throughout Europe, an example of
what Anthony Smith has identified as the need by nationalists to draw upon a "golden
age." The use of the ancient past allows nationalists "to locate and *re-root* the community in its own historic and fertile space. Like the community itself, the golden age (or
ages) possesses a definite historical location and clear geographical dimensions in the
land of the ancestors. The land is an arena for the enactment of the heroic deeds and the
contemplation of eternal verities which are among the main achievements of the heroes
and sages of the golden age. It is also a landscape and soil that influences the character of
that age, not only by giving birth to its heroes and sages, but also by forming and mold-
ing the community of which they are members. Hence the need, in the eyes of nationalists, to re-root the community in its own terrain and liberate the land of the fathers and
mothers, so that it may once again give birth to heroes and sages and create the conditions for a new collective efflorescence. Only by re-rooting itself in a free homeland can a
people rediscover its 'true self', its ethno-historical character, in habitual contact with its
sacred places and poetic landscapes." Anthony Smith, "The 'Golden Age' and National
Renewal," in Geoffrey Hosking and George Schöpflin, eds., *Myths and Nationhood*, 49.

[27] On Taubes, see his autobiography, op. cit., as well as his short biography in Shlomo
Bickel, ed., *Pinkas Kolomey* (New York, 1957), 266–8. See also Gershom Bader's unpublished biography of Taubes in his "Galician Celebrities" manuscript, op. cit.

[28] Herzl checked up on Taubes as soon as he received his proposal. On March 10, he wrote
to both Nathan Birnbaum and Saul Landau to ask for their impression of the publicist,
expressing his desire to have both the Yiddish and Hebrew translations published as

already prepared the Yiddish transliteration, which the paper published at a deep discount.[29] Taubes even offered *Ha'am-Dos Folk* to be the new organ of Herzl's Zionist Organization, an offer which Herzl could never accept.[30]

Nevertheless, Taubes's Jewish national identity always remained focused on the needs of Jews in Galicia. It was he, after all, who in 1894 founded the "Jewish national" association Beis Yisroel in Kolomea in opposition to the local branch of Birnbaum's Palestine-colonization society Zion. Taubes's papers maintained this stance. Despite Taubes's conversion to the idea of a Jewish state, *Ha'am*'s detailed program statement did not include any hint of political Zionism and did not discuss Palestine. In fact, its first review of *Der Judenstaat* praised the work precisely because Taubes felt that it did not insist that the Jewish state be located in Palestine.[31] The paper addressed instead the "political, national, religious, and economic" questions of Jewish life in Galicia. It sought the realization of Jewish civil rights as guaranteed by the constitution, as well as national minority rights for the Jews, which were theoretically protected by the constitution, but only if Jews could win recognition as a nationality. The principal objective of the paper, it concluded, was to "awaken" the Jews' national pride and convince them that they must claim their national rights.[32]

Ha'am, as well as all of the other papers, repeatedly called for unity, *akhdes*, among Jews. Such calls not only made the Jewish nationalist

quickly as possible. Landau did not publish his response, but Birnbaum responded that he did not think highly of Taubes's literary ability, nor did others in Galicia. (As the quality of Birnbaum's own Yiddish at that point – and thus his ability to judge Taubes – is questionable, Birnbaum's response may have been driven by personal animosity toward Taubes for establishing Zionist organizations in competition with Birnbaum's own groups in East Galicia.) Birnbaum also seemed to question the usefulness of a "Jargon" translation overall. Herzl's letter to Birnbaum, and Birnbaum's negative response the next day, reside in the Nathan and Solomon Birnbaum archives in Toronto, Canada. (My thanks to David Birnbaum for providing me with copies.) Landau reprints his letter from Herzl in his memoirs. S. R. Landau, *Sturm und Drang im Zionismus* (Vienna, 1937), 65.

[29] On Taubes's decision to transliterate the book rather than translate it outright, see Chapter 4. Taubes advertised the book on the front page of every issue of *Ha'am-Dos Folk* for just 25 kreuzer.

[30] Jacob Toury, "Herzl's Newspaper: The Creation of *Die Welt*," *Zionism* 1, no. 2 (Autumn 1980): 163–4. Herzl's organ, with which he wanted to target the "upper echelons" of Jewry in the West as well as Western governments, had to be fully Western, bourgeois, and German. See Chapter 5.

[31] *Ha'am-Dos Folk*, March 10, 1896.

[32] *Ha'am-Dos Folk*, September 24, 1895.

movement the key to unity, a traditional Jewish value, but it inherently placed these editors and their papers above political division. It made the Yiddish press the focus of Jewish national identity. In other words, the ideology of Jewish unity presented by these papers was most often based in support of the papers themselves. Subscribing to these "genuine" Jewish organs became the hallmark of a true, national Jew. *Ha'am* said as much in concluding its program statement.

We hope and expect that all those who have good intentions towards our People, that all who are moved by the present terrible condition of the Jews and strive to improve it, all true friends of our People will stand by us with their payment and also with their action, that all will support us and our undertaking.[33]

The following summer, Taubes apologized for an issue's late publication by reminding readers that the paper existed on a very narrow margin and that it needed the constant and punctual support of all friends of the "people."

If only a small part of our Jews would want to know their duty for the "people," if at least one Jew in a thousand would want to feel the necessity for an organ for the people's interests, written in the people's language, if at a minimum every subscriber would want to know that the punctual appearance of our paper depends on the punctual payment [of dues] and that when one does not pay, the true friend of our people, the one who pays punctually, suffers punctually.[34]

The *Izraelitishes folksblat* and its sister paper the *Yidishe folkstsaytung* even linked its subscribers to the "holy" project of resettling the land of Israel, and supporting "our unfortunate Russian brothers," by donating one tenth of its profits to the colonies.[35] In this light, delinquent subscribers, an endemic problem for all of these papers, did not merely threaten the viability of the newspaper. They endangered the persecuted Russian Jews whom the papers supported.

Now dear readers and subscribers to our paper! You deserve credit for the great thing you do in subscribing, and particularly that you pay promptly. Know that with that alone you support the Russian refugees who are so unfortunate that no pen can describe the circumstances of their troubles. And he who reads the paper and does not pay ... he should know that he thus robs hundreds of thousands of unfortunate families who are wandering with such difficulty in darkness before the entire world.[36]

33 *Ha'am-Dos Folk*, September 24, 1895.
34 *Ha'am-Dos Folk*, July 10, 1896.
35 *Izraelitishes folksblat*, July 8, 1891.
36 *Yidishe folkstsaytung*, July 1, 1891. Apparently the appeal failed, for this was the *folkstsaytung's* last issue.

PAPERS FOR THE JEWISH FOLK: NURTURING
AN ORTHODOX READING PUBLIC

In order to establish their authenticity, the papers carefully positioned themselves as "organs for the People" written in "simple" Yiddish to represent "Orthodox" interests.[37] Like the Polish rural press, whose peasant nationalist agenda had only recently become dominant, these Yiddish papers drew on popular religious beliefs to translate secular nationalist ideas and locate the Jewish nation specifically among traditional Jews.[38] Thus whereas *Selbst-Emanzipation*, courting largely secular Jews, remained obsessively focused on the radically pro-Polish assimilationist association Agudas Achim, gloating over its final demise in 1893, the Yiddish press rarely mentioned it. It focused more often on the decline of religious observance, especially among Jewish girls, who were frequently sent to state schools, which it equated with national betrayal. Generally, the papers portrayed themselves as the solution to this malaise. This rhetoric parallels campaigns in other nationalist movements to prevent "their" children from being lost through their enrollment in another nation's schools. As in those cases, Jewish nationalists felt tremendous frustration at their perceived co-nationals' indifference to this imagined crisis.[39]

Taubes was especially vexed by the issue of education but was more progressive than Knöbel. While Knöbel's papers were expressly Orthodox in orientation, Taubes's opposed religious reform but also anti-modern ultra-Orthodoxy. He described his efforts as "the golden middle road" between religious "indifference" and religious "exceptionalism." "We cannot accept as good," he explained, "when one closes himself to every innovation, every modern institution which contemporary times demand, without which one almost cannot live."[40] In 1892, he had tried to establish a modern Jewish elementary school that unlike the existing Jewish schools would teach Hebrew language and include secular subjects, but was blocked by local rabbinic leaders.[41] Taubes presented himself to

---

[37] This is self-evident, above all, in the papers' names themselves: "The People's Paper," "The People's Friend," "The Jewish People's Paper," and so on.

[38] Keely Stauter-Halsted, *The Nation in the Village* (Ithaca, 2001), 186–92.

[39] Tara Zahra, *Kidnapped Souls: National Indifference and the Battle for Children in the Bohemian Lands, 1900–1948* (Ithaca, 2008); Pieter Judson, *Guardians of the Nation* (Cambridge, Mass., 2006), esp. 19–65.

[40] *Ha'am-Dos Folk*, September 24, 1895.

[41] *Selbst-Emanzipation*, September 19, 1892.

traditional readers as a greater defender of the faith than his rabbinic opponents. He particularly blamed them for what he considered the catastrophic consequences of Jewish attendance at public schools. One of his lead articles, for example, began simply, "Who is guilty?"

On the question, "Who is guilty?" we have a very short but true explanation: the rabbi is guilty! We mean namely, our rabbis, the sages and *tzadikim*, as well as the rabbis who sit on their lofty thrones who concern themselves with religious questions and with sermons twice a year, and equally the *tzadikim* who have under them thousands of adherents who hear their words. They alone, yes only they alone are guilty that tens of thousands of Jewish children are openly violating Sabbath and holidays in the public schools. On them alone, yes on them alone weighs the guilt that tens of thousands of Jewish children in their most tender youth, when they still don't know how to differentiate between good and evil, are estranged from their religion and nation.

It is unfortunately a sad truth that the instruction and upbringing which our Jewish youth enjoys in the public schools is, under present conditions, not directed that they should be raised as Jews, just as the children of other confessions and nations are raised in their religion and nationality. Even more, not only they are not raised Jewish, but on the contrary they are raised anti-Jewish.

Children who work on *shabbes* and Jewish holidays while celebrating Sundays and Christian holidays, he argued, will learn that the "holy Torah" applied only to their parents and will ultimately abandon Judaism and the Jewish nation – the two being inextricably linked – altogether. Taubes blamed the rabbis because Austrian law dictated that Jews could not be required to write on Saturdays, but most parents were too timid to fight against school administrators. If the rabbis would harness their influence and lead a campaign to enforce Jewish rights, charged the paper, it would have a big impact.[42]

Shevach Knöbel (1863–1938), the editor of two papers, both extremely short-lived, is perhaps the best example of this convergence of religious orthodoxy and national unity (see Figure 3.1).[43] Knöbel was the son of the head of the religious court in Roznitov and an extremely learned man in his own right. He specifically promoted his papers as "Orthodox" and even managed to advertise them in the ultra-Orthodox *Machsike Hadas*, itself printed in Hebrew.[44] In the summer of 1894 Knöbel traveled

---

[42] *Ha'am-Dos Folk*, November 15, 1896.

[43] The *Yidishes familienblat* lasted from November 1893 until October 1894, the *Yidishes folksblat* from February to September 1894. Knöbel also made frequent contributions to other Yiddish papers as well.

[44] See, for example, *Machsike Hadas*, February 1, 1894, 7. Knöbel identifies himself as the son of the "great" rabbi Eliezer Lipman, head of the religious court in Roznitov. For a

FIGURE 3.1. Shevach Knöbel (1863–1938), here as an older man.

throughout eastern Galicia to encourage subscriptions to his papers. An article signed by his "friend" "Shmilkye Hasid" describes the visit to his hometown. Welcoming Knöbel to his *shtetl* dressed in Sabbath clothes, signifying the great importance he placed on the visit, Shmilkye arranges a meeting with the wealthy Jew, "Reb Shakhne." Knöbel tries to explain that he is the *redaktor* (editor) of a newspaper, but Reb Shakhne hears him say *dokter* and wants to know what Knöbel wants. "No, Reb Shakhne," he explains, "I am a *redaktor*, that is, one who publishes a newspaper.

brief biography, see Meir Wunder, *Meorei Galitsye: Encyclopedia L'Chachmei Galitsye* (Jerusalem, 1978), 569–72.

I publish a Jewish newspaper, the *Yidishes familienblat*, which represents Orthodox interests, and as you are a genuine Jew, you must support such a paper and order it." But Reb Shakhne doesn't understand what Orthodox means either, and so Knöbel explains, "That is those Jews who hold fast in their faith and don't demand any innovations." Knöbel tells him to ask his daughter about such issues, and the rich man responds, "What should I ask my daughter. She is continually reading *Menores hame'or* [a traditional devotional text], and there it does not talk about this." Finally Knöbel loses his temper, exposes the girl's dangerous reading material and argues that without his paper's guidance she would ultimately abandon Jewish observance.

An honest Jew like yourself is always engaging in Torah and acts of kindness, but needs sometimes to have this world in mind also, for by having nothing [of this world] in mind and neglecting your children, especially your daughters, they will soon not be as religious as you. Since you don't look into this at all, she is not reading the *Menores hame'or*, she is reading a German book, and such a book that makes no good impression on the young people ... [until] the daughter wants only a "doctor" for a husband and laughs off all of Judaism and Jewish customs.

One must be more attentive to one's children, he continues. Not all such books are harmful, but one has to be alert, and the *Yidishes folksblat* with its Orthodox orientation helps parents reach their children, for example, with its biographies of great Jews. "For the young people know the biographies of Schiller, Goethe, Shakespeare, and Chekhov, as well as of the apostates Heine and Börne, but [not] of great Jews." In the end he convinces the man, who immediately subscribes to the paper and goes to look at what his daughter is reading.[45]

In all likelihood, this entire story was fabricated. It provided Knöbel with a subtle means of explaining to his readers what an editor did, what it meant to be Orthodox, and what services an Orthodox newspaper could provide. Elsewhere, he defined assimilationism as well, a term other papers also had to teach their readers. For example, when *Der Folksfraynd* printed Zion's letter disclaiming its partnership with the paper because of the latter's support of "a known assimilationist personality" for Parliament, the editors added parenthetically, "Assimilationist means one who wants that Jews should mix-in among the other nations."[46]

Similarly, an article in the *Yidishes familienblat* written in a heavy Galician dialect (perhaps in order to suggest authenticity) blamed parents

---

[45] *Yidishes folksblat*, June 29, 1894.
[46] *Der folksfraynd*, February 1, 1891.

for sending their children to schools that neglected Jewish learning. Again the newspaper presented itself as the solution. "The best cure temporarily is the newspaper, which can teach them who they are, to make them a little familiar with Jewish history."[47] Knöbel did not invent the idea that a newspaper constituted religious literature vital to every "genuine" Jewish home. Indeed, the very first Galician Yiddish papers, the *Izraelitishes folksblat* and the *Yidishe folkstsaytung*, joined together so that subscribers "should have a paper [to read] every Sabbath." In this way, the editors subtly introduced the newspapers into the religious canon appropriate for Sabbath study.[48]

The idea of influencing traditional Jews through the press was not an original one, even in Galicia. The ultra-Orthodox party Machsike Hadas had attempted this over a decade earlier, on the eve of the 1879 elections. But that party published its paper (other than its first issues) in Hebrew, and thereby limited its impact – important though it was – to the educated, traditional elite.[49] Even in the 1890s the idea of a Yiddish-language paper was still considered radical. The Galician Yiddish papers had to justify their use of Yiddish, not to any government censor, but to the Jewish public itself. The papers fought to transform traditional Jews into newspaper readers, as well as acculturated Jews into Yiddish newspaper readers, and therefore had to explain to the public the purpose of a Yiddish paper. Knöbel's papers repeated such explanations in nearly every issue.

We know that there are many who laugh at a jargon newspaper; give them [a paper] to understand and to explain the use of this newspaper. One can read a newspaper in all languages of the world, [the opponents say], but they must not disgrace themselves with the language which one speaks with their parents, with

---

[47] *Yidishes familienblat*, December 8, 1893.

[48] Significantly, the rebbe of Ger, Rabbi Avraham M. Alter, despite endorsing the formation of an Orthodox daily (*Der Yid*), specifically asked his Hasidim *not* to read the paper on the Sabbath. Gershon Bacon, *The Politics of Tradition: Agudat Yisrael in Poland, 1916–1939* (Jerusalem, 1996), 62.

[49] Its impact on yeshiva students and the traditional elite was profound. Religious students who had been forbidden to read modern newspapers or to study Hebrew as a modern language were suddenly exposed to a new world in that paper. Inevitably, such readers made their way to other Hebrew-language papers as well, some even becoming *maskilim* and writers themselves. "This fanatic Hasidic paper," wrote its editor Isaac Ewen many years later, "which dared not mention a word about the Zionist Congress, stirred Hasidic youth from their lethargy and propelled them out of the prayer houses, first into the tents of the *maskilim*, and then into the arms of the Zionists." Isaac Ewen, *Fun dem rebns hoyf: zikhrones un mayses, gezen, gehrt un nokhdertseylt*, translated by Lucy Dawidowicz, *The Golden Tradition* (Boston, 1967), 199.

their families, with their people. Such a paper can bring much use for the people; this depends only on the wish of every Jew.[50]

Ha'am, too, felt compelled to explain its purpose. In a lead article in November 1895, the paper complains that the Jew is too interested in foreign politics and human interest stories from abroad and argues that he needs to focus more on Jewish politics, "that is the politics that he does not have." This was the purpose of a Yiddish newspaper. "The Jew does not yet know and does not want to know what he has to look for in a Yiddish newspaper. Therefore the Yiddish newspapers have fewer readers and their effect is small; therefore they have less support and their existence is miserable." The author describes how he went to a certain businessman, a "modern, educated Jew," and asked him to subscribe. "I already get the *Neue Freie Presse*," the man responded. The writer was indignant: "As if we want to compete with the 'Presse.' As if we consider that our poor, small paper for 70 kreuzer a quarter should, God forbid, threaten the *Neue Freie Presse,* which costs 8 gulden a quarter." The papers have different purposes, he explains. A Yiddish newspaper is a mirror to the Jewish nation, a wake-up call to a people so oppressed it doesn't even recognize its oppression, so beaten it has become indifferent to the humiliation which it suffers.[51]

Knöbel intuitively sensed the importance of a Yiddish paper as an instrument to strengthen Jewish nationalist feeling. A lead article in his *Yidishes familienblat*, essentially a subscription appeal, reasserted the need for the "jargon paper" along these lines. Against those who say that foreign-language papers are enough, he writes,

But in truth he who can read a newspaper in other languages must first understand that every People must have a newspaper that every single person can understand, for not everyone can understand Hebrew, German, or Polish – but jargon everybody understands, the most highly educated as well as the ignorant.

Indeed, Knöbel went even further, suggesting that his paper had the potential to form a new public sphere to unite the Jewish people. "To what purpose are all newspapers founded?" asks the paper. Not to bring the news – that was incidental. Rather, it was either to advance a party goal or else simply to unify a people.

Our Galician Jews still need a newspaper to join the people together, to discuss in the paper what they lack, how exactly one can help. A newspaper is such, for

---

[50] *Yidishes familienblat*, January 19, 1894.
[51] *Ha'am-Dos Folk*, November 1, 1895.

example, that if one is having a meeting, one can give advice, one can discuss in every city or association what the meeting needs [to accomplish]. Likewise a newspaper is a meeting place for many [people] from hundreds of cities. With the newspaper one can unite small strengths and, most importantly, advise individuals together.... [For] each person who reads the newspaper, all the news that is happening in the world [and] the life stories we present will awaken in that reader an honorable feeling [that] he is proud to come from such a People, such greats, such sages and geniuses.[52]

Other papers defined themselves in precisely the same terms. *Der folksfraynd*, for example, in its mission statement, emphasized above all its role as a public forum.

It is already, to be sure, no new thought. It has already been felt for a long time in many – very many – quarters that we Jews in Galicia need to have our own Jewish newspaper, which is not specifically about the news normally conveyed in the newspapers. No, not only about this – this is totally a side issue; the main thing is, we Jews need to have an organ for our People, a newspaper for our own interests, in order to hear one another's opinions and advise each other about our situation, our position, our economic situation, our communities, and the like.

But now, after every nation has begun to consider how exactly it should acquire a good position, a good image in the land and in society, now it is truly already high time that we Jews should also do something for ourselves. We should also strive to improve our position, our situation, [especially] our economic situation, to organize our communities.

We must unite. We must hold together. Consult together. Strive together. Work together – and we will. With God's help we will carry out everything together.[53]

The papers often referred to other nationalities, especially the Ruthenians, who had already begun to challenge Polish domination through effective political organization. Jewish nationalists noted that the Ruthenians had begun to secure national rights only because they had organized themselves and demanded such rights; the Jews needed to do the same.

Politics must "be made," political rights must be demanded. This we see most clearly among our neighbor nation – among the Ruthenians. All the time that the Ruthenians did not "make" any politics, all the time that they did not demand their political and national rights, they also had absolutely nothing and stood very low, almost equal with us. But scarcely did they begin "to make" politics, scarcely did they begin to demand political rights and, well, well, what do you think? If only a year from now it will be said of us Jews. It seems to us that everyone is familiar

---

[52] *Yidishes familienblat*, January 19, 1894.
[53] But for this the Jews need their own paper, and this is the one, it concluded. *Der folks-fraynd*, January 1, 1891.

with what the Ruthenians have achieved in recent years. Ruthenian *Gymnasia* appear more and more, the Ruthenian language is becoming recognized in school and in government offices. All labels and signs which used to be [printed] only – among us in Galicia – in Polish or German, are today also in Ruthenian. We meet Ruthenian civil servants in every government office, professors in every school.... Lately, we are seeing the same among the Romanians (as well as the Ruthenians) in Bukowina. And yet even the worst Jewish enemy will recognize that in terms of intelligence we tower above both of these nations. We are in general much more intelligent than the Ruthenians and the Romanians. Then why is it that we are so low politically! Simple – political rights are not demanded so we don't have them; since we don't demand them, they don't give them.[54]

Note that the comparison is based not on admiration, but embarrassment. Instead of arguing that Jews ought to learn from the other nationalities, the paper emphasized that *even* these others, who ranked so much lower than the Jews, had won minority rights – how much more so the Jews ought to have them. Other "non-historical" nations, that is, nations with no history of political independence, fell victim to similar arguments. The following appeal, for example, came from the *Izraelitishes folksblat* several years earlier.

The Serbians and Bulgarians who are simple, crude pigs who stand thousands of rungs below us, they are moved to struggle for a nationality and for a fatherland, to achieve their freedom, yet we Jews who have the most glorious history of all Peoples, with our holy fatherland which is respected and held to be holy by all nations... we are totally sleeping – we are completely unmoved also to achieve some kind of freedom.[55]

As noted in Chapter 2, such comparisons were especially pronounced in the Habsburg Empire, where Jews could point to other nonhistorical nations who had won recognition as nations and conclude that the Jews' claim was at least as sound.[56] Thus the tenacious Zionist claim of direct continuity between the "glorious" past of ancient Israel and contemporary Jewry, a connection which the papers' appropriation of Hebrew and Erets Yisroel as symbols essentially sought to strengthen, would ultimately form an important basis of the Jews' claim to nationhood.

Rather than merely arguing that the Jews constituted a nation, however, the papers simply assumed it as a given and mocked the Jewish secular intelligentsia for denying the obvious. Because the rhetoric of this national identity was based on a traditional vocabulary (Jewish unity, Hebrew, the

54 *Ha'am-Dos Folk*, September 24, 1896
55 *Izraelitishes folksblat*, July 8, 1891.
56 Almog, op. cit., 32.

land of Israel), it was relatively natural to claim that all "genuine" Jews believed in Jewish nationhood; it merely entailed transforming the language of an existing identity. By associating denial of Jewish "nationhood" with the secular Jewish elite, and confirmation of it with the ordinary, streetwise Jew, the newspapers greatly eased this transformation. "There are small things which a simple farmer who has a healthy human understanding will understand well," wrote a lead in the *Yidishe folkstsaytung*, "while people who have some education, yes even great sages can't bring down into their head the simplest part of such a concept."

Suddenly great sages have begun to break their philosophical heads and have discovered a new type of question about Jews, a question at which every simple Jew totally laughs, poking at him while he laughs. Have you heard such a question: Are the Jews a People or just a religious community, that is, only a society which has its own statutes? Obviously the people who argue such nonsense are simply crazy; they ought to be sent to the mental asylum. Again! Everyone who looks at just the first pages of world history knows that we are the oldest People among all the Peoples who exist today, that at that time when we had our land and our government, our king and our laws, all the other peoples did not yet exist.[57]

Thus wealth and secular education are linked to assimilation and national betrayal. In one article the *Izraelitishes folksblat* actually defines "intelligentsia" as "the assimilationists."[58]

An article in the *Yidishe folksblat* tells a similar story. Knöbel approaches an educated (*gebildete*) Jew, who already subscribed to the Viennese *Neue Freie Presse*, the *Vaterland*, and the Polish *Curier Lvovski*, and asks that he subscribe also to his paper. "Should I also subscribe to a jargon paper," he asks. "And one from a Jewish editor who goes out dressed Jewish? No, that doesn't go for me. Anyway, what do Jewish newspapers write? Nonsense, trivialities – no, I will not subscribe." Ignoring his scorn of authentic Jewish costume, Knöbel responds by mocking his support for an allegedly anti-Semitic paper.

You will please forgive me, if you will not subscribe to the paper, I cannot say anything to that. But how regrettable it is that a Jew reads the *Vaterland*, the first anti-Semitic paper in Austria you do like, for this you send money.... How long will our enlightened Jews not have any self-respect [*selbst-gefiel*] ... to take the enemy into one's home?

"What does a Jew with a long caftan understand," Reb Zecharya answers, "a little ashamed." Knöbel replies with a long, humorous story

---

[57] *Yidishe folkstsaytung*, December 1, 1890.
[58] *Izraelitishes folksblat*, July 23, 1891.

praising the honor of the Orthodox and after a good laugh convinces the man to subscribe.[59] Naturally, as above, the entire story was probably fabricated.

The papers' self-created image as "organs for the people" played a critical role in their attempt to transform Jewish nationalism into a popular ideology. For this reason, all of these papers, but especially Knöbel's "Orthodox" press, emphasized their role as a popular forum for all of the people. To this end they did not print just polemical editorials but also included nature articles, essays on Jewish history, serialized fiction, and even word puzzles for which readers could send in solutions and win prizes.[60] In this way the publishers created a complete newspaper culture, a new public sphere in which traditional Jews could safely participate. Above and beyond the papers' platforms, the very act of transforming religious Jews into newspaper readers was in itself a political act. It implied not only a cultural transformation but also a transformation in the Jews' perception of themselves as members of a larger community. The papers, after all, included news about Jewish communities from throughout the world. This naturally fostered a broader sense of a transregional Jewish national identity. Benedict Anderson's emphasis on the role of "print-languages" in laying the foundation for national consciousness is instructive here. The print media, he writes, allowed otherwise isolated individuals or communities to become aware "of the hundreds of thousands, even millions, of people in their particular language-field, and at the same time that *only those* hundreds of thousands, or millions, so belonged. These fellow-readers, to whom they were connected through print, formed ... the embryo of the nationally imagined community."[61] The editors of these papers were engaged in a self-fulfilling prophecy; the process of popularizing the notion of a Jewish national community

---

[59] *Yidishe folksblat,* July 13, 1894.

[60] Again, Knöbel's papers pioneered this format much more than the others. The first three papers, founded largely to fight for Joseph Bloch's 1891 reelection included very few such features, while Knöbel's *familienblat* practically catered to them. Nature articles included lessons about "exotic" animals such as elephants and crocodiles; history pieces discussed the biography of Maimonides, the history of Jewish migration to Poland, and the story of Napoleon's Sanhedrin; *Ha'am* even serialized a story by Sholem Aleichem. The word puzzles were a *familienblat* exclusive; winners received ten *seforim* (books on religious subjects). Ironically, the paper insisted that all solutions be submitted in "pure Hebrew." *Yidishes familienblat,* December 22, 1893. Unlike *Machsike Hadas,* none of these papers included regular Torah lessons.

[61] Benedict Anderson, *Imagined Communities: Reflections on the Origin and Spread of Nationalism* (London, 1983), 44.

actually created that community. In other words, the papers helped forge the Jewish nation by allowing traditional Jews to imagine it.[62]

Moreover, beyond these "family" features, the main editorials (most of the articles were little more than editorials) were carefully constructed in order to convey a sense of comfort and familiarity to the average Jew. There is no better example of this than the *Yidishes familienblat*'s biggest admirer, "Shmueli Hasid." Shmueli (sometimes called Shmilkye, a Galician accented diminutive of Shmuel), a frequent contributor to both of Knöbel's papers, was most likely the editor's *persona*. His use of such a pseudonym recalls how the "grandfather" of modern Yiddish literature, S. Y. Abramovitsh, adopted an invented persona, Mendele the book-seller, to distance himself from the Yiddish literature with which he was still uncomfortable and to mask his work with a sense of tradition.[63] Shmueli, unlike Moykher-Sforim, was not trying to distance himself from a language in which he was embarrassed to write. However, he does suggest the same strategy of using an invented persona to frame his articles more comfortably for the paper's traditional readership.

In his debut, Shmueli writes sarcastically that he is, unfortunately, only a *Hasid*, and has been rejected by both German and Hebrew papers. But he wanted so much to write for a paper and was overwhelmed when he saw that finally a jargon paper had appeared which would accept his submissions, namely the *Yidishes familienblat*.

For a long time I have had the desire to be a contributor to some newspaper, for it is a real pleasure to be published in a paper, so that the whole world knows that I also exist in the world. But I am – and it shouldn't happen to you – an unlucky person. I have had the misfortune to be born to such a father who is called by the German name "Hasid" and so I must really also be called Shmueli Hasid – now, how do you like that, dear editor? I tried to write an article for a German paper, [but] they answered me plainly and simply: we take no articles from a Hasid. I turned red like a beet with shame. I had, *nebekh*, to burn the article in shame. I then tried to write articles for Hebrew newspapers, but everyone mistreated me, giving me the same answer. I saw that a Hasid remains a Hasid, and that I must sit with my articles and blow wind at home – such troubles, such worries.... But how I thrilled, all of my limbs simply became limp, that I saw the *Yidishes familienblat* had such a tolerant editor who takes articles from a Chanak, *nu*, he will surely accept an article from a Hasid – said and done.[64]

---

[62] Again, this mirrors closely the role of the Polish rural press. Stauter-Halsted, op. cit., 188–9.

[63] Miron, op. cit., 16 and passim. This is the central argument of the work.

[64] *Yidishes familienblat*, May 4, 1894. Chanak refers to Zvie Chanak, a regular contributor to the paper.

It should be clear from the folksy tone that this was a populist style designed to convince its readers how a Yiddish paper could be a forum for the common people and thus worthy of support.[65] Indeed, it could be a forum not only for the common people, but for *hasidim* who constituted the majority of Galician Jewry. The article itself is a bitter lament over the problem of declining religious observance, but even here it managed to infuse this typical contemporary anxiety with populist significance. At that time, the government was considering legislating, as in Russia, that all community rabbis be required to attend state-sponsored seminaries. Shmueli attacks these so-called doctor rabbis, that is, the university-educated (*gebildete*) rabbis, not for their lack of a proper Jewish education but because of their distance from the people. The article questioned their ability to speak Yiddish and make "simple Jews" feel at home.

It has always been a puzzle to me why the three, a medical doctor, a lawyer, and a rabbi, are all given the title "doctor." Only when I look at the contemporary "educated" rabbi are all three questions answered for me: the first knows the disease, the other makes the disease, and the third is the disease! Only in the meantime, until the fresh [modern] rabbis are ready, I am yet still a bit of a human being. I [can still] come to the rabbi with my friends, we drink a bit of wine and say "*lekhaim*," we hear words of *Torah*, we celebrate with him and he with us; he doesn't look to whether I am dirty, or [have] a torn caftan. I am a hasid; I may go as I please. When I come to the rabbi to ask a question, he answers me as I understand in a simple Yiddish. Ah, how bitter and dark will it be for me that I will have to come to the doctor rabbi, knock on the door, my hat under my arm; maybe I will even have to give him a kiss on the hand. *Nu*, and how exactly will I express myself in Polish: *Es hot gegebn a kap kheylev ofn kigl, a shprits milkh of der yokh?* [A candle made of unkosher animal fat dripped into the pudding, a drop of milk into the chicken soup? (daily questions of kosher food typically brought to the town rabbi)]. Honestly, I don't know where to begin. Will he possibly understand Yiddish? I am highly doubtful![66]

Similarly, *Der folksfraynd*'s objection to these "rabbis of the future" included their "German" pronunciation of Hebrew (the *komets* vowel, pronounced "u" in Galicia, being turned into a *patah*, pronounced as a long "a"), which was "not like us" in Galicia.[67] These rabbis were rejected not merely because of inadequate training, but because they were disconnected from the common Galician Jew.

[65] It was typical of this press that each new paper claimed finally to fill the need of the Jewish people for a Yiddish paper, ignoring its predecessors, some of which were still in print.

[66] *Yidishes familienblat*, May 4, 1894.

[67] *Der folksfraynd*, May 1, 1891.

Of course, not only acculturated Jews laughed at the idea of a Yiddish newspaper. Taubes himself recognized that even traditional Jews tended to view Yiddish as inherently less sophisticated than German or Polish. This is why he deliberately chose to transliterate Herzl's *Der Judenstaat* into Hebrew script, rather than to translate it outright, in order to preserve a sense of seriousness and realism that he hoped Herzl's status would invoke. In his unpublished papers, Gershon Bader recalls that Taubes confessed fearing that had he produced a true Yiddish translation, Galician Jews would have viewed it as, "laughable, to treat in jargon such a deep diplomatic question as the founding of the Jewish state."[68] This rather open confession by this pioneer in Yiddish-language literature, and later the vice-president of the 1908 Czernowitz Yiddish-language conference, highlights the extent to which the highly colloquial Yiddish used in Taubes's other publications was deliberately designed to create a populist image and avoid association with modern Jewish circles.

Many of these papers, by declaring in their manifestos that they were filling the need of "Orthodox" Jewry for a "kosher" paper in a "simple" Yiddish, could later assert near-religious authority in calling their readers to political action. In other words, the early nationalist papers were Orthodox not just to promote sales, important though this was, but also because the idea of genuine Jews standing up against assimilationists coalesced Orthodox and nationalist interests.[69] If a paper kept a distance from secular, anti-religious rhetoric and associations, it could successfully promote the strengthening of Jewish national identity and Jewish national institutions.

A good example of such a "kosher" campaign by the papers was their call for Jews to declare Yiddish their *Umgangssprache* in the 1890 census, the cause which led Taubes to launch his first Yiddish paper, the *Yidishe folkstsaytung*.[70] As Eric Hobsbawm has noted, the census forced Austrian citizens to "choose not merely a nationality, but a linguistic

---

[68] Bader, op. cit., 4.

[69] Michael Silber has pointed out the peculiar congruence of ultra-Orthodoxy and modern Jewish nationalism in Hungary based on the ideologies' shared rejection of acculturation. This congruence synthesized in the person of Akiva Hirsch Schlesinger, who had already developed a full-fledged Zionist ideology in the 1860s and 1870s. See Silber, "The Beating Jewish Heart in a Foreign Land" (Hebrew), *Cathedra* (1995), 84–105. Recall also Rafael Mahler's account of Hasidic leaders from the Napoleonic period who opposed Austria's attempt at Germanization on similar grounds. R. Mahler, *Hasidism and the Jewish Enlightenment* (Philadelphia, 1985), 14.

[70] Gelber, "History of the Jews in Kolomea" (Hebrew) in Dov Noy and Mark Schutzman, eds., *Sefer zikaron li-kehilat Kolomeyah veha-sevivah* (Tel Aviv, 1972), 44. Recall that *Selbst-Emanzipation* did not take up this cause.

nationality."[71] Traditional Jews, who might have felt uncomfortable identifying themselves as members of the Jewish "nation," probably felt more
at ease identifying their language of daily use as Yiddish. In a society in
which linguistic singularity defined nationhood, this could not help but
have a transformative effect on Jewish identity, despite the fact that the
campaign was unlikely to succeed in winning recognition for Yiddish.
(Polish census-takers would simply mark "Polish" instead.)[72] Indeed,
Joshua Fishman's study of "positive ethnolinguistic consciousness" identifies such calculations among a wide range of nationalist groups. Such
campaigns may entail a difficult struggle, he writes, "but the struggle itself
presents possibilities for both direct and indirect rewards. Not only may
the avowed beneficial end goals of the struggle ultimately be attained,
but the very process of pursuing such a struggle for dignity is community
creating, consciousness raising and language stimulating."[73]

The census campaign also provided an opportunity to remind Jews
of the practical benefits of achieving recognition as a nationality, that
although Jews enjoyed equal civil rights, they still suffered from inequality because Yiddish was not recognized as an independent language. As
a result, the government was not required to publicize proclamations in
Yiddish, as it was required to do in other languages, and even Yiddish contracts were not legally binding. But Jews cannot blame the government,
cautioned *Der folksfraynd*. "We are ourselves guilty" for not answering
census-takers truthfully.

Nu, so when all of us Jews who speak Yiddish and write Yiddish should ourselves
not be foolish [but] should clearly tell the census-taker what is the truth – that we
are Jewish Jews, that is, we belong to the Jewish nation and we speak Yiddish;
then the government will know that the Jewish nation lives and our language is
not dead. Our Yiddish documents will become valid and the ledgers of Jewish
businessmen will have a bit of worth.[74]

The papers' obvious frustration with traditional Jews' lack of interest in
nationalist issues mirrored the frustration of many nationalist movements

---

[71] E. J. Hobsbawm, *Nations and Nationalism since 1780* (Cambridge, 1990), 110, and Brix
(Vienna, 1982), 114.
[72] The 1869 census law, reaffirmed several times by ministerial ordinances, leveled a 40
kronen fine against those who failed to answer one of the nine approved languages and
directed that the answer automatically be changed to that of the majority population.
Polish census-takers in predominantly Ruthenian East Galicia had no intention of giving
up those numbers to the Ruthenians. Rosenfeld, *Die Polnische Judenfrage*, 83.
[73] Fishman, *In Praise of the Beloved Language* (New York, 1997), 76.
[74] *Der folksfraynd*, January 1, 1891.

toward their respective peasantries. As Pieter Judson has noted, nationalists simultaneously praised peasants as heroic "repositories of traditional national values," while despairing over their "unreliability" and "ignorance." Peasant indifference to the census was especially profound. "For many rural respondents," notes Judson, "the language question (not to mention the nation question) simply did not hold the kind of personal significance that nationalists attributed to it."[75] The *Yidishe folkstsaytung*, annoyed at Jewish indifference toward the census, sharply attacked Jews too lazy to do their national duty for their people. Here it tries to explain the pernicious results of their apathy, namely, the Jews' false registration as Poles.

[The census-taker] asks "What is a Jew?" "A Jew is a Jew!" [the Jew answers]. He writes "Mosaic religion." Then comes the other questions, for example, "What language do you speak Mr. So and So?" "To what nation do you belong my dear Jew?" But these other questions the Jew doesn't hear at all, or he is indifferent to them. "Write whatever you want. I have no time; I need to get ready for the Sabbath. My wife is already getting angry with me for dawdling so long." The Jew was not at all moved to answer, "nationality, Israel," "language, Yiddish." Understand that one must do this, for otherwise how is one supposed to know that a Jew is a Jew from the people Israel and speaks the Yiddish language? But the official who sets the law that Jews are not a nation and their language is not a language already knows exactly how to fill in the census card: he writes "nationality, Polish," "language, Polish" or, very rarely, "language, German."[76]

Another campaign of the papers was their call, after an 1891 blood libel in Corfu, to boycott the island's *esrogs* [citrons], required by Jews for the *Sukkoth* holiday each fall. Calls to forbid the ritual use of these fruits, allegedly grafted with lemons, date back several centuries.[77] Although by the mid-nineteenth century most rabbinic authorities permitted the use of the Corfu esrogs, Zionists in the 1870s and 1880s increasingly called for banning the fruit in order to support the emerging esrog market in Palestine. While this argument hardly swayed most rabbinical authorities,[78] the 1891 blood libel and subsequent mass exodus of many of the

---

[75] Pieter Judson, *op.cit.*, 23, 32.

[76] *Yidishe folkstsaytung*, December 1, 1891. Taubes surely knew that there was no nationality category on the census, only language.

[77] On the history of the controversy over the Corfu *esrogim*, see Yosef Salmon, "The Controversy over Etrogim from Corfu and Palestine, 1875–1891" (Hebrew), *Zion* 65 (1990): 75–106.

[78] Indeed, many of those who actually preferred the Palestinian *esrogs* had refrained from declaring so publicly in order not to support the Zionists. Salmon, op. cit.

island's Jews led to an international boycott against the Corfu produce supported by some of the greatest religious authorities of the generation, some of whom had previously opposed the ban.[79]

For Jewish nationalists, the boycott was designed both to punish Greek farmers for the attacks as well as to support Jewish colonists in Palestine. For these Yiddish papers, however, it was above all an opportunity for the papers to draw traditional Jews into a political campaign, to appropriate a religious activity and fill it with political meaning. *Der folksfraynd*, among others, assumed religious authority in calling for the boycott, claiming that it was an extra *mitzvah* (religious merit) to use esrogs procured only from the land of Israel.

For the [Greek] field in which the *esrog* grew is mixed with Jewish blood which was innocently murdered. There where one can help one should take [one's *esrog*] from the land of Israel by which one will, first of all, have a *mitzvah* that one supports Jews, and second, [the fact] that it is from "the land of Israel" is an extra *mitzvah*, and third, one should not give such money to such enemies of Israel.

Basing themselves on the support of the chief rabbi of Vienna, Moritz Güdemann (not someone whose authority traditional Jews in Galicia would normally have respected), the paper assumed the authority to demand that Galician rabbis forbid the use of Greek esrogs not only on political grounds, or even on nationalist grounds (i.e., to support Jews in Palestine), but on religious grounds, that Greek esrogs should be declared *posl*, ritually unfit for use.[80] A month later, the *Yidishe folkstsaytung* announced that the Hungarian rabbis had forbidden the purchase of Corfu esrogs, and called on merchants to buy only from Jewish colonies. It even included a five-stanza poem in support of the campaign.[81] The same day an anonymous article in the *Folksfraynd* chastised Galician rabbis for remaining silent, claiming that all Jews had agreed that esrogs should be purchased only from Palestine.[82]

Only in September, when the editors may have sensed that they were being ignored, did they modify their view. A notice in *Der folksfraynd* on the first of September from a group of rabbis who refused to forbid the use of the Greek esrogs explained that most people would simply be unable

---

[79] Those who supported the ban included Isaac Elchanan Spector, Naftali Zvi Yehuda Berlin (the *Nitsiv*), Samuel Mohiliver, David Friedman and others. Salmon, op. cit., 106.

[80] *Der folksfraynd*, June 1, 1891. Both Ashkenazic and Sephardic rabbis in Palestine had issued similarly worded rulings, condemning Greek esrogs as *posl*, but the Yiddish papers did not draw on them. Salmon, op. cit., 106.

[81] *Yidishe folkstsaytung*, July 1, 1890.

[82] *Der folksfraynd*, July 1, 1891.

to uphold such a ruling.[83] Two weeks later, the paper conceded that Greek Jews would also suffer from a boycott and that in any case the supply from the Jewish colonies could not meet European demand and a boycott could drive up the price of esrogs beyond the means of many Jews.[84]

Even Knöbel's papers, which specifically defined themselves as Orthodox, appropriated religious values for nationalist purposes. A story from his *Yidishes familienblat*, for example, tells of two sons of a wealthy Jew who attended a gymnasium (secular secondary school). The younger son remained religious, while the older one Polonized his name and left Judaism altogether, except on visits home so as not to jeopardize his inheritance. The article praises the younger brother's piety, but also his patriotism to the Jewish people, while the older brother is reminded that Christians do not really love him. They hate him even more than his brother, whom they at least respect for not trying to ape them and deny who he is. Here the younger son chastises his brother:

You patronize your Christian comrades, who can only call you a stupid Jew that you press on them too much; believe me that they hate you much more than me that I do not flatter them and I don't want to be like them.... They do not love you, they love your deep pockets, your good heart, but not because you are called by a Polish name just like them.

His fidelity to the religious commandments, he explains, was in order to demonstrate that the Jews constituted a single people, with the longest and most glorious history of all peoples in the world.

As a Jew I must hold on to all commandments and prohibitions; with this I show that we are a People. The *tefilin* [phylacteries] show that 4,000 years ago we were already teaching all Peoples the faith in the One, and that, before all other Peoples, we were a civilized People. We learned from the past for the future that we were created for greatness, and just as putting on *tefilin* shows that God is One, so are we a single People![85]

In other words, the younger brother does not rebuke his sibling for denying God's Torah; rather he focuses on his brother's denying the glory

---

[83] *Der folksfraynd*, September 1, 1891.

[84] *Der folksfraynd*, September 15, 1891. Taubes raised the issue again in 1896, when he repeated his "ruling" that God intended the commandment only for an esrog from Israel. As in the first campaign, Taubes deftly presented a nationalist argument in religious form. "God, may He be blessed, commanded us through Moses our rabbi that we should take on Sukkoth an esrog (*V'lakachtem lachem b'yom harishon*, etc.). He said this at the time we were entering the land of Israel and [He] certainly did not intend a Corfu esrog." *Ha'am-Dos Folk*, July 30, 1896.

[85] *Yidishes familienblat*, September 21, 1893.

of the Jewish national language and mocks his attempt to assimilate into Polish circles – this from the *Yidishes familienblat*, a declared defender of Jewish Orthodoxy.

Other papers were even more inclined to view Jewish religious observance in nationalist terms. A lead article in the *Izraelitishes folksblat*, for example, explains that while Christian holidays merely celebrate religious memories, Jewish holidays celebrate the Jewish nation, "springing out of its achievement of political, material, and spiritual freedom." Thus, Passover, according to the paper, was principally about political freedom, Sukkoth was to thank God "for the bounty of our Fatherland," and so on.[86] These were not radical interpretations, but they were narrowly focused to elicit nationalist meaning.

Still, the fact that they did not stray far from normative religious values highlights the sincerity of the publishers of these papers. These were not assimilated Jews cynically manipulating religious themes in order to entice traditional Jews into their movement. Rather, they were Jews raised in a traditional milieu, who had come to Zionism as a means of entering the modern world without abandoning their deeply entrenched Jewish identities. They genuinely viewed Zionism as the natural and most authentic interpretation of Judaism, just as *maskilim* of the previous generation understood their ideology as a renewal of Judaism in its "pure and unalloyed form."[87] The Zionists' strong support of Jewish colonies in Palestine, for example, grew naturally from religious liturgy which prayed for the return to Zion. Of course, the added component of human action to hasten such a return was an important innovation.[88] Nevertheless, they still saw such action as fulfilling the Divine plan, and opposition to it as hindering that plan.[89] "Jewish nationalism," notes Ehud Luz, "drew

[86] *Izraelitishes folksblat*, October 8, 1891. Nationalists latched on especially to the tradition that the Israelites merited redemption from Egypt because they did not change their names, clothes, or language.

[87] Immanuel Etkes, "Immanent Factors and External Influences in the Development of the Haskalah Movement in Russia," in Jacob Katz, ed., *Toward Modernity* (New Brunswick, 1987), 29.

[88] Note, however, that the proto-Zionists Zvi Hirsch Kalischer and Yehuda Alkalai had already set a precedent for such a position by reconciling human endeavors with traditional sources, effectively opening Zionism to the Orthodox. See Shimoni, op. cit., 77–81.

[89] Recall Zion's first Yiddish publication, for example. Subtitled "Lamentations for *Tisha B'av*," it described the prayers of religious Jews who mourned the destruction of Jerusalem without supporting its rebirth as "chatter without heart and feeling." *Der Kantchik* (Lemberg, 1890), 17.

its legitimacy from the Jewish religion."[90] Nationalist ideas and religious motifs formed a seamless whole, upon which the writers drew freely; it was therefore not at all disingenuous for Jewish nationalists to frame their nationalist identity within religious themes. Of course this was not a peculiarly Jewish tendency but was rather typical of contemporary national movements.[91]

One need not rely on Knöbel to emphasize this point. In fact, the phenomenon is exemplified by Laibel Taubes much more so. Taubes, raised in a strictly religious environment, was the scion of generations of respected rabbis on both his paternal and maternal sides; both his father and grandfather served as community rabbis. Moreover, Taubes remained at least moderately observant his entire life, strongly protesting, for example, the scheduling of the 1905 Austrian Zionist conference over the Shavuoth holiday.[92] His conversion to Zionism, he later wrote, was a result not of his abandonment of traditional Judaism, but rather of a new conviction that the national idea was a natural and integral part of traditional Judaism.

Even as a very young man, I began to feel on my own that the standing of our Jews is not so good. I felt that we lacked something only I didn't know the right name for what it was that we lacked. For a long time, as a consequence of my upbringing, of my environment, and of my entire Jewish milieu at that time, I felt that Jews merely lacked proper fear of Heaven. With time, however, I began to feel that aside from "world-to-come" issues, we actually lacked our complete "I", our complete soul. We lacked the feeling and the understanding for the "Jewish spark" – that which we call today Jewish nationhood [*national Judentum*].[93]

Despite this later testimony, Taubes's actual path to Jewish nationalism seems to have been born as much out of his desire to improve the Jews' economic situation, made worse by the failure of Jews to organize their own financial resources for the benefit of the community, as out of

---

[90] Ehud Luz, *Parallels Meet: Religion and Nationalism in the Early Zionism Movement (1882–1904)* (Philadelphia, 1988), x.

[91] "In a world where religious values still predominated," notes Raymond Pearson, "what was later revealed as embryonic secular nationalism naturally found expression in religious form. A blurring of religious and nationalist motivation was often characteristic.... In the modern period, religion and emerging nationalism became mutually reinforcing interests, with religion gradually losing its status as senior partner to nationalism." R. Pearson, *National Minorities in Eastern Europe 1848–1945* (London, 1983), 21.

[92] *Die Welt*, June 16, 1905, 9. He did dress "German," however, at least where he felt safe in doing so. See Chapter 5.

[93] *Zichrones fun Laibel Taubes*, 6.

his search for a more "complete soul."[94] Nevertheless, Zionism remained for Taubes a movement that strengthened Torah rather than one which opposed it. Zionism proclaimed, he once wrote, that "a Jew is not 'unfortunately a Jew' but a proud son of his great ancestors Abraham, Isaac and Jacob, a true follower not of new teachings, of a *Torah Chadasha*, but only of our ancient, holy exalted *Torah* of Moses."[95] While he applauded Western Jews for joining the Zionist movement, he was careful to frame their activity as a return to traditional Judaism itself, thereby preempting ultra-Orthodox opposition that Zionism constituted a modern ideology antithetical to Judaism. On the contrary, he argued, Zionism was itself an extension of traditional Judaism. "Naturally, we Orthodox Jews believe more than the progressives in the rebuilding of the Jewish state," he wrote.

It fills us with special joy that we see our ancient, lofty hope and the belief in the rebuilding of the Jewish kingdom winning supporters among the modern, educated, progressive Jews. We celebrate that our educated Jews are becoming familiar with the *Volksidee*. We are proud to hear from a man like Dr. Herzl: We are a people. We are not Germans, not Poles, not Frenchmen, not Russians, and also not *Timchas* (?). We are a people, a people, Jews. *Yisroel Goy Echad*!

Boldly referring to the Jewish state as "Olam haBa," the world to come (i.e., the Messianic age), Taubes confidently concluded that faith and nationalism were natural bedfellows. "We know that 'every Jew has a place in the world to come' – all Jews may have a share in the future Jewish state, in the future Jewish world. Nationalism leads to faith, faith leads to nationalism."[96]

FROM READERS TO VOTERS: THE HOLY CAMPAIGN TO REELECT JOSEPH BLOCH

The papers also engaged local political contests, especially those which would directly impact their traditional readership. The election of a new chief rabbi in the capital city Lemberg, for example, drew endorsements from this press. *Der folksfraynd*'s choice for the office indicates again how these papers used orthodox rhetoric carefully to draw traditional readers into the modern world.

[94] Bader, op. cit., 1–3.
[95] From his report on the third party conference of Galician Zionists, *Ha'am*, November 15, 1895. Taubes described the official dinner following the conference as being truly "a table on which were said words of Torah."
[96] *Ha'am*, June 1, 1896

Lemberg must have a rabbi with all advantages, namely he should be extraordinarily learned, he should be of great lineage, he should be God fearing, and [in addition] to all of these advantages he must also be a little familiar with the "outside" wisdom that he should be able to behave as the representative of Galician Jews.

The deceased Rabbi Ettinger, it claimed, had all of these characteristics, and the paper reviewed the three candidates to replace him. The first was rejected because he was a Lithuanian Jew, and his accent made him difficult to understand. The second was too old, and so the paper endorsed the third candidate, whom it was certain would be elected. Within a single sentence, the paper demanded traditional learning, piety and lineage, appealed to popular resentment of "foreign" Jews trying to win local positions, and broached the possibility of secular learning as a requirement of a Jewish spiritual leader.[97]

Perhaps the most obvious example of this mixture of religious authority and nationalist rhetoric was the 1891 campaign of Joseph Bloch for reelection to the Austrian Parliament. A battle of major political significance, it helped stimulate the emergence of the Yiddish press in the first place; in Kolomea alone at least three new Yiddish papers began publication during the campaign.[98] No Jewish nationalist entered Parliament before 1897 or came close to matching Bloch's widespread popularity. Despite his by-then opposition to Zionism, Bloch's outspoken Jewish pride made him the darling of the early nationalist movement and his election campaigns generated tremendous activity among Jewish nationalists in Galicia, as noted above. Support for his reelection was increasingly seen as a religious duty, a badge which proved one's Jewishness. The 1891 election in particular highlighted how the Yiddish press linked religious authenticity and Jewish unity on the one hand, and support for their papers and their candidate on the other.

In 1891 Bloch again faced his "eternal contra-candidate" Emil Byk, whom he and his supporters again portrayed as a lackey of the Polish Club.[99] The papers allotted tremendous space to the campaign; two full

---

[97] *Der folksfraynd*, March 1, 1891.

[98] These were the *Yidishe folkstsaytung*, the *Izraelitishes folksblat* and *Der folksfraynd*. Toury also locates the roots of these papers in Bloch's reelection campaign, coverage of which constitutes the bulk of his analysis, although Gelber claims that Taubes launched the *folkstsaytung* (which he mistakenly calls the *Yidishe folksblat*) to promote his census campaign. Toury, op. cit., 133 and Gelber, op. cit., 44. Note that the 1892 Kolomea tallis-weaver strike did not have such an effect. All three of these papers had folded by then, and the next would not appear until the following year.

[99] Bloch was also challenged by a wealthy Parisian Jew named Ber Meisels.

FIGURE 3.2. Salomon Buber.

supplements to the third issue of *Der folksfraynd*, for example, were filled
with endorsements of Bloch. Letters such as the following from Salomon
Buber (1827–1907), the celebrated scholar of Midrash and a powerful
member of the Lemberg Jewish community,[100] added a religious imperative to supporting him (see Figure 3.2).

[100] Salomon's grandson, whom he helped raise, was Martin Buber. His granddaughter Nelli
(Martin Buber's sister) married Mordechai Braude. In using Buber, the paper hoped to
ground its religious imperative to support Bloch in a traditional rabbinical authority.

It is a holy obligation according to the law that all rabbis and sages of Galicia stand by the wise Herr Dr. Bloch, and preach in public in every city that every person who fears God in his heart should choose only the rabbi Dr. Bloch, and every person who opposes him is sinning against God and man. Because God has sent him for our sustenance, he is an angel sent to his nation, and he is putting his life in danger to wage God's war against those who rise up against us.[101]

Similarly, at a political rally held in the large synagogue in Kolomea, the president of the community council, H. Shlomo Hirsch, and the deputy mayor, Joseph Funkenstein, spoke on the vital necessity of reelecting Bloch for the good of all Israel. They compared it to the choice God gave the Israelites between the blessings and the curses (for following or disobeying His will), only now the imperative to do good was not to obey Mosaic law but to vote correctly.

The entire group of Jews agreed with one voice that anyone who steps outside of the community and gives his vote for someone else – he should suffer all the curses in the rebuke [of Moses] in the holy Torah. And he who votes for the Jewish fighter, the rabbi Dr. Joseph Samuel Bloch, he should receive all the blessings in the Torah – to this the entire auditorium said "Amen" and then they blew the *shofar* – the holy effect which this had on all of those gathered is indescribable.[102]

The preacher at the main synagogue in Buczacz likewise delivered a series of sermons on behalf of Bloch, which he published later that year in a Hebrew chapbook titled *Sefer Milhamot Bloch* (the Book of the Wars of Bloch). The book's title overtly plays on the biblical verse about the "Book of the Wars of the Lord" (*Numbers* 21:14), which discusses the miracles wrought by God for the Israelites. Here, the author (Judah Leisner) waxes on about the miraculous services wrought by Bloch for contemporary Jews. Drawing on other biblical verses, he describes Bloch as the one whom God dearly desires, as a man whose "lion's heart" fights anti-Semitism with divine might. The book's approbation by a member of Buczacz's wealthy elite praised the author for his heartfelt sermons which, "entered the heart

---

Besides, Buber was also a prominent banker in Lemberg, a one-time president of the Lemberg Chamber of Commerce, and had been a board member of the Lemberg Jewish Community Council since 1870. See Meir Wunder, *Meorei Galitsye: Encyclopedia L'Chachmei Galitsye* (Jerusalem, 1978), Vol. 1, 413–15, and Mayer Balaban, "Shalshelet hayachas shel mishpachat Orenstein Braude," in *Sefer Hayovel lekhevod Dr. Mordechai Zeev Braude* (Warsaw, 1931), 47.

[101] *Der folksfraynd*, February 1, 1891. Buber's letter, as well as several others, was written in Hebrew. Buber, a board member of the progressive Temple, was directly challenging the position of the Belzer Rebbe, an extraordinarily charismatic and influential figure.

[102] *Yidishe folkstsaytung*, March 1, 1891.

of the entire people, so that everyone united as one man, sealed a covenant, and bound a strong and firm resolution to elect Dr. Bloch."[103]

According to one paper, even Byk himself supported Bloch's candidacy. Why, then, was Byk opposing him? Putting words into Byk's mouth which he clearly never uttered, the *Izraelitishes folksblat* suggested a reason.

The party of Dr. Emil Byk, however, says thus: Yes, it is admittedly true, we know this [that Bloch needs to be re-elected] and we want Dr. Bloch to enter parliament again as before, for we also know how necessary [it is that] one must have him as a Representative; *we feel just as Jewish as all Jews.* Only, there are electoral districts besides our own: let another electoral district also show that they know what Dr. Bloch is – not just Kolomea, which has already shown it twice. [emphasis added][104]

In other words, only those who support Bloch are true Jews. Similarly, when Byk decided to drop out of the election and run instead in the Brody-Zloczow district, *Der folksfraynd*, which had been defaming his character for weeks, suddenly began to applaud his noble action, which somehow returned him to the Jewish fold. Writing that Byk had acted so honorably, so Jewish, "as a true son of our holy fathers Abraham, Isaac, and Jacob," the paper called on all of his supporters to back Bloch. Dr. Byk's withdrawal from the race, it concluded, was done for the sake of *akhdes*, unity, in order that Jews would not fight one another. Thus the way to national unity, including interclass unity, was by supporting the nationalist candidate:

We may be proud of our representative, who saved the honor of God and all Israel, the honor of our holy Torah and our sages, the honor of our rich Jews and our poor working men, the skilled handworkers; we may be proud of our Representative who is known by all of Jewry, from one corner of the world to the other.[105]

Byk's withdrawal from the race left just one other Jewish candidate, a wealthy Parisian Jew named Leon (Ber) Meisels, grandson of the famous

---

[103] Judah Leisner, *Sefer Milhamot Bloch* (Lemberg, 1891), 7, 9. In 1879, *Machsike Hadas* celebrated Simon Sofer's election in strikingly similar language. "A voice was heard in the camp of the Hebrews," declared the headline. "Who should be sent? Who will go for us? Behold a voice calls out. **Simon! Simon!** And who calls Simon? The Holy, blessed be He!" (Bold in original.) *Machsike Hadas*, July 23, 1879, 3.

[104] *Izraelitishes folksblat*, February 8, 1891.

[105] *Der folksfraynd*, February 15, 1891. Byk won the Brody seat that year and held it until his death in 1906. Once Byk switched to Brody, the *Drohobyczer Zeitung* – which had endorsed Bloch in 1883 and Byk in 1885, could heartily endorse both men and celebrate both of their victories. *Drohobyczer Handels-Zeitung*, March 6, 1891, 1.

rabbi of the same name. Curiously, although the Yiddish press concerned itself far more with Byk, Bloch's reminiscences focused almost exclusively on Meisels.[106] Bloch accused Ignacy Schreiber, the personal secretary of the Belzer Rebbe (Yehoshua Rokeach), of concocting Meisel's candidacy and securing the Rebbe's endorsement for Meisels as the candidate of Orthodox Jewry because Bloch refused to "contribute" 5,000 gulden to *Machsike Hadas*, a fantastic sum which Bloch did not possess.[107]

Ultimately, the rebbe's endorsement of Meisels, under the guise of the "Electoral Committee of Machsike Hadas," did not carry much weight.[108] Meisels allegedly spent nearly 60,000 florins in the district and yet could not muster even 100 votes, while Bloch won over 2,000. Voters seemed to view Meisels, who allegedly earned his fortune by refusing to grant his ex-wife a divorce until she paid him a one million florin ransom, as an opportunistic outsider.[109] A campaign ballad championing Bloch's cause was even composed, which one *Galitsyaner* recalled being sung by a Yeshiva student at his Sabbath table. The first verse went as follows:

Faithful children,	*Kinderlach, getraje*
the whole community,	*die ganze chewraje*
we should all another year live.	*mir solln alle über e' Jahr erleben.*
We must go already,	*Ma derf scho gehen*
to Meisel's funeral,	*zu Meisels lewaje*
and to Bloch our votes give.	*Und for Blochn die stimm abgeben.*

In one of the following verses Meisels is called "a Parisian Frenchman at whom stones had been thrown and for whom a sad fate is prophesized."[110]

---

[106] Similarly, Gelber's history of Kolomea Jews does not even mention that Byk had initially opposed Bloch in 1891, writing only that Byk supported Bloch in this campaign. Gelber, "History of the Jews in Kolomea" (Hebrew), 53.

[107] Bloch, *My Reminiscences*, 263.

[108] *Machsike Hadas*, February 7, 1891, and February 22, 1891; *Kol Machsike Hadas*, March 1, 1891. A. L. Shusheim recalls incorrectly that the rebbe endorsed the Polish Christian candidate against Bloch. A. L. Shusheim, "Yidishe Politik un Yidishe Partein in Galitsye," in *Pinkes Galitsye* (Buenos Aires, 1945), 44. In 1895, when Bloch ran for reelection after having been forced to resign his seat earlier in the year, *Machsike Hadas* blamed Bloch for the recent rise in anti-Semitism and claimed to have recognized this fault in him already ten years before. They strongly endorsed Bloch's pro-Polish Jewish opponent, Maximilian Trachtenberg. *Kol Machsike Hadas*, November 28, 1895, 5.

[109] Bloch, op. cit., 260–1, 267 and *Oesterreichische Wochenschrift*, March 13, 1981, 1–3. This accusation was repeated by all three Yiddish papers then in print.

[110] Bloch, op. cit., 266–7. The spelling is as it appears in that source. The Galician Jew recalling the song sought out Bloch on a cruise in 1921 to retell it.

As noted, the Yiddish papers focused far more on Byk than Meisels. To the extent that they discussed Meisels at all, they tended to dismiss him as a tactless outsider. Meisels's endorsement by *Machsike Hadas,* however, led one of the papers to frame its opposition to Meisels as a populist rally of religious Jews against the Orthodox organization. In a March 1 endorsement of Bloch, the *Yidishe folkstsaytung* printed a five-stanza poem praising Bloch as a Jewish savior. Defend the "honor of the Torah," declared the poem, but "don't look towards the 'Mazikei Hadath,'" a subtle drop of one letter that changed the meaning of the Orthodox group's name from "Upholders of the Faith" to "Harmers of the Faith." "Voters, don't be an ass. Away with the Meyzel, long live Dr. Bloch."[111]

Judging by the election results, the campaign was a resounding success. Election day violence, already infamous through the empire, could not overcome Bloch's popularity. Despite an outbreak of anti-Jewish violence in Kolomea and Sniatyn, and an extraordinary degree of electoral corruption, ultimately the district's Jewish majority united behind Bloch, who won with 2,128 votes, defeating the "Christian" candidate by 350 votes.[112] Note that coverage of the election tended to distinguish only between Christians and Jews, often failing to differentiate between Poles and Ruthenians, and that it avoided reference to such contentious concepts as "nations." This was quite typical of this press. In referring to Jewish nationhood, the papers initially tended to employ the more comfortable terms "*Am*" (people), or its Yiddish equivalent "*Volk*," and "*Uma*," which roughly translates to "nation" but avoided the need to employ the modern term more threatening to their traditional readership.

CONCLUSION

Ultimately, it is difficult to quantify the impact of the Yiddish nationalist press on Galician Jewry. Clearly, none of these papers could claim serious financial success. Aside from the obvious fact that they only lasted for short periods, all of the papers made it painfully clear that they were struggling to survive. They all complained bitterly in nearly every issue of their dire financial straits, about the problem of insufficient subscriptions and of subscribers who had not paid their dues; *Ha'am* even printed a blacklist of delinquent subscribers. That paper may actually have survived

---

[111] *Yidishe folkstsaytung,* March 1, 1891.
[112] *Der folksfraynd,* March 15, 1891.

longer than the others thanks to revenues from its graphic advertisement of Quaker Oats on the front page of most issues. (Interestingly, the same advertisement appeared on the cover of some Ruthenian nationalist papers, possibly suggesting earlier cooperation between those camps than previously thought.[113])

Absolute circulation of the papers is difficult to gauge because government bureaucrats, unable to distinguish between Hebrew and Yiddish papers, compiled circulation statistics for the "Hebrew or Hebrew letter" press as a whole. As a result, Hebrew, Yiddish, and German papers printed in Hebrew characters all appeared as a single statistic. Fortunately, however, the statistics did classify papers according to frequency of publication, and because all of the Yiddish papers appeared as bi-weeklies, it is possible to estimate the extent of their circulation. Over the course of the years 1890–7 the "Hebrew letter" press averaged between 10,000 and 14,000 bi-weekly papers each per year, roughly the same as the Ukrainian bi-weekly press during those years, although dwarfed by the Polish bi-weekly press, which printed between 50,000 and 100,000 papers each per year.[114]

Other evidence also suggests that the Yiddish papers enjoyed some influence. Zionist and other reading halls, where a single subscription would be picked up by large numbers of readers, figured among the list of subscribers. In addition, papers circulated informally among friends. An agent for the *Yidishes folksblat* described how he had had difficulty selling subscriptions in a certain *shtetl* because the entire town shared a single subscription.[115] Moreover, although short-lived, many of the papers achieved widespread distribution. The *Yidishes familienblat*, for example, listed agents in Rumania (Bakui and Jassi), Stryj, Boryslaw, Przemysl, and Cracow. One can assume it was also sold in Lemberg (the provincial capital) and Kolomea, among other reasons because firms from both cities advertised in the paper, as did some from Vienna. To this extent, the papers' claim to have forged a single Jewish community across Galicia a la Benedict Anderson seems justified.

In sum, the Yiddish nationalist press of the early 1890s represented a revolutionary advance for the Jewish nationalist movement. Written in a

[113] I would like to thank Harald Binder for this information.

[114] See Jerzy Myslinski, "Issues of the socio-political press in Galicia during the years 1881–1913" (Polish), *Rocznik Historii Czasopiśmiennictwa Polskiego*, 4.1 (1965), 115–33 and 4.4 (1965), 80–98. My thanks to Harald Binder for bringing this source to my attention.

[115] *Yidishes folksblat*, July 13, 1894.

populist style, often in a heavy Galician dialect, these papers proclaimed themselves to be "organs for the people," defenders of Orthodoxy and the common Jew. They appropriated religious themes in order to convince traditional Jews to view themselves as a modern nation and to organize politically to secure national minority rights. In this way, they attempted to transform the basis of Jewish identity from religion to nation. This press highlights the central role of Jewish nationalism, first and foremost, as an identity, a *Weltanschauung*, beyond any particular political program which its parties advocated.

4

A Broadening Audience

Organizational and Ideological Change, 1896–1904

The Jewish nationalist movement in Galicia did not enjoy spectacular growth during the mid-1890s. Summing up the 1894–5 year for the Galician Zionists' first annual yearbook, Adolf Stand wrote bitterly that he had little news to report regarding the Zionist movement in Galicia. The fault, he wrote, lay with the provincial associations, which ignored the leadership in Lemberg and refused to support its activities. Letters from the province complained that a Galician colony had not yet been founded, and in the meantime their short-lived Yiddish-language party organ (*Das Jüdische Wochenblatt*) had folded because only two of the provincial associations sent in their required two Gulden support for the paper.[1] Stand could not know that in just half a year, Galician Zionism would be completely transformed by the publication in Vienna by a popular feuilletonist named Theodor Herzl of a short book entitled *Der Judenstaat*, the Jews' State.

Galician Zionists flocked to Herzl in the aftermath of *Der Judenstaat*'s publication, although they briefly attempted to maintain organizational autonomy. Most groups belonged either to the provincial organization based in Lemberg or else to the new practical Zionist federation Ahavath Zion based in Tarnow. The latter attempted to rally traditional, especially Hasidic Jews to Jewish nationalism by establishing a colony of religious Jews in Palestine under the strict leadership of David Moshe Friedman, the Czortkower rebbe. By 1901, however, both of these federations had collapsed and nearly all Galician Zionist groups had become affiliates of

---

[1] Adolf Stand, "Review of the year 5655" (Yiddish), *Jüdischer Volkskalender* (Lemberg, 1895), 92–3.

Herzl's Zionist Organization (ZO). As such, they temporarily renounced their "double program" in favor of political Zionism. Even the 1897 electoral reform, which added a fifth curia open to all adult men, failed to motivate many Jewish nationalists to mobilize politically, as it did for other nationalist movements in the empire.[2]

More important than this organizational history is the transformation of Jewish nationalist propaganda during this period. While membership in Zionist clubs still drew mainly from the secular intelligentsia, Jewish nationalism during this period began to penetrate into traditional communities throughout Galicia. Yiddish-language propaganda grew dominant, while synagogues and study houses emerged as important venues for Zionist events. The timing and content of their events likewise reflected their growing concern with attracting traditional Jews as well. This activity was expanding rapidly by the turn of the century, precisely the moment in which scholars have identified the solidification of a sharply anti-Zionist position among the Orthodox, especially Hasidic leadership.[3] Critically, as Orthodox hostility toward Zionism mounted, traditional Jews grew increasingly influenced by the Jewish national idea. Like other nationalists, Zionists (in print and at rallies) emphasized their violent struggle with conservative forces in order to inflame nationalist passions in their audience.

HERZL, THE ZIONIST CONGRESS, AND GALICIAN REORGANIZATION

In February 1896 a popular feuilletonist from the Viennese *Neue Freie Presse* named Theodor Herzl (1860–1904) published a short book entitled *Der Judenstaat*, the Jews' State, which from its first appearance rocked the Zionist movement.[4] Although the work contained few ideas not already articulated by other ideologues, as Gideon Shimoni notes, no one else had so "boldly and lucidly propounded the outer limits of the nationalist idea as applied to the Jews, namely, the complete congruence of the Jewish entity with a sovereign polity, a *Judenstaat*, a state of Jews

---

[2] See, e.g., King, *Budweisers into Czechs and Germans* (Princeton, 2002), 901.

[3] Yosef Salmon, *Religion and Zionism: First Encounters* (Jerusalem, 2002), 306ff; Aviezer Ravitzky, *Messianism, Zionism, and Jewish Religious Radicalism*, 14–19ff.

[4] The volume of scholarship on Herzl is staggering. See, e.g., Jacques Kornberg, *Theodor Herzl: From Assimilation to Zionism* (Bloomington, 1993); Steven Beller, *Herzl* (London, 1991); Amos Elon, *Herzl* (New York, 1975); Alex Bein, *Theodor Herzl* (Philadelphia, 1941); and Michael Stanislawski, *Zionism and the Fin de Siecle* (Berkeley, 2001), 1–18.

... no one until that time had so straightforwardly articulated the will to full sovereignty."[5] Within a very short period, Zionism would be transformed from a collection of diverse associations throughout Europe into an organized and increasingly prominent movement, with Herzl its virtually uncontested leader.

Precisely because of Herzl's position as one of Vienna's most famous journalists, *Der Judenstaat* made a tremendous impression among the small group of Galician Zionists, as it did among their Viennese counterparts.[6] Yehoshua Thon, writing a decade after Herzl's death in 1904, still found it difficult to describe fully the extent of Herzl's impact on the Zionists of the time.

Today's Zionist generation can not grasp the concept of the enormous impression which that book then made on us, the activists, who stood in the middle of Zionist activity. It was for us a sharp word of agreement, encouragement and empowerment, which came to us from some great height, perhaps from the most heavenly heights.[7]

Herzl taught Galician Zionists to "think in millions," recalled Thon in a memorial volume dedicated to the Zionist leader, suggesting "a plan of such scope and of such daring that I became dizzy."[8] Already in March 1896, a meeting of Zionist students in Lemberg composed a letter of gratitude to Herzl, lauding his great book and placing themselves at his service. Gershon Zipper, then editor of *Przyszłość*, sent a similar letter of support on April 4, informing Herzl that Galician Zionists identified entirely with *Der Judenstaat* and assuring him that they were ready to fight by his side.[9]

[5] Gideon Shimoni, *The Zionist Ideology* (Hanover, 1995), 89.
[6] The Viennese Zion federation passed a resolution calling on Herzl to accept leadership of the group already in March 1896. Herzl initially hesitated, but after the group's president Moritz Schnirer (1860–1942) presented him with a petition signed by thousands demanding that he reconsider, Herzl acquiesced and accepted leadership of the federation. Moses Landau, *Geschichte des Zionismus in Oesterreich und Ungarn* (unpublished dissertation, University of Vienna, 1925), 97–8.
[7] Julian Hirshaut, *In Gang Fun Der Geshichte* (Tel Aviv, 1984), 259.
[8] Osias Thon, "The First Big Visions: When Herzl Taught the Zionists to Think in Millions," in Meyer Weisgal, ed., *Theodor Herzl: A Memorial* (New York, 1929), 53. Thon was deeply impressed by Herzl's presence, his "aristocratic manliness," but noted that the same quality which ultimately made him such a powerful leader – namely, his incredible ego – also undermined the practical work needed to implement his vision. Following a disagreement with Thon over the trustworthiness of a certain individual, whom Thon noted later proved him to be correct, Herzl rebuked Thon with these words: "Take note of this, Dr. Thon, and bear it in mind for the future: When Dr. Herzl says something, he is always in the right." Thon, op. cit., 54.
[9] Nathan Gelber, *Toldot ha-tenuah ha-tsiyonit be-Galitsyah, 1875–1918* (Jerusalem, 1958), 287–8. Gelber reprints Zipper's letter in Hebrew translation with Herzl's response.

Despite the fact that Herzl, a man who at one time considered solving the "Jewish problem" via the mass conversion of all Jewish children at the Vatican, clearly sat in the camp of "disillusioned integrationists," his appeal in Galicia was not at all limited to other secular intellectuals. On the contrary, Taubes and other Zionists more closely connected to traditional Jewish society hoped that Herzl – precisely because of his secular credentials – could convince religious leaders, inspired by the grand scale of his proposal, that Zionism was not a utopian fantasy. For this reason, Taubes sought to have Herzl's book published in Yiddish as soon as possible, but rather than translating it into Yiddish he chose simply to transliterate the German text into Hebrew script, which he felt would preserve a sense of seriousness and realism.[10]

Another key traditional figure captivated by Herzl was Ahron Marcus (1843–1916), a brilliant student from a modern Orthodox family in Hamburg who as a young man made his way to Cracow where he became a committed Hasid.[11] Marcus strongly believed in projects to settle Jews in Palestine and had supported Zionist groups in Cracow since the early 1880s. Herzl made a fantastic impression on Marcus, who once admitted kissing a letter from Herzl, "as though it was a prayer book."[12] *Der Judenstaat*, Marcus wrote on April 27, 1896, "came like a lightning bolt in the darkness of night in both of the camps, assimilationists and Hasidim." Like Taubes, Marcus found strength rather than weakness in Herzl's secular credentials. Hasidim, he continued, were "completely beside themselves with astonishment that our ideals, our utopias, our hopes and aspirations, which over generations and millennia have become flesh and blood, were found worthy of recognition by men who in sagacity and sober judgment rival the leading statesmen of Europe."[13]

Marcus was one of twenty-three Galician delegates to the First Zionist Congress in Basel, whose clearly secular nature he later worked to obscure.[14] Marcus worked tirelessly to persuade the Zionist leader

---

[10] See above, Chapter Three.

[11] On Marcus, see Joshua Shanes, "Ahron Marcus: Portrait of a Zionist Hasid," *Jewish Social Studies* 16, no. 3 (Spring/Summer, 2010): 116–61, and the sources cited there.

[12] From a letter of Marcus to Herzl. An English translation appears in Willy Aron, "Herzl and Aron Marcus," *Herzl Year Book* 1 (1958), 190. I would like to thank Marcus's great-great-grandson Israel Marcus for providing me with copies of the original correspondences.

[13] Aron, op. cit., 188. Marcus delivered a fifteen-page lecture to a Zionist group on January 10, 1897, that largely focused on the compatibility, indeed inseparability, of political Zionism and Judaism, with multiple proof texts brought from major rabbinic figures. Ahron Marcus, *Dr. Theodor Herzl's "Judenstaat" besprochen in der Generalversammlung der "Chowewe Erez Israel" in Krakau am 10. Januar 1897* (Cracow, 1897).

[14] Yosef Salmon, op. cit., 291.

that the key to their success lay with the Hasidic masses, whom Marcus intended to deliver through the conversion to Zionism of the major Hasidic *zaddikim* of his day, particularly David Moshe Friedman, the rebbe of Czortkow (1828–1900).[15] Marcus persuaded Herzl to send a letter to the rebbe, which he attempted to do via Leibel Mendel Landau (1861–1920), a well-known Galician rabbi and early Zionist. Although this letter did not make its way to Friedman, efforts by Marcus to win the support of the rebbe would not be in vain.[16]

Herzl's most devoted supporter in Galicia was probably Adolf Stand.[17] In a letter to Herzl dated September 17, 1896, Stand commented that despite a decade of Zionist activity in Galicia, the movement had made little progress. The problem, he wrote, was the lack of a leader to unite the disparate forces. Herzl's conversion to Zionism, Stand was certain, would finally change that. Herzl replied that he wanted to organize all Zionists under the umbrella of the Zion federation in Vienna, and Stand promised to work toward integrating Galician Zionists into Zion.[18]

The Galician infatuation with Herzl extended beyond letters of support. The entire orientation of Galician Zionism was transformed by the publication of *Der Judenstaat*. This is plainly evident in the lead editorials of the Galician Zionists' annual Yiddish-language *Folkskalender*, first published in 1895. In that year, the lead article by Mordechai Ehrenpreis ("What We Want") explained to readers that while Zionism did call for the eventual establishment of a Jewish home in Palestine, Galician Zionists were primarily concerned with improving the spiritual, material, and political life of Jews in Galicia.[19] In 1896, just one year later, the journal's orientation had changed dramatically. Adolf Korkis wrote in that calendar's lead article ("Zionism: What It Is and What It Wants") that the only solution to the Jewish problem in Europe was Palestine. Korkis's article, which at fifteen pages was nearly four times the length of Ehrenpreis's, makes absolutely no reference to any Diaspora-agenda or to Galicia's "double program."[20]

[15] Shanes, "Ahron Marcus," 133–6 ff. Herzl later abandoned both Marcus and his project to recruit Friedman, leading Marcus to withdraw from the ZO and ultimately to support the establishment of the Orthodox party Agudath Israel. Shanes, "Ahron Marcus," 140–5.

[16] On Friedman, see later in the chapter. A copy of the letter and its history appear in Y. Rapaport, "The Letter from Theodor Herzl to the Rebbe of Czortkow" (Hebrew), *Zion* 4 (1939): 351–2.

[17] Gelber, op. cit., 302–4 ff.

[18] Gelber, op. cit., 304, 308.

[19] Mordechai Ehrenpreis, "What We Want" (Yiddish), *Jüdischer Volkskalender* (Lemberg, 1895), 1–4.

[20] Adolf Korkis, "Zionism: What It Is and What It Wants" (Yiddish) *Jüdischer Volkskalender* (Lemberg, 1896), 1–15. In the last paragraph, Korkis does mention Ahad Ha'am and the program of cultural Zionists, but he dismisses it as wrong-headed.

Not all Zionists flocked to Herzl, to be sure. Among Herzl's most important opponents in Galicia was Jacob Samuel Fuchs, editor of the important Hebrew paper *Hamagid*, then based in Cracow. Fuchs had initially joined the rush of Herzl enthusiasts, requesting permission from Herzl to translate *Der Judenstaat* into Hebrew. When Herzl ultimately gave the rights to David Berkowitz instead, Fuchs and his paper turned on Herzl and remained a bitter opponent of the Zionist leader.[21] While Taubes hoped that Herzl's prestige would help Zionists to reach traditional Jews, Fuchs argued instead that Herzl, a highly acculturated "German" Jew, would merely alienate them. On the eve of the Galician Zionists' fourth provincial conference in October 1896, Fuchs warned the delegates against accepting Herzl's leadership over their movement, arguing that he was an outsider with no connection to the province. The conference, still in the midst of deep enchantment, ignored Fuchs and openly embraced Herzl. Adolf Stand, Herzl's point man in Galicia, was elected chairman of the provincial board.[22]

At the same time, however, the conference did support Fuchs on a more important issue. Anticipating the dispute about to erupt between "practical" and "political" Zionists, between those who sought the immediate colonization of Palestine and those like Herzl who insisted on first securing international recognition of a Jewish state, Fuchs contended that only direct colonization work would succeed in attracting traditional Jews to the Zionist cause. Herzl's vision of directing all resources toward laying the political foundation for a Jewish state, he argued, was simply inappropriate for Galicia, because only pure settlement activity would inspire the masses without offending their religious sensibilities.[23] This argument proved to be far more persuasive to Galician Zionists at their 1896 conference, where delegates discussed the need to capitalize on popular sentiment for the founding of a Galician colony in Palestine. To this end, they agreed to found a Galician colonization organization, headed by the Tarnow association Ahavath Zion.[24] Reconstituted in late December 1896, the organization numbered over 600 members by the time of its first general meeting in May 1897.[25]

[21] For a detailed account of Fuch's dispute with Herzl, see Gelber, op. cit., 292–6ff.

[22] Gelber, op. cit., 296.

[23] Gelber, op. cit., 300.

[24] Adolf Gaisbauer, *Davidstern und Doppeladler* (Vienna, 1988), 195. Ahavath Zion was originally founded by Abraham Salz in 1891. See earlier and Chapter 2.

[25] *Die Welt*, June 4, 1897, 9–10. See the group's official statutes, *Statuten des Vereines für Colonisation Palästinas "Ahawath Zion" in Tarnow*, approved by the government on June 28, 1899.

Obviously, the establishment of a Galician colonization federation constituted another step toward full Galician autonomy from Vienna. Ahavath Zion had been merely a local branch of the Viennese Zion colonization federation. The break from Zion came at the tail end of many years of conflict, based on what the Galician Zionists perceived as Viennese insensitivity toward Jewish conditions in Galicia.[26] Nevertheless, Ahavath Zion still declared itself to be in full cooperation with the Viennese Zion federation (soon to be transformed into the core of Herzl's Zionist Organization), and it voted to send a delegation to the upcoming Zionist Congress.[27] Moreover, delegates at the constituting meeting agreed not only not to hinder the establishment of new Zion branches in Galicia but actually to aid them, provided that Vienna permitted those branches to direct their funding to Ahavath Zion.[28] (Zion could not agree to divert their funding to a competing organization, and the question of funds would ultimately cause a series of crises between the two groups.)

Indicative of the ambiguous relationship between the new society and Vienna was the activity of its dominant personality, Abraham Salz, the founder of the original Ahavath Zion which formed the basis of the new group. Despite his leadership position in Ahavath Zion, Salz at first enjoyed quite good relations with Herzl. In January 1897, just days after Ahavath Zion broke from Vienna, Salz was invited to the Austrian capital by Herzl to discuss the Jewish situation in Galicia. Salz spoke about the need to raise money for a Yiddish-language newspaper and especially about the need to start a colony. (Stand had voiced the same priorities to Herzl in his letter the previous fall.)[29]

They also discussed the upcoming parliamentary elections, which for the first time would include a fifth curia, open to all adult men. As a result of the reform, Galician Zionists for the first time discussed nominating Jewish nationalist candidates for Parliament. Already in November 1896, Taubes had asked Herzl himself to run in Kolomea. Now, at a meeting with Herzl in February 1897, both Salz and Stand urged Herzl to consider the option. Salz, in fact, recommended to Herzl that he run in three different districts (Kolomea, Tarnopol, and Stanislau), where he felt certain

---

[26] Gelber, op. cit., 340.

[27] *Die Welt*, June 4, 1897, 10. The Congress was moved to Basel at the last moment due to local opposition in Munich. In July, the group elected the following delegation: Salz, Sigmund Bromberg, Ahron Marcus, Julius Hochfeld, and David Tieger. *Die Welt*, August 13, 1897, 6.

[28] Gelber, op. cit., 339.

[29] Abraham Salz, "Cooperation Conflict with Herzl" (Polish) in *Pięćdziesiąt Lat Sjonizmu* (Tarnow, 1934), 51–2.

of victory. In the meantime, Nathan Birnbaum also approached Herzl seeking an endorsement for his election bid in Sereth-Suczawa-Radutz, as did Joseph Bloch for his bid in Kolomea, where he had been pressured to resign two years earlier. Herzl refused either to run himself or to support Birnbaum's or Bloch's candidacies. (Herzl despised Birnbaum, whom he had basically replaced as leader of the Zionist movement, and Bloch had already come out against Zionism.) Herzl did at first support nominating several other Zionist candidates, including Salz, but soon decided that uncertain results risked Zionism's "mystical power" in Galicia. He proposed a scheme to Salz whereby an electoral committee would nominate four Zionist candidates (including Birnbaum), all of whom would decline the nominations. In this way, he wrote, they could save the "prestige of our party" in Galicia. Indeed, none of them ultimately ran for election.[30] Only Bloch – undeterred by Herzl's rebuff – actually competed. Bloch ran in Brody against his old nemesis Emil Byk who finally managed to defeat him in a landslide, 1,021 to 161 votes, allegedly because the county prefect (Bezirkshauptmann) did not admit Bloch's supporters to the ballot boxes.[31]

In 1900, just before the next elections, Stand again suggested that Herzl compete, this time in Kolomea. Herzl again refused.[32] In fact, he actually opposed the only Jewish nationalist who did run, Saul Landau, in favor of Byk, a leading opponent of the Zionist movement, due to a personal conflict with Landau, who ran on a strictly Diaspora nationalist platform.[33] Although he won few votes (22 against Byk's 936), at least one Jewish nationalist group took heart. The *Jüdisches Volksblatt*, organ of the Jüdische Volksverein, noted that "for the first time since the constitutional era, a struggle was waged between bearers of two important streams in Judaism: the assimilationist and the Jewish-national idea." The author described Landau as the first candidate to run for Parliament

---

[30] Herzl had recommended that Salz run in Kolomea and Leon Kellner in Drohobycz, but when Kellner proved unable to run, he proposed the alternate scheme to save face. Salz described the exchange, and reprinted Herzl's letters about the matter, in a *festschrift* celebrating fifty years of Zionism in Tarnow. A. Salz, "Cooperation and Conflict with Herzl" (Polish), 53–5. Herzl described his opposition to Birnbaum in his diary on March 10, 1897, cited in Jess Olson, "A Tale of Two Photographs," in Kalman Weiser and Joshua Fogel, eds., *Czernowitz at 100* (Lanham, 2010), 27.

[31] S. R. Landau, *Sturm und Drang in Zionismus* (Vienna, 1937), 188.

[32] Dov Noy and Mark Schutzman, eds., *Sefer zikaron li-kehilat Kolomeyah veha-sevivah* (Tel-Aviv, 1972), 37. The election was held in January 1901.

[33] Ignacy Daszyński opposed him as well, describing Landau – a champion of Jewish workers – as a leader of the Jewish bourgeoisie. S. R. Landau, op. cit., 27, 200.

in Brody-Zloczow exclusively as a representative of the Jewish people, ignoring Bloch's 1897 attempt to unseat Byk.[34]

Although they did not nominate any candidates, the added curia did give Galician polemicists an opportunity to educate Jews about the electoral system and the importance of political activism. Taubes, whose Yiddish-language paper *Ha'am-Dos Folk* was still in print at the time of the election, was one of the few to realize the importance of the opportunity. Taubes printed numerous articles, such as the following, explaining the significance of the electoral reform and challenging Jews to take advantage of the moment.

As long as the "simple" Jew will not grasp, and will not at all want to grasp, that an election is not God forbid a "decree" which the "kingdom" has decreed against "Jews" that they must once in several years go to the magistrate and give a piece of paper, as long as the "intellectual" Jew will want again to exploit the decree for his private interests, to ingratiate himself with the Germans in order to become an important person, a mover, and the like, as long as these same conditions continue to rule among us Jews and we continue to exercise the voting right under the same circumstances as until now, it makes absolutely no difference for us to have four curias or five.[35]

Taubes called for the establishment of a Jewish electoral committee in order to nominate Jewish candidates in all districts with Jewish majorities, and even suggested the formation of a Jewish Club in the Austrian Parliament, years before any other Jewish nationalist dared to campaign for this. To his Orthodox and Liberal opponents who argued that a small club of just a few Jews could not accomplish anything, or rather to traditional Jews influenced by those opponents, Taubes explained the power of small parties in a parliamentary system ruled by coalition governments.[36] Although neither of these goals would be achieved in 1897, the insertion of these ideas into Jewish political discourse would bear fruit ten years later, when Parliament passed electoral reform granting universal manhood suffrage.

Despite Ahavath Zion's break, cooperation between Galician Zionists and Herzl increased dramatically in the months leading up to the First Zionist Congress, scheduled for August 1897. In February, Herzl informed Stand confidentially that he would serve on the Congress's organizing

[34] *Jüdisches Volksblatt*, December 14, 1900.

[35] *Ha'am-Dos Folk*, February 28, 1897.

[36] Taubes first called for the formation of a Jewish Club in a two-part series about the nature of the Austrian Parliament in early 1896. *Ha'am-Dos Folk*, February 18, 1896. He reiterated the idea during the 1897 elections. *Ha'am-Dos Folk*, March 1, 1897.

committee as the East Galician representative, while Salz would serve as the representative from West Galicia.[37] Stand was especially interested in milking popular excitement for the Congress as a means of reaching out to traditional Jews. To this end, he sent David Malz on a speaking tour visiting nearly every community in Galicia to rally support for the Congress. He also entered into negotiations with various Orthodox leaders to support and even attend the Congress.[38]

Twenty-three delegates from Galicia attended the First Zionist Congress, where they achieved significant prestige. Salz served as a vice-president of the assembly, and he and Adolf Korkis were elected to the Greater Executive Committee, the group that actually headed the movement. As per Herzl's request, Ahavath Zion presented a petition to the conference with 10,000 signatures from Galician Jews ready to move to Palestine.[39] Herzl, who opposed efforts by practical Zionists to settle Palestine prematurely, before having secured international recognition for their state, did not actually intend to move them. Rather, he wanted to make an impression among world leaders that the Zionist movement was a serious solution to the Jewish problem.

Among the most important results of the First Zionist Congress was the passage of the so-called Basel Resolution, the guiding principle of the Zionist movement to which all subsidiary associations were required to subscribe. The short declaration, which remained the Zionist movement's official statement of purpose for over half a century, read as follows:

Zionism aims at the creation of a home for the Jewish people in Palestine to be secured by public law.

To that end, the Congress envisages the following:

1. The purposeful advancement of the settlement of Palestine with Jewish farmers, artisans, and tradesmen.

2. The organizing and unifying of all Jewry by means of appropriate local and general arrangements subject to the laws of each country.

3. The strengthening of Jewish national feeling and consciousness.

4. Preparatory moves towards obtaining such governmental consent as will be necessary to the achievement of the aims of Zionism.[40]

---

[37] Gelber, op. cit., 309.

[38] Gelber, op. cit., 314.

[39] Abraham Salz, "Herzl und das Basler Programm," in *Theodor Herzl Jahrbuch* (Vienna, 1937), 221–2, and A. Salz, "30 Years of Zionism" (Polish) in *Pięćdziesiąt Lat Sjonizmu* (Tarnow, 1934), 14.

[40] *Stenographisches Protokoll der Verhandlungen des I Zionisten-Kongresses in Basel* (Vienna, 1897).

It is difficult to overestimate the importance of the Zionist Congress in the history of the Zionist movement. As Michael Berkowitz has discussed at length, the Congresses provided

the single most powerful force in transmitting Zionist goals and ideals to the party faithful and the broader Jewish audience. Their inspirational impact was not only to direct participants; it also enabled delegates and spectators to represent the movement enthusiastically in their communities as living extensions of Zionist culture.[41]

Berkowitz's conclusion is probably as true for Galicia as it was for Vienna or Germany, but here it was a mixed blessing. On the one hand, Galician Zionists certainly recognized the value of the Congress as a tool for dramatically increasing their recruitment. Immediately upon their return from Basel, Salz, Stand, and Malz began a speaking tour throughout the province, which succeeded in attracting many traditional Jews into the Zionist camp.[42] Naturally, the secular tone of the Congress was obscured while statements by Herzl and others that out of context suggested a religious sensibility were stressed.[43]

At the same time, however, Galician Zionists also recognized that there was a definite mismatch between the Basel program and their own 1893 platform, which focused much more on work in the Diaspora than on the securing of a national home in Palestine. Viennese Zionists themselves had to resolve a number of differences between their own program and Basel, which they did shortly after the conclusion of the Congress.[44] Galician Zionists had a more difficult time than Zion bridging the gap between their program and Basel. While Zion was essentially being converted into the core of Herzl's Zionist Organization (ZO), Galician Zionists were being asked once again to relinquish their autonomy to Vienna. Moreover, the Basel Resolution's deliberate vagueness regarding Jewish nationalist work in the Diaspora had to be reconciled with Galician Zionists' Diaspora-oriented outlook. At the other extreme, the growing importance of practical colonization efforts, which many Galician Zionists viewed as vital propaganda for recruiting traditional Jews to the Zionist movement, contradicted Herzl's insistence on securing an international charter for a state before beginning any settlement activity.

---

[41] Michael Berkowitz, *Zionist Culture and West European Jewry before the First World War* (Cambridge, 1993), 8.
[42] Gelber, op. cit., 318.
[43] Salmon, op. cit., 289–91.
[44] Gelber, op. cit., 318.

For all of these reasons, reconciling their differences with the Basel program constituted the principal function of the sixty delegates at Galicia's fifth provincial Zionist conference held on December 26–27, 1897.[45] Heinrich Gabel's opening report on the status of the Zionist movement in Galicia emphasized that since the third and fourth conferences, the idea of settling the land of Israel had become increasingly central to Galician Zionists, particularly among traditional Jews. This was clearly evident in the breakdown of Zionist groups in the province. While Zion in Lemberg could boast nineteen branches, and the Vienna-based Zion federation now had just eight, the Tarnow-based colonization society Ahavath Zion had grown to eighty-five branches in less than one year. (There were in addition roughly half a dozen independent Zionist societies spread throughout the province.)[46]

The central issue of the conference was the extent to which Galician Zionists would retain their autonomy under the auspices of Herzl's new Zionist Organization. This was a particularly crucial question in light of the growing importance of "practical colonization" efforts in recruiting new Zionists, efforts that Herzl of course opposed. What was to be the relationship between Ahavath Zion and the Greater Executive Committee in Vienna? Osker Kokesh (1855–1905), originally from Brody but now representing that committee, expressed deep concern that a failed Galician colony would set back the world Zionist movement. Salz, however, despite his own position on the Greater Executive Committee, stated bluntly that the group did not intend to stop its efforts toward founding a Galician colony. Salz reiterated his group's general support for the Basel Resolution but insisted that the activity of Ahavath Zion would not at all undermine it. Most conference delegates agreed. The final resolution (accepted by Kokesh as well) affirmed that the Galician Zionists stood by the Basel Resolution and acknowledged the position of the Viennese Executive Committee as the highest authority in all Zionist affairs, yet it simultaneously declared practical colonization activity to be "excellent agitation material" and therefore "temporarily indispensable."[47]

The stakes of this disagreement were not merely programmatic. The question of Galician autonomy, a leitmotif in Galician-Viennese relations since the 1880s, now took on an added importance in regard to the

[45] On the conference, see *Die Welt*, December 24, 1897, 13; December 31, 1897, 10; January 21, 1898, 10, and *Ha-Melitz*, January 11, 1898, 2–3.

[46] Gelber, *op. cit.*, 324–5.

[47] *Die Welt*, December 31, 1897, 10.

allocation of the shekel, the annual dues collected by all Zionist associations. The Greater Executive Committee in Vienna naturally demanded that all funds be sent to them, while local Zionists (above all Salz) insisted that at least some of the money stay in the province for local agitation. (Salz wanted at least half of all funds to remain in Galicia for such activities.) Ultimately, a divided vote secured one quarter of all funds for Galician use, although the Viennese Executive Committee continued to oppose the decision.[48]

The conference also decided that the Lemberg Zion society would constitute the new provincial Zionist body and converted all independent Zionist groups, as well as branches of the Viennese Zion federation, into branches of Lemberg Zion for the purpose of "spreading the idea of the colonization of Palestine with Jews on a legal basis." This formulation obviously reflected the Basel program, which they here clearly accepted despite their constituting themselves as an organization separate from the ZO. Finally, the conference constituted a twenty-one-member provincial committee (*Landes-comite*), which would from then on direct all Zionist activity in the province and act as liaison with the leadership in Vienna.[49]

By the end of 1897, Galician Zionism was thus divided between three organizations with overlapping mandates and membership: Ahavath Zion, the autonomous provincial organization based in Lemberg, and the Zionist Organization based in Vienna, which opened branches in Stanislau and Kolomea. Nominally, all Galician Zionists still recognized the authority of the ZO. Nevertheless, serious tensions had already emerged between many Galician Zionists and Vienna. For example, the Lemberg-based provincial organization successfully resisted Viennese opposition to their retention of part of the shekel.

More dramatically, Ahavath Zion ignored Zion as well as a clear directive from Herzl himself when Salz negotiated with Baron Rothschild to purchase land for a Galician colony in Palestine. Zion demanded that all funding be directed toward existing settlements only, but Salz argued that the Basel program never forbade the establishment of new settlements. More fundamentally, Salz insisted that he had every right to buy the land according to the agreed statutes of Ahavath Zion. When Zion refused to help fund the deal, Salz came up with the money from elsewhere and succeeded in founding the settlement Machanayim.[50]

[48] *Die Welt*, December 31, 1897, 10; Gelber, op. cit., 328–31.
[49] *Die Welt*, January 21, 1898, 10.
[50] On the foundation and development of the settlement, see Shimshon Stein, *Machanayim* (Jerusalem, 1978).

The rift with Herzl and the ZO over Machanayim only worsened during the ensuing months. At Ahavath Zion's 1899 general meeting, held April 25 and 26, delegates changed the group's statutes to include the right to open branches throughout Austria. When one delegate pointed out the obvious, that this would create competition with other Zionist organizations, Salz insisted that the committee that composed the new statute had no such ulterior motive and merely wanted to expand the organization's support base. At the same time, the conference also recognized the importance of a unified Galician organization and directed all of its branches to facilitate this by sending delegates to the upcoming Galician provincial conference.[51]

Pressure against Ahavath Zion and Salz (now president) began to mount. Many leading Zionists, particularly Max Nordau, accused Salz of betraying the Zionist movement. As a result, *Die Welt* published an editorial questioning Salz's and Ahavath Zion's commitment to the Basel program. To these claims Salz replied that both the First and Second Zionist Congresses explicitly called for the colonization of Palestine, and he argued that the editors' question ought to have been directed at those who had failed to take up such activities, an obvious reference to his Viennese critics.[52] Salz's increasingly hostile stand toward the Viennese leadership, capped by an article he wrote for the *Österreichische Wochenschrift* in which he openly attacked political Zionism, sparked an argument on the pages of *Die Welt* between Salz and his friend (and vice-president), Julius Hochfeld, over whether or not Salz had the backing of Ahavath Zion's governing board in attacking Herzl and the ZO leadership so virulently.[53] Hochfeld and others on the board, including Taubes, wrote in *Die Welt* that they wanted a more conciliatory approach toward Herzl and the ZO. Nevertheless, all of their names appeared the next month on a double-page advertisement in a Yiddish paper in Cracow calling for donations toward their new colony that would settle starving workers from Boryslaw.[54]

Despite the impressive financial and organizational success of Ahavath Zion in 1898 and 1899, the group's strength began to crumble in the months following its April 1899 conference. On the one hand, increasing numbers of subsidiary associations defected to the Galician branch of the ZO.[55] At the General Conference of Galician Zionists, held on July 19

[51] *Die Welt*, May 5, 1899, 12.
[52] *Die Welt*, May 5, 1899, 13.
[53] *Die Welt*, July 14, 1899, 9; July 28, 1899, 9–10; April 4, 1899, 9–10.
[54] *Jüdische Volksstimme*, May 25, 1899.
[55] Gaisbauer, *op. cit.*, 201.

and 20, 1899, the vast majority of the 100 delegates present expressed their full allegiance to Herzl and the ZO, and moved to organize themselves in line with the doctrine of political Zionism.[56] At the same time, the group's colony Machanayim suffered from financial collapse and had to be transferred to the network of settlements controlled directly by Rothschild. By 1901, Ahavath Zion had once again become a local branch of the Galician Zionist organization.[57] Salz largely withdrew from any leadership role in the Zionist movement at this time, not to return until after Herzl's death in 1904.[58]

The defeat of Ahavath Zion left essentially two competing organizations in Galicia: the Lemberg-based provincial organization and the Galician representation of the ZO. This situation continued until the Third Zionist Congress (August 1899) finally settled the question of organization. The Congress directed Zionists to establish a single organization for each country (*Landesorganization*), which in turn represented its constituents through the mediation of local districts. In Austria, the Viennese Zion federation took the lead in establishing an Austrian Zionist Organization by calling for an all-Austrian Zionist conference to be held in Olmütz on March 24–25, 1901. The conference platform affirmed that Austrian Zionists stood in full agreement with the Basel Program, declaring the acquisition of a national home in Palestine to be its ultimate goal. Regarding *Gegenwartsarbeit*, Diaspora work, the

[56] *Die Welt*, July 28, 1899, 11.

[57] Gelber, op. cit., 377. For an "obituary" of the group, which focuses on its accomplishments in nationalizing traditional Jews rather than the colony itself, see R. Superman, "On the Grave of a Galician Society" (Hebrew), *Hamagid*, April 18, 1901, 5, and April 25, 1901, 4–6. "And you extreme opponents of Ahavath Zion in Tarnow, do not rejoice in its downfall but rather weep! Do not see in this a victory for 'political' Zionism but rather the fall of Zionism in general among Galician Jews. Do not rejoice that you found a grave for this society, which accomplished in four years more than other societies and foundations that have been in existence for decades. Weep, weep at its departure, for with it is lost a great part of the hope of the development of the Zionist and national idea among our brothers in Galicia!"

[58] He remained informally active, however, and in 1905 was elected head of a committee charged with uniting the many different Zionist organizations in Tarnow, including Poalei Zion. *Hamicpe*, February 24, 1905, 5. An interview with Salz, in which he explains his withdrawal from the Zionist Organization as well as the reasons for his return after Herzl's passing, appears in *Hamicpe*, April 7, 1905, 3–4. Essentially, he argues that practical and political Zionism needed to work together, which they were unable to do as long as Herzl still lived. A far more cynical announcement of Salz's return appears in *Zion*, No. 1, 1905, 4 (*Beilage* to *Die Welt*, No. 11). Here, the West Galician District reported in March 1905 that Salz again "declared himself a convinced supporter of the Basel Program," but suggests Salz had swallowed his pride and caved into the demands of his former opponents.

platform did outline various programs for the economic, spiritual, and physical advancement of the Jews, but (to the chagrin of many Galician delegates) it stopped short of advocating any domestic political activity (*Landespolitik*). Delegates established seven districts for Austria, including two for Galicia (West Galicia, with its seat in Cracow, and East Galicia, with its seat in Lemberg).[59]

On June 16–17, 1901, 112 Zionist delegates from across Galicia met in Lemberg to reorganize their party as an integral part of the new Austrian Zionist organization, and to voice their reaction to the decisions reached at Olmütz. Indicative of the new balance of power, the conference was convened not by the Galician provincial organization, but by the newly constituted Austrian organization, which was exercising its authority to organize provincial districts. Although many Galicians expressed frustration that *Gegenwartsarbeit* did not receive more prominence in the Olmütz Program (Mordechai Braude spoke at length about the need for Landespolitik in Galicia), they did ultimately accept its authority. All Galician Zionist associations were directed to join the Austrian Zionist Organization. The conference established seven Galician sub-districts (*Kreise*), which enjoyed autonomy regarding economic and cultural activities, subject to the approval of the district committee.[60]

REACHING TRADITIONAL JEWS

While all of these political struggles took place at the organizational level, Zionist activity on the ground began to undergo a critical transformation as well. Galician Zionists had consistently focused their outreach on the so-called assimilationist intelligentsia. Individual figures such as Laibel Taubes and the other Yiddish publicists did attempt to reach traditional Jews not yet committed to the anti-Zionist Orthodox line. The official Zionist organizations, however, deliberately avoided such activity. Reflecting on this period years later, Gershom Bader described the phenomenon in almost pathological terms.

Until after the second Zionist Congress in Basel, the Orthodox [*sic*] circles in Galicia could not be organized. However much one endeavored to win the

---

[59] Gaisbauer, op. cit., 97–103. A third South Galician district, based in Stanislau, was added at the Second Austrian Conference, held in Bielitz on May 18–19, 1902.

[60] *Die Welt*, May 31, 1901, 7; June 7, 1901, 1, 4; June 14, 1901, 4–5; June 21, 1901, 2–6; June 28, 1901, 6.

Orthodox circles for the Zionist movement, it helped very little. One could then find individual Orthodox Zionists in almost every Galician city, but one struggled fruitlessly to bring together these people and organize them as a group. It's hard to know today whose fault it was that up until that time we consistently concentrated our entire agitation on winning the assimilationists and the student youth. These efforts of ours then went so far that on account of them we ignored other Jewish groups, middle class [*balabatishe*] and proletariat, who wanted to join us, when we thought for a moment that we had a chance to win over some new assimilationist "big shot."[61]

As Bader indicates, the situation began to change at the end of the century. Although Zionist efforts generally remained focused on students and other members of the secular intelligentsia, growing signs of outreach beyond this elite began to emerge during this period. On the one hand, Zionist lectures, rallies, and periodic celebrations such as the Maccabee festivals – the events that constituted the backbone of Zionist activity – continued largely to service the intelligentsia throughout the Herzlian period. Zionist speakers generally conducted such events in Polish and German, for example, and reports suggested that attendees generally came from various segments of the secular intelligentsia.

Nevertheless, beginning in the late 1890s, signs of outreach beyond this limited group do begin to emerge. For example, the Jewish National Party made two short-lived attempts to publish a Yiddish-language organ, *Der Carmel-Der Wecker* in 1893 and the *Jüdisches Wochenblatt* in 1895.[62] Also in 1895, Galician Zionists launched their first Yiddish-language yearbook, an annual journal that continued to appear until the First World War. Edited by Bader, the *Yidisher Folkskalender* included not only polemical articles, but also cultural material from contemporary Yiddish literature and poetry, as well as many pages of practical information such as postal rates, addresses of Jewish doctors and lawyers by city, and a list of all Galician communities' Jewish populations and elected community leaders. Like the Yiddish papers discussed in Chapter 3, these journals affected Yiddish readers both directly through their polemical

[61] See Gershom Bader's biography of Eliezer Meir Lipshitz in his unpublished manuscript of "Galician Jewish Celebrities," YIVO Institute for Jewish Research.

[62] The *Wochenblatt* often described itself as "the" organ of Galician Zionism, although as noted this honor belonged to *Przyszłość*. The paper reprinted many times the party's resolution from its February 1895 conference obligating all Zionist groups to designate a correspondent to the *Wochenblatt* and to donate two gulden monthly to its maintenance. The resolution was passed at the end of the meeting, and the motion by one delegate to have the matter debated earlier in the evening was resoundingly defeated, suggesting that the paper may not have been as important to Zionist leadership as its editors had hoped. *Jüdisches Wochenblatt*, March 7, 1895, 1, 3.

articles and indirectly by contributing to Galician Jewry's sense of constituting a single, national community.

In 1894, Galician Zionists also established the so-called Political
Association (Politischen Verein) to "improve the economic and cultural
position of our brothers in Galicia." Fearing its organizational weakness,
the group did not see itself as a party designed to nominate candidates,
nor did they intend even to advise traditional Jews for whom to vote,
"because he [the simple Jew] does not at all know how the elections even
affect him." Rather, they viewed the association as a "political school"
designed to teach the public the nature and significance of politics.[63] Even
this was a significant achievement. Moreover, the group rejected Abraham
Salz's motion at its constituting meeting that only Zionists be permitted
to serve on its board in favor of Gershon Zipper's counterproposal, that
non-Zionists be welcomed as long as they fully supported the group's
statutes.[64] Zionists thus established as early as 1895 a Jewish nationalist
association designed to reach out to traditional Jews without demanding
Zionist allegiance, even of its board members.[65]

Around this time, Zionist activists also began to hold events in synagogues rather than in their own meeting halls or in municipal buildings,
and in Yiddish rather than German or Polish. On June 16, 1897, for
example, David Tieger spoke in Yiddish in one of Czortkow's synagogues.
He was scheduled to speak also in the town's large "Israelite Synagogue"
(the modern synagogue of the Liberal elite), but the rabbi refused to
allow it, and so he held his second lecture in the small synagogue of the
local butchers instead.[66] In September, another Zionist speaker addressed
700 Jews in Horodenka's main synagogue, citing passages from the Bible
and Talmud to prove Zionism's validity as a solution to Jewish suffering. Following a commotion during which organizers forcibly removed
a group of Social Democrats who had attempted to disturb the meeting, the speaker led the assembly to resolve to purchase their esrogs only

---

[63] Editorial response to Adolf Stand, "Review of the Year 5655," 93. See the group's program in *Przyszłość*, May 2, 1895, 57, reprinted in Gelber, op. cit., 211–12.

[64] *Jüdisches Wochenblatt*, March 7, 1895, 2. The meeting was held on February 28, 1895.
For a list of its first board members, see *Jüdisches Wochenblatt*, March 7, 1895, 5. Zipper
was elected Polish-language secretary.

[65] Of course, they certainly hoped and assumed that the newly politicized Jews would ultimately become Zionists. Explaining that the basis of the new association, self-help, itself
constituted the heart of Zionism, the *Wochenblatt* wrote a fortnight after its founding
that the group's very openness to non-Zionists "is itself a little piece of Zionism, Zionism
in the future." *Jüdisches Wochenblatt*, March 14, 1895, 2.

[66] *Die Welt*, July 16, 1897, 14.

from Palestine.[67] And in October, a rally featuring Laibel Taubes, among others, attracted some 2,000 participants at a synagogue in Bolechov. The event sparked the formation of local committees to establish a variety of Zionist organizations, including a women's Bnos Zion Verein (Daughters of Zion Association).[68]

Scores of other examples appear throughout the Herzlian period, culminating in dozens of Herzl memorials held in synagogues throughout the province following the Zionist leader's death in July 1904, as well as the following year on the first anniversary of his passing.[69] Correspondents described auditoriums overflowing into courtyards and streets and attracting the participation of broad segments of the Jewish community, well beyond the local Zionist population. Some specifically mention the heavy participation of Hasidim or other traditional elements, such as a correspondent from Zbarow who estimated that over one thousand men and women attended his local memorial.[70] In Zlotchov, the Zionist correspondent described a "wonder" in his community when the once hostile chief rabbi joined in the mourning.

The chief rabbi here, the famous genius Rabbi Feivel Rohatyn, who never had one word with Zionism, eulogized Herzl in the main synagogue in front of a huge audience drawn from all parties. The mourning of the Zionists transformed itself here into the mourning of all Israel. The sexton instructed [the community] in the name of the rabbi to close the stores during the eulogy – I could not believe my eyes.[71]

Services typically incorporated traditional mourning liturgy and customs, such as the *Kaddish* and *El Malei Rachamim* (Oh God of Mercy) prayers. In Stryj, participants vowed even to abide by the mourning rites of *shiva* and *shloshim*, the seven- and thirty-day periods of restrictions traditionally observed only for one's immediate family. Black flags hung on so many houses that the Polish papers questioned why this "Polish city" was mourning for a "Jewish king."[72] These events seemed to have affected many of their listeners very powerfully. Herzl's funeral service in

---

[67] *Die Welt*, September 24, 1897, 14.
[68] *Die Welt*, October 22, 1897, 9. The event was held on October 13.
[69] See, among others, *Die Welt*, August 11, 1905, 11.
[70] *Hamicpe*, July 28, 1904, 3. This and the previous week's issue include descriptions of memorials in over two dozen other cities.
[71] Ibid., 3. The rabbi continued to speak on Zionism as well, which he described as "pure from defilement [*shmutz*]," and declared it forbidden to "sit on one's hands and wait for miracles."
[72] *Hamicpe*, July 21, 1904, 4.

Gliniany (Gline), for example, was recalled by one participant as being one of the largest in the shtetl's history. The speakers spoke with such sincerity, he wrote, that they moved the entire audience to tears, although local Hasidim later denounced one of the speakers for comparing Herzl's death to that of Moses.[73] To be sure, not all Zionist groups enjoyed such glowing success. A long correspondence from Przemysl, for example, bemoaned the poor attendance at their memorial, which he felt reflected the almost total absence of Zionist activity in the city.[74] Such reports were certainly the exception, however, and were far outnumbered by reports to the contrary. Even taking into consideration the correspondents' tendency to exaggerate attendance, these events indicate a growing trend of outreach toward traditional Jews.

Not only did Zionists succeed in penetrating into traditional synagogues, but the timing and content of their lectures reflected their growing concern with attracting traditional Jews as well. On September 26, 1903, for example, the president of the Zion association in Zaleszezyki (Eliyahu Glaser) delivered the most important and well-attended sermon of the year, that of the Sabbath preceding Yom Kippur, at the large house of study (*Bes Medresh*) in town.[75] Glaser's twenty-three-page lecture (later published in Judeo-German and sold cheaply by the group) drew heavily on rabbinic texts to prove that the purpose of repentance, or *teshuva* (literally "return"), was ultimately to shorten the length of the exile and achieve a national return to a Jewish state. This had to be actively pursued, he insisted; the Hasidim who remained politically aloof were not acting in accordance with Torah. What the Zionists want, he concluded, is that Jews should have in their own land, "a city hall with a *mezuzah*, a courthouse with a *mezuzah*, a tax office with a *mezuzah*, a post office with a *mezuzah*."[76] Thus Glaser not only managed to portray Zionism as a movement primarily concerned with the dictates of the Torah, but he did so in a forum and with proof texts that automatically invested his argument with religious significance.

Zionists also took advantage of synagogues for fund-raising purposes, an effort that like Glaser's sermon endowed this basic organizational

---

[73] Henoch Halpern, *Megiles Gline* (New York, 1950), 147.

[74] *Hamicpe*, July 28, 1904, 4.

[75] Known as Shabbes Shuva, the Sabbath of repentance (literally "return"), this was traditionally one of two Sabbaths on which a town rabbi would be expected to deliver a sermon. Its purpose is to inspire feelings of penitence by Jews in preparation for the upcoming Day of Atonement.

[76] Eliyahu Glaser, *Rede* (Cracow, 1903), 22.

necessity with religious significance. The Stanislau branch of Zion, for example, reported in 1896 having raised a considerable portion of its annual earnings from Erev Yom Kippur collection plates placed in almost two dozen synagogues, study houses and other minyans on the eve of this most important Jewish holiday. These plates are traditionally placed in synagogues to enable Jews a final opportunity to sweeten God's judgment against them before His verdict is sealed on Yom Kippur itself. Among Hasidim the practice is especially pronounced. Zion's addition of their own plates to the tables not only raised funds toward their project to establish a Galician-Jewish colony in the land of Israel. It also spread awareness of this project throughout the local Jewish community in a manner that sanctified it as *tzedaka*, a cause to which one's contribution fulfilled the religious obligation of giving charity.[77] Zionists likewise designed the blue-and-white Jewish National Fund charity boxes to mimic the traditional box of "Rabbi Meier Baal Haness." Shlomo Blond recalled his mother in Tysmienica, for example, dutifully putting money in both boxes on special occasions, especially Friday night at candle lighting time. In this way, he wrote, the "idea of Zion" grew widespread in Tysmienica, "especially in the homes in which a traditional spirit dominated."[78]

While activists did not succeed in founding very many specifically Orthodox Zionist associations,[79] Ahavath Zion, by far the largest Zionist organization in Galicia before 1900, had been specifically established for the purpose of disseminating the Jewish national idea to the religious masses. In 1895, the group published a Hebrew- and Yiddish-language brochure, *Ahavath Zion*, which printed approbations by leading Galician rabbis (including the late Simon Sofer) on behalf of efforts to settle the

---

[77] *Ha'am-Dos Folk*, November 15, 1896. The correspondent, who listed the amount raised from each minyan by name, also noted his group's resolution to distribute collection boxes to all members, "so that they should by every possible opportunity gather [money] for this purpose." A correspondent from Przemysl in 1904 wrote that a new *academic* Zionist fraternity in his city likewise placed the plates in all of their local synagogues, aside from the main one, which prevented them from doing so by force. *Hamicpe*, September 23, 1904, 5.

[78] Shlomo Blond, *Tismenits: a matseyveh oyf di hurves fun a farnikhteter Yidisher kehila* (Tel-Aviv, 1974), 88.

[79] Several branches of the international Mizrachi organization (est. 1902) were founded in Galicia, as were several Orthodox-Zionist synagogues, but the Zionists' most successful "Orthodox" organization was the Haschachar federation, charged with attracting hasidic youth to the Zionist movement. Over half a dozen Haschachar associations were founded in 1905–6, and the group even managed to put out a short-lived monthly journal in Hebrew. Gaisbauer, op. cit., 225–7.

land of Israel.[80] The group's report of its first regular meeting in May 1897 described its purpose in just these terms, praising itself for bringing together traditional rabbis with progressive Jews.[81] The conference elected Rabbi Feibush Schreier its honorary chairman, and the chief rabbi of Czernowitz, Binyamin Weiss, its president. At the group's constituting meeting the previous December (1896), the delegates accepted a resolution proposed by Schreier that members of any settlement founded by the new society would have to behave according to Jewish law, including observance of any custom that had achieved widespread acceptance.[82]

Nor did the group's leadership ever lose sight of its raison d'être. Salz's defense against Herzl and the others who opposed his colonization efforts turned largely on his argument that only a purely settlement association could succeed in attracting traditional Jews to the Zionist movement. In a letter to Herzl dated October 31, 1897, Salz reminded the Zionist leader that Galician Zionists had always leaned more toward political than practical work. But, he argued, the movement was floundering because of religious opposition to political Zionism. Practical settlement was therefore absolutely necessary in order to recruit the traditional masses. To prove his point, Salz confidently pointed to the spectacular growth of his association in its first months, attracting 4,000 members in eighty branches. The group published the names of hundreds of small contributors in the Hebrew section of its German-Hebrew organ, *Mittheilungen des Vereines "Ahawath Zion,"* and in a long letter penned by a scion of Hasidic aristocracy boasted of the broad support for Zionism among contemporary *zaddikim*.[83] "The quiet and true Zionism of the Hasidic rebbe," argued Salz, "is more important to us than the activity, or more correctly inactivity ... of proper Zionists."[84]

Salz's provocative declaration was not hyperbole. He had a specific rebbe in mind in making this statement, namely, David Moshe Friedman, the rebbe of Czortkow. Friedman, a long-time supporter of efforts to settle Jews in Palestine, was an early member of Ahavath Zion, a fact widely published at that time. Ahavath Zion openly published the conditions of

[80] For a review, see *Jüdisches Wochenblatt*, January 24, 1895, 6. Through such efforts, wrote the reviewer, the group hoped to highlight "the relationship of Orthodoxy to Zionism and the settlement of the land of Israel." The book was similar to Avraham Slutski's *Shivath Zion* (see note 88) but consisted exclusively of Galician rabbis.

[81] *Die Welt*, June 6, 1897, 9–10.

[82] Gelber, op. cit., 337.

[83] *Mittheilungen des Vereines "Ahawath Zion,"* July 21, 1898, 6–9. *Hamagid* printed the organ as a supplement from 1898 to early 1899.

[84] Gelber, op. cit., 356, 358.

Friedman's support, including his appointment of the future settlement's rabbi and *shochet* and supervision over the future settlers to ensure that they lived according to "Torah and Mussar."[85] Friedman's involvement was quite substantial. In fact, it was Friedman's directive that led some members of the group to sever their ties with the ZO the previous December (1897), demanding that the Viennese leaders make good on promises to establish a rabbinic committee.[86] Herzl's attempt to reach Friedman in 1896, by contrast, was thwarted by the rebbe's attendant who refused to deliver Herzl's letter.[87] The group also proudly reported that its decision to send copies of the religious Zionist tract *Shivat Zion* (Return to Zion) to community rabbis throughout the province succeeded in recruiting twenty rabbis to the cause.[88]

Despite the group's success at recruiting numerous rabbis from small and medium-sized communities, it could not stem the rising anti-Zionist tide among most Orthodox leaders.[89] Ahavath Zion assumed, probably correctly, that its recruitment of major Hasidic leaders would bring along many of their traditional followers, but it could not convince anyone else of Friedman's stature to join. In particular, special efforts to win over Yechezkel Halberstam (1813–98), the rebbe of Sieniawa, failed completely.[90] Friedman's support is so noteworthy precisely because it was so rare. Despite the best efforts of Salz and several other Galician Zionists, most Orthodox Jewish leaders continued to oppose the Zionist movement vehemently, particularly among Hasidim, where the opposition was likely to be more widespread. Indeed, Yosef Salmon describes Machsike Hadas as the "most active anti-Zionist element among ultra-Orthodox Jewry in eastern Europe" during the 1890s.[91] As Jewish

[85] *Krakauer Jüdische Zeitung*, February 13, 1898, 5; *Hamagid*, January 6, 1898, 5. See also Salz's memoirs in *Pięćdziesiąt Lat Sjonizmu*.

[86] *Ha-Melitz*, April 29, 1898, 2, cited in Salmon, op. cit., 297.

[87] Rapaport, op. cit., 352 and Y. Austridan, *Sefer Yizkor le-hantsahat kedoshe Kehilat Ts'ortkov* (Haifa, 1967), 66–9. The rebbe's son and successor, Israel Friedman, granted an interview in 1897 in which he expressed his support for Zionism if it could offer the Orthodox certain religious guarantees. Soon afterward his father joined the renegade Ahavath Zion federation. *Die Welt*, December 17, 1897, 13.

[88] Gelber, op. cit., 341. This was a well-known Zionist work that attempted to prove the compatibility of Zionism with traditional Judaism. Essentially, it was a collection of letters of approbation from various rabbis (most without much authority in the rabbinic community) for the settlement idea. For a discussion of this important text, see Yosef Salmon, op. cit., 177–99. See also Salmon's introduction to the recent reprint, "The Book *Shivat* Zion and Its Historical background" (Hebrew), in A. J. Slucki, *Shivat Zion* (Jerusalem, 1998), 7–60.

[89] Salmon, op. cit., 297.

[90] Gelber, op. cit., 345.

[91] Yosef Salmon, op. cit., 258.

nationalists increasingly turned their attention to traditional Jews, and increasingly attracted some of them, tensions between them and their Orthodox opponents only worsened.

Numerous Zionist reports from the province attest to this growing conflict, and served to provoke it. As Peter Judson documented in the Czech-German "borderland" press, these reports were designed to generate and inflame the very passions they assumed to be latent in the population.[92] For example, embedded among the glowing reports of successful Herzl memorials from dozens of larger cities is a lead editorial bemoaning the failure of such memorials in many of the smaller towns of Galicia, where Orthodox and assimilationist opposition to the Zionists combined to prevent the use of the main synagogue for the service. Religious Jews (*Adukim*), this author worried, were growing increasingly anti-Zionist. Most knew nothing about the movement or its dead leader but simply opposed it for its tendency to draw young Jewish men out of the study house, literally and metaphorically, and into the modern world.[93] In at least one case, a Herzl memorial allegedly provoked a violent reaction on the part of Hasidim. In Rzeszow, about a week after Zionists held a Herzl memorial in the main study house, one that reportedly attracted many Jews previously unfamiliar with the Zionist ideology, several Hasidim grabbed a young Zionist who happened to be passing by their study house, dragged him inside and beat him "murderously" shouting, "Kill the Zionist! Skin him!" The boy barely escaped with his life and the looming Zionist retribution was prevented only by the arrival of the police.[94]

This animosity is particularly reflected in Zionist memoirs of this period, whose descriptions of childhood homes nearly all recall the strong Orthodox opposition to the Jewish nationalist movement. M. D. Berl, for example, one of the first Zionists in Sanz, paints a portrait of unbridled hatred and fear of the newly arrived Zionists by the Orthodox establishment, which particularly resented the group's appropriation of Hanukah as a secular national holiday. In Sanz, a city dominated by Hasidim of the local rebbe and absolutely free of Zionist activity until the first years of the twentieth century, the Zionists' first Hanukah festival raised a storm of protest by local Hasidic leaders.[95] "The Zionists desanctified the

[92] Pieter Judson, *Guardians of the Nation* (Cambridge, Mass., 2006), 177–218.

[93] *Hamicpe*, August 5, 1904, 1.

[94] *Hamicpe*, July 29, 1904, 3, and August 12, 1904, 5. The latter correspondent drew no connection between the two events.

[95] "When I settled in Sanz in 1900," recalled M. D. Berl, "I found the city sunken in ignorance, almost without any ray of light, without any cultural institute, without any

Hasmonean holiday," they allegedly declared; "they defiled the Hanukah miracle." Men and women gathered and sang together at their club, complained the Hasidim, but above all they objected to the defilement of the Star of David. The symbol until then had appeared only over the Holy Ark in the synagogue and on phylactery bags, but now it hung brazenly in the window of the Zionist hall facing the market. In response, the community's leaders directed the men to tear the Star of David from their bags, for it had now become the emblem of the Zionists. When one Zionist broke into the study house and carved a Star of David into the rabbi's lectern, the rabbi had it thrown outside, declaring, "This is worse than a crucifix." When the culprit was discovered, he had to flee the city and eventually settled in Germany.[96]

This incident not only speaks to the history of Orthodoxy as a response to modernity but also suggests that the Zionists' well-known tendency to adopt traditional Jewish symbols, a phenomenon with parallels in virtually all modern nationalist movements, was a double-edged sword. "The new nationalism," writes Israel Bartal, "made extensive use of traditional symbols that had been consciously and sometimes unconsciously expropriated from their traditional society, who did not always discern the novelty hiding behind the seemingly familiar words."[97] Clearly, this assessment reflects the situation in Galicia. Nevertheless, many members of Orthodox society did discern the novelty and it fortified their resistance to the new movement.

This violent energy did not always remain a threat in potentia. In Gliniany (Gline), Zionists who had long held festivals on all of the Jewish holidays one year managed to secure permission from the officers of the synagogue to hold a festival in that holy space. When their placards advertised that Mayer Balaban (1877–1942/3)[98] would be playing klezmer between the afternoon and evening services, local Hasidim were outraged and started tearing down the signs as fast as the Zionists could replace

organization. Its only portion was Hasidism. The entire intelligentsia of the city consisted of two or three Jews who didn't wear *shtreimels* on the Sabbath." M. D. Berl, "The Zionist Movement in Sanz" (Hebrew), in R. Mahler, *Sefer Sanz* (Tel-Aviv, 1970), 357.

[96] M. D. Berl, op. cit., 359.

[97] Israel Bartal, "Responses to Modernity: Haskalah, Orthodoxy, and Nationalism in Eastern Europe," in *Zionism and Religion* (Hanover, 1998), 21.

[98] Balaban, then a young teacher at the Baron Hirsch school and the most important local Zionist speaker, later became the most celebrated and influential historian of Polish Jewry in the world. During the interwar period, he occupied chairs in Polish Jewish History and World Jewish History at the Free Warsaw University and the University of Warsaw. Incarcerated by the Nazis in the Warsaw Ghetto, his exact date of death is unknown. See Israel Biderman, *Mayer Balaban: Historian of Polish Jewry* (New York, 1976).

them. The event itself was absolutely packed and at first proceeded with few problems. Balaban's Polish-language lecture was received with wild calls of "bravo" that ended only when a concerned Jew insisted that such behavior was inappropriate in a synagogue. However, shortly thereafter, when Balaban and his partner began playing Hatikva, someone threw a lit lamp right next to him, which quickly ignited a fire in the building. Panic ensued as Jews tried to save their synagogue and for months afterward tension lingered from the incident. Although witnesses clearly identified the perpetrator, neither the Hasidim nor the Zionists pressed for his prosecution for fear of opening up old wounds.[99]

The tensions did not dissipate, however, and in the summer of 1905 Gliniany was the scene of an even more rancorous battle between the young Zionists and the Hasidic establishment. (The element of youth rebellion against an established and older communal leadership was not lost on the memoirist, who cited it as a prime cause of the underlying tensions.) The Zionists intended to establish a modern Jewish school, teaching "Hebrew in Hebrew" as the slogan went, and that summer they secured permission for a Zionist speaker then traveling in Galicia from Russia to speak on the subject in the main synagogue. To thwart this effort, Hasidim arranged for the local rebbe himself to speak in the synagogue during the Sabbath morning services, a rare occurrence to say the least. The rebbe's speech, delivered to an absolutely packed synagogue, blamed Jews lax in their religious observance for the poverty and starvation rampant among local Jews.[100] Although the rebbe did not mention the Zionists by name, the entire auditorium knew whom he meant. When a small group of Zionists and their sympathizers catcalled the rebbe, demanding that he name names without insinuation, a riot broke out. The entire town swarmed to the synagogue until the police and local garrisons arrived and with great effort managed to end the battle.[101]

Asher Korekh, also from Gliniany, equally emphasized the strong opposition to Zionism by his hometown's Hasidic population. He likewise focused on a particular Sabbath battle, when a famous Zionist preacher (Abramson) spoke at the main synagogue. (It's not clear what year this occurred, but the details are sufficiently different that it does not seem

---

[99] Halpern, op. cit., 148.
[100] The accusations allegedly included married women who refused to cover their hair or observe the laws of family purity, young men and women who danced together, and Jews who desecrated the Sabbath.
[101] Halpern, op. cit., 152–6. The event became known as the Farshterten Shabbes, the spoiled Sabbath.

to be an alternate version of the story just related.) Fearing his influence, the local rebbe came to the synagogue with his followers and demanded to speak on the *bima* (the elevated platform on which the Torah is read). When he was denied this right, he called one young man a *shaygetz* (literally, a non-Jewish man, but colloquially a sharp insult), who responded by punching the rebbe in the chest. The Hasidim fled the scene, but the simple Jews of the town, although not followers of the rebbe, turned on the Zionists when they heard about the attack. Here again one sees the distinction between Orthodox anti-Zionists and traditional Jews sympathetic to Zionism but not when construed as anti-clerical or radical. Following the attack, it became dangerous for Zionists to step outside. When Korekh and a friend, "wanting to be heroes," went out later for the late afternoon prayer service, they were surrounded by a mob. A wagon driver told his son to "rip out their guts" and the young men only just managed to escape. The next morning, Zionists found their clubhouse walls smeared with feces.[102]

Meir Gottesman, who grew up in the East Galician oil town of Bolichov, similarly described his community's condemnation of the Zionists as religious heretics.

I remember in my childhood years, when Zionism first emerged and was still in the beginning of its development that in our city among the religious Jews Zionism was [considered] unkosher and forbidden. At that time, among them a Zionist was a sinner of Israel [*poshea Yisroel*], even worse than one who ate pork. They said that one was not allowed to force the end of days. One must do nothing on one's own for *Eretz Yisroel*, but only wait until the Messiah will come.[103]

Gottesman's father strictly forbade him to join the Zionists out of fear that he too would become a heretic. Unfortunately for him, however, the local Zionist club was located across the street from his home. Once, when Meir was playing ball with some friends and he accidentally got close to the Zionist club, his father beat him and warned that the next time he would simply throw him out of the house. His father's concern seems well warranted, for as a teenager, Gottesman managed to sneak into the clubhouse unbeknown to his father and soon thereafter became a shekel-paying Zionist.[104]

---

[102] Asher Korekh, *Bagola uva-moledet* (Jerusalem, 1941), 105–12.
[103] Meir Gottesman, "How Exactly Did I Become a Zionist?" (Yiddish), in Yona and Moshe Hanina Eshel, eds., *Sefer ha-zikaron li-kedoshe Bolihov* (Haifa, 1957), 268. Herzl, he wrote, they would call a "*goy, a treifnik*, etc."
[104] Gottesman, op. cit., 269.

Joachim Schoenfeld, a child of Sniatyn, recalled his town in similar terms. "The Zionist organization in our shtetl," he wrote, "was anemic and dormant due to the opposition of the Chassidim."

They represented the majority and held the upper hand. Herzl's *Der Judenstaat*, for example, was circulated secretly from hand to hand. The Chassidim asserted that the Zionists were following the path of the *maskilim*, and with all the doctors and the *daitschen* (Germanized Jews) at the helm of the organization [they] were paving the way to assimilation and were a threat to Judaism. Zionists in our shtetl had to go underground with their activities. The youth, boys and girls, had to hide the fact that they were interested in Zionism. They couldn't keep any Zionist literature at home, for it was anathema to their Chassidic parents.

In fear of their elders, the young Zionists met in the forest outside of the city, usually on Saturday afternoons.[105]

Schoenfeld credited the flood of Russian refugees between 1903 and 1905 as extremely important in the town's subsequent transformation. Although most of the migrants continued to America, a few stayed behind, particularly the well educated, versed in both traditional and secular knowledge. This mixture of *maskilim*, Zionists, socialists, and other revolutionaries revitalized political life, according to Schoenfeld, and within a short time a Zionist organization was founded. The group soon rented an apartment and founded a library, a staple of nearly every Zionist society.[106]

The influence of Russian émigrés figured prominently in other recollections of young Zionist converts as well. Kalman Mahler, for example, credited one such refugee with his own conversion. As a young Talmudic student in Sanz, a city in 1901 still largely void of any secular Jewish life, Mahler headed a charity to support impoverished yeshiva students. One day a friend brought him and the other members of the group to a Russian refugee, learned in both Talmud and secular subjects, who needed help to emigrate to Palestine. At first they refused out of hand to aid a Zionist. The next day, however, the young émigré sang some Hebrew songs for the local boys. The songs moved them not only to help the young man but also to learn more about Zionism and, after becoming convinced supporters, to purchase shares in the Jewish National Fund. The boys were soon among the first members of the local Zionist association Ezra, at whose library they discovered the *maskilic* writers Shulman, Graetz, and

---

[105] Schoenfeld, *Jewish Life in Galicia under the Austro-Hungarian Empire and in the Reborn Poland 1898–1939* (Hoboken, N.J., 1990), 118.

[106] Schoenfeld, op. cit., 121.

Mapu. "Zionism awoke in us a search for knowledge," wrote Mahler, "to study Hebrew and Yiddish literature, Jewish history and also general knowledge. In Zionism we heard a call to the people to take its destiny in its own hands."[107]

In all of these narratives, the centrality of the Zionist clubhouse itself, particularly its library, stands out. Although other factors such as the influx of Russian refugees clearly played a role, it was at the clubhouse that young traditional Jews became exposed to new ideas and possibilities. The Zionist clubhouse had long been established among young *acculturated* Jews as the preferred social hangout, even among those with no interest in joining the Zionist party. Such was the case of Hirschl Hurvitz, for example, the fictional protagonist of S. Y. Agnon's classic novel, *A Simple Story*, set in fin-de-siècle Buczacz.

Like other boys from well-to-do homes who had studied to be rabbis and stopped, Hirschl joined the Society for Zion. The society owned a large room to which its members came to read newspapers and journals, or else to play chess on a board that stood on a table in a corner. Not all the newspapers and journals dealt with Zionism, nor was everyone who read them a Zionist. There were some who came to the clubhouse simply to read, just as there were others who came to socialize, for one way or another it was never a dull place.[108]

A contemporary Zionist report from Kolomea describes Zionist motives in the province in almost exactly the same terms, albeit in a derisive tone lacking Agnon's brilliant subtlety. Most so-called Zionists were Zionist in name only, he wrote, and joined the groups "for some small position, to read newspapers cheaply, for a game of chess, to sit around lazily and play stupid games, or simply for belching and yawning, but not to support the return to Zion or to spread the Zionist idea among the people."[109]

This social aspect of the Zionist clubhouse, coupled with the availability of abundant reading material, represented a critical mode of outreach to traditional Jews once the barrier was broken between them and the movement's acculturated leaders. Partially this was an economic issue. Early visitors to the Zionist club, Agnon informs us, consisted of "those Jews [who] were already comfortable enough off to have put away a nest egg and to have no worries about making ends meet."[110] More important,

[107] Kalman Mahler, "How Exactly Heder Boys Became Zionists" (Yiddish), in *Sefer Sanz* (Tel-Aviv, 1970), 354–6.
[108] S. Y. Agnon, *A Simple Story*, translated by Hillel Halkin (New York, 1985), 17.
[109] *Hamicpe*, August 5, 1904, 1.
[110] Agnon, op. cit., 15.

though, was the attitude of the Zionists themselves, who in the first years of the new century increasingly sought to attract traditional, Yiddish-speaking Jews to their facilities. In Kolomea, for example, the Zionist association Beth Israel transformed its library into a *Folksbibliothek*, opening it to the Jewish public and advertising its availability with Yiddish-language placards. The group also opened a Toynbee Hall (an undergraduate residence hall that also offered lectures and social activities) at its headquarters, offering lectures every Saturday night by speakers "well versed in Yiddish literature."[111]

Zionists were at the forefront of the movement to establish Jewish libraries and Toynbee Halls in Galicia, even beyond their own facilities. The libraries, which housed not only books but also sponsored periodic lectures on Jewish history, literature, and popular science, did not necessarily support Zionist agitation directly. But they clearly contributed to the Zionists' broader agenda of nurturing a modern, national identity among Galician Jews. The completion of the Jewish library in Lemberg, for example, for which Gershom Bader served as custodian, drew the following report from local Zionists:

The erection of the Lemberg Jewish library signifies a victory of the Zionist idea. The Lemberg Jewish Community Council, which can be viewed as the high mountain of assimilation, had to bow before the Zionist idea.... We hope that the library will bring an end to the official assimilationist indifference of the local Jews.[112]

Zionists took complete credit for the establishment of the Lemberg Jewish community library in November 1900. The committee which directed its construction, however, was headed by Samuel Horowitz, president of the community council and an outspoken opponent of Zionism.[113] (He also happened to be Mordechai Braude's uncle.) To be sure, Zionist claims of having forced Horowitz, Byk, and the rest of the community oligarchy to build the library, in light of those leaders' repeated refusals to address the issue in community council meetings, are not unreasonable. (Salomon Buber, vice-president of the kehilla and a key Zionist supporter in the council, apparently played a critical role

---

[111] *Hamicpe*, May 17, 1905, 4; *Die Welt*, November 14, 1902, 13. When maintaining the Toynbee Hall grew too difficult for Beth Israel, responsibility was assumed by all of the town's Zionist groups collectively. See *Hamicpe* for a list of recent lectures.

[112] *Die Welt*, December 12, 1900, 7.

[113] The committee also included Rabbi Caro of the Lemberg Temple and the prominent traditional rabbi Isaac Schmelkes, as well as known Zionist supporters such as Salomon Buber. See the board's call for donations in *Die Welt*, February 1, 1901, 8.

in overcoming opposition to the project. He donated the larger part of his personal collection to the new library and served as vice-president of its governing board.)[114] A more dispassionate analysis of the situation would suggest, however, not that Horowitz and the others succumbed to Zionist pressure, but rather that they were genuinely affected by the growing importance of Jewish nationalism in Jewish political discourse. Horowitz, in fact, donated 1,000 volumes of his personal collection to the new library. His speech at the library's opening ceremony, which Zionists argued was forced and insincere, probably reflected the Jewish leader's genuine support for Jewish literacy and collective identity. After noting that "assimilations march into battle ... against Jewish tradition and the love for Jewish literature," he continued:

But surprisingly and unexpectedly a completely radical change has occurred in the last decade. The epoch of the modern Jewish movement and the happy rebirth of Jewry [*Judenthum*] has arrived. We have freshly encountered and discovered our Israel [*sic*], we stand again united on the map. We have learned the value of our Jewish character during this period. We do not want to collapse, assimilate [*aufgehen*] and disappear among other nationalities [*volksstammen*]. We are for ourselves alone and so want to remain.[115]

On October 26, 1901, Zionists in Lemberg also succeeded in establishing a Jewish "Toynbee Hall."[116] In its first five months of activity, a total of 6,687 Jews attended forty-two bi-weekly lectures at the Hall. The best-attended lectures discussed "popular medicine," followed by lectures of historical and literary-historical content, and finally legal, economic, and natural science presentations. The gap between Zionist leaders and their audience was especially obvious at the Toynbee Hall, for while most of the lectures were held in German, most of the audience preferred Yiddish. Apparently, the association simply did not have enough Yiddish-speaking lecturers to satisfy demand.[117]

Cracow Zionists also succeeded in opening a Toynbee Hall, although not until 1905. This hall was specifically designed to meet the needs of traditional Jews, who Zionists felt had grown alienated from the

[114] *Die Welt*, December 12, 1900, 7. On Buber, see earlier in the chapter and Chapter 3.

[115] *Die Welt*, February 1, 1901, 8. Byk, whose speech opened the ceremonies, was similarly (and in this author's view unfairly) dismissed by the Zionist paper. Similarly, see *Hamagid*, June 9, 1898, where a correspondent from Tarnow expresses "bewilderment" that local Jewish leaders of the Polish Club met to celebrate *Ahavat Zion*'s upcoming exploratory visit to Palestine for the purpose of establishing a Jewish settlement.

[116] *Die Welt*, November 1, 1901, 12. The president of the association was a young Zionist named Heinrich Loewenherz.

[117] *Die Welt*, February 8, 1903, 7.

city's Jewish library because of its increasingly pronounced modern character.[118] Originally slated to be housed in a section of the local Temple of "Progressive Israelites," this option was closed by an opponent in that organization. (But note that the Temple did house the first anniversary celebration of the Hebrew literature Sefat Emet – language of truth – association, in 1898.)[119] Zionists eventually managed to raise money for their own hall, whose opening celebrations they announced with Yiddish-language placards around the city. Five hundred guests, mostly from the poorest segment of the Jewish community, gathered at Hotel Keller to celebrate, where the president of the Toynbee Hall association greeted them with a Yiddish-language speech. The Zionist leader Ludwig Goldwasser gave the keynote speech, "What Is Education [*Bildung*]?" Regular lectures were to be held Friday, Saturday, and Sunday.[120] A correspondent to the Hebrew-language *Hamicpe* especially rejoiced that by providing the poorest Jews with this facility, these Jews "will not need to join the socialist groups and be lost to our people."[121]

Zionist leaders not only reached across religious divisions during these years but also began to cross class lines. Lectures and events specifically targeting workers appeared increasingly frequently in the Zionist press as activists attempted to organize Jewish workers within the Zionist movement. Naturally, local socialists were highly interested in these workers also. At first, however, Zionists faced little direct competition from the Galician socialist party (since 1897, the Polish Social Democratic Party of Galicia and Silesia, or PPSD [Polska Partia Socjalno-Demokratyczna]), whose growing Polish nationalist orientation led it to drop its Yiddish-language paper in 1899 and oppose all "separatist" efforts to organize Jewish workers. Among the most radical spokesmen for this policy was Herman Diamand, the one-time president of Zion who now advocated the total assimilation of the Jews into the Polish nation. Other Jewish voices within the PPSD favoring the establishment of a separate Jewish division to meet the specific needs of Jewish workers were persistently defeated. Although future leaders of the independent Jewish Social Democratic Party of Galicia (Żydowska Partja Socjalistyczna, or ŻPS)

---

[118] *Hamicpe*, February 3, 1905, 5.
[119] Andrzej Żbikowski, "The Impact of New Ideologies: The Transformation of Kraków Jewry between 1895 and 1914," *Polin* 23 (2010): 159.
[120] *Die Welt*, February 10, 1905, 11.
[121] *Hamicpe*, February 3, 1905, 5. On the opening of the Stanislau Toynbee Hall, housed in the local Baron Hirsch school, see *Hamicpe*, May 13, 1904, 5. A committee of Zionists including Braude stood behind the success.

already began working secretly to organize Jewish workers by 1902, until the group formally broke from the PPSD in 1905, Zionists faced little competition from this corner.

Galician activists in Lemberg had already founded the first union of Zionist workers called Ivria in Austria in 1897. The following year, with the support of Saul Landau, several other unions of Zionist clerks formed in Galicia, most prominently in Cracow and in Stanislau. While Landau's German-language *Jüdischer Arbeiter* served as a central organ for Zionist workers in Vienna, activists in Galicia published the Yiddish-language *Halvri* in Lemberg with the support of the Zionist party. In 1899, just as the PPSD was discontinuing its Yiddish paper, activists formed the Union of Jewish Commercial Employees. The group declared its allegiance to the Basel Program but also dedicated itself to "work in the present" for the material needs of Jewish workers. Other organizational efforts culminated in the establishment of Poalei Zion (Workers of Zion) in 1904, a Zionist socialist organization based heavily in white-collar workers that would play a significant role in Jewish nationalist activities in the coming years.[122]

Jewish gymnastics associations, or *Turnvereine*, constituted yet another aspect of Zionist outreach.[123] Such groups flourished in Central Europe beginning in 1898, famously celebrated by Max Nordau's call for Zionists to forge a new breed of "muscle Jews," although in Galicia they struggled for survival at first.[124] The Jewish gymnastic movement's (*Turnbewegung*) strong rhetoric of Jewish national renewal made it a natural ally of the Zionist movement. In fact, unlike in Central Europe, where at first such groups generally avoided any direct relationship with the Zionist movement, in Galicia the Jewish Turnbewegung was an openly Zionist project. The province's very first Jewish *Turn* association, for example, called itself the Jewish Nationalist Youth Gymnastic Club. The Zionist student organization Hashachar voted to dedicate its revenue from the

---

[122] On the formation of Poalei Zion and its predecessor organizations, see Shabtai Unger, *Po`ale-Tsiyon ba-kesarut ha-Ostrit, 1904–1914* (Tel-Aviv, 2001), 32–54.

[123] On the Jewish gymnastics movement in Galicia, see Joshua Shanes, "National Regeneration in the Ghetto: The Jewish *Turnbewegung* in Galicia," in Jack Kugelmass, ed., *Jews, Sports, and the Rites of Citizenship* (Urbana, Ill., 2007), 75–94.

[124] Just a handful of Jewish Turnvereine were formed in Galicia before 1907, most with just dozens of regular members. The groups suffered from two obstacles largely absent further West: widespread impoverishment, which limited their ability to acquire equipment and hall space, and strong resistance from religious leaders, who opposed pedagogical innovation. E. M. Zweig, "Einige Notizen über die körperliche Lage der Juden in Galizien," *Jüdische Turnzeitung*, March 1904, 45–9.

Maccabee celebration that year to the new *Turnverein*. In Lemberg, the Zionist leader Alexander Waldmann lectured as early as 1901 about the necessity of the physical regeneration of the Jewish People. Waldmann founded that year the short-lived Jewish Gymnastics Association, headed by Heinrich Gabel (1873–1910), chairman of the East Galician District of the Zionist movement and later a Zionist delegate to the Austrian Parliament. It was also Zionist agitation, a short while later, that built the Jewish youth center (*Studentenheim*) in Lemberg, designed to serve as a gymnastics and tournament hall as well. It thus comes as no surprise that when the First Jewish Turnverein of Galicia was finally re-founded on November 1, 1903, its postal address was the East Galician District Committee of the Zionist movement. Similarly, in Cracow it was Sam Wahrhaftig, a member of the West Galician District Committee, who led the agitation for a Jewish *Volkshaus* with a gymnasium.

Jewish nationalists in Galicia well recognized the usefulness of the Turnbewegung for their own propaganda. Galician Zionists, for example, sought to portray themselves as the great builders of unity among Jews, and Galician *Turner* tapped into the same language. Israel Zinn, president of the Lemberg Turnverein, speaking to a packed house at that group's March 1908 show tournament, described the great importance of physical education for the regeneration of the Jewish people, how it unified "the entire Jewish youth without consideration of class and occupation." *Turner* were especially interested in bannering their "Orthodox" membership, which signaled both their victory over religious opponents and their role as Jewish unifiers.

One athlete received especially hearty applause due to his appearance. It was a young man from the orthodox circles of the city. The curly, dark black *peies* [sidelocks], proud and self-aware, muscular and full of energy, he marched in the rows of athletes. Our association has succeeded in winning over a great number of Orthodox youth and their number grows from day to day. In our associations, where the student youth forms the overwhelming majority, they feel themselves very much at home.[125]

Opposition to the Jewish gymnastics associations from "assimilationist *kahalniks*" who controlled Jewish community funds also invited Zionists to bring their struggle against these "Poles of the Mosaic Confession" to the

---

[125] *Jüdische Turnzeitung*, April 1908, 67. Of course, despite such rhetoric, the fact remained that the secular, student youth did form the "overwhelming majority" of the Turnbewegung, as it did of the Zionist movement itself. The vicious rhetoric against the heders, after all, was not likely to win over a large number of traditional Jews to the movement.

Jewish Turnbewegung. The *Turn* and Zionist leader Israel Waldmann, for example, viciously attacked the "*Moszkos*" in a letter bemoaning Bethar Tarnopol's grave financial situation. Repeating the Zionist mantra, he described how the Poles and Ruthenians respected those Jews who show Jewish pride, and blamed anti-Semitism on assimilationist sycophants who disgust the Christian nations. "The Poles and Ruthenians approve of these ideas, only Mauschel, here called Moszko, appear to us unfriendly. And with right. Moszko knows: strengthen the hand of a Jewish *Turner* – so it goes above all on the Moszko's throat!"[126] ("Mauschel," a corruption of Moses, was a common anti-Semitic pejorative.)

Countless reports from Galician *Turner* described how the Polonized Jewish elites who controlled the community councils refused to let the aspiring gymnasts use Jewish community facilities, often successfully blocking the formation of a Jewish Turnverein. Israel Zinn, for example, reported that the Lemberg Jewish Community Council twice denied his group the use of the orphanage for their meetings. After one lone member of the board finally helped them find a space, they went ahead and bought all of the necessary equipment, but were then closed down because other councilmen feared that the Poles would suspect Jewish separatism. "The gentlemen of the Community Executive Board probably came to be convinced," wrote Zinn angrily, "that the support of an association with 'separatist' tendencies could threaten their position with the Polish nobility."[127]

The Jewish Turnbewegung also highlights the Zionist movement's difficult position vis-à-vis the Orthodox community. While Jewish *Turner* were very interested in recruiting traditional Jews to their movement, their ideological commitment to "regenerating" Galician Jewry was founded upon a total rejection of the traditional form of Jewish education, the *heder*. Rare was the *Turner* report from Galicia which did not emphasize the backwardness and immoral character of the traditional heder. A 1904 report on the movement's progress in Galicia, for example, focused almost entirely on this issue. Its author complained that although the public primary schools, which did offer physical education, were theoretically opened to Jews, they were scarcely used, partly because of the difficulties of the Ruthenian language (in Eastern Galicia), but mostly because of the Jews' "religious exceptionalism." He then described at

---

[126] *Jüdische Turnzeitung*, March 1908, 40. Waldmann signed the letter with the traditional Zionist signature, "Mit Zionsgruss."

[127] *Jüdische Turnzeitung*, April 1905, 62.

length the conditions of a traditional heder, which represented to him the precise antithesis of the *Turn* ideal.

So are the Jewish children in the *heders* raised – cramped, dark and dusty rooms, in which one finds a place for a table with a bench next to the enormous oven and the family bed of the teacher. On this bench the students crouch crooked, in ages from 5, 4 even 3 years old until the age of 12 years old.... So are the *hedarim* a source of physical and mental depravation.[128]

More bluntly stated, wrote Josef Katz several years later, "When a child does not visit the *heder*, his education is the better for it."[129]

Jewish *Turner*, in short, were attempting to recruit traditional Jews while sharply criticizing their Orthodox leaders. Despite Israel Zinn's claim to have attracted "orthodox" Jews to the movement, his own campaign against the heders and those who supported them indicate that his "orthodox" members were actually traditional Jews not yet committed to anti-Zionist Orthodoxy. In any case, with both the Polonized elite and the Jewish religious leadership opposed to their movement, it is not surprising that it failed to achieve any foothold in the province in its first years of activity. Only after the parliamentary elections of 1907 would the movement achieve any real growth.

REFASHIONING NATIONALIST LITERATURE

Indicative of the Zionists' increasing turn toward traditional Jews is a pair of Yiddish-language People's Books (*Folks-bikhlech*) published by Cracow Zionists in 1903 and 1904. In length and style, the booklets recall Zion's *Volksbibliothek* series, published by the Lemberg group in 1890–91.[130] A closer look at their content, however, reveals an important transformation in the Zionist program over the course of the decade. The earlier books had attacked traditional religious authority together with the assimilationists, hoping thereby to attract to Zionism modernizing religious students who had similarly rejected strict orthodoxy. Now, ten years later, Zionists were increasingly attempting to reach not only modernizing religious students but also members of the traditional community itself. Their propaganda, therefore, could not attack the religious establishment so easily, but rather had to highlight more respectfully the compatibility of Zionism with Judaism.

---

[128] Zweig, op. cit., 45.

[129] Josef Katz, "Bericht über die Turnbewegung in Galizien," *Jüdische Turnzeitung*, August 1909, 128.

[130] These were *Der Kantchik* (1890) and *Der Wecker* (1891). See earlier and Chapter 2.

The first booklet, *Chanukah*, presents itself as a traditional telling of the Chanukah story, based on Talmudic and Midrashic sources, which it conspicuously cites. The author explains that at the time of the Chanukah story three parties existed among the Jews: "The *Hasidim*, the fully religious [*ganz frume*], the Sadducees, those who held strong in the Jewish religion, and the Hellenists, those who wanted all Jews to become true Greeks."[131] This innovative, if counterfactual version of history, particularly its subtle distinction between the Hasidim and the Sadducees, set up a vitally important argument for the author when, halfway through the booklet, he turns to the question, "What do we learn from this history?" Predictably, the author attempts to draw direct parallels between the "parties" during the Hellenist period and the Jews in contemporary Galicia.

Today's Hellenists were, of course, the assimilationists, "mostly educated [*gebildete*], doctors, civil servants, merchants and (their) apprentices [*meshartim*], small bankers and other such wealthy people." These misguided people blame the Jews' incomplete assimilation for the rise in anti-Semitism, he writes, and therefore seek total assimilation. Notably, the crimes of the assimilationists that the author lists focus on their religious laxities (Reform Temples that look like churches, neglect of *kashrut*, Sabbath- and Chanukah-lights, etc.), matters that would have most offended traditional Jews. Some "enlightened" houses even shame themselves with Christmas trees, adds the author for good measure.[132]

The most important innovation of the book is its critique of the "Hasidim," a name he inaccurately applies to the masses of "simple" Jews in Hasmonean times who were "too afraid" to oppose Greek rule.[133] Today's Hasidim, he concludes, are the same. Unlike *Der Kantchik* and *Der Wecker*, however, *Chanukah* does not accuse the religious masses of hypocrisy because, for example, they pray for redemption but don't support the Zionists. On the contrary, the author praises their sincerity at great length. The Hasidim, he writes, "are true, good Jews, who want with their whole heart that they and their children should remain Jews."

They have not yet given up hope that Jews must one day be redeemed from exile. They have not removed from their prayer books the words "Zion" and "Jerusalem." They still pray three times a day and ask God to lead them to the land of Israel and renew them as a People, as a free and independent People in

---

[131] M. Henes, *Chanukah* (Cracow, 1903), 6.

[132] Ibid., 12.

[133] In fact, the ancient Hasidim formed the core of the Maccabean resistance movement, although in one famous incident a group was slaughtered when it refused to fight on the sabbath. See Robert Goldenberg, *The Origins of Judaism* (Cambridge, 2007), 77–80.

their own land, as God had promised them.... We do not want to suspect any Jew that he means any differently in his heart as he prays in his mouth. We want to recognize that not only do the majority of religious Jews mean this with their whole heart, but that all of them, all religious and "genuine" Jews [are sincere]. Just one thing is difficult for us: what are they waiting for? And how exactly do they suppose that God will help ... when one holds his hands in his pockets and does not want to do anything himself?[134]

Ultimately, the booklet – like its predecessors a decade earlier – argued for actively speeding the redemption through human agency, something that did contradict Jewish tradition, at least as interpreted by most religious authorities at the time. Unlike its predecessors, however, *Chanukah* portrays the religious masses extremely sympathetically, suggesting that their resistance to Zionism was based on a mild misunderstanding of Torah, namely, the role of human agency in bringing the redemption. The Maccabees provide just the case of religious Jews actively fighting to restore national sovereignty which the author needed to prove his religious credentials.

Haven't they learned anything from those "Hasidim" in the Hasmonean time, who hid themselves in the desert ... while the "Hellenists" in Jerusalem turned the world upside-down, converting young and old, contaminating the Temple, until the Hasmoneans came and began to fight, to make war – even on the Sabbath, just to save the land from the enemy and to be able to live free, as God intended.

Finally, the author points to unnamed religious authorities who have seen the truth of Zionism and embraced the new movement. In other words, the booklet argues, religious Jews need not fear that they would be joining a heretical movement, as most religious leaders in fact argued. "Many religious, great rabbis and sages have understood this as common sense," the booklet concludes, "that God only helps those who do something themselves, and He sends his blessings only where there is already something there." That is why they have joined the Zionists, "just as the 'hasidim' who joined the Hasmoneans."[135]

In 1904, Cracow Zionists produced a second *Folks-bikhlekh* entitled "What Is Zionism?"[136] Although twice the length of its predecessor, and written mostly in Judeo-German rather than in Yiddish, it too sought to reach out to the Hasidim who constituted the overwhelming majority of the Jewish population. Goldberg begins with a brief history of the Zionist movement, describing the contribution of the "true Jewish

---

[134] Ibid.
[135] Ibid., 13.
[136] Shmuel Goldberg, "What Is Zionism?" (Cracow, 1904).

sages" Moses Hess, Leon Pinsker (famous, readers are told, for quoting the Talmudic dictum "If I am not for myself, then who will be for me"), and, of course, Theodor Herzl ("a great sage, welcomed in the courts of kings"). Evidently, the author hoped to convince religious Jews unfamiliar with these extremely secular thinkers that they were in fact Orthodox. Similarly, Goldberg calls the First Zionist Congress a gathering of "Jewish sages from around the world" who met to decide whether Herzl's plan was feasible. "Since the destruction of the Temple," he writes, "since the Jews have been in exile, this was the first time that Jews were gathered from all four corners of the world to advise openly about the situation of the Jews, and to consider by what means to help the Jews." Thus the Congress is portrayed as a sort of Sanhedrin which lent religious support to Herzl's plan, rather than an assembly of confirmed, mostly secular Zionists already committed to Herzl's leadership.[137]

Throughout the work, Goldberg strives to prove the feasibility of Zionism. He writes, for example, that non-Jewish intellectual leaders were nearly universal in their positive assessment of the movement.[138] More disturbingly, he misrepresents foreign governments, particularly the Sultan of the Ottoman Empire, as being entirely favorable to the enterprise. The only problem, writes Goldberg, is that the Sultan feared not enough Jews would come; he demanded proof that the Jews would all come. This is why the shekel, the annual dues owed by every Zionist, was set at one mark, one frank, and so on. Beyond the funds it raised for organizational expenses, it gave a headcount of committed Zionists, "just as the Jews of long ago used to give a shekel to the Holy Temple."[139]

This point was quite true. The Zionist shekel was another appropriation of Jewish tradition – the original shekel collection (all military-aged men paid one half-shekel) was God's preferred method of counting the Jews after the biblical exodus from Egypt and the practice continued as an annual tax. The religious suggestion that Herzl constituted today's Moses, or that the shekel counted not Zionists but Jews (i.e., genuine "Jewish" Jews) was absolutely deliberate. "What Is Zionism" goes so far as to calm those who doubt the feasibility of Herzl's plan by citing the biblical passage in which the Jews in Egypt mistakenly doubted Moses's declaration that the time of their redemption had come.[140]

---

[137] Ibid., 9.
[138] Ibid., 15.
[139] Ibid., 12.
[140] Ibid., 31.

"What Is Zionism?" concludes much like its predecessor (*Chanukah*), by lavishing praise on the piety of Galician Jews while insisting that the Torah demands of Jews that they take action themselves in order to receive God's blessings. Only Divine blessing brings our sustenance and healing, writes Goldberg, yet no one would sit idly by without working for food or going to doctors.[141] The same is true of the Jewish return to the land of Israel. At the same time, however, in an attempt to disarm Orthodox critics who still accused Zionism of false messianism, Goldberg candidly admits, "In truth, Zionism will not bring redemption for the Jews like the exodus from Egypt or the redemption from the Babylonian exile." Rather, he writes, it is an attempt to find a safe haven (*makom menucha*) for persecuted Jews throughout the world who simply cannot go on suffering. "The true redemption will first be with the coming of the Messiah." Nevertheless, he concludes, if all the Jews will join together (i.e., under the flag of the Zionists), and everyone will give according to his ability, in this merit perhaps the promise of the prophets will be realized and the true redeemer will come.[142] Thus he manages to appropriate prophetic language even as he disavows this very messianism.

Such efforts at outreach, which followed in the tradition of the Yiddish press of the previous decade, did influence many Jews to accept various tenets of Zionism. While few Jews were inspired to join the Zionist movement (the number of shekel payers remained a paltry few thousand), their polemics did contribute to the gradual transformation of the identity of many traditional Jews from a religious to a modern nationalist conception. A good example of Zionist influence on traditional Jews is the short-lived Yiddish-language newspaper *Der Emes'r Yid* (The Genuine Jew), "organ for all Jewish affairs," published in 1904.[143] At first glance, the paper seems to be an exact replica of the Zionist-affiliated Yiddish papers of the 1890s discussed in Chapter 3. Like many of those papers, it described itself as a religious organ, which was to report Jewish and political news from around the world in a "simple" Yiddish, for those unable to read Polish or German newspapers. It was written for "our religious brothers, who have not yet lost their true Jewishness [*emese Yidishkayt*], who are strengthening our religion and holy Torah, and leading their children in the straight path."[144] In short, it presented itself as an "Orthodox"

---

[141] Ibid., 29.

[142] Ibid., 32.

[143] The paper's banner was also printed in German as *Der Wahre Yid, Organ für die Gesammtinteressen des Judenthums.*

[144] See the complete program of the paper in its first issue, *Der Emes'r Yid*, February 5, 1904.

paper, and under that guise worked toward politicizing traditional Jews and encouraging them to think of Jewish national concerns beyond their local interests. It included extensive coverage of the Russo-Japanese war, for example, as well as news from Congress Poland and elsewhere outside of Galicia. Its editorials, like those of its predecessors, emphatically declared that Jews constituted a nationality and they goaded Jews to become politically active and to organize and demand Jewish representation in the various governmental bodies.[145] So far, so familiar.

Unlike the Yiddish papers of the 1890s, however, *Der Emes'r Yid* was not an "Orthodox" front for openly Zionist editors. In fact, it was launched by the editor of *Machsike Hadas* and *Kol Machsike Hadas*, organs of that ultra-Orthodox organization, and thus remained outspokenly opposed to the Zionist movement.[146] The paper's editor, Osias Wilf, saw Zionism adopting religious forms and symbols in order to create a secular, Jewish identity in their stead. For this reason he opposed the movement, despite his endorsement of Jewish nationalism as the basis of an activist Jewish politics. Editorials like the following appeared frequently in the paper.

In recent times a new movement is becoming noteworthy among the Jews in Galicia and Russia. The youth has begun to feel Jewish. They interest themselves more with Jewish things, [they] learn Jewish history and Hebrew, they are no longer disgraced by the name Jew, they no longer hide themselves, they no longer disguise themselves. In short, they have become much more Jewish than before – and this movement is growing stronger and more widespread in wider and wider circles.

But nevertheless we see, to our great regret, that in regards to *Yiddishkeit*, that is to say in simple language, in regards to piety, in regards to religious observance and reverence [*shmiras hadas v'hayirah*], the situation has not improved whatsoever. Our youth, who speak the whole day only about "*Yiddishkeit*," who found Jewish clubs, organize and listen to Jewish lectures, learn Hebrew and speak of

---

[145] See, for example, the quotation at the beginning of Chapter 5. Another editorial chastised religious Jews for not organizing in order to take control of the Jewish Community Council away from the liberal elite. "Regarding a triviality, for example who should be the editor of "Machzikei Hadas" there were meetings and hearings held, one ranted and screamed.... But about such an important thing as the Community Council elections, one finds not a single person who will undertake something, who will do something." *Der Emes'r Yid*, April 29, 1904.

[146] Wilf first announced the Yiddish paper in a full-page ad in *Kol Machsike Hadas*, originally a newspaper used to circumvent Austrian restrictions on weekly periodicals but by then simply an alternative voice for the ultra-Orthodox party. *Kol Machsike Hadas*, January 15, 1904, 8. His decision to launch the new Yiddish paper, however, cost him his support by the party leadership. See later.

being more Jewish than our old pious Jews – this very same youth is much less than pious. They are desecrating the Sabbath, they do not observe the important commandments, they are not at all concerned for the commandments of the holy Torah and [they] live just as before, when the youth was of an assimilationist mind, that is, they wanted to mix-in with the other peoples and live equally with them.

Blaming the lack of proper religious instruction for the problem, the article continues by criticizing the Zionists' replacement of the *heder* with modern pedagogical institutions.

Our Jewish youth, which wants to be so-to-speak Jewish, to feel and think Jewish, [they] struggle to learn Hebrew, but not through learning Torah ... not through busying themselves with Torah and thereby [passively] learning Hebrew. Only in order to arrive at the goal more quickly they learn Hebrew through certain methods, which appear every day new and different, that one doesn't know already which is better. To be sure, they learn through the path of Hebrew, but they have no concept of the Torah and know absolutely nothing of what it states inside.

They want only the stories, the article concluded, and none of the morality and laws. If one wants to raise pious children, he strongly suggested avoiding such institutions.[147] This fixation on education again mirrors the Yiddish populist press of the 1890s, as well as similar campaigns in other nationalist movements to prevent "their" children from being lost through enrollment in the wrong schools.[148] Note also his need to define "assimilationist," which likewise recalls the Yiddish press of the 1890s.

Although the paper never mentioned here the Zionist movement by name, it was clear to whom it was referring. Furthermore, other times it did attack the Zionist movement by name. When the Lemberg *Togblat* printed an article attacking the Haluka, the organized system of charity that supported religious Jews living in Palestine and a symbol to the Zionists of Jewish unproductiveness, the paper went on the offensive. The *Togblat* had accused the Haluka of lacking any accountability. In response, the *Der Emes'r Yid* argued that the Zionists' National Fund was no different.

So who gives an accounting for the national fund? Perhaps what it states every week in *Die Welt* that whoever gives the money buys himself a great *mitzvah* and whoever gives 240 kronen will be written up in the Golden Book; is that called an

---

[147] *Der Emes'r Yid*, April 22, 1904.
[148] See earlier, Chapter 3; Tara Zahra, *Kidnapped Souls: National Indifference and the Battle for Children in the Bohemian Lands, 1900–1948* (Ithaca, 2008), and Judson, *Guardians of the Nation*, esp. 19–65.

accounting? And who are the caretakers of the money? Is perhaps the great rabbi and famous sage, of perfect reverence, our teacher Isaac Leib Schreiber *shlita*[149] in Drohobycz not as trustworthy as Dr. Farbstein[150] in Zurich, and is the Rabbi, sage and saint from Atinia perhaps not such a trustworthy man as (they shouldn't be compared) Dr. Werner, or is the Rabbi and saint, *shlita* in Kosov not so believable as some sort of another doctor?

Criticizing the entire Zionist project of collecting money in order to buy land eventually in Palestine, the paper contrasts the administrators of the Haluka, who were supporting "thousands of families in the land of Israel toiling in Torah," to the "big shots" at the National Fund, who were sitting on "millions" and just "waiting for the Messiah to come" rather than supporting the poor Jews who needed immediate assistance.[151]

Wilf's position highlights the success of Jewish nationalists in convincing many traditional Jews that they needed to organize politically as a national community and fight for their rights as such; but it also underscores the limits of this success. Despite its anti-Zionist credentials, *Der Emes'r Yid* cost Wilf his job as editor of *Machsike Hadas*. The party leadership fired him from his position at the paper, which thereafter repeatedly denounced both *Der Emes'r Yid* and *Kol Machsike Hadas* (both of which were owned by Wilf) as the private enterprise of a possibly heretical Jew, charges that Wilf furiously denied. Letters to both *Machsike Hadas* (supporting the ousting of Wilf) and *Kol Machsike Hadas* (defending him) in the spring of 1904 attest to the deep emotions that the crisis engendered and to the still controversial nature of Wilf's attempt to politicize and nationalize traditional Galician Jews despite his fierce anti-Zionism and support for a Torah-centered Jewish identity.

Still, that a man in Wilf's position could launch a paper genuinely committed to an activist nationalist politics suggests that this stance had begun to spread not only among religiously observant Jews but also among their Orthodox leadership. Of course, Zionists cannot take complete credit for

---

[149] *Shlita*, literally "he should live many long and good days," is an acronym traditionally ascribed to men whose leadership or saintliness is being emphasized. Schreiber was the millionaire president of Machsike Hadas whom Joseph Bloch accused of attempting to extort 5,000 florin in exchange for the endorsement of the Belzer Rebbe. See earlier, Chapter 3, and Bloch, *My Reminiscences* (New York, 1973), 263–6.

[150] Dr. David Tzevi Farbstein, an early Zionist, helped to organize the First Zionist Congress. He was also elected to the Swiss National Council as a leader of the Social Democratic Party. (His brother, Yehoshua Heshel Farbstein, was a prominent leader of the Mizrahi movement.) Geoffrey Wigoder, ed., *New Encyclopedia of Zionism and Israel* (New York, 1994), 410.

[151] *Der Emes'r Yid*, September 9, 1904.

this transformation. Aside from other political groups operating simultaneously on similar principles, some of which we will consider shortly, the hyper-nationalist Zeitgeist itself moved many traditional Jews to a nationalist position. Nevertheless, Zionists certainly hastened this process and moved many traditional Jews to reject the Orthodox establishment's continued support for *shtadlanut* (lobbying) as the best means of protecting Jewish interests. These activities clearly indicate the changing direction of Galician Zionist outreach, and the nature of the movement's relationship to traditional, non-Zionist Jews.

RETURN TO DIASPORA POLITICS

By 1901, Congress Zionism had become the dominant Zionist voice in Galicia. Practical Zionism largely died with the bankruptcy of Ahavath Zion, while the autonomous Galician provincial organization had submitted to the authority of the Austrian leadership in Vienna. As a result, Galician Zionists agreed to limit their domestic activities to those programs outlined in the Olmütz Program and, more generally, in the Basel Resolution. Domestic political activity was, therefore, specifically forbidden. The only exception was the struggle to "conquer" the Jewish Community Councils (*Kultusgemeinden*), a program specifically endorsed by Herzl and the Zionist Organization.

Despite their submission in 1901, however, many Galician Zionists continued to resent both the strong-handed administration by the Austrian leadership in Vienna and their inability to pursue domestic programs, especially political programs, more freely. In an attempt to forestall the fragmentation of the Zionist organization, Viennese leaders at the Austrian Landesorganisation's third annual conference in June 1903 pushed through resolutions demanding strict party discipline. Any association that did not stand by the Basel Resolution without any alterations whatsoever would be considered "philo-Zionist," at best, and excluded from the organization.[152]

Such rule by force could not last long. At the Austrians' fourth conference, in June 1905, Viennese Zionists were besieged by demands from the provincial districts for autonomy from the central Action Committee. This time they were successful. Conference resolutions essentially truncated the power of the central committee, leaving total control over party

---

[152] Gaisbauer, op. cit., 112.

funds in the hands of individual districts.[153] The era of Viennese dominance in Galicia ended as quickly as it arrived.

Much of this had to do with broader trends within the Zionist movement as a whole. Following the death of Herzl in 1904, opposition to strict political Zionism grew increasingly more confident. Herzl died without having achieved his coveted international guarantee for a Jewish state and without having left a successor likely to do any better. His death also essentially ended the question of accepting a territorial solution outside of Palestine, the so-called Uganda Scheme. Delegates at the Seventh Zionist Congress in Basel (1905) emphatically declared that no territory outside of Palestine would be considered for the Jewish homeland, and essentially supported practical colonization activity. As a result, much of the vanguard of the political Zionist faction followed Israel Zangwill out of the Zionist Organization, soon to establish the rival Jewish Territorialist Organization (ITO). Political Zionism thus discredited, the path was cleared for practical and cultural Zionists to assert their program.

At the same time that the Zionist organization underwent this internal transformation, alternative Jewish nationalist associations grew in importance. Jewish nationalist opposition to this position began to emerge already at the time of the First Zionist Congress, and not only in Galicia. *Jüdische Volksvereine*, Jewish nationalist associations focused exclusively on promoting Jewish national awareness and Jewish political and economic advancement in Austria, first appeared in Vienna in December 1897 and spread quickly throughout the empire.[154] In Galicia, none other than Reuven Bierer reestablished the now defunct Shomer Israel society as a *Jüdische Volksverein*. In January, 1902 these groups met to constitute a Jewish Diaspora-nationalist party, the Jüdische Volkspartei, headquartered in Vienna. Their program emphatically declared that the Jews constituted a nation and not merely a confessional community, and the party pledged itself to work for their cultural, political, and economic betterment. It demanded Jewish national autonomy as well as the introduction of universal, direct suffrage with proportional minority representation.[155]

---

[153] Gaisbauer, op. cit., 120–4. A resolution adopted without opposition reiterated, however, that the Zionist party did not constitute an Austrian political party and that participation in inner-political struggles was left up to each individual.

[154] See Gaisbauer, op. cit., 459–64, and Rozenblit, *The Jews of Vienna 1867–1914* (Albany, 1983), 170–6.

[155] "Programm der Jüdischen Volkspartei," *Jüdisches Volksblatt*, January 10, 1902, 1.

Jewish nationalist students likewise continued to focus on domestic issues. The program of the first Zionist Student Day, held in Lemberg on July 24–25, 1899, for example, focused on issues such as sports clubs and other cultural activities, the socioeconomic problems of Jews in Galicia, and the political recognition of a Jewish nationality.[156] The same held true for their second meeting in 1902, where students also discussed the need to bring enlightenment to the Hasidic youth, and their 1903 meeting, where the police informant did not even use the word *Palestine* in his report. The students were far more concerned about reforming Jewish community government and cultural activities like Hebrew courses and gymnastics associations.[157]

Despite Galician Zionism's heritage of embracing Diaspora politics, by the first years of the new century such a position had become far more contentious. Gershom Bader, one of Galicia's most important Zionist spokesmen and publicists, came out with a scathing attack on the Jüdische Volkspartei in his lead contribution to the 1902 Jüdischer Volkskalender which he edited. "Jewish Nationalism" and "Zionism," he wrote, were interdependent and could not be separated. "The beginning of *Zionist* is *Jewish nationalist*, but the consequence of *Jewish nationalist* must be *Zionist*."[158] In other words, Zionism, the movement to achieve a Jewish state in Palestine, begins by strengthening Jewish national consciousness in the Diaspora. The ultimate purpose of Jewish nationalist work in the Diaspora, however, must be Zionist. It must be the realization of a Jewish state in Palestine.

Bader did not oppose Diaspora nationalist activity. On the contrary, he supported the foundation of economic associations to improve the lot of Galician Jewry. "But when you want to play in politics," he wrote, "then we have to shout loud and clear: no, kiddies, you are playing with fire!"[159] In other words, it was their intention to engage in Landespolitik which he opposed. There was nothing to be gained by such activity, but everything to be lost. In the city council, he argued, Jewish nationalists were not needed because even the assimilationists will defend Jewish rights, while in Parliament, he asked, how could a dozen or fewer members of a Jewish Club possibly accomplish anything? "One must understand that the best

---

[156] *Die Welt*, June 23, 1899, 8 and November 11, 1899, 8–9.
[157] *Die Welt*, November 7, 1902, 7, and OSA/AVA, Innenministereum, Präsidiale, 22/ Galizien 1906, Karton 2110.
[158] G. Bader, "Jüdisch-nationaler oder Zionistisch?" in G. Bader, *Jüdischer Volkskalender* 8 (Lemberg, 1902), 37.
[159] Ibid., 40.

means is to sit quietly and not to mix-in between the parties, because they are like Yent's parable about the stone and the glass: if the stone falls on the glass, it hurts the glass. If the glass falls on the stone, it also hurts the glass."[160] Above all, however, Bader opposed the Jüdische Volkspartei not on practical, but on ideological grounds. "Any nationalist ideology," he wrote, "which does not envision a Jewish national home as its final consequence, is foreign to the Jewish people's soul.... A nation without its own land is only a caricature of a nation, nothing more."[161]

Zionist leadership in Vienna certainly shared Bader's reservations about Landespolitik. Nevertheless, political expediency suggested that compromise would prove more fruitful than competition. In October 1902, negotiations between representatives of the Austrian Zionist organization and the Volkspartei led to a breakthrough agreement which essentially enabled the absorption of the later group by the former. In the agreement, the Zionist party committed itself to promote the "spiritual, economic and physical advancement of the Jewish People," while at the same time to tolerate members who pursued programs on which the two groups disagreed (i.e., Landespolitik), and even to support them as much as was feasible (*nach tunlichkeit*). The leaders of the Volkspartei, in exchange, accepted the legitimacy of the Basel Program ("the acquisition of an open-legal secured homeland in Palestine for the Jewish People") and agreed to pursue this goal through all appropriate means, including its recommendation to party members that they contribute to the shekel fund. (Beyond its financial implications, by paying the shekel, Volkspartei members signified their membership in the Zionist party.) The groups declared themselves united, particularly regarding cooperative activities such as community elections, but in effect the larger and better organized Zionist party simply absorbed its former rival.[162]

Partially as a result of the above agreement, Galician Zionists felt emboldened to reconsider the temporary abandonment of Landespolitik imposed upon them in 1901. Already in November 1903, delegates at the Zionists' East Galician district meeting in Lemberg passed resolutions favoring an engagement with Landespolitik, noting above all its importance in their campaign to politicize Galician Jewry, "to raise the Jews to a higher level of political maturity." The resolution that ultimately passed left it to the individual associations to choose tactics based on

[160] Ibid., 43.
[161] Ibid., 43–4.
[162] *Die Welt*, October 31, 1902, 5.

local conditions, but recommended supporting whichever candidate, Jewish or not, most sympathized with the Zionist movement. The conference thus represented a limited endorsement of Landespolitik. On the one hand, the resolution did not call for the nomination of Zionist candidates in Austrian elections, and it specifically recommended complete neutrality in the Polish-Ruthenian struggle. "The Zionists must content themselves," exclaimed one delegate, "with the training of the Jews to political maturity, [and] thus pursue more educational rather than political aims." Still, the group did call upon its members to participate as Zionists in Austrian elections (principally through voter rallies), its resolution formally opposed an expansion of Galician autonomy (which it feared would endanger Galician Jews), and it reiterated the call to conquer the *kehillas* and turn them into true "People's Organizations."[163]

Despite this partial acceptance of Landespolitik, Austrian Zionists in Galicia and elsewhere continued to maintain that the Zionist party should not directly participate in domestic political struggles. All of this would suddenly change at the end of 1905 when the emperor, greatly alarmed by the first Russian revolution, hoped to defuse proletarian dissent in Austria by calling for the reform of the voting franchise. The entire curial system was to be dismantled and replaced by a one-man, one-vote system throughout the empire. Austrian Zionists quickly recognized the great potential for both educational and political advancement which the suffrage reform promised and resolved to engage in the domestic political struggle full force.

[163] *Die Welt*, November 27, 1903, 10. A speech by Adolf Stand strongly denouncing the East Africa plan was received with wild applause.

5

Fort mit den Hausjuden!

The 1907 Parliamentary Elections and the Rise of Jewish Mass Politics

It was a pathetic tale that was told by a poor Jew in Galicia a fortnight ago during the riots, after he had been raided by the Christian peasantry and despoiled of everything he had. He said his vote was of no value to him, and he wished he could be excused from casting it, for indeed casting it was a sure *damage* to him, since no matter which party he voted for, the other party would come straight and take its revenge out of him. Nine percent of the population of the empire [*sic*], these Jews, and apparently they cannot put a plank into any candidate's platform! If you will send our Irish lads over here I think they will organize your race and change the aspect of the Reichsrath.

Mark Twain, "Concerning the Jews," *Harpers Magazine*, March 1898

The Jew must begin to play a "Jewish politics." He must begin to strive that before everything he does he should ask himself: what use can come out of this [against] me? ... [In Galicia], where the Jews constitute a majority of the population in many cities – and in many other cities, although they do not alone form a majority, they are present in a sufficiently large number that they can affect a certain influence on the political process through uniting with other parties – there the Jews must not retreat from political life, there they must participate and represent their interests – but they must represent *Jewish politics*, they must [represent] above all their own interests, naturally in those places where they are not against the interests of the land in general. When the Jews as state citizens must participate in the political life, they must not be Czechs or Germans, or Poles or Ruthenians – only Jews.

Der Emes'r Yid, June 17, 1904

INTRODUCTION

Galician Zionism began as a movement oriented toward normative nationalist goals: the fostering of a Jewish national identity among

Galician Jewry through cultural and educational projects, as well as an engagement with domestic politics to protect and improve the Jews' economic and political position. In the brief intoxication following Theodor Herzl's ascendancy to leadership, political Zionism's nearly exclusive focus on achieving a Jewish state enjoyed a temporary dominance over the Jewish nationalist movement in Galicia as well. By 1903, however, this had begun to wane, and in the following years Galician Zionism increasingly returned to its "Jewish nationalist" roots.

Even Austrian Zionists had begun to move toward an engagement with *Gegenwartsarbeit* as early as 1903, although this still largely entailed traditional Diaspora issues: conquest of the Jewish community councils (a program initiated by Herzl himself) and the cultural and economic progress of Cisleithanian Jewry. *Landespolitik*, domestic national politics, was still considered a dangerous diversion from Zionism's ultimate goal. With the November 28, 1905 pronouncement by the prime minister of the emperor's decision to support universal manhood suffrage, however, most Austrian Zionists dropped their past opposition to Landespolitik and voted to run candidates in national elections. Naturally, such a decision carried the most importance in Galicia, whose heavily concentrated Jewish communities offered the most obvious chances of electoral victory.

Galician Zionists had, of course, already committed themselves to participate in Landespolitik in the 1890s. This was made clear in Zion's first program brochure in 1892, whose "outer" program explicitly called for Landespolitik and was ratified at the first conference of the Jewish National Party of Galicia. Nathan Birnbaum's short-lived Austrian Zionist Party, which sought to unite Jewish nationalists and Zionists in both Galicia and Vienna, also passed resolutions favoring Landespolitik "in principle" in response to rumors of Prime Minister Taafe's (ultimately aborted) suffrage reform.[1] And Laibel Taubes had boldly called for the formation of a Jewish Club in the Austrian Parliament as early as 1896, while in 1897 he proposed the establishment of a Jewish electoral committee in order to nominate Jewish candidates in all districts with Jewish majorities. Put on hold by Herzl, these Diaspora-oriented tendencies could no longer be suppressed.

The realization of universal male suffrage transformed the stakes of Zionist outreach. Not only did every male Jew (at least twenty-four years old) become a potential voter, but the general atmosphere of mass mobilization throughout the province (voter rallies, the growth of

[1] Gelber, *Toldot ha-tenua ha-tsiyonit be-Galidsyah*, 1875–1918 (Jerusalem, 1956), 201.

mass-circulation newspapers, etc.) provided an unprecedented opportunity for Zionists to penetrate into the traditional and still largely nonpoliticized Jewish masses.[2] To this end, the period saw a sharp rise in the number of Zionist papers published in Yiddish, including *Der Jud*, *Di Yidishe Folks Politik*, and above all the *Togblat*, a daily Yiddish paper (the province's first) published in Lemberg well into the interwar period.[3] Like the populist press discussed in Chapter 3, these papers were designed not simply to provide news to the Yiddish-reading public, but also to politicize Galician Jewry in favor of the Jewish nationalist position.

To achieve any influence among traditional Jewry, however, Zionists had to adjust the nature of the nationalist vision that they put forth. Galician Zionism in the first years of the new century by and large remained a movement of the secular, Polonized intelligentsia. To be sure, Zionist activists had attempted to reach out beyond the intellectual elite, through the Yiddish press in the 1890s, and increasingly through hosting rallies in synagogues and other religious venues. Nevertheless, the Zionist movement's core constituency remained the Jewish intelligentsia, and its leaders, including those with religious backgrounds, were modern, largely Polonized Jews. Zionists had become so associated with Polish culture and the acculturated intellectual elite that their socialist opponents could actually point to their Polonization in challenging their claim to national leadership. For example, *Der Sozial-Demokrat*, organ of the Jewish Social Democratic Party of Galicia (Żydowska Partia Socjalno-Demokratyczna, or ŻPS), frequently pointed out how Zionist orators spoke in Polish, while their own speakers always used Yiddish.[4] As early as 1905, a member of the ŻPS, relishing his group's successful infiltration of a Zionist rally, later bragged: "It didn't help that on the Polish placards

---

[2] At the time of the elections, writes Leila Everett, "the vast majority of Galician Jews were Yiddish-speaking, unassimilated and to a large extent politically uninvolved." L. Everett, "The Rise of Jewish National Politics in Galicia, 1905–1907," in Andrei S. Markovits and Frank E. Sysyn, eds., *Nationbuilding and the Politics of Nationalism: Essays on Austrian Galicia* (Cambridge, Mass, 1982), 154.

[3] *Der Jud* was published by the Zionists' West Galician district from 1905 to 1906, while the *Yidishe Folks Politik* was an independent Zionist paper published in Kolomea in 1906. Only the daily *Togblat* achieved a solid subscription base. Founded by Gershom Bader in 1904, it became an official organ of the Galician Zionist movement on January 1, 1907. The *Togblat* did appear at times somewhat erratically, but usually it did not skip more than one day in succession. The *Togblat* was wrested from Bader's control in 1906. See note 81.

[4] See, for example, *Der Sozial-Demokrat*, May 1, 1907, 3, where the paper writes that Zionists never even bothered to train Yiddish speakers until forced to do so by the upcoming elections.

they wrote that the meeting begins at two-thirty in the afternoon and on the Yiddish at three in the afternoon, so that the Jewish workers who don't read Polish would arrive late and not find a seat at the meeting."[5] The discrediting of Zionists as bourgeois reactionaries by Jewish socialists was standard fare throughout Eastern Europe. Here, however, they are portrayed as cultural aliens as well, their Polish education starkly contrasted to the Yiddish-speaking Jewish workers who constituted the "true Jews." (Of course, many of the socialists' own leaders had to learn Yiddish as adults as well and never truly mastered the language.[6])

In order for Galician Zionists to appeal to Jews beyond the Polonized intelligentsia – as well as to forge an alliance with the Ruthenian nationalist leadership (as they ultimately needed to do in order to win rural seats) – they would clearly have to overcome this image. At the same time, however, they could not afford to antagonize Polonized Jews whose support they aggressively pursued, nor did they relish the prospect of provoking a Polish anti-Semitic backlash. The possibility of achieving a Jewish political presence in the Austrian Parliament provided Jewish nationalists with a solution. For the first time, Jews could choose political neutrality by voting for Jewish nationalist candidates. With Jewish national representatives in Parliament, the Zionist vision of Jewish integration into Austrian society as one of the empire's recognized nationalities seemed more promising than ever. No better opportunity could have presented itself for Jewish nationalists to take their message to the people.

UNIVERSAL SUFFRAGE AND ZIONIST POLITICS

"Fort mit den Hausjuden!" So began Saul Landau's call to wrest the Jewish "mandates" in Galicia from "assimilationist lackeys" of the Polish Club, the so-called House Jews who had dominated Jewish politics since 1879.[7] Since that year, only one Jewish Member of Parliament from Galicia had successfully opposed the dominance of the Polish Club.[8] Even the introduction of a fifth curia in 1897 was not able to bring an independent

---

[5] *Der Sozial-Demokrat*, November 24, 1905.

[6] Rick Kuhn, *Henryk Grossman and the Recovery of Marxism* (Urbana, 2007), 17. On the foundation of the ŻPS, see later in the chapter.

[7] S. R. Landau, *Der Polenklub und seine Hausjuden*, 1. Jewish "mandates" were electoral districts in which Jews comprised the majority of the population and thus were theoretically assured of a Jewish representative.

[8] This was Nathan Kallir in Brody, who served from 1873 until his death in 1886. He was replaced by Moriz Rosenstock, who faithfully joined the Polish Club. Even Joseph Bloch, the candidate of Jewish national pride, joined the Polish Club, later resigning his seat under Polish pressure in 1895. (See Appendix A.)

Jewish candidate to Parliament.[9] Then, in the wake of the 1905 Russian Revolution, the emperor decided that he could best avert the threat of a socialist revolution in Austria by conceding the principal demand of the Austrian proletariat, namely, universal suffrage. The lower house of Parliament, the so-called House of Representatives (*Abgeordnetenhaus*), immediately began debate on its introduction.[10]

Parliament intended its new electoral system to alleviate nationalist tensions which had paralyzed legislative activity. Generally speaking, districts were supposed to be as nationally homogeneous as possible. In practice, this meant that not all districts would represent an equal number of constituents. In Galicia, for example, Ruthenian districts included almost double the number of voters as found in their Polish counterparts.[11] In addition, a minority protection system was introduced which added a second representative to rural Galician districts. The first mandate would go to the candidate who won an absolute majority of all votes cast, the second to the one who received at least a quarter of the votes. This was designed to protect the Polish minority in Eastern Galicia, largely concentrated in urban areas (which received just one mandate, neutralizing the Ruthenian and Jewish urban minorities) but spread out in smaller numbers throughout the province. It also, in contradiction to its supposed purpose of avoiding nationally mixed mandates, doubled the Polish representation in West Galician rural districts while leaving the substantial Jewish urban minorities in Western Galicia without the possibility of separate representation.[12] In this way, the so-called minority protection system actually protected the already powerful position of the dominant Polish camp from losing too much control. This provision was included so as to earn the necessary support of the conservative Polish Club to pass the reform.

---

[9] Benno Straucher, running as an independent Democrat and not as a Jewish nationalist, was elected that year in Czernowitz (Bukowina), but from a different curia.

[10] For a general study of the suffrage reform, see William Jenks, *The Austrian Electoral Reform of 1907* (New York, 1950). On the 1907 electoral system in Galicia, see Harald Binder, "Die Wahlreform von 1907 und der polnisch-ruthenische Konflikt in Ostgalizien," *Österreichische Osthefte* 38 (1996): 293–321.

[11] Polish districts averaged 46,276 residents versus 103,057 residents in Ruthenian mandates. Polish urban dwellers were especially well represented (often registering just a few thousand voters, versus 25,000–50,000 in rural districts), but even Polish rural districts far surpassed their Ruthenian counterparts. West Galician rural districts spanned from 101,000 to 151,000 people, while East Galician districts ranged from 160,000 to 279,000. See Binder, op. cit., 310, and *Summarische Ergebnisse der Statistik der Reichsratwahlen von 1907* (Brünn, 1907), 44–9.

[12] Jenks, op. cit., 119. Jenks incorrectly writes that the minority protection system was only applied to Eastern Galicia. For a corrective discussion, see Binder, op. cit., 298–300.

For Jewish nationalists, the national mandate system, particularly with its extra protection of national minorities in East Galicia, exacerbated the desperate situation of Austrian Jews who were still not considered a nationality, or *Volksstamm*, in their own right. With so many potential urban electoral districts in Galicia comprised of Jewish majorities or pluralities, the stakes of such recognition rose considerably. If in the past the recognition of Yiddish as a legal *Umgangssprache* would have guaranteed state support of Yiddish schools and recognition of Yiddish contracts, now it could mean a guaranteed Jewish presence in the Austrian Parliament, and a considerable one at that.

The first speaker in Parliament to demand recognition of the Jews as an official Volksstamm was not a Jew but a Ruthenian, Iulian Romanczuk (1842–1932), one of the leaders of the Ruthenian faction.[13] As we have seen, Romanczuk's group understood that the recognition of a Jewish nationality would spell the end of Polish demographic dominance in Galicia. On December 1, 1905, toward the end of a long speech during the debate over suffrage reform, Romanczuk digressed briefly to note that "in his own purely personal opinion" the Jews ought to be added to the list of nationalities recognized by the government. He did this not by advocating that Yiddish be recognized as a language in its own right, a notion unlikely to receive much support, but rather by citing the example of the Irish, universally recognized as their own nationality even though their everyday language was English. In other words, he challenged the entire linguistic conception of nationality that had governed Austrian policy since 1867.

I would like now to suggest whether it should not also be left up to the Jews to consider themselves in political respects a separate nation (tumultuous laughter). Naturally, this would not be able to have any influence on the linguistic conditions…. (Representative Daszyński:[14] As a religion?) Is then the linguistic factor the only decisive [factor] in national affairs? (Representative Daszyński: Should the Jews be constituted as a religion or as a race? – Outcry: As a race!) Whether as a race or as a religion is unimportant.

It is well known, Herr Colleague, that the Irish are considered their own nation, as a different nation than the English, although they speak the same language as

---

[13] Romanczuk was a National Democrat. For an explication of the Ruthenian parties, see Ivan Rudnytsky, "The Ukrainians in Galicia Under Austrian Rule," in Andrei S. Markovits and Frank E. Sysyn, eds., *Nationbuilding and the Politics of Nationalism: Essays on Austrian Galicia* (Cambridge, Mass., 1982), 42–60.

[14] Ignacy Daszyński (1866–1936), parliamentary representative from Cracow, was the powerful leader of the Polish social democrats and by 1905 a strong opponent of Jewish national recognition. He later served as the first prime minister of interwar Poland. On his relationship to the Jews in the 1890s, see Chapter 2.

the English. (Representative Daszyński: Good, but the Jews! How should they constitute themselves? On what grounds?)

Just as the Irish have constituted themselves.... How the Jews constitute themselves, this we can already leave to themselves [to decide] – naturally, coercion cannot be exerted in this regard. But when a Jew wants to consider himself as a member of a particular Jewish nation, than this cannot be denied to him; one cannot compel the Jews to confess a different nationality. (Representative Daszyński: But how will one distribute the mandates?)

Just as it would be among all of the other nations, just as in the case of the Germans, who are spread out in small colonies, just as in the case of the Poles, who live spread out in many districts of East Galicia, and among all of the other nations![15]

Romanczuk then returned to a different topic. Evidently, this was no spontaneous aside by Romanczuk. It seems rather to have been a carefully planned maneuver between Romanczuk and the Jewish nationalists, for the very next speaker scheduled on the agenda was none other than the independent representative from Czernowitz, Benno Straucher (1852–1940), a well-known Zionist leader.[16] The Zionists apparently assumed that the motion would carry more weight if first raised by a Christian and then seconded by their own man. As Straucher was absent when his name was called, it was not until the next parliamentary meeting on December 4 that he could emphatically reiterate the call to designate Jews as a Volksstamm.

It is known, that at present in Jewish circles a movement rules, which argues that the Jews should also be allowed to enjoy national autonomy.... The Jews claim their own national representation in Parliament as an individual national political entity, as which they want to be considered. The number of the Jewish representatives will correspond to their population and economic power. (Representative Daszyński: Does one want a Jargon *gymnasium* or not?) The question has nothing to do with this. There can also exist a People, which besides its own written and literary language uses the language of another cultured People in its outside, civic activities, as well as in its education, and yet possesses its own national-political individuality.

Regarding this I refer, as Representative Romanczuk has already done, to the Irish. It is the demand as well as the wish and the endeavor of a large number of Jews not only in Galicia and Bukowina, but also in Western Austria, to be present in the new parliament according to their own Jewish national representation. This is a fact.... The Jews constitute a particular nationality [*Volksstamm*].[17]

---

[15] *Stenographische Protocolle des Abgeordnetenhauses*, Session 17, 32509.

[16] On Straucher, see Gaisbauer, *Davidstern und Doppeladler* (Vienna, 1988), 511 ff.

[17] *Stenographische Protocolle des Abgeordnetenhauses*, Session 17. In March 1906, Straucher made a much longer and more impassioned plea for proportional Jewish national representation, reprinted in *Die Welt*, March 23, 1906, 9–11.

Less than a month later, under Romanczuk's chairmanship, the annual meeting of the Ruthenian National Democratic political association Narodna Rada unanimously passed a resolution demanding that Galician Jews be allotted Jewish-national electoral districts.[18] (The "radicals" also supported the recognition of a Jewish nationality. A separate police report describes a meeting of Ukrainophile students whose resolution demanded recognition of the Jewish nationality at the University of Lemberg, noting the Jewish student's steadfast support for their struggle for an independent Ruthenian university.)[19] Romanczuk also joined Straucher, Nathan Birnbaum, and other Jewish nationalist leaders on December 12 at a mass rally in Vienna of 2,000 Jews to demand national autonomy for Austrian Jewry.[20]

Straucher and Romanczuk faced steep opposition, of course. They were opposed not only by Germans, who needed the Jews to bolster their numbers in Bohemia-Moravia and Bukowina, and by Poles, who needed them in Galicia, but also by Social Democrats like Victor Adler (himself born Jewish) and Daszyński, who argued that the Jews constituted only a religious group and not a nation.[21] Jewish Liberals opposed the measure for the same reason, of course, especially those sitting in the Polish Club. Already in December 1905, Emil Byk, the consummate "House Jew," convened a "conference of notables," as Zionists sarcastically described it, consisting of Jewish parliamentary and diet representatives, *kahal* representatives from the larger Jewish communities in Galicia, and a few other select guests. The conference, which according to Zionist reports included just eighteen to twenty participants, declared itself resoundingly against Jewish national autonomy or the formation of a Jewish national curia, arguing that it would undermine Jewish civil equality.[22]

---

[18] *OSA/AVA*, Innenministerium, Präsidiale, 22/Galizien 1903–5, Karton 2109. The meeting was held on December 26.

[19] *OSA/AVA*, Innenministerium, Präsidiale, 22/Galizien 1906, Karton 2110.

[20] *Die Welt*, December 15, 1905, 7–8.

[21] Austro-Marxism demanded national autonomy for all nationalities in Austria under the auspices of a Social Democratic federation, but argued that Jews, who lacked territorial concentration, did not constitute a nationality. Polish socialists naturally denied Jewish nationhood as well and called on Jewish workers to join the Polish Social Democratic Party (PPSD). See Robert Wistrich, *Socialism and the Jews* (London, 1982), 299–348.

[22] *Die Welt*, December 29, 1905, 5–7, and January 5, 1906, 12–13. According to Munio Wurman, there were originally more participants, but when a mass demonstration of Jews burst into the hall – protesting the exclusion of Zionist representatives – Byk cleared the room of all but twenty-four delegates, half of them from Lemberg itself. When the delegate from Tlumacz "assailed" Byk for his support of the Polish Club, Byk had the police remove him. Munio Wurman, "Tlumacz Jewry and the Nationalist Movement" (Hebrew), in Shlomo Blond, ed., *Tlumacz: Sefer Edut V'zikaron* (Tel-Aviv, 1976), 65.

Predictably, the Zionist press argued that the conference had no right to speak in the name of the Jewish people. They reserved this privilege for themselves, based not merely on their ideological commitment to the Jewish people but on what they perceived as their growing influence among the people. *Die Welt*, for example, hastened to point out that at the same time that Byk was hosting his two dozen guests in Lemberg, the Zionists organized a rally with roughly five hundred participants who declared themselves in favor of Jewish national autonomy and Jewish electoral districts.[23] Zionists in Rzeszow, boasted the paper one week later, led over one thousand Jews in a protest march against Byk's *gemeindetag*.[24] And in early January, *Der Jud* happily contrasted the eighteen to twenty assimilationist oligarchs who met with Byk to the Zionists' successful organization of several hundred mass rallies on a single day, January 7. The rallies had been ordered by the Lemberg-district Action Committee, in consultation with the other districts, which sent out hundreds of telegrams throughout the province as soon as they caught wind of Byk's conference.[25]

The January 7 rallies did not merely protest the undemocratic *kahal* leadership, but helped to position the Zionists as the natural choice for Jewish national leadership. Responding to assimilationist *and Orthodox* arguments that only by working within the Polish Club could Jews achieve anything in Parliament, Zionists pointed out that even the six Jewish mandates to which the Polish Club eventually agreed were only a result of Zionist rallies and not of internal agitation by the "House Jews." Only after Zionist pressure led the government to form Jewish electoral districts, wrote *Der Jud*, did the Polish Club quickly call Byk back to Vienna to claim the achievement.[26] Indeed, the entire reason Byk organized his "conference of notables," according to *Der Jud*, was to cover up his embarrassment over the fact that his "masters, the Poles" did not originally allow him to speak on behalf of Jewish electoral districts in Parliament, leaving that honor to a non-Jew (i.e., Romanczuk). "Forced to remain silent in Parliament, he spoke at home instead."

[23] *Die Welt*, December 29, 1905, 6.
[24] *Die Welt*, January 5, 1906, 12.
[25] *Die Welt*, January 5, 1906, 13. The availability of the telegraph was clearly vital to Zionist efforts in these years. Gaisbauer quotes the number of rallies as over 400, while *Die Welt* calls it at about 100. Ber Borochov later recalled 260 mass rallies on that night. Gaisbauer, op. cit., 466; *Die Welt*, January 12, 1906, 11; Ber Borochov, *Ketavim*, Vol. 3 (Tel Aviv, 1955–66), 58.
[26] *Der Jud*, February 22, 1906.

On January 7, 1906, however, there was in Galicia something more than one meeting, and in the rallies there was a bit more people than 20-something and there was also a bit more celebration and excitement, than in the Lemberg *kahal*-house. And to whom did the hundreds of Jewish people's rallies [*Volksversammlungen*] express their thanks, their trust and their respect? – Not to Dr. Byk!

Oh, vengeance is sweet![27]

Byk, of course, hardly took this abuse silently. "If the Galician Jews were responsible, mature people [*mentchn*]," *Der Jud* quoted him saying, "they would make rallies and agree with my opinion and [would] throw into excommunication those crazies who say that the Jews are a People."[28] Byk did not content himself merely with rhetoric, however. In response to a slander campaign against him led by the Zionist press, Byk allegedly encouraged the Polish authorities to suppress Zionist clubs, many of which (especially among the socialist Poalei Zion) were closed down altogether.[29] Zionists were quick to point out that other than Straucher himself not a single Jewish representative signed the protest motion raised in Parliament over the illegal closures. Even the social democrats, whose representatives protested civil abuses of every sort throughout the empire, remained silent now.[30] The message was clear: neither Jewish Liberals nor Social Democrats could be counted on to defend Jewish interests. (Romanczuk, of course, did appear among the motion's signatories.)

Zionists attacked Byk throughout this entire affair, from the moment his convention was announced. They were infuriated that as a "lackey" of the Poles he refused to speak on any Jewish issue until now, when as a self-proclaimed "Jewish leader" he came out against Jewish national interests, at least as they perceived them.[31] Nevertheless, as in 1885,

---

[27] *Der Jud*, May 3, 1906.

[28] *Der Jud*, May 3, 1906.

[29] For details on the closures and other actions taken against Zionist associations, see *Die Welt*, February 23, 1906, 9–10. Poale Zion responded to the closures simply by renaming those branches that had been shut down and thereby quickly securing permits to reopen. "The Union of Commercial Clerks Poalei Zion," the previous official name of the societies, now became, "The General Jewish Union of Workers in Austria," while the independent group Achdut (Unity) in Cracow replaced the now defunct Achva (Brotherhood). Shabtai Unger, *Po`ale-Tsiyon ba-kesarut ha-Ostrit, 1904–1914* (Tel-Aviv, 2001), 50.

[30] *Die Welt*, February 23, 1906, 6 (the motion is reprinted on page 10). The protest (signed by fifteen Representatives) was raised by Ernst Breiter, a non-Jewish representative from Lemberg who frequently defended Jewish rights in Parliament. In the aftermath of the 1907 elections, during which Jewish nationalists strongly promoted Breiter's reelection, Breiter signed nearly every motion protesting electoral abuse in Galicia.

[31] See especially *Die Welt*, December 29, 1905, 5.

the Zionists' portrait of Byk as a stooge of the Polish Club is not fair. Just weeks before his death, for example, Byk fought against the club in demanding that the minority protection system be applied not only to rural districts but also to urban ones in order to guarantee Jewish representatives in the many towns and cities in which they formed a large percentage of the population.[32] Byk also protested in Parliament the decision of the Viennese city council to prohibit kosher slaughter, although *Die Welt* still whined that he did so only in his own name and not in the name of the Polish Club.[33] Byk had also led a crusade against the Sunday-rest law, which devastated Jewish businessmen and workers; because they were closed Saturday for their own Sabbath, they thereby lost two days of work.[34] In 1903, Byk even took up an international Jewish cause when he sent a letter of gratitude to the mayor of London who, in protest against the Romanian pogroms, had excluded the Romanian consular-general from an affair of foreign dignitaries.[35] And that same year, he led an international conference in Lemberg (joined by Zionists and several leading rabbis) to address the problem of Jewish girls in the white slave trade.[36] Such activities by Byk again point to the complexity of the so-called assimilationist camp, which was able to defend Jewish collective interests while voicing anti-nationalist ideas.

A PRELUDE TO THE COMING BATTLE

Jewish nationalists, and their Jewish and Polish opponents, began preparing for the 1907 confrontation even before the passage of suffrage reform. In early 1906, for example, Jewish students fought over the recognition of Jewish nationhood at the University of Lemberg, which

[32] *Beilagen*, April 24, 1906, quoted in Jenks, op. cit., 120.

[33] *Die Welt*, May 19, 1905, 12.

[34] See, for example, *Stenographische Protocolle*, June 12, 1903 (Session 17), 21244. *Der Jud*'s front-page obituary of Byk, surprisingly congenial considering how viciously they had been slandering him, noted in particular Byk's struggle against the Sunday rest law. *Der Jud*, June 28, 1906, 1. Likewise, in 1905, the Zionist-leaning *Drohobyczer Zeitung* celebrated twenty-five years of Byk's public service. Quoting Isaiah, it wrote that all of Byk's good work for the Jewish community would serve as the true legacy for the childless leader, and wished him many more years of leadership. *Drohobyczer Zeitung*, May 26, 1905, 3.

[35] *Jüdische Volks-zeitung*, February 4, 1903.

[36] *Allgemeine Zeitung des Judentums*, September 25, 1903, 461–4. Other participants included Yehoshua Thon, Gedalia Schmelkes, and his uncle, Rabbi Isaac Schmelkes (1828–1906), a leading rabbinic authority at the time and a former Reichsrat candidate for Machsike Hadas in 1879.

registered students according to nationality. Four hundred students, plus the rector of the school and several professors, attended an open rally on February 14 to debate the issue. Zvie Aschkenase spoke for those students proposing a resolution to demand that the university recognize the Jewish nationality, while another student (Kohl) spoke against the resolution in the name of the "Polish Students of the Mosaic Confession." Aschkenase's resolution was accepted by majority vote. (Unlike most Zionist coverage of rallies, the police report does not hide the presence of dissenting voices.) In response, a group of six hundred invited guests rallied on February 23 to oppose the resolution and "condemn its harmfulness to Jews living on Polish ground."[37]

More dramatically, in the summer of 1906, the two sides clashed in the battle over Emil Byk's vacated seat in the Brody-Zloczow district. Byk, who died on June 24, had been a loyal member of the Polish Club since it arranged his victory in 1891. Capturing his seat carried tremendous symbolic meaning for Galician Zionists, although at first most of them almost ignored the election, choosing instead to take their regular vacations. A sudden awakening by Braude led to their recall and the establishment of a Jewish electoral committee based in Brody. Braude himself took charge of the organization, ultimately leading to his dismissal from the Stanislau Temple.[38] The Zionists nominated Adolf Stand to replace Byk and serve the final year of his term (see Figure 5.1). Stand energetically declared that if elected he would not join the Polish Club but would serve instead as an independent Jewish nationalist candidate, possibly even establishing a Jewish Club in Parliament. The Polish Club, on the other hand, had no intention of allowing "their" mandate to leave their midst, even for just one year, despite the fact that Brody itself had the most concentrated Jewish population of any city in Galicia, about 80 percent.

The principal candidate of the Polish Club was Josef Gold (1864–1939?), a doctor and the deputy mayor of Zloczow (see Figure 5.2), although several others also ran briefly, including the mayor of Brody, Stanislaus Rittel. Although the results would ultimately be decided under the old restricted suffrage system (Byk sat as the representative of the third, or Chamber of Commerce curia), the campaign clearly anticipated the "mass politics" of the following year's elections. Jewish nationalists staged numerous mass rallies, for example, which served not only to raise support for Stand, but

---

[37] *OSA/AVA*, Innenministereum, Präsidiale, 22/Galizien 1906, Karton 2110.
[38] Mordechai Braude, "Memoirs of Rabbi Dr. Mordechai Ze'ev Braude (1870–1908)," (Hebrew) in Dov Sadan, ed., *Zikaron Mordechai Ze'ev Braude* (Jerusalem, 1960), 193–7.

FIGURE 5.1. Adolf Stand.

also helped generally to raise the political consciousness of Galician Jewry, often in favor of the Jewish nationalist position. Unencumbered by other races throughout the province, as they would be a year later, Galician Zionists could invest all of their energy and best speakers in this single district, particularly Benno Straucher, whose prestige as a parliamentary representative carried considerable weight.[39] "Election fever," wrote *Der Jud*, was growing hotter every day, and not only among the voters. Daily

---

[39] Braude, op. cit., 195–6.

FIGURE 5.2. Josef Gold.

rallies were held in both cities, including four over the weekend before the election.[40] Similarly, a correspondent from Brody wrote to the Viennese *Neue Zeitung*, "The prospects of Adolf Stand rise from hour to hour," above all due to the great voter rallies. Zipper, Malz, Waldmann, Taubes, and others all made tremendous impressions, he wrote. "The Sunday rally, however, at which the Jewish national candidate presented himself and gave a brilliant speech, was totally spectacular. His statement, that he will not join the Polish Club, but rather will work to found a Jewish Club in Parliament, was received with storming applause."[41]

Zionists emphasized, as they had for Bloch in 1885 and 1891, how Stand would serve as a true Jewish representative and not sit as a stooge for the Poles. A lead editorial in *Der Jud*, for example, was titled simply, "A Jew Campaigns!"

---

[40] *Der Jud*, August 30, 1906.
[41] *Neue Zeitung*, September 14, 1906.

A Jew is a candidate and he is running as a Jew, not as something else. He knows that he can count on the votes of many conscious Jews and he hopes that the votes will be victorious.

We also hope so. But hoping alone is not enough. One must do. He who doesn't live in the electoral district [but] perhaps has relatives and friends there, his obligation is to move them through words or letters that they should work for the election of Adolf Stand. And he who has money, his obligation is to support the agitation fund in Lemberg and in this way to support the Jewish People's interest.

Jews! Celebrate, because the time has already come when a Jew can campaign as a representative of Jews.

Jews! Work, do what lies in your power, and the candidate will be elected.

Jews! The prize is great; try to win it![42]

Thus the election provided an opportunity to draw Jews into a political campaign not in Byk's district alone, but throughout Galicia. Indeed, Stand's election was portrayed as a matter of grave importance for the entire Jewish world, just as Bloch's election in 1891 had been. The Jewish masses are looking to this election as a sign of hope, wrote the *Togblat*. "The hopes of Zionism do not rest in this election, but rather [the hopes] of the Jews of Brody-Zloczow, and temporarily also of all of Austria."[43] *Hamicpe*, a Hebrew weekly based in Cracow, described the election as deciding the fate of Jews even beyond Austria, declaring that Jewish electors in Brody-Zloczow were choosing between blessing or cursing all Israel.[44] Recalling Bloch's 1885 campaign over two decades before, Stand portrayed himself as the candidate of the Jewish masses against their oppressors, of democracy against oligarchy, and of youth against anachronism. So he concluded his final campaign speech.

Gentlemen! Do you know the difference between me and the other candidates who have suddenly discovered their Jewish heart? Theirs is a struggle for individuals, mine is a system. I personally may fall, but behind me stand hundreds and thousands of young Jews, and this young-feeling People will later give us the mandate. We will get it as a mandate of the Jewish people! (Wild applause).[45]

Most important, for the first time, the Zionists completely severed the creation of a Jewish homeland in Palestine from their domestic political agenda. They made it clear that although Stand was proud to be a Zionist, he was running not as a representative of the Zionist party, but

---

[42] *Der Jud*, August 30, 1906.
[43] *Togblat*, September 14, 1906, 1.
[44] *Hamicpe*, September 7, 1906, 1–2.
[45] *Der Jud*, September 6, 1906.

rather as a representative of all Jews. Zionists, in a remarkable departure from their normal propaganda, candidly admitted that most Jews did not agree with their ideology and hoped thereby to convince them that voting for Stand did not necessarily imply support for Zionism.

> The Zionists, as a party, also have a narrow party task – to build a Jewish state in the land of Israel. And in this point, it may be that not all Jews are in agreement with the Zionists. Many simply do not believe in the possibility of realizing such a great idea, [while] others believe that it can only happen through miracles, supernaturally, etc.... [Therefore], when [Stand] goes into Parliament, it is not as a representative of the Zionist party, but rather as a representative of Jewish interests in the broadest sense.

Zionists are the most qualified to lead the Jewish people, wrote the paper, because they feel their suffering more than the other politicians and they have through their actions proven their commitment to alleviate it. "Therefore we rightfully demand that you should give us your vote, even if you are individually not a Zionist.... [W]e demand the votes not only of Zionists, but of all Jews, because we represent in domestic politics not only the Zionist position, but rather the general-Jewish [position]."[46]

To a large extent, the strategy worked. In the final weeks before the election, Stand picked up a number of important endorsements. Joseph Bloch's *Österreichische Wochenschrift*, for example, published passionate endorsements of Stand, albeit via correspondents to the paper. "All Jews who feel themselves as Jews," one declared, "in whose hearts lies the good of the Jewish People, must go together on September 14 as one man, friends, and elect the goal-minded [*zielbewussten*] Jewish politician, the candidate Adolf Stand."[47]

Whereas Bloch's support may have been predictable, Stand also received the endorsement of the fiercely anti-Zionist *Machsike Hadas*, organ of that ultra-Orthodox political party. The paper carried an endorsement of Stand on its front page just a week before the election.

> Among the candidates in Brody-Zloczow, none of whom we particularly like, we find the candidate Adolf Stand [to be the best]. Despite all of our opposition to Zionism, nevertheless we recognize that this candidate is the most desirable [compared] to the other opportunists whom the assimilationists nominated with the strength of the anti-Semites' fist. While their candidature is strengthened by heretics to their people and by those who are ashamed to utter the Jewish name on their lips, Stand proclaims his Jewishness up front [*b'reish gli*] and shows pride in it before all other nations.

---

46 *Togblat*, August 28, 1906, 1.
47 *Dr. Bloch's Oesterreichische Wochenschrift*, August 31, 1906, 9.

Time will tell if he lives up to his promises in Parliament, admits the paper, but Gold will certainly be of no use there. "He is a stranger to us," and here the paper echoes the Zionists themselves, "who does not know the needs of his people, because he never came as a friend to share in their troubles. Only now that a Jewish mandate was opened is he pushing himself in front of [our] faces to take the crown for himself."[48] That the ultra-Orthodox paper could criticize the assimilationist candidate in a populist, nationalist tone and endorse a completely secular Jew in his stead indicates a profound transformation in that group's political identity. Despite the fact that the paper respected those who, unable to vote for a Zionist, planned on staying home election day, Stand could not have asked for a better endorsement from that group.

Unlike Machsike Hadas, the parties of the Left did not unite behind Stand as the lesser of two evils. On the one hand, the labor Zionist party Poalei Zion, which at this stage was far more Zionist than socialist, had just cemented an agreement with the Zionists to support the independent Jewish National Party in the upcoming general parliamentary elections. Although few of their supporters were eligible to vote for Stand in 1906, the group did print a reluctant endorsement of him on August 31, about two weeks before election day. "Adolf Stand is no friend of *Poalei Zion*, but this is not important right now. Among all of the candidates he is the most Jewish [and] the most democratic, and therefore he deserves our support."[49]

In contrast to Poalei Zion, the Jewish Social Democratic Party of Galicia (ŻPS), despite its recent addition of national cultural autonomy to its platform demands, refused to endorse the Zionist candidate. Equally appalled by both candidates, its party organ *Der Sozial-Demokrat* wrote in its September 14 lead that for the Jewish workers it made no difference which candidate won. Both were bourgeois stooges with no ability or interest to better the conditions of the Jewish workers.[50]

The Zionist press often accused the Polish Club of intimidating Stand's supporters, charges which – whether true or not – Zionists utilized to rally support. For example, a Brody correspondent to the *Neue Zeitung* alleged that the Polish Club threatened local Jews that if Stand were elected, they would lower the number of Jewish mandates they had "conceded" in the distribution of electoral districts for the coming 1907 general elections.

---

[48] *Machsike Hadas*, September 7, 1906, 1.
[49] *Der Jüdischer Arbeiter*, August 31, 1906, quoted in Unger, op. cit., 82.
[50] *Der Sozial-Demokrat*, September 14, 1906, 1.

The accusation enabled him to declare confidently that such "election maneuvers" would scare nobody, adding that if they actually made good on the threat it would merely strengthen the Jewish nationalist camp.[51] A Zloczow activist's complaint in the same issue that Zionist opponents simply shut them down by force occasioned similar rhetoric. Allegedly, a voter rally scheduled for the Sabbath in the Zloczow synagogue was forbidden by order of the county prefect (*Bezirkshauptmann*) on request of Josef Gold, taking advantage of his position as deputy mayor of that city. Those present refused to disperse and wanted, according to the correspondent, to wait "as worshipers in the house of prayer" for the speaker to come. At this point the chairman of the Jewish Community brought garrison forces with bayonets into "God's house" to clear the hall. In the end, the meeting took place on Sunday instead, with Laibel Taubes as its main speaker. "Perhaps," he concluded, "perhaps the Zloczower Jews will one time finally get tired already of being the electoral slaves of the Polish Club."[52]

Stand, ironically, was among those Zionists who felt closest to Polish culture. Zionism was for Stand – a disappointed integrationist – a means of transforming Polish romantic nationalism into a Jewish context.[53] Thus, despite his strong opposition to joining the Polish Club, Stand openly admitted and even highlighted his Polish qualifications. In fact, he used them to distinguish himself from a popular Viennese rabbi named Rosenmann who also ran briefly for the parliamentary seat. At a rally on September 8, Rosenmann spoke in German while Stand spoke in Polish. Although he reiterated that, if elected, he would not join the Polish Club, Stand also spoke in favor of Polonizing Brody's German gymnasium.[54] (Gold, who had also been invited to the debate, excused

---

[51] *Neue Zeitung*, September 14, 1906, 2.

[52] *Neue Zeitung*, September 14, 1906, 2. The correspondent added for good measure that as deputy mayor Gold allowed the dead to vote, registering several hundred of them in Zloczow. Braude also describes the authorities' attempts at censoring Zionist placards and prohibiting Zionist rallies. Braude, op. cit., 193–7.

[53] At a Maccabee celebration that December, for example, Stand mocked the Hellenists for wanting to assimilate despite his praise for Greek culture! "They did not appreciate the beautiful and lofty [aspects] of Greek culture; they liked only the dirty and immoral [aspects] of the Greek land." *Togblat*, December 25, 1906.

[54] The Brody city council had already agreed to change the language of instruction to Polish in 1896, but negotiations to begin Polish instruction were still wrapping up. The council supported this less for nationalist reasons (that is, to integrate the school's graduates into Galician society and universities) than for financial reasons, as the change freed them from their obligation to contribute to the school. The high school, originally founded in 1818 as a Jewish community technical school (Realschule), began teaching the first grade

his absence, merely reiterating in a statement that if elected he *would* join the Polish Club.)

Considering Stand's strong Polish feelings, it is not at all surprising that no Ruthenian-Jewish alliance reached Brody at this stage. On the contrary, the Ruthenians, who formed a small minority of this urban district, actually nominated their own candidate. Recognizing the necessity of Ruthenian support for the Jews, Nathan Birnbaum used his short-lived paper, the *Neue Zeitung*, as a platform from which to plead with Jewish national- ists not to ignore the importance of Ruthenian support and to come to an agreement with the Ruthenians. "They express their sympathies to the Jewish nationalists in many meetings," he wrote, "and maybe they will also in the end vote for Stand.... [But] it seems that one has not yet found the right methods vis-à-vis the Ruthenians with which to bind ourselves into a strong political interest group."[55] A week later, he noted that the stand of the Ruthenians still remained uncertain, but that "the guilt lies absolutely on the Jewish side."[56] By then, of course, it was too late.

Despite high hopes, Stand did not win election to Parliament in 1906; the seat went instead to Gold who won with 855 votes to Stand's 454. (The Ruthenian candidate received 132 votes.) Zionists after the election immediately cried foul. "In the election commission they would not accept a single Jewish Jew," complained *Der Jud*. "In the streets they positioned garrison and military forces, they dragged the dead from the graves and bought votes as widely as they were allowed." But the fact that 454 Jews bravely voted for him despite all of that, concluded the paper, demon- strated the victory of the Jewish national spirit. "The national candidate Adolf Stand fell but the national idea was victorious."[57] The *Togblat* also described the results as a moral victory for the Zionists over the assimila- tionists, noting that considering the terrorism and corruption on the part of Gold, Stand's several hundred votes constituted a true victory. Indeed, in a careful calculation of all of the mitigating factors, the paper con- cluded that a majority of the voters actually chose Stand.[58]

in Polish in September, 1907. Börries Kuzmany, "Center and Periphery at the Austrian- Russian Border: The Galician Border Town of Brody in the Long Nineteenth Century," *Austrian History Yearbook* 42 (2011), 80–3. Recall that Brody Jews a generation earlier had fought against the Polonization of the public schools, arguing at that time that *as Germans* they had the right to a German-language school.

[55] *Neue Zeitung*, September 7, 1906.
[56] *Neue Zeitung*, September 14, 1906.
[57] *Der Jud*, September 19, 1906.
[58] *Togblat*, September 16, 1906, 1, and September 18, 1906, 1. The Kolomea *Yidishe Folks Politik* drew a similar conclusion. It too praised the "self-sacrifice" and "bravery" of the

The anti-Zionist Jewish socialists (ŻPS) drew exactly the opposite conclusion from the results. Zionists, particularly Poalei Zion, clearly constituted a major source of competition for Jewish socialists among recently politicized Jews. Although they obviously opposed Gold as much as the Zionists themselves, the ŻPS celebrated Stand's defeat as proof of the Zionists' misguided ideology. Despite the exhaustive agitation of the doctors, rabbis, and lawyers (i.e., the bourgeois professionals) for Stand, wrote the *Sozial-Demokrat*, not to mention the agitation of the Zionist press, the failure of the Zionists to win more votes was quite remarkable. Mocking Zionist propaganda, the *Sozial-Demokrat* argued that Stand's defeat proved that "the Zionists are not only not the 'only representative of the Jewish people' but they are not even [the only representative] of the Jewish bourgeoisie."[59]

The election itself certainly had little practical significance. Byk's replacement would fill his predecessor's post for just one year, with practically the only business of Parliament being the passage of the reform bill, already past its first reading, and the timing of new elections. With the new electoral system essentially delegitimizing the entire curial arrangement, it is hard to imagine a more lame duck session than this one. Stand might have put up a bigger fight for Jewish national mandates, but he was unlikely to have accomplished much more than Straucher.

The campaign's larger significance was its role as a prelude to the elections one year later. It was, first of all, an early opportunity to begin the 1907 campaign for the general election of Jewish national candidates throughout Galicia. The daily mass rallies and extensive newspaper coverage, which reached throughout the province and even Vienna, certainly made an impact on many previously disinterested Jews. Jewish nationalists also learned an important lesson about the critical role of Ruthenian support, even in such a densely Jewish city as Brody. How much more would they need help to win in less densely Jewish cities, let alone the minority mandate in rural districts?

Immediate post-election coverage already began using the defeat as material toward the more important battles to come. Jewish nationalists, as with Bloch's populist crusade more than twenty years earlier, sought to portray themselves as democratic liberators struggling against

---

454 Jewish voters for Stand, despite having previously questioned the wisdom of spending so many resources on this small election. *Di Yidishe Folks Politik*, September 14, 1906, 3; September 21, 1906, 1.

59 *Der Sozial-Demokrat*, September 19, 1906.

oligarchic oppressors. *Die Welt*, for example, wrote of Stand's defeat, "Instead of a fighter for the rights of the Jewish people, a new slave of the Polish Club has come into the Austrian parliament." The district's high number of Jewish voters signified to the paper the betrayal of the Jewish people by assimilationist voters, rather than the actual might of Polish rule.

The Poles? Oh no, they would have not been able to achieve the victory from their own strengths. But there is yet a class of Jews who without thought for their interests, without understanding the social interdependence [of all Jews], sacrifice their last and best on the altar of Polish assimilation. For in the election campaign between the Zionists and the "Poles" the national element alone was not authoritative. Not only the Jew Stand should have come into Parliament, but rather the Democrat. The victory of the Zionists would have meant the victory of democratic, free men over the power hungry, enslaving and slavish *Szlachta*. The victory of the Zionists means simultaneously the victory of an oppressed people over the oppressor. For the Poles are the rulers in Galicia – Jews and Ruthenians are in their service. The election of the Zionists could have achieved this social significance.[60]

Whether Stand's election would have signified such a momentous victory is unclear. In any case, such arguments would soon become ubiquitous as Jewish nationalists and their opponents prepared themselves for empire-wide elections the following spring.

THE JEWISH NATIONAL PARTY OF AUSTRIA

Galician Zionists continuously struggled with their Viennese counterparts over the question of Landespolitik. They wanted to work toward alleviating the physical misery of Galician Jewry and at the same time hoped that an active engagement with political campaigns would raise Galician Jewry's "political maturity." Nevertheless, before the announcement of universal manhood suffrage, even in Galicia support for Landespolitik did not entail running candidates in national elections, but merely supporting those candidates who pledged to defend Jewish rights and, heeding Herzl's call, to "conquer the *kehilla*."[61]

As late as October 1905, representatives of all three Galician districts (Lemberg, Stanislau, and Cracow) meeting in Lemberg to discuss their

---

[60] *Die Welt*, September 19, 1906, 6–7.
[61] Recall that the Galician Zionists' so-called Political Association (Politischen Verein), established in 1895 to introduce traditional Jews to the nature and significance of politics, avoided even political endorsements.

position on Landespolitik still did not question this approach. On the one hand, the group agreed with the delegate (Leon Reich) who argued that the Basel Program, focused entirely on the acquisition of a homeland in Palestine, was not sufficient for Galician Jews, who needed instead to work toward the improvement of conditions in Galicia. The conference agreed, therefore, that Zionists were obligated to engage in domestic political struggles and to include the Jewish masses in these struggles as much as possible. However, as Jewish life in Galicia was heavily governed by the Jewish community councils, the delegates called on Zionists to concentrate their efforts on conquering those bodies. Regarding national politics, Zionists were instructed to ally themselves with whatever party recognized the equal rights of the Jews as individuals and as a nationality.[62] The calls of the Jüdische Volkspartei to nominate Jewish-national candidates to the provincial Diet and national Parliament still did not achieve a large following, even in Galicia.[63]

By early December, the situation had changed dramatically. Electrified by news of imminent suffrage reform, Austrian Zionists in Galicia and Vienna began a vigorous agitation campaign demanding recognition of the Jews as an official nationality and the assignment of Jewish electoral mandates in proportion to their percentage of the population. In early 1906, Isidor Schalit (1871–1954), head of the Austrian Zionist organization after Herzl's death, met twice with Minister of Interior Count Bylandt-Rheidt to press these demands, which were flatly rejected. Nevertheless, the meetings helped Schalit solidify his role as leader of the Jewish national movement in Austria.[64] To this end, Schalit also went on a speaking tour as early as December 1905 to encourage provincial Zionist districts to adopt resolutions favoring an active engagement with national politics. Thus it happened, ironically, that the leader of the once staunchly anti-Diasporist Viennese Zionists came to Cracow on December 17 to convince a conference of representatives from all three Galician districts to adopt such a resolution. The Galician delegates of course fully agreed to pursue Jewish national autonomy by all possible means and empowered several delegates (Stand, Goldwasser, Braude, et al.) to oversee the campaign.[65]

---

[62] See the police report of the meeting in *OSA/AVA*, Innenministereum, Präsidiale, 22/ Galizien 1906, Karton 2110.

[63] See, for example, "Jüdische Nationalpolitik in Galizien," *Jüdisches Volksblatt*, May 6, 1904, 1. On the Volkspartei, see earlier and Chapter 4.

[64] Rozenblit, *The Jews of Vienna: 1867–1914* (Albany, 1983), 176.

[65] *Die Welt*, December 29, 1905, 3.

By now, the influence of the Ruthenians had begun to be felt as well. Iulian Romanczuk, the Ruthenian leader who first broached the subject of Jewish national mandates in Parliament, responded to a wave of telegraph messages of gratitude from various Zionist groups by appealing to the Zionists to organize themselves for the coming elections. Zionists, he wrote, needed to petition ministers both within Parliament and outside it. They needed to prepare Zionist candidates throughout Galicia and, above all, they needed to organize mass meetings to rally Jewish support for these candidates and the Jewish national idea itself. His letter was translated and reprinted in Gershom Bader's Yiddish Zionist daily, the Lemberg *Togblat*, which tried to convince its readers, including the Zionist leadership itself, to support the campaign to win nationality recognition.[66] Bader was especially concerned about rallying the Zionist leadership behind the campaign. He later recalled that his publication of Romanczuk's letter was against the wishes of the Zionist leadership at the time, "which would have slept through the opportunity."[67]

In May 1906, leaders of all Austrian Zionist districts as well as representatives of the Jüdische Volkspartei (which by then had merged with the Zionists) met in Vienna to decide how to organize themselves for the campaign. Rather than running candidates directly, they decided to form an independent and united party called the Jewish National Party of Austria to run candidates in the national elections. A conference of Austrian Zionists was hastily convened in Cracow on July 1 to debate the resolution calling for the formation of the new party. The resolution demanded state recognition of the Jewish nation in Austria, and called for measures to strengthen Jewish national feeling as well as improve day-to-day life. Leadership of the party was to be held only by members of the Zionist party, although non-Zionists would be allowed to join if they accepted the party's platform.[68] A Viennese Zionist who opposed Landespolitik insisted that the resolution note that the Zionist party itself did not constitute a political organization, a compromise accepted by the conference.

[66] The letter is reprinted in *Die Welt*, December 15, 1905, 6–7.

[67] G. Bader, "Political Activity in Exile" (Yiddish), in *Yidisher folkskalender* 14, 1908–9, 46–7. Ironically, Bader himself had sharply denounced the Jüdische Volkspartei's plans for precisely this campaign just five years earlier (see Chapter 4), but now he admitted the vital importance for Zionists to win recognition as a nationality in Austria because it allowed a place in the European mind-set for Jews to have their own state in Palestine.

[68] This latter point was the subject of serious debate. This policy had precedent in Galicia in the form of the Political Association, which welcomed non-Zionists on its board as long as they accepted all of the association's statutes. See earlier, Chapter 4.

The new party, headed by Benno Straucher and based in his Viennese office, was saturated with Galician Zionist leadership, including Adolf Stand, Gershon Zipper, Abraham Salz, Yehoshua Thon, and others. Galicians accounted for 92 of the 135 delegates who constituted the party in Cracow on July 2, 1906, as well as three out of the five board members (Stand, Zipper, and Braude; Schalit and Straucher were the others). The party set up offices in Vienna and later in Lemberg, the latter established principally to coordinate the electoral campaigns in the province.[69]

The establishment of an independent Jewish nationalist party not only avoided awkward questions about the nature of the Zionist organization; it also facilitated the integration of non-Zionist nationalists into the movement, both as voters and as candidates. On the one side, traditional Jews sympathetic to calls for Jewish national rights in Galicia but opposed to Zionism for religious reasons could now support the Jewish national candidate more safely, without compromising their opposition to the Zionist organization. (Recall Stand's similar positioning just a few months earlier in Brody.) The Galician Zionist leadership, in fact, expressly forbade any reference to the Zionist program at any rally of the Jewish National Party, an order apparently obeyed, if grudgingly by some.[70]

At the same time, the separation of the new party from the Zionist organization also facilitated the support of the socialist-Zionist party Poalei Zion, founded just two years earlier in 1904.[71] Poalei Zion had broken from the general Zionist organization in 1906, but in 1907 the group endorsed the candidates of the Jewish National Party, although they refused to join that party outright. A spokesman for Poalei Zion explained the decision as obvious:

For the Jewish worker there is no question for whom to vote in those districts where a socialist assimilationist is competing with a democratic Jew. Assimilation is a reactionary stance that damages the interests of the people. The [assimilationism]

---

[69] For a transcript of the conference deliberations, see the report in *Die Welt*, July 13, 1906, 7–10. See also the police report of the conference in OSA/AVA, Innenministerium, Präsidiale, 22/Galizien 1906, Karton 2110.

[70] So charged Israel Waldmann at the Eighth Zionist Congress a few months after the election. In response to catcalls denying the charge, Waldmann claimed to have spoken personally at eighty-six rallies at which no mention of the Zionist program was made, and he invited those who doubted him to ask Adolf Stand, present at the Congress, to confirm the order forbidding such references. Stand's failure to go on record against Waldmann suggests that it was true, as does the lack of "Zionist" rhetoric in rally reports during the campaign itself. *Stenographisches Protokoll der Verhandlungen des VIII Zionisten Congress* (Vienna, 1907), 105.

[71] For a recent history of *Poalei Zion*, see Unger, op. cit. On the 1907 elections, see 131–40 ff.

of the PPSD, despite its red color, is no less dangerous than regular assimilationism; at its essence it is anti-socialist. To oppose it is not chauvinism, but rather concern for the national interests of the Jewish worker.[72]

Despite their extensive organizational infrastructure, Zionists clearly suffered from a distinct disadvantage in their late recommitment to Landespolitik. Just as Zionists themselves ridiculed pro-German assimilationists like Emil Byk in the 1880s for suddenly switching to the Polish camp, so too their own opponents now attempted to expose them as hypocrites for contradicting their own ideological rejection of Jewish national life in the Diaspora. This was especially true of the socialists, of course, who had been demanding universal suffrage since the movement's foundation in the early 1890s, even through Yiddish-language propaganda.[73] Writing a decade later, the ŻPS, whose party organ *Der Sozial-Demokrat* had displayed a front-page banner calling for direct, universal suffrage since its founding in October 1905, fiercely mocked the Zionists for their "sudden discovery" of the importance of Landespolitik for Galician Jewry. As early as January 1906, a lead article in the *Sozial-Demokrat* attacked the Zionists for spending all of their energies simply convincing the world that they were the only representatives of the Jewish people, and to get two or three "kosher" Jews into Parliament.

These same Zionists, who have preached their entire lives that the Jews are an abnormal People, that they cannot develop culturally in exile and that in order to become a People equal to all they must have their own territory, and that the only place where Jews can lead an independent cultural and economic life is *Erets Yisrael*, these same Zionists come today and explain to us that the Jews are a normal people equal to all. They show us today that theoretically a territory and even a language are not the only basis for the concept of a People, and consequently the Jews have the same rights (in exile) as the other Peoples and they state special demands in the name of the Jewish People. And it is characteristic how the Zionists throw themselves before the fashions of every time without looking to find any remedy for their insanity.

They have no program at all, claimed the paper, "so that one doesn't yet know today exactly what they want, one only hears their crying. In their press and also in their meetings they discuss national autonomy,

---

[72] *Der Jüdischer Arbeiter*, April 4, 1907, quoted in Unger, op. cit., 134.
[73] *Der Arbeter*, the Yiddish-language organ of the Galician Social Democratic Party from 1893 to 1896, regularly printed articles demanding universal and equal suffrage. The party even organized Jewish rallies toward this purpose. Jacob Bross, "The Beginning of the Jewish Labor Movement in Galicia" (Yiddish), in F. Kursky et al., eds., *Di Yidishe sotsyalistishe bavegung biz der grindung fun "Bund"* (Vilna, 1939), 497–503.

which they have perpetually combated, [as well as] national curias and proportional suffrage. It is thus no wonder they alone don't know what they want."[74]

Obviously, this is a gross oversimplification of the Zionist movement, which was far more complex. Zionists had never "combated" national autonomy. Indeed, Galician Zionists in particular had from the beginning committed themselves to cultivating Jewish national life in the Diaspora. In fact, it was not the Zionists but the socialist ŻPS that suddenly reversed itself, adding Jewish cultural autonomy to its party platform just one year earlier as a result of the electoral reform.[75] Clearly, however, Zionists were popularly associated with a nationalist vision that broadly called for Jews to leave Europe and settle in Palestine, and Zionist opponents could and did capitalize on this apparent inconsistency.

Zionist leaders, in fact, were themselves painfully aware of the need to reeducate Jews about their Jewish national vision. Nearly a full year later, they recognized their failure to get their message across to the Galician Jewish masses. The people do not yet know, complained one Zionist in a late 1906 editorial, that Zionists are even engaged in Landespolitik.

The people, to whom we want to come now, don't know us. It is well known that there exists something of a Zionist party, which wants to lead the Jews back to Jerusalem – but it is not known that this party also has a *Landes*-program, a *gegenwarts*-program. Several months ago it formed a Jewish-political party asso-ciation, but who knows it and its program? Who knows something about it and its strivings? – The offices, which the political association has built in Lemberg and in Vienna, probably do their work completely, earnestly and keenly. But that is not enough. A political association must not be satisfied with bureaucratic work. It must go out to the people, it must speak to the people, it must agitate, organize – and for what is our political association waiting? For that time when it will already be too late, when the other parties will already have everything divided up among themselves and for us nothing at all will remain.

The election in Brody-Zloczow proved what strong agitation could accomplish, he continued. (Recall that Zionists had portrayed Stand's defeat as a victory.) But then it was just one election and Zionists could send all of their best speakers there. The new elections required much greater organization in order to spread throughout the province.[76] Despite this and other Zionist pleas, however, only in the final months before the

---

[74] *Der Sozial-Demokrat*, January 12, 1906, 1. For similar rhetoric by the Austrian Social Democratic Party, see *Arbeiter Zeitung*, May 7, 1907, 3–4.

[75] The party specifically rejected any nationalist program in its 1905 founding meeting and manifesto. Rick Kuhn, op. cit., 40, 50.

[76] *Der Jud*, November 29, 1906.

election did the Jewish National Party finally begin to campaign seriously for election.

THE 1907 CAMPAIGN

When the suffrage reform bill was signed into law on January 26, 1907, Jewish mandates were not apportioned according to their population. Under pressure from Galician Jewry, however, the Poles did allow for the formation of six urban electoral districts with Jewish majorities.[77] It should be noted, however, that Jews constituted over 11 percent of the Galician population and thus from a nationalist perspective deserved eleven or twelve of Galicia's 106 districts. Moreover, it was unlikely that urban electoral districts could have been constructed at all without some falling to Jewish majorities, and Galician Zionists complained that the mandates formed were specifically chosen because they were the home bases of known "Polish lackeys."[78] Nevertheless, the battle lines for Jewish nationalist candidates had been drawn.

In Galicia, Zionists saw the 1907 campaign as the most important struggle ever of Jewish nationalists against the assimilationist establishment. "Away with the 'house Jews'!" cried Saul Landau (1870–1943) in an election-year propaganda book subtitled, "Foundations of a Jewish People's Politics."

After decades of domination, now finally the People will themselves have the word. The teacher's aids, movers and water carriers, coachmen, *tallis* weavers, match factory workers and other thousands of the proletariat who lead a miserable, joyless life in the ghetto, will soon become parliamentary electors.... And when these masses step into the voting booth, then they will raise the battle cry from the Vistula until the Prut: *Away with the vampires of the Jewish People, away with the house Jews of the Polish Club!*[79]

Frustrated with Galician Zionists during the Herzlian period, whom he felt had strayed from their program of Diaspora-nationalism in favor

---

[77] These were (1) one of the Lemberg districts, (2) one of the Cracow districts, (3) Stanislau, (4) Kolomea, (5) Brody (city), and (6) Drohobycz-Turka-Bolechow-Skole. According to the Polish Club spokesman, in seven other districts Jews constituted a plurality of the population, and in a few others they cast the deciding vote between the Polish and Ruthenian majorities. *Die Welt*, August 10, 1906, 7–8.

[78] These were, according to an early report in *Der Jud*, Dr. Rosenblat in Cracow, Emil Byk in Lemberg, Nathan Löwenstein in Brody, Heinrich Kolischer in Przemysl, and Elias Goldhammer in Tarnow. *Der Jud*, January 18, 1906. Przemysl and Tarnow were still expected to be Jewish mandates in early 1906.

[79] Landau, op. cit., 19. Italics in original.

of Palestine-work, Landau now praised the "wise political" decision of the Zionist District Committee of Galicia to put off the "purely Zionist questions" and energetically engage domestic politics.[80]

Of course, the decision by the Zionists to participate in Landespolitik came very late indeed, and the first concrete steps to enter the campaigns came even later, although to be fair the elections were only set in January 1907. It took the Zionists about one to two months after the passage of suffrage reform to mobilize their forces fully. The Jewish National Party initially nominated just half a dozen candidates, mainly in the districts set aside as "Jewish mandates." Indicative of its Galician focus, the party's main newspaper was the Yiddish-language daily, the Lemberg *Togblat*, which became the official organ of the Galician Zionist organization as of the first of January.[81] Despite the fact that it was nominally based in Vienna, the party only established a German-language organ (the *Jüdische Zeitung*) in mid-May, just days before the election.[82]

On December 19, 1906, the Zionist leadership met in Vienna to discuss the upcoming parliamentary elections. To present a united position at the Vienna conference, the Galician delegates (forty in all) met the previous Sunday in Lemberg. They adopted a number of resolutions that essentially shaped the nature of their campaign the following spring. The conference decided, first of all, that Zionist candidates, in the event of election, were obligated to try to form a Jewish Club and were in any case forbidden from joining any other national club. Second, electoral compromises with other parties were permitted only if the candidates' Jewish national individuality was preserved. Above all, the delegates agreed that the upcoming electoral campaign should be exploited as an opportunity to awaken the "national awareness" of the Jewish people, as well as to struggle against all forms of political corruption. Finally, the conference determined that not only Zionists were to be nominated in the upcoming

---

[80] Landau, op. cit., 27.

[81] The party's Polish-language paper, *Wschód*, was not discontinued, however. The *Togblat* was no longer under Bader's control. For personal reasons, Zionists had pushed Bader out of the paper in 1906 and likewise denounced his Hebrew-language paper *Haeth* (The Time) in 1907. *Haeth* appeared three times a week in early 1907, lasting only twenty issues. For a candid history of the *Togblat*, and its contentious relationship with the Zionist party, see Bader, "A Self-accounting" (Yiddish), *Yiddishe Folkskalender* (1908), 95–102 as well as a supplementary letter Bader attached to his final issue of *Haeth*, March 17, 1907.

[82] The paper was edited by Isidor Schalit, the former chairman of the party and parliamentary candidate in the heavily Jewish fifth Viennese district (Leopoldstadt I). Benno Straucher replaced Schalit as chairman just before the election.

election but also any Jewish national candidate who accepted the authority of the Zionist leadership. The delegates directed the Viennese conference to nominate Jewish candidates not only in districts with Jewish majorities but in all districts with concentrated Jewish populations. The conference closed by nominating its first candidates: Zipper in Lemberg, Malz in Drohobycz-Stryj, Braude in Stanislau, and Schalit in Kolomea.[83]

The decision to nominate candidates in all districts with significant Jewish populations was based on the premise that the main purpose of the campaigns was not to win election, although they expected to do so in the districts with the highest Jewish concentrations, but to exploit the opportunity to agitate among Galician Jews. As with the early Maccabee festivals and the Yiddish press, Jewish nationalists sought to create a politicized national community by campaigning for its defense. "The main thing was the nationalist propaganda," recalled Braude in his memoirs, "the awakening of the people and their organization for independent political struggle." Still, he wrote, they did expect to win in at least seven districts (Brody, Tarnopol, Stanislau, Drohobycz, Stryj, Kolomea, and Buczacz) in which Jews constituted a majority or plurality of the population and where, he assumed, Zionists could also expect the support of the Ruthenians.[84]

The mass rallies, which by May had become daily events in large and small communities throughout Galicia, formed the backbone of the Zionist campaigns, as it did for those of the other parties. Each day the *Togblat* announced upcoming rallies and their featured speakers in a large-print advertisement on its first page. In light of the election, the party announced on February 22 (and repeated in subsequent issues of the *Togblat*) that all rallies through election day would be free of charge. By late February, they had begun holding rallies in the major Jewish centers, especially Lemberg, although as late as April – just a month before the elections – correspondents in many smaller Jewish communities still complained that Jews in their area remained indifferent to electoral

---

[83] *National-Zeitung*, January 25, 1907. Thon would soon replace Schalit as the party's candidate in Kolomea.

[84] Braude, op. cit., 203. On the question of Ruthenian support, see later in the chapter. In contrast to Braude's later recollections, Gershom Bader wrote at the time of the campaign that Zionists did not at first expect to win Stryj but grew more optimistic following a wildly successful rally led by Adolf Stand. *Haeth*, March 14, 1907, 3. In a fascinating example of how linguistic acculturation did not match political alliances or ideologies, the rally – filled with religious Jews (*adukim*) – was conducted in German and Polish but held at the Ruthenian *Volkshaus*, which they subsequently reserved for use once a week for the remainder of the campaign.

politics. Once again, nationalist frustration at popular "indifference" to its "national" interests parallels other nationalist movements.[85] It highlights the constructed quality of the national community but also suggests the incredible accomplishment of the nationalists in the growing consensus among Jews that they did in fact constitute a community deserving of national rights.

Zionist rallies typically attracted a few hundred to 2,000 participants, although they were generally closer to the 2,000 mark, and several exceptional rallies brought in up to 5,000 Jewish voters.[86] Zionist speakers – candidates and others – raced throughout the province to promote their Jewish national vision and endorse their party's candidate. They often spoke for two to three hours about the necessity for "genuine" Jewish representatives who would not sacrifice their own people's interest as the assimilationist oligarchy had allegedly done until then. Typically, each rally ended with a "unanimous" resolution to support the Jewish national candidate of that district. Critically, the candidates did not limit themselves to their own districts but rather tried to reach as many different areas as possible. As a result, most rallies, at least until the final days of the campaign, did not even feature that district's own candidate.

Of course, descriptions of rallies and the choice of which rallies to describe varied wildly from one newspaper to the next, depending on its partisan publisher. Coverage of the rallies by the Zionist press should be read with an awareness of each paper's agenda. As noted, nationalist papers exaggerated the extent of violent struggle and framed all conflicts as nationalist in nature, even if other motivations (religious or even personal) underlay them.[87]

Zionist papers, above all the *Togblat*, not only provided coverage of their own rallies but also took care to note the failure of their assimilationist opponents to attract more than a few score attendees to their gatherings. (Socialist rallies, which could not be so easily dismissed as elitist and anti-democratic are mentioned far less frequently, and then usually those of the Polish socialist party. Jewish socialist activities are virtually ignored.) On April 18, for example, a local Zionist activist happily reported that just thirty of Zolkiew's 1,600 Jewish voters attended

---

[85] Judson, *Guardians of the Nation* (Cambridge, Mass., 2006), 23 ff.
[86] Leila Everett mentions one such rally in Drohobycz, but there are other examples as well. Everett's estimation that the rallies attracted from 400 to 2,000 participants seems to agree with reports in the local Zionist press, which she does not reference, although as noted they leaned toward the larger number. Everett, op. cit., 174.
[87] Judson, op. cit., 177–218.

a "*Moszko*-Polish" rally, and most of them were Zionist hecklers.[88] Zionists often tried to infiltrate the assimilationist rallies, but most were usually kept out, a fact the Zionist press happily contrasted to their own party's open "Volk" rallies. "Last night we had two meetings," wrote a correspondent from Tarnopol on April 7. "One [consisted] of Jews, the other by contrast [*l'havdil*] of Israelites. One was a voter rally, the other by contrast a conventicle."[89]

As during Stand's election campaign in 1906, Zionists portrayed themselves as the party of the "people" and their opponents as an oligarchic anachronism. As long as their only real competition was the Jewish candidate of the Polish Club, this strategy worked well. In Stand's second attempt to win election in Brody, for example, it worked splendidly. Stand's chief opponent was an opportunist named Szymon Wollerner. Wollerner, a wealthy man with apparently no real ideological conviction other than his own desire to win election, had initially approached the Zionists to secure his nomination. In a letter to Gershon Zipper, Wollerner promised the Jewish National Party thousands of crowns for their election coffers as well as his commitment to adopt their political platform as long as he did not have to do so openly until after his election. Only after they rejected him did he turn to the Jewish assimilationists, that is, the Jewish Electoral Organization.[90] After hearing of his nomination, Zionists contacted the Polish-Jewish party and informed them of Wollerner's pathetic attempt to buy his nomination as well as of their proof of this fact. (Braude self-importantly recalled doing so to avoid disgracing the Jewish people.) That party refused to budge, however, and the letter proved to be Wollerner's undoing.

The Zionists waited to expose the letter until just a week before the election, at which time they held a massive rally to which they invited the entire population of the city – Jews, Poles, and Ruthenians. Even Stanislaus Rittel, the pro-Polish Jewish mayor of the city, attended the meeting. Braude was given the job of releasing the evidence. "In my speech, I tried not only to develop the main points of Zionism and our political program, but also to prove that our movement had nothing

---

[88] *Togblat*, April 28, 1907, 3. The paper hints that most of the district's Jews, devout Hasidim, would however support the Polish candidate, despite his being a "known anti-semite."

[89] *Togblat*, April 12, 1907, 1. In this case, Zionists did manage to infiltrate the "Israelite" meeting, and with Israel Waldmann at their head they reportedly responded forcefully to all of the speaker's arguments.

[90] On this body, see later in the chapter.

against the true interests of the Poles, that we strived for real peace and cultural competition [i.e., pluralism] among the three nations who dwell in Galicia." After an emotional speech that described the long history of Jewish-Polish coexistence, in which he insisted the Polish state never expected the assimilation of the Jews, Braude revealed the letter. He noted the "wretched" state of the assimilationist party, that it could find no other candidate than Wollerner even after Zionists warned them about his character. The Zionists later distributed hundreds of copies of the letter throughout the city. "This speech was one of the most successful of my life," Braude later recalled, although the election proved to be close nonetheless.[91]

A frequent theme of Zionist reports was the opposition's resort to military force to suppress Zionist popularity. These allegations were utilized by the Zionist press to forge a sense of righteous uprising against oligarchic oppression. On April 21, for example, 200 Jews were arrested in Bolechow for trying to force their way into a rally of Nathan Löwenstein (1859–1929) – Jewish candidate of the Polish Club – guarded by police, garrison forces, and municipal firemen. The group immediately formed their own rally nearby. Apparently, just fifty people were allowed into Löwenstein's meeting and even they voted against a resolution to support his candidacy. By contrast, a Zionist rally organized at a kloiz (Hasidic prayer house) in the city attracted over 1,000 Jews who voted "unanimously" to support the Jewish national candidate, Gershon Zipper.[92]

Similarly, when Kolomea's pro-Polish candidate Heinrich Kolischer came to the city for a rally, barely 300 of the town's 6,000 voters showed up, including just fifty Jews.[93] Fearing violence from anti-Kolischer sentiment, garrison forces were stationed throughout the city to guarantee

---

[91] Braude, op. cit., 208–10. Braude's account is partially corroborated by a letter from Wollerner to the *Landesmarschall* (head of the *Landesausschuss*), following his defeat in 1907, where he complains that he didn't get enough support from the local county prefect [*Bezirkshauptmann*]. He adds that his whole campaign cost him 32,000 Kronen and that he had become financially and morally ruined. My thanks to Harald Binder for sharing that source with me.

[92] *Togblat*, April 21, 1907, 2.

[93] According to one local Zionist, Kolischer was a totally unknown figure in Kolomea and had to sneak into the city in order to be nominated by an assembly of local notables in the first place, subsequently disappearing before most Jews even discovered his arrival. A. J. Brawer, "In the Austrian Parliamentary Elections in the Year 5667 [1907]" (Hebrew) in Dov Noy, ed., *Sefer zikaron li-kehilat kolomeyah* (Tel-Aviv, 1972), 61. Brawer describes Kolischer as a "real assimilationist," a wealthy industrialist who identified with the Polish nobility.

order.[94] By contrast, the Jewish national candidate Yehoshua Thon spoke to a cheering crowd of thousands on Tuesday night and then again on Wednesday night. Friday night (Sabbath evening) he spoke at the study house, and Saturday (Sabbath day) at two separate synagogues, both packed. Thousands attended rallies held on Saturday afternoon and Saturday night, each pledging to support his candidacy[95] (see Figure 5.3).

An important sign of the growing influence of the Jewish nationalists was their now frequent use of synagogues and study houses for rallies, as well as for more informal lectures. Obviously, this allowed them to gain access to a much greater number of Jews than would have been possible were all meetings held in Zionist locations. Moses Rat, who spoke at several synagogues in Kolomea on behalf of the local Jewish national candidate (Thon), was even permitted to speak at the kloiz of the Boyaner Hasidim, despite their opposition to Zionism.[96] Nathan Birnbaum was likewise allowed to hold a Sabbath-day rally at the Sadigora kloiz in Zolishtshik. "The kloiz," reported the *Togblat*, "was already filled wall to wall at 7:30 with Hasidim, *balabatim*, workers and citizens from all classes, as well as Ruthenians." Birnbaum recounted how Jews had been politically "unripe" and allowed representatives who represented other people's interests; now was the time for Jewish national representatives, he concluded to tumultuous cheers. After the second speaker again blasted the "moshkos," the assembly passed the standard resolution "unanimously" supporting his candidacy.[97]

Often synagogues and study houses constituted the only large meeting hall in a city. Even in larger Jewish communities that did boast community halls, however, Zionists were often denied their use by anti-Zionist forces in the *kahal*. Jewish nationalists used the smaller study houses and synagogues as a means of circumventing their opponents in the community hierarchy, including at times the town rabbi himself.

[94] Kolischer, whose wife happened to be Braude's cousin, had been previously nominated in his home town of Przemysl as well as in Brody. According to Braude, in both cases he was forced to "flee" after just one rally when Zionists responded to his speech with such convincing erudition that he simply could no longer remain a candidate. Braude, op. cit., 208. If this is true, then universal suffrage certainly affected his political fortunes, for Kolischer had previously served as parliamentary representative from both of those districts. (See Appendix A.)

[95] *Togblat*, May 16, 1907.

[96] The Vishnitz Hasidim, however, did not permit him to speak at their kloiz. Moses Rat, "*Haredi* Judaism in Kolomea" (Hebrew) in Dov Noy, ed., *Sefer zikaron li-kehilat kolomeyah*, 86.

[97] *Togblat*, April 2, 1907.

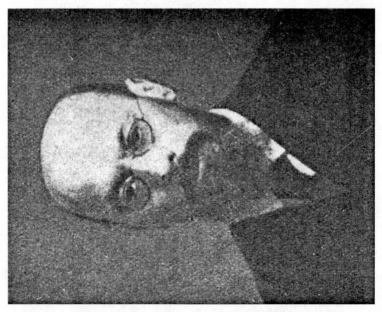

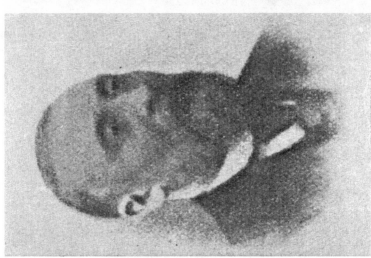

FIGURE 5.3. Heinrich Kolischer (left) and Yehoshua Thon.

Such a scenario occurred in Sniatyn, whose Jewish-national election committee, in honor of the party's nomination of Nathan Birnbaum, organized the city's first rally on Sunday, March 24.[98] The president of the *kehilla*, intending to block the rally, cynically responded to the Zionists' request for permission to use the main synagogue by insisting that they ask the rabbi whether it was permissible to use a synagogue for political purposes. According to the correspondent, the president knew full well that the rabbi would never give his permission, not because Jewish law forbade such a gathering, but because the rabbi was a strong supporter of the Polish candidate. When the Zionists received permission from the caretakers of a smaller study house to hold the rally there, the *kehilla* president allegedly managed to have the authorities declare the gathering illegal – supposedly because it biased the study house in favor of one party – and garrison forces were stationed to block the hall's entrance on the Sunday afternoon in question. Enraged, the Zionists issued a thinly veiled threat that such actions would lead to violent unrest by the town's Jews, and in the end the president agreed to open the main synagogue for the rally.[99]

Other times, the Zionists were less successful. At a rally led by Yehoshua Thon at the synagogue in Sniatyn, for example, a representative of the Polish county prefect closed the meeting on the grounds that no permission for the rally had been granted. When the organizers protested, pointing out that gatherings in synagogues did not require special permission, the official allegedly replied, "So what, the meeting is now closed because the building is not fit to hold such a large crowd." Thon attempted to deliver his speech outdoors, but "gangs of hooligans" suddenly appeared and beat up those assembled, thereby ending the meeting.[100]

---

[98] The Jewish National Party had previously nominated the popular rabbi Gedalia Schmelkes for that district but his candidacy was switched to a rural district instead. The nomination of Birnbaum was actually quite contentious. The party had initially hesitated to nominate him for any district both because he was not a native Galician and because he had by then become an opponent of Zionism. Birnbaum personally traveled to Buczacz to agitate among local Jews where he "won the heart" of the local Jewish national election committee, which requested from the executive in Lemberg that they accept his nomination. The party leadership acquiesced to this request and even allowed Birnbaum complete autonomy to run his campaign as he saw fit. Braude, op. cit., 204. Birnbaum's campaign to replace Schmelkes also enjoyed the active support of Poalei Zion. In fact, this was the only case of Poalei Zion opposing the candidate of the Jewish National Party. See Unger, op. cit., 134.

[99] *Togblat*, April 2, 1907, 2.

[100] Joachim Schoenfeld, *Jewish Life in Galicia under the Austro-Hungarian Empire and in the Reborn Poland 1898–1939* (Hoboken, N.J., 1990), 123.

Pro-Polish Jews often recruited the Polish authorities to block Zionist rallies. In Zborow, for example, about a week before the election, the Polish county prefect forbade the use of the town synagogue for a political rally by a known Zionist speaker on the grounds that the "Mosaic religion" forbids the use of a prayer house for political speeches. Violators were threatened with a 200 Kronen fine and fourteen days' arrest.[101] Polish authorities abused their municipal power in others ways as well. "Taxes of persons known or suspected of voting for the Jewish candidates," recalls Joachim Schoenfeld, "were suddenly raised, with no installment payment granted. The health department displayed vigorous activity inspecting shops, stores, and *khaydorim*. Some voters were called in to the authorities and were promised favors in the form of concessions and licenses if they would vote for the Polish and not the Jewish candidate."[102]

Not always did anti-Zionist Jews need to draw on the resources of Polish authorities. In Kolomea, for example, the Jewish deputy mayor Joseph Funkenstein essentially ran the city himself, serving under a puppet Polish mayor. Ironically, Funkenstein had once been a powerful supporter of Jewish nationalists. In 1891, for example, he publicly supported Joseph Bloch over Leon Meisels, signing his name to a placard demanding local Jews vote for Bloch.[103] As late as 1898, he addressed a meeting of Jewish nationalists in Kolomea and blessed their activities in the name of the entire Jewish community.[104] Highlighting the extent to which personal ambition rather than ideology and lofty ideals sometimes determined political behavior, Funkenstein now apparently feared that a victory by the Jewish nationalist candidate (Thon) would lead to his boss's replacement by a legitimate administrator and for this reason he became "enemy number one" to the Jewish nationalist cause. He recruited dozens of small businessmen to join his crusade, as well as a secret society of secular, wealthy merchants known ironically as "the good boys" due to their rare attendance in synagogue and public desecration of Jewish law.[105]

[101] *Neue National-Zeitung*, May 24, 1907, 7.

[102] Schoenfeld, op. cit., 123. These accusations are repeated by other sources as well, albeit mostly Zionist ones. For similar reports from the 17th electoral district (Kolomea), for example, see Brawer, op. cit., 61–2. For an extensive contemporary account of such abuses in the 29th electoral district (Rohatyn-Brzezany), see note 204. As noted later, extant police files corroborate some of these accusations.

[103] A copy of the placard appears in S. Bickel, ed., *Pinkas Kolomey* (New York, 1957), 83. See also Funkenstein's declaration of support for Bloch earlier, Chapter 3.

[104] Gelber, "History of the Jews in Kolomea" (Hebrew), in Dov Noy and Mark Schutzman, eds., *Sefer zikaron li-kehilat Kolomeyah veha-sevivah* (Tel Aviv, 1972), 45.

[105] Brawer, op. cit., 61. Brawer does not acknowledge Funkenstein's past support of local Zionists and his angry description of the deputy mayor may have been exaggerated. On

On Passover, just over a month before the election, Zionist speakers flooded the synagogues and study houses of Galicia, which were generally packed with worshipers during the holiday. In Lemberg, for example, twenty speakers went to different study houses throughout the city on the first night of Passover alone to speak about Zionist goals for the elections.[106] In Buczacz, Zionists held no less than ten voter rallies in the study houses and synagogues during the eight-day holiday.[107] Against pro-Polish opponents who cynically charged Zionists with violating the sanctity of synagogues (despite the fact that they did the same throughout Galicia), Zionists confidently asserted that the political rallies in fact constituted a holy activity perfectly fitting for a synagogue. A correspondent from Bolechow, for example, sent the following report of that town's first rally, held in the main synagogue.

It is noteworthy that despite the pamphlets of the community-clique [*kahalniks*] which argued that it is a desecration of God's name to speak out about politics in the synagogue, the people unanimously cried out that [Adolf] Stand should speak not on the cantor's platform but specifically [*davka*] next to the Holy Ark, next to the Holy Torah. And with right! Because they consider the matter to be a truly Jewish, holy thing that belongs precisely in the synagogue and especially [*taka*] next to the Holy Ark.[108]

Even the *Sozial-Demokrat*, in its surprisingly congenial report of Zionist outreach on Passover, expressed disgust at the Jewish oligarchs who tried to prevent the use of synagogues by Zionist agitators. According to the report, presumably reliable considering the paper's strongly anti-Zionist position, the "kahalniks" hung placards with a warning that the synagogues should not allow any Zionist to speak because this would only bring pogroms. The placards were signed "the government-true Jews."[109]

Zionists and socialists had good reason to protest against charges that they desecrated the synagogue by using it for such purposes. Not only did such accusations fly in the face of historical reality – these spaces had long been used for political purposes – but they displayed a coarse hypocrisy, for those who raised this charge simultaneously used the synagogues for their own campaigns. Nathan Löwenstein, for example, presented himself as a "democratic" candidate in Drohobycz dressed in a prayer

the other hand, Funkenstein's history also confirms Brawer's assessment that his anti-Zionist crusade had a purely personal rather than ideological basis.

[106] *Togblat*, April 2, 1907.
[107] *Togblat*, April 16, 1907, 2.
[108] *Togblat*, April 11, 1907, 1. 800 Jews reportedly attended the rally.
[109] *Der Sozial-Demokrat*, April 4, 1907, 2.

shawl during a service at the synagogue. His speech, seeking to bolster his populist credentials, noted that his father and grandfather were both rabbis.[110]

The Zionist appropriation of synagogue space was strengthened by the party's decision to include three pulpit rabbis among its nominations (Braude, Thon, and Schmelkes), whose posts offered a distinct advantage in that they provided the candidates with a captive audience every week. (Unfortunately, Braude lost his position on account of his nationalist activities.)[111] The decision drew criticism from some Zionists that it made them look like a clerical, anti-democratic party, and thus undermined their support among Jewish workers and intellectuals.[112] Jewish socialists in fact did capitalize on Zionist appropriation of religious positions. An anti-Zionist attack in the *Sozial-Demokrat*, for example, mocked Jewish nationalists for defining their program in terms of religious observance, here exaggerating their use of religious rhetoric. "Eat matzos, learn Torah, [eat] properly salted kosher meat, keep the Sabbath – to issue such demands amounts to the stupification and clericalization of the people!" Worse, the paper continued, "the gentlemen Zionists themselves are the greatest heretics and hold very little by religion." Thus, by their actions they seemed to prove the manipulative intent of their use of such rhetoric.[113]

Nevertheless, Braude and Thon had argued for years that the role of a preacher and his synagogue included the encouragement of political activism among the congregants.[114] Such rhetoric now assumed an even

---

[110] *Arbeiter Zeitung*, May 7, 1907, 3. Löwenstein's father was the Lemberg preacher Bernhard Löwenstein, discussed in Chapter 2. His wife was apparently the sister or daughter of Samuel von Horowitz, with whom he led the pro-Polish Jewish Electoral Organization. Joseph Margoshes, *A World Apart* (Boston, 2008), 45.

[111] Thon, who had avoided openly Zionist activity since assuming his post in Cracow, limiting himself to Zionist-oriented sermons, barely held on to his job in the face of opposition to his candidacy. Nella Rost Hollander, *Jehoshua Thon: Preacher, Thinker, Politician* (Montevideo, Uruguay, 1966), 28. Hollander recalled that Braude's dismissal occurred some time after he presented himself as a candidate in Stanislau, but Braude's memoirs make it clear that it had happened already in 1906. Braude, op. cit., 197–215.

[112] *Neue National-Zeitung*, May 10, 1907, 2.

[113] *Der Sozial-Demokrat*, April 4, 1907, 1.

[114] "The postulate that a rabbi cannot have a political opinion of a definite party was false," wrote Thon's daughter of her father's philosophy. "The moment has already come that the synagogue stops being the synagogue as of old, the preacher will not be the same as before, all this will not be any more God's memorial only, it will rather be a place to preach the revolution of the contemporary generation." Nella Rost Hollander, op. cit., 14.

greater importance. On the last day of Passover, Braude gave a sermon at the Stanislau Temple to thousands of Jews which highlighted Hosea's teaching that a preacher must teach Jews to struggle, and thus that politics do indeed belong in the synagogue.

It is a mistake to think that the Temple should be limited to prayer. "The dead cannot praise the Lord, nor any who descends into the silence [of the grave]." [*Psalms* 115, 17] And who are the dead? These are the wicked ones who even when they live are called dead. A truly live person cannot and must not close his eyes and remove himself from everything.[115]

Braude, raised in a strict religious environment, hardly limited himself to progressive Jews in preaching political activism. At a Sabbath afternoon rally in Lemberg, for example, Braude spoke to over 1,000 Jewish voters (over 200 were sent away for lack for space), "the majority in *shtreimels* [fur hats worn by Hasidim on Sabbaths and holidays] and gray beards." There was reportedly great applause when Braude entered, despite the fact that most of those present were still unacquainted with the Zionists or their program. Braude, who apparently spoke in German, was followed by a Yiddish speech from Fischel Waschitz and then the customary "unanimous" resolution of support for Braude's candidacy.[116]

In Stanislau, Braude's only serious opponent was his one-time friend Edmund Reich, the most powerful member of the Temple board who in 1900 had been the chief supporter of Braude's selection as rabbi.[117] Despite his dismissal from his rabbinical post, Braude remained a very popular figure among Stanislau Jews. According to Zionist reports, 8,000 people greeted him at the train station as he returned for the first time as a candidate.[118] Braude later recalled men and women of all ages calling out endlessly, "Long live our candidate, Dr. Braude." Half of the crowd, about 4,000 people, allegedly accompanied him to the courtyard outside the headquarters of the Erez Yisrael association in order to hear his candidate speech. As his opponents saw the mass of people marching with Braude to the Zionist offices, Braude later wrote, they "recognized for the first time the full elementary power of the national idea."

Braude did not pretend that all of these Jews had become convinced Zionists. Reflecting on these years in his memoirs, Braude admitted that these Jews lacked "national political awareness in the modern sense of the idea."

[115] *Togblat*, April 17, 1907.
[116] *Togblat*, May 7, 1907, 2.
[117] Braude, op. cit., 154.
[118] *Togblat*, May 9, 1907, 3.

The masses did not yet at all understand the difference between religion and nationalism within Judaism, and the idea of secular nationalism was foreign to them. I would say that even our program of organizing the Jews of Galicia and in Austria generally as a united nation among other nations, which already then found itself many movers among the young members of the intelligentsia who constituted the foundation of our movement, did not yet penetrate into the consciousness of the wider ranks among the people.

Instead, he insisted, their emotional support for his candidacy reflected a primal feeling in "the soul of the simple person" that the Jewish national movement would stem the tide of religious assimilation through its outspoken Jewish pride. He compared his own support to that enjoyed by Bloch, whose supporters similarly possessed no great political maturity.[119]

Gedalia Schmelkes, then a rabbi in Przemysl and a candidate of the Jewish National Party in the urban district of Tarnobrzeg-Nisko-Mielec, enjoyed far more influence over traditional Jews than either Braude or Thon, both of whom preached in progressive Temples. (Schmelkes, at least externally a more traditional rabbi, was also the nephew of Rabbi Isaac Schmelkes of Lemberg, a leading rabbinic authority until his death in 1906.) An even more important rabbinical supporter of the Jewish nationalist position was Israel Friedman (1854–1934), the new rebbe of Czortkow. Although he refused Herzl's invitation to join the Zionist Organization, Friedman and his father David Moshe had been vocal supporters of practical Zionism since the heydays of Ahavath Zion.[120] In 1907, the city of Czortkow fell in Arthur Mahler's electoral district. Not surprisingly, one of Mahler's first stops after arriving in Czortkow to present himself as the Jewish national candidate was at the court of the rebbe, where he was received for an "interview." Afterward, the Jewish nationalists publicized a "secret" instruction from the rebbe to all Czortkower Hasidim in Galicia to support the Zionist candidate.[121]

On the other hand, not all Hasidim were so receptive to Zionist ideas. Violent tensions already present between the two groups hardly dissipated in the charged atmosphere of parliamentary elections. The Zionist press seized on reports of conflict in its portrayal of Jewish nationalists as democratic heroes fighting hypocritical "religious" opponents. The *Togblat*, for example, reported that on the first night of Passover a young "Zionist Hasid" named Horowitz was brutally attacked in the synagogue

---

[119] Braude, op. cit., 211–12.
[120] See earlier, Chapter 4.
[121] Yeshayahu Austridan, *Sefer Yizkor le-hantsahat kedoshe Kehilat Ts'ortkov* (Haifa, 1967), 91. See also *Jüdische Zeitung*, May 11, 1907, 7.

by half a dozen of his co-religionists as punishment for inviting another Hasid to join the Jewish election committee during the dancing and singing which preceded the evening service. The paper blasted the attack as a "small pogrom, led by hooligans dressed in *shtreimels*, grandfatherly caftans and coarse [ritual] belts." Horowitz suffered under doctor's care for several days, the paper reported, and court proceedings against the attackers were under way.[122] (Of course, as we shall see, Zionists were not wholly innocent of using such tactics themselves.)

Zionist rallies not only raised support for specific nationalist candidates but also served to politicize Galician Jewry more generally and in particular to convince Jews that they constituted a nationality to which national minority rights were due. The vast majority of rally speeches focused nearly exclusively on the nature of Jewish suffering in Galicia, on the corruption of the current community leadership, and on the program of the Jewish National Party. Only in conclusion would the speaker mention the local candidate and his particular qualifications. Since most candidates ran in districts in which they did not even live, the party program in any case constituted a far more influential and interesting message to local Jews than the local candidate, of whom they had probably never heard.[123] For many, it was the first time they had ever been exposed to such political rhetoric. Laibel Taubes (see Figure 5.4), one of the party's most important and prolific speakers, here describes his impact when he spoke at a small hamlet in northeast Galicia.

I recognized that with this crowd one would have to begin from the political abc's, that the poor, oppressed Jews had no understanding of the most primitive political concepts – but I also recognized that this was an audience thirsting for enlightenment. And when I spoke I saw how the audience really came to life and listened eagerly and tensely to every word. Every word was for them a revelation, a sort of prophecy.... After I finished my lecture around midnight, an old Jew came to me and said, "Mr. Taubes! Admittedly, what you have told us is, truly, very interesting and completely correct. I want to ask you one question, however. Why are we hearing this now for the first time?"[124]

Taubes himself was also a candidate of the Jewish National Party (in the Przemyslany-Zloczow rural district), nominated during the Zionists'

---

[122] *Togblat*, April 16, 1907, 2.

[123] At times, the party held rallies before they even nominated any candidate. For example, a correspondent from Krshanub wrote that local Jews were so excited about the Jewish national candidate that they held a rally for him despite not yet knowing who it would be. *Togblat*, April 3, 1907.

[124] Taubes, *Zichrones fun Laibel Taubes* (Vienna, 1920), 20-1.

FIGURE 5.4. Laibel Taubes.

eleventh-hour spree of nominations in late April and early May. Taubes
was a critical figure for Galician Zionism because he helped it to overcome its image of being a movement of disillusioned secular intellectuals, an image made only worse by the rise of Herzl. Zionist propaganda
emphasized Taubes's religious upbringing and populist credentials to

highlight his connection to the common Jew. Taubes is no disillusioned integrationist, wrote the *Togblat* in its announcement of his candidacy, but rather is one of the people.

He was and remains a child of the People, one of the great Jewish masses. His parents left him no great inheritance, he made no *fachstudium* [i.e., university degree] in order to acquire a privileged "higher" status in society, and when Laibel Taubes became a Zionist, he did not "go down" to the people, but rather came up from the people. He did not come from a different world; he was not pushed to Zionism through rejection, through anti-Semitism, but only from inside [himself], from his soul of the people [*Folks-neshama*] he generated his enthusiasm for Zionism and for everything that is Jewish. Laibel Taubes thus became a Zionist not like many of our intellectuals, through his head, but through his heart.[125]

Taubes himself cultivated this populist image very deliberately. Henoch Halpern, who grew up in Gliniany, later recalled that although Taubes generally dressed "*Deitsch*," when he came to "Gline" for a Sabbath visit he entered the synagogue wearing a caftan with a *gartel* [ritual belt worn by Hasidim during prayer] and *shtreimel*, "exactly like all the Jews in the *shtetl*," in order that his Western dress should not undermine his influence before he even had a chance to speak. (Asher Korekh similarly recalled that Zionist preachers in Gline were careful to dress with a caftan and *shtreimel*.)[126] When he did finally speak, recalled Halpern, Taubes's striking dark hair, European manners, and beautiful, soft Yiddish won over the town. He was so beloved, Halpern wrote, that eventually he did not have to trade his German clothes for Hasidic ones.[127] In this personal appeal just before the election, Taubes again portrayed his candidacy as that of a Jew who knows his people's suffering, and knows what they need to overcome it.

I am a Jew who lives with the Jewish People, who lives with the great, poor, enslaved, oppressed but honorable Jewish *Folksmassen*. I don't consider myself, God forbid, any higher, any more honorable, any greater than the People. I am one of the People.... I know the pain of our People, our oppressed condition, our

[125] *Togblat*, April 28, 1907, 2. For Taubes's own description of his Zionist conversion, see earlier, Chapter 3.

[126] Asher Korekh, *Bagola u'vamoledet* (Jerusalem, 1941), 111.

[127] Henoch Halpern, *Megiles Gline* (New York, 1950), 142. Unfortunately, Halpern does not date any of these visits. The only rally by Taubes in Gline that could be confirmed took place on May 13, 1899. According to the local correspondent, the entire population of the shtetl showed up at the synagogue for Taubes's three-hour lecture, with the exception of the local Hasidic rebbe and "his followers." One wonders how large a group that represented and whether they objected primarily to the content of his lecture or to the fact that he held it on a Sabbath. *Die Welt*, September 16, 1899, 10.

difficult struggle for existence, our desperate needs, our wishes and our demands
not just in theory from books alone. No, I know this all from life, from our hard,
difficult Jewish life. I feel our People's pains, I feel them with all of my senses....
And that is why I have the courage, my brothers, to ask for your trust to enable
me to work for the good of our *Folksmassen* at that place where one must go
work: in the parliament. Therefore I am running [for Parliament].[128]

Jewish nationalists certainly did not shy away from exploiting religious imperatives in defense of their candidates, as they did on behalf
of Bloch in 1891. This was especially ironic in the case of thoroughly
secular and acculturated figures such as Adolf Stand, on behalf of whom
the Hebrew periodical *Haivri* printed a double page Yiddish-language
supplement just before election day. The extra-large header "Ne'ilah!"
refers to the final prayers of Yom Kippur before the gates of heaven are
closed. These final days before the election, it explains, are just such a
time. Thus the final moments of the campaign are elevated to the status
of the holiest day of the year. "The day of action has arrived," declares
the paper, echoing the solemn declaration of the prayers "The day of
judgment has come," but with the important difference that on election
day our fate would not rest in heaven. "Our fate lies in our own hands,"
it notes, "may it be for a blessing and not a curse!" This final phrase,
repeated throughout the page, is also liturgical, as are other appropriated
aphorisms such as "all Jews stand as guarantors for each other" and the
now familiar Zionist call for *akhdes*, unity, behind the Jewish national
candidate. On the left-hand column, the name of the local candidate,
Adolf Stand, appears three times in a large, bold font. The concluding
words declare, "Jews! Brothers! Have mercy on your honor, on the honor
of the entire people! Don't sell your right for money! Consider that your
fate lies in your own hands! Toss the fate such that it should fall for a
blessing and not for a curse!"[129]

Aside from the actual content of the speeches, the rallies themselves
served as a critical agent in forging a common sense of national community among Galician Jews. Rallies attracted Jews from all classes, men and
women, young and old, religious and secular. All stood together and often
intermixed by all of those criteria as they listened to speeches calling for
Jewish solidarity and national struggle. This photograph (Figure 5.5) of a
mass rally in Buczacz for the Jewish national candidate Nathan Birnbaum
(standing in front row center), for example, shows men and women of

---

[128] *Togblat*, May 12, 1907, 2.
[129] *Beilage zum Haivri*, Nr. 7, 1907.

FIGURE 5.5. Nathan Birnbaum at a rally in Buczacz on May 25, 1907 in support of his candidacy for the Austrian Reichsrat. Photo courtesy of the Nathan and Solomon Birnbaum Archives, Toronto.

clearly middle-class dress, women with uncovered hair, and shaved men with "German"-style hats, standing and sitting together with Jews of an obviously much lower social class, many of whom were women who covered their hair or men who wore long beards.[130] Where else would such Jews stand together? Where else would women with children stand among men, as many do in this picture? The rallies thus created a new national public space, in the case of this outdoor rally quite literally, in which all Jews could safely participate.

To be sure, not always could rallies accommodate such large numbers of people. Toward the end of the campaign, by which time rallies rarely attracted less than a thousand participants, organizers facing inadequate hall space occasionally limited attendance to voters alone, meaning that women and children were not admitted. In response, several districts organized rallies specifically for women, although men were also allowed to attend. Such a rally was held in the public soup kitchen in Brody on May 6, for example, featuring no less than Adolf Stand as its main speaker. Fishel Washitz first spoke on the importance of the moment for the recognition of the Jewish people in Austrian law, on the danger to Jews posed by the assimilationist clique, and on the importance of the Jewish women's movement and women's agitation for Jewish national candidates. Stand spoke on the Jewish national program, interrupted frequently by wild applause. In the discussion that followed, Mrs. Landau complained about a lack of Zionist support for socialists and used the opportunity to explain socialist theory at length.[131]

Another women's rally was held in Bolechow just before the election, at which over 600 women and men showed up. This time, both scheduled speakers were women. The first, Mrs. Heizelkam, spoke for over two hours about Jewish suffering and "*moszko*" politics. Filled with biblical references, her speech moved many in the audience to tears. Mrs. Feferbaum, who followed, discussed how all of the anti-Jewish laws impacted first and foremost women, who feel their families' hunger most pressingly. (A recent study of the Ukrainian women's movement makes the same exact point.)[132] Feferbaum emphasized the power that women can wield by using their influence over their husbands. Although women

---

[130] The picture appears alongside a list of participants (including S.Y. Agnon) in Israel Cohen, ed., *Sefer Buczacz* (Tel Aviv, 1956), 136.

[131] *Togblat*, May 16, 1907, 2.

[132] "Since women, to a greater degree than men, confront the minutiae of daily existence and family life, these minutiae become the primary concerns of women deflecting interest in feminism as such." Martha Bohachevsky-Chomiak, *Feminists Despite Themselves: Women in Ukrainian Community Life, 1884–1939* (Edmonton, 1988), 212.

could themselves not vote, she admitted, "we must at least exert all of our influence on our husbands that they should not let themselves be frightened by the terror of the enemies of Israel, because this is a matter of our very existence. We must do everything [in order to ensure] that our husbands should vote as one man for Dr. Gershon Zipper."[133]

ZIONIST OPPOSITION: SOCIALIST, INDEPENDENT, ORTHODOX, AND ASSIMILATIONIST

Although they eventually nominated nearly two dozen candidates, the Jewish National Party did not constitute the entire Jewish opposition to the conservative Polish Club. On the contrary, Jewish nationalism by this time had reconfigured the entire spectrum of Jewish politics, from the socialists on the Left to the Polish nationalist Jews on the Right. Certainly much of the credit for this went to the Zionists themselves, whose many years of agitation had begun to bear fruit. Competition in the market-place forced Zionist opponents to adopt some sort of national program, just as socialist pressure forced Zionists to establish Zionist workers' associations and to include various progressive social and economic programs in their platform. The hyper-nationalist atmosphere then dominant in Galicia surely played a role in the transformation of Jewish political discourse as well. In short, by 1907 no party could hope to mobilize Jewish voters without some sort of program demanding Jewish collective representation.

The Zionists' best-organized competitors for the anti-Polish Club vote were the socialists. In fact, Zionists actually faced two separate opponents in the social democratic movement. On one side stood the Polish Social Democratic Party (Polska Partia Socjalno-Demokratyczna, or PPSD), an opponent of the Polish Club but a staunch advocate of Jewish assimilation nonetheless. Herman Diamand (1860–1931), the one-time president of Zion who now served as one of the PPSD's highest ranking leaders, was one of the Polish party's most vocal spokesmen for Jewish assimilation (see Figure 5.6). Diamand described his party's position vis-à-vis the Jewish question as follows:

There are no special Jewish traits worth preserving. All retention of Jewish traits is deleterious. Although it is difficult for us to dispose of Jewish habits, we must

---

[133] *Togblat*, May 16, 1907, 2. Perhaps influential here was a well-known *midrash* that credits two wives during the time of Korach's rebellion against Moses with saving or dooming their husbands, by preventing or instigating their husbands' participation in the revolt.

FIGURE 5.6. Herman Diamand.

adopt new forms and not allow the difficulties that we encounter in Polish society to deter us. We must make every effort that all manifestations of Jewish uniqueness disappear as soon as possible.[134]

[134] Joseph Kisman, "The Jewish Social-Democratic Movement in Galicia and Bukowina" (Yiddish), in G. Aronson et al., eds., *Di Geshikhte fun Bund*, Vol. 3 (New York, 1960), 361. An abbreviated English translation appears in Jacob Hertz, "The Bund's Nationality Program and Its Critics in the Russian, Polish and Austrian Socialist Movements," *YIVO Annual of Jewish Social Science 14* (1969), 63.

Such rhetoric placed Diamand largely outside the pale of Jewish political discourse by 1907. The main spokesmen for the Social Democrats among Jews in 1907 did not come from the PPSD, however, but from the ŻPS, which had split from the PPSD in 1905.[135] Like the Jewish labor Bund in Russia, which provided a model for the ŻPS and supplied both ideological and material support for the new group,[136] the ŻPS insisted that as Jews constituted their own nation, Jewish workers needed to be addressed in their own language (i.e., Yiddish) and they needed to be represented by their own party. The group immediately joined the socialist campaign for universal suffrage, even before the emperor's November 1905 proclamation, but only at its second party congress in 1906 did it commit itself to the struggle for Jewish national cultural autonomy in Galicia. Both of these positions certainly lent the group a certain attractiveness and authority by 1907, not to mention the general appeal of socialism to many Jewish workers.

The establishment of a separate Jewish party was sharply denounced by the PPSD as well as the Austrian Social Democratic Party. Both argued that Jews did not constitute a nation and therefore had no right to an independent party which, they felt, would merely weaken the general movement. The PPSD – recognizing the growing appeal of Jewish nationalism to Jewish socialists – had actually tried to avert the split by forming its own Jewish division in 1903. Headed by Diamand – an avowed assimilationist – and largely devoid of any real autonomy, it did little to appease separatist sentiment and was eventually disbanded altogether.[137]

Despite the Polish party's relentless attacks against the Jewish "separatists," however, the Jewish party continued to express its full support for the PPSD, which it hoped would respond with a more favorable position toward Jewish national rights.[138] Thus, in 1907, while the

[135] The group announced its formation during May Day celebrations in 1905 (at which time publication began of *Der Yidisher Sozial-Demokrat*), but it did not officially constitute itself until June 9–10, 1905. See the police report of the group's first congress in *OSA/AVA*, Innenministerium, Präsidiale, 22/Galizien 1903–5, Karton 2109. For a history of the movement, see Bross, op. cit.; Kuhn, op. cit.; and Henryk Grossman, *Der Bundizm in Galizien* (Cracow, 1907).

[136] Rick Kuhn, "The Jewish Social Democratic Party of Galicia and the Bund," in Jack Jacobs, ed., *Jewish Politics in Eastern Europe: The Bund at 100* (New York, 2001), 133–54.

[137] *OSA/AVA*, Innenministerium, Präsidiale, 22/Galizien 1903–5, Karton 2109. *Der Arbeiter*, the Yiddish-language paper of the Polish Socialist Party published in Cracow, similarly denounced the new party and predicted its failure. *Der Arbeiter*, January 1905, 30.

[138] See the party's six-page response to the PPSD, "An Answer to the Polish Social Democratic Party," in its anonymous June 2, 1905, pamphlet, *Farn Kongress: Oisgabe fun di yidishe*

labor Zionist federation Poalei Zion fully endorsed the candidates of the Jewish National Party, the ŻPS refused to back down from its position that Zionism, as inherently bourgeois and reactionary, could never be supported. Despite its common cause with the Zionists of advancing Jewish national rights in Galicia, and despite the Polish party's open hostility toward the ŻPS, the latter group agreed in the name of socialist solidarity to endorse the candidates of the PPSD.[139]

Although the ŻPS did not enter any candidates of its own in 1907, the group took a very active role in the campaigns, organizing voter rallies throughout the province, many attracting thousands of participants. Like the Zionists, the Jewish socialists hoped not only to promote their individual candidates (in this case, the candidates of the PPSD) but also wanted to take advantage of the opportunity to penetrate into the Jewish masses and to educate them about their party's program. While socialist anti-clericalism obviously limited their appeal among traditional Jews, ŻPS rallies did attract some such Jews nonetheless, and not by accident. For example, on at least one occasion the group deliberately held a rally on a Sunday to attract those Jews who refused to attend political rallies on the Sabbath. The hall was packed with Jews of all classes, wrote the *Sozial-Demokrat*, including some "gray old Jews, for whom this was certainly the first time in their lives in which they attended a rally on a Sunday." Note the author's obvious contempt for traditional Jews, while simultaneously boasting of their attendance.[140]

While such rallies certainly constituted an important source of competition for the Jewish National Party, which inevitably received the sharpest criticism from the Jewish socialists, they also made an important contribution to the broader Zionist project of politicizing traditional Jews and strengthening their sense of themselves as constituting a national community. Zionists, in fact, recognized the benefit of socialist

---

Soz.-Dem Partei in Galizien. The group never hid its frustration and resentment against its erstwhile ally. Its spokesmen often complained how the ŻPS was actually squeezed between two groups: Polish socialists, who refused to recognize the ŻPS and allow it to develop, and the "Jewish bourgeoisie." By agitating for the Jewish vote, the group hoped to influence both of these groups. On the one hand, it pressured the PPSD to adopt at least temporarily a more favorable position toward Jewish national rights. At the same time, it forced the Jewish "bourgeois" parties to take the socialist position into more serious consideration. See, for example, *Der Sozial-Demokrat*, April 12, 1907, 3.

[139] Shabtai Unger suspected that Daszyński's explanation was closer to the truth, namely, that the ŻPS's decision was based less on socialist solidarity than on their lack of any suitable candidate over thirty years old, the minimum age. Unger, op. cit., 132.

[140] *Der Sozial-Demokrat*, April 19, 1907, 4.

agitation and in at least one dramatic instance even joined with them in a mass demonstration against their assimilationist enemy, even though they had each nominated their own candidate in that district. This occurred in Kolomea, just three days before the election, in response to Joseph Funkenstein's refusal to distribute voting cards as required by law. The Sabbath-morning march on city hall was organized by Aaron Schorr, the local socialist candidate, but was supported by Zionists as well and, most important, spontaneously attracted thousands of Hasidim walking home from synagogue. Still dressed in their *shtreimels*, they simply joined them as they marched. Although the crowd only secured about a thousand voting cards before being dispersed, the rally – like the one for Birnbaum pictured in Figure 5.5 – surely had a powerful impact on those who participated in it. These traditional Jews may have marched more in protest against Funkenstein than in support of either of the alternate candidates. The crowd was heard to shout both "Long live Dr. Schorr" as well as "Long live Dr. Thon!"[141]

Zionists not only faced stiff opposition from the Left. In Cracow, Zionist popularity was dwarfed by that of a local group known as the Party of Independent Jews (Partia Niezawiślych Żydow), headed by its parliamentary candidate, Adolf Gross.[142] Gross (see Figure 5.7) was the editor of *Tygodnik*, a Polish-language weekly in Cracow, which added a special Yiddish-language supplement to support his parliamentary campaign in the weeks before the election.

Jewish nationalists questioned Gross's credentials on two points. First, they noted his wavering commitment not to join the Polish Club, an accusation vindicated four years later when Gross in fact did join the Polish Club after his 1911 reelection. More important, they questioned his ability to build support among the Jewish masses because of his strong, outspoken anti-clericalism.[143] Gross's primary opponent was not the Zionists, however, but rather Józef Sare (1850–1929), the Jewish deputy mayor of Cracow and the candidate of the community oligarchy and of the Polish Club. Indicative of the times, Sare also turned to the Yiddish press in his

---

[141] For an impassioned first-hand account of these events, see Levi Grebler, "Social Democracy in Kolomea on the Eve of the 1907 Elections" (Yiddish), in Shlomo Bickel, ed., *Pinkas Kolomey*, 182–9. This story is roughly confirmed by a contemporary report in the Austrian socialist *Arbeiter Zeitung*, May 31, 1907, 3.

[142] On Gross and the Party of Independent Jews, see Andrzej Żbikowski, "The Impact of New Ideologies: The Transformation of Kraków Jewry between 1895 and 1914," *Polin* 23 (2010), 140–53.

[143] *Neue National-Zeitung*, April 19, 1907, 5; May 3, 1907, 7.

FIGURE 5.7. Adolf Gross.

bid to influence Cracow's traditional Jews. From April 26 through election day, Sare published a daily paper in Yiddish (the *Jüdische Mittag-Zeitung*), which he distributed free of charge.

Gross portrayed himself as a populist crusader for the Jewish people, a man who would "rather stay home in Cracow with his family" than run for office, but who was called for a higher purpose to serve the Jewish people. In particular, Gross sharply attacked the wealthy oligarchy that dominated community politics. "The Jewish People needs to have its representative [in Parliament] who will not simply do favors for individuals, but will work for the entire Jewish People." He energetically declared himself to be this true Jewish representative, although his speeches more often emphasized his defense of middle-class and lower middle-class interests. In the weeks before the election, Gross organized a number of mass rallies, each boasting thousands of participants "from all Jewish classes: *hasidim, balabatim* [bourgeoisie], workers as well as non-Jews."[144] In fact, Gross received a wide variety of endorsements – from assimilationists in L'viv, from the PPSD and the ŻPS, and even from *Wschód*, the Zionists' Polish-language paper based in L'viv! (The Jewish National Party, and its Viennese organs, obviously endorsed their own candidate.) Gross truly represented a form of Jewish solidarism, advocating the strengthening of Jewish communal institutions through their democratization.[145] Thus, although he opposed the idea of Jewish "nationhood," he certainly promoted secular notions of Jewish identity and the defense of Jewish collective rights. Like the Zionists, Gross declared that he would not join the Polish Club because it served only Polish interests. But neither did he intend to form a Jewish Club. Instead, he called for the establishment of a "Galician Club" to represent all of the province's interests in Parliament.[146]

Gross's populist rhetoric was of course designed to counter Sare's position as a member of Cracow's wealthy elite. Perhaps aware of the similarity between his own populist rhetoric and that of the Zionists, however, Gross focused much of his campaign on slandering the Zionists, whose recent successes in *kahal* elections allowed him to categorize them as members of the establishment. Indeed, when Zionist "hooligans" allegedly tried to disrupt a rally for Gross, *Tygodnik* described the Zionist infiltrators as even worse than the community establishment.

The foundation of political life is the rallies ... and those who would disrupt a rally are even worse than the *kahalniks*. We openly struggle against our obvious enemies the *kahalniks*, but against the Jesuit hidden enemies, the Zionists, we must struggle even more energetically.[147]

Because the Zionists' most important leader in Cracow, Yehoshua Thon, was nominated in distant Kolomea instead of at home, Gross could easily attack the Jewish nationalists as fearful of Gross's righteous candidacy. (He may have been right; the Jewish national candidate in Cracow would barely muster a hundred votes in the election.)

Zionists also faced tough opposition from the Right. The ultra-Orthodox *Machsike Hadas*, which had uncharacteristically supported the Zionists in Brody-Zloczow the past year, now withdrew their support and energetically entered the campaign in favor of the ruling Poles, their

---

[144] *Beilage zum 'Tygodnik'*, No. 18, 1907, 1. This particular rally attracted over 2,000 voters (nonvoters were turned away).

[145] Żbikowski, op. cit., 150, 153.

[146] *Beilage zum 'Tygodnik'*, No. 20, 1907, 1. In fact, Gross moved closer to the Polish Club during his first term in parliament and joined the faction outright in his second term.

[147] *Beilage zum 'Tygodnik'*, No. 18, 1907, 1.

traditional allies. Beginning in February 1907, the party (as well as Osias Wilf's now independent Orthodox paper *Kol Machsike Hadas*) printed repeated warnings against opposing the government, a charge they leveled at Zionists for refusing to support the ruling Polish Club.[148] The party strongly urged the nomination of suitable Orthodox candidates in all districts with Jewish majorities or pluralities. When one was forced to choose between Zionists and assimilationists, however, they advised readers to choose "the lesser of two evils" and vote for the latter, "friends of the Poles and lovers of the government," and not for the Zionists.[149] Their papers expressed deep fear about antagonizing the dominant Poles and mocked the Zionists' goal of establishing a Jewish Club in Parliament. "It is forbidden to go on an unstable bridge, and the plan of the Zionists to separate from the Polish Club is far worse than a shaky bridge."

What will a Jewish Club of six Representatives be able to accomplish in the next parliament? On the other hand, what will Jewish Representatives be able to accomplish within the Polish Club? ... Our splitting from the Poles will not hurt them in any case; even if the Polish Club loses some Representatives, their place in the coming parliament will be strong and it will be one of the pillars of the next government. But this split will hurt only us, for we will have no brother in the government during troubled times.[150]

The Poles constitute the Jews' only hope for an ally, wrote one article just before the election. After all, the Poles promised six of "their" mandates for the Jews, while the Ruthenians did not offer a single one of their twenty-eight mandates.[151] This was a gross distortion of the political situation. The twenty-eight Ruthenian mandates to which the paper refers were comprised nearly exclusively of Ruthenian constituencies, while the six mandates which the Poles "offered" were in any case comprised of clear Jewish majorities. In fact, the Poles generally opposed the formation of Jewish mandates and claimed all non-Ruthenian mandates as their own.

Despite their fierce denouncement of the Zionists, Machsike Hadas (like the "Independent Jews" in Cracow) also actively contributed to

---

[148] *Kol Machsike Hadas*, February 11, 1907. The paper called on Jews to support the Poles and not anti-government assimilationists, a category that included Zionists in ultra-orthodox rhetoric.

[149] *Kol Machsike Hadas*, March 28, 1907; *Machsike Hadas*, April 12, 1907; *Kol Machsike Hadas*, April 19, 1907; *Machsike Hadas*, April 26, 1907; *Kol Machsike Hadas*, May 3, 1907.

[150] *Machsike Hadas*, April 26, 1907.

[151] *Kol Machsike Hadas*, May 3, 1907.

the Zionist goal of Jewish political mobilization. The Orthodox party was mobilizing Jews in favor of the Polish Club and their Jewish allies, to be sure, but not because they opposed Jewish national rights but rather because they supported them. Indeed, Wilf's paper once stated as obvious the need for Jews to win equal national rights alongside their neighbors.[152] Thus even here, Zionist assumptions about the need for Jewish national representation were being confirmed; merely the tactics were in question.

Importantly, while Zionists clearly recognized the benefit of socialist agitation among the Jewish masses, few seemed to have grasped the significance of the Orthodox position. Zionist historians and memoirists tend to accuse Orthodox leaders of pathetic foolishness at best, traitorous self-centeredness at worst. Such writers generally portray the Orthodox-Polish alliance not as a positive political choice designed to advance Orthodox Jewry's own legitimate collective interests but as cowardly submission to the Polish authorities whom they feared and whom they thereby strengthened. Orthodox Jews thus appear as tools of the Polish authorities. Joachim Schoenfeld, for example, recalled, "The authorities put all types of pressure on the Jewish voters to induce them not to vote for the candidate of the Zionist party." He then immediately continued with an example of these authorities, namely, the Hasidic rebbes. "The rebbes asked the Hasidim to vote for the candidate favored by the authority and not by the Zionists. One shouldn't go against the will of the government [they argued] but should try to achieve relief only by requesting, petitioning, and asking."[153] Similarly, an article in the *Neue National-Zeitung* – the Yiddish *Togblat* would never dare to print something so anti-clerical – decried how the Belzer rebbe was allegedly "bought" by the Polish Club to support their candidate, an anti-Semitic professor, although Jews in his district comprised 67 percent of the population. "So goes Jewish fanaticism with Christian clericalism hand in hand."[154]

In Sanz, a Zionist activist actually composed a ballad, whose message of anger and disgust at the Jewish elites (identifying some by name, including the Belzer rebbe) recalls the anti-Meisels poem sung at Sabbath tables in 1891. The song was written for the Purim holiday and plays on the traditional prayer "Shoshanat Yaakov." It begins by recalling Haman, the villain of the Purim story, but then turns to describe the

[152] *Kol Machsike Hadas*, February 11, 1907.
[153] Schoenfeld, op. cit., 123.
[154] *Neue National-Zeitung*, May 17, 1907.

Hamans of today, "vile youth who denounce Jews at court" and despite defending "a goy against a Jew" become president of the Jewish community's Bikur Cholim society. The composer saves his most derisive comments for the rebbe of Belz, whom he compares to Emil Byk, Byk meaning also "bull" in Yiddish and Ukrainian. In the original Yiddish, the poem's rhyme requires a Galician pronunciation, "wonders" being pronounced *vinder* instead of *vunder*, for example, in order to rhyme with *kinder*.

> Something new has happened in the world,
> That nobody has yet before seen.
> That a Byk should wear a *shtreimel* and a *pelz*,
> It is actually the Rebbe, the holy man [*Tzadik*] of Belz.
>   *Shoshanat Yaakov* ...
>
> Once rebbes used to show wonders
> That [barren] women should have children.
> Even greater miracles show the Belzer
> That bulls [*Byks*] have calves.
>   *Shoshanat Yaakov* ...[155]

Such depictions are unfair. Certainly, many Jews were pressured, financially and otherwise, to support the pro-Polish candidate. But many were probably genuinely persuaded by the argument that Jewish leaders working within the Polish Club stood the best chance of protecting Jewish interests. Aside from the fact that all political choices are designed to defend those issues most important to the individual voter, many traditional Jews honestly viewed the Jewish candidates of the Polish Club, despite their secular credentials, as the best representatives for the Jewish community in non-Jewish society. Whereas Zionists were viewed as a secularizing force among the Galician Jewish youth, the Polonized Jewish elite promised protection against secularization, for example, by promising educational autonomy. Meir Gottesman, raised in a Hasidic family in Bolechov, recalled his father's response when Meir asked him to support the Jewish national candidate, Gershon Zipper. "What? I should give my vote to a Zionist, a sinner of Israel [*poshea Yisroel*]? No, I will give my

---

[155] Kalman Mahler, "A Political Purim-*Shpiel*" (Yiddish), in R. Mahler, ed., *Sefer Sanz* (Tel-Aviv, 1970), 538–9. Mahler dated the poem to the 1907 battle between Zionists and the "Moshe Rabbeinu's Poles," but perhaps confused by the reference to Emil Byk wrongly connects it to a nonexistent contest between Byk and Adolf Stand. Byk, of course, was dead by 1907. Mahler might have been remembering Stand's 1906 attempt to replace Byk, and if so it again highlights the extent to which that match truly constituted a prelude to the upcoming general elections.

vote to Dr. Löwenstein. He is a good Jew. He wins favors for Jews from the government."[156]

In fact, this perception was not at all unreasonable. The so-called assimilationists often cared quite deeply about the quality of life of Galician Jewry. Recall the activity of Emil Byk, the enemy of Jewish nationalists for over twenty years who nevertheless fought sincerely on behalf of Galician Jewry. The same may be said of Samuel Horowitz, the assimilationist leader in Lemberg who donated 1,000 volumes to the Zionist-sponsored Jewish community library and gave a stirring speech at the building's inauguration on the importance of Jewish awareness. Indeed, Mordechai Braude, who happened to be Horowitz's nephew, admitted that his uncle always remained supportive of his family despite his opposition to Jewish nationalism. Horowitz supported the appointment of Braude's father as rabbi and head of the religious court in Lemberg and had even taken a positive interest in his nephew's development and progress.[157]

The Zionists' problematic dismissal of assimilationists is especially ironic in the case of Tobias Aszkenaze, the so-called assimilationist opponent of Abraham Salz in Stryj. Aszkenaze, an unfailing advocate of Polish-Jewish integration with no ties to religious Judaism, eventually earned such a reputation as a defender of Jewish interests that anti-Zionists actually accused him of joining that movement.[158] Following the Polish pogrom in Lemberg in November 1918, Aszkenaze published an article in the Polish press recalling his long-standing support for the Polish cause but now demanding recognition for the Jewish nationality.[159] Similarly ambiguous is the case of Elias Goldhammer, whom a *Selbst-Emanzipation* correspondent endorsed for Parliament in 1891 (noting that "for all his Polish-national views he possessed a warm, full Jewish heart and had the courage to fight for what was good for the Jews") but whom *Der Jud* now decried as the "House Jew" of Tarnow.[160] The Zionist historian Raphael Mahler likewise described him fifty years later as a refined and educated

[156] Meir Gottesman, "How exactly did I become a Zionist?" (Yiddish) in Yona and Moshe Hanina Eshel, eds., *Sefer ha-zikaron li-kedoshe Bolihov* (Haifa, 1957), 268.

[157] Braude, op. cit., 206.

[158] See Gershom Bader's biography of Aszkenaze in his unpublished manuscript at the YIVO collection, op. cit.

[159] N. M. Gelber, *The National Autonomy of Eastern-Galician Jewry in the West-Uukrainian Republic 1918–1919*, in Isaac Lewin, ed., *A History of Polish Jewry during the Revival of Poland* (New York, 1990), 240. Nathan Löwenstein likewise grew much more engaged in Jewish issues following the postwar pogroms. G. Bader, *Medinah va-ḥakhameha* (New York, 1934), 136.

[160] *Selbst-Emanzipation*, March 2, 1891.

person, as did Salo Baron in his memoirs of Tarnow.[161] And Rudolf Gall, the Jewish candidate of the Polish Club in Tarnopol, organized and raised funds in 1906 for a short-lived cooperative for local destitute carpenters who lacked sufficient work tools.[162]

It is well worth remembering that Braude and Thon, two of the highest ranking leaders of the Jewish nationalist movement in Galicia since its foundation in 1883, both received appointments at progressive Temples controlled by so-called assimilationists. So did Samuel Gutman, the author of the Zionist chapbook *Der Wecker*, who was appointed assistant rabbi of the Lemberg Temple in 1903.[163] True, Braude was fired when he ran for Parliament in 1907. But Thon was not, despite the Temple's disapproval of his decision, and even Braude – an outspoken Zionist leader – served for seven years before his dismissal from the Temple. Moreover, his sponsor at the Temple, Edmund Reich, whom Braude described as a "powerful man who was always considered an extreme assimilationist and a man who did his public work in active partnership with the Polish authorities," continued to praise Braude and treat him with "devotion and affection," despite his Zionist activities. In fact, Braude admitted, Reich was in general "very sympathetic with the aspirations of the young Zionists," although he turned into Braude's "enemy" after the latter's decision to manage Stand's 1906 campaign.[164]

Thon similarly had an assimilationist sponsor in Cracow, Leon Horowitz, head of the Cracow Jewish community and brother of Samuel Horowitz. Leon Horowitz, whom even his nephew Braude described as a "moderate assimilationist who recognized the power and value of Zionism," loved Thon dearly and permitted him to promote Zionism in his speeches and sermons as long as he distanced himself from active Zionist politics. Thon respected this condition for ten years, until the

---

[161] R. Mahler, ed., *Sefer Sanz*, 538. Salo Baron recalled Goldhammer as a distinguished lawyer who, according to "popular local consensus," was robbed of his electoral victory by illegal machinations. Baron, *Under Two Civilizations: Tarnow, 1895–1914* (Palo Alto, CA, 1990), 2.

[162] Leopold Lourie, "Geschichte des Galizischen Hilfvereins," in Adele von Mises, ed., *Tante Adele erzaehlt … 1858–1931* (unpublished manuscript, Leo Baeck Institute, New York), 4. The cooperative dissolved shortly after its founding when its members, who did not understand the idea of a cooperative, divided up the tools among themselves.

[163] See Chapter 2. Recall that Gutman's principal function, ironically, was to deliver Polish-language sermons on alternate weeks, which the senior rabbi (Ezekiel Caro) found too difficult.

[164] Braude, op. cit., 156–7, 197. One can imagine the impact of Braude's decision to oppose Reich in parliamentary elections in 1907.

elections in 1907.[165] The suggestion by one of Thon's biographers that Thon's congregants merely tolerated his semi-Zionist sermons, which tried to "plant a seed of national pride" and build an interest in Hebrew culture, on account of his great erudition and spiritual depth is simply not sufficient. Other gifted preachers must have been available without the Zionist baggage. Aside from enjoying his oratorical talent, Thon's congregants probably appreciated Thon's deep love for Jewish people and Jewish culture, and his ability to instill this love in the members' children, despite their disapproval of his political ideas. More than just a few of them still possessed a "warm, Jewish heart."[166] Thon himself recognized this. In 1901, Thon publicly slammed Adolf Stand – and Cracow Jews – for celebrating Horowitz's defeat in that year's elections to the Galician Diet. Horowitz at least ran as a Jew, wrote Thon, while his democratic opponent who happened to be Jewish ran "only" as a democrat. "The last elections signify – admittedly only indirectly – a defeat for Zionist work.... [Horowitz's defeat indicates that] Jewish community feeling [*Gemeingefühl*] is strongly, strongly dying. This is incredibly sad."[167]

Like the Zionists, the so-called assimilationists also shared a vision of Jewish collective leadership, albeit in a form very different from what the Zionists had in mind. On January 6, 1907, almost one year after Byk's infamous "conventicle," approximately 250 Jewish leaders (parliamentary and diet representatives together with other members of the secular intelligentsia) met in Cracow for the purpose of establishing a Galician-Jewish political organization. The conference was led by Samuel Horowitz (see Figure 5.8), president of the Lemberg Chamber of Commerce, long-time advocate of Jewish-Polish integration, and staunch ally of the Polish Club.

In his keynote speech, preserved in a police report of the meeting, Nathan Löwenstein (see Figure 5.8), son of the late rabbi of the Lemberg Temple and now candidate of the Polish Club in Drohobycz, spoke about the new living conditions [*Existenzbedingungen*] that the electoral reform made possible for Jews. (Löwenstein was also the one-time editor of *Ojczyzna*.) As the leaders of Galician Jewry, he insisted, it was their obligation to establish a strong organization charged with defending the interests of the Jews. A resolution calling for the establishment of an organization to defend the political and economic interests of Galician

[165] Braude, op. cit., 203.
[166] Hirshaut, *In Gang Fun Der Geshichte* (Tel-Aviv, 1984), 260–1.
[167] *Die Welt*, October 10, 1901, 4–5. Stand's article appeared September 20, 1901, 7.

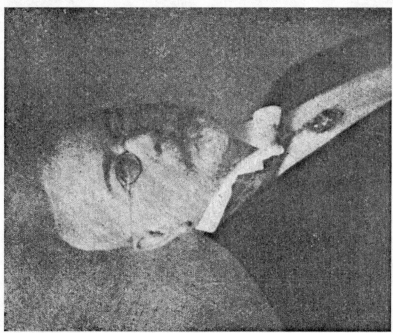

FIGURE 5.8. Samuel Horowitz (left) and Nathan Löwenstein.

Jewry was soon passed with the provision that general and national-Polish interests were also served. (In case the point was missed, a series of speakers proceeded to denounce the Zionists' anti-Polish politics.) The assembly elected an executive committee headed by Horowitz with local representatives throughout the province and charged it with preparing a program that would articulate the demands of the Jews in political and economic regards and "begin the necessary steps by which these demands will find consideration."[168]

The Jewish Electoral Organization, which set up branches in several towns, constituted the core of an independent Polish-Jewish organization that clearly belied Zionist claims that these leaders were simply Polish stooges.[169] To be sure, its proponents always repeated at their meetings that they supported Polish solidarity (i.e., the Polish Club), and Löwenstein, the group's leading figure, was also a member of the Polish Electoral Committee (Rada Narodowa), as was Artur Nimhin, the mayor of Stanislau. Still, in at least one case a branch of the organization opposed the candidate of the Polish committee,[170] and the group's paper, *Jedność* (Unity), demanded more than the seven Jewish mandates granted by the Polish Club. The Polish National Democrats in particular attacked the Jewish organization for its alleged "separatism," to which *Jedność* replied that such separatism was justified because of Jewish collective interests.[171]

Józef Sare, whom even *Jedność* opposed in favor of Adolf Gross, similarly emphasized his primary allegiance to his Jewish brethren. As noted above, Sare published a free daily afternoon paper in Yiddish during the election season to spread this message (see Figure 5.9). It argued, like *Machsike Hadas*, that only by working with and within the powerful Polish Club could a Jew accomplish anything for his community.[172] Describing the great impression he made at a rally, for example, the paper quoted Sare, emphasizing his Jewish credentials.

[168] See police report of the meeting in *OSA/AVA*, Innenministereum, Präsidiale, 22/Galizien 1907, Karton 2111.

[169] For a long critique of the organization, see Saul Landau's lead article, "Moschko mit dem Revolver," *Neue National-Zeitung*, March 8, 1907, 1–2. Among other comments, including a long description of what constitutes a "Moschko," Landau conspicuously and repeatedly notes that the organization's placards calling for support of the Polish candidates were issued in German (with Hebrew characters), suggesting again their supposedly insincere and opportunistic Polonization.

[170] *Jedność* endorsed Gross over Sare in Cracow. *Jedność*, 1907, nos. 5, 11, cited in Andrzej Żbikowski, op. cit., 150.

[171] Harald Binder, *Galizien in Wien: Parteien, Wahlen, Fraktionen und Abgeordnete im Übergang zur Massenpolitik* (Vienna, 2005), 160.

[172] *Jüdische Mittag-Zeitung*, May 3, 1907, 1, and May 4, 1907, 1.

In this moment, when I come to you to apply for your mandate, I must first say who I am. First of all, I am a Jew (Wild Applause). I have been a Jew, I am a Jew and I will remain a Jew. (Bravo). I have never been ashamed of this. I have at every opportunity openly declared it and will continue to do so. In my long-standing public activity, I have always stood up for the rights of my coreligionists, and I will continue to do so.[173]

As election day drew close, the paper ramped up its populist rhetoric with language virtually indistinguishable from its independent and Zionist competitors. "**Whichever Jew** has a warm Jewish heart," demanded the paper on May 8. "**Whichever Jew** has a clear mind. **Whichever Jew** understands the interests of his brothers. **Whichever Jew** wants their well being. **Whichever Jew** strives so it should be better for the Jews. He must strive to agitate for the election of the vice mayor, Mr. **Józef Sare**![174] Even if such rhetoric was insincere political pandering, which is not at all certain, it clearly reflected and strengthened a popular groupist mood on the Jewish street.

POLES, RUTHENIANS, AND JEWS

The key to Zionist success in many Galician districts, in which the Jews constituted only a strong minority and not a majority, would be the support of the Ruthenians. In seven East Galician rural districts in particular, Jewish nationalists competed with Poles for the second mandate, awarded to the candidate with at least 25 percent of the votes. In the likely event that neither minority candidate could muster a quarter of the votes, the winner would be decided in a runoff election, thus effectively decided by whichever candidate the Ruthenian majority supported.

Whether Jews could expect this support was not entirely clear. To be sure, evidence of cooperation between the two nationalist movements went back several years. As early as 1903, for example, Zionist leaders in Waszkiwci (Bukowina) and Stryj sent delegates to help celebrate the inauguration of a local Ruthenian gymnastics (*sokol*) association, something the Ruthenians clearly appreciated. A report in the *Ruthenische Revue* noted that the Zionist speaker was "energetically applauded" when he discussed the necessity of national reconciliation between Jews and Ruthenians. The paper noted optimistically that such reconciliation

---

[173] *Jüdische Mittag-Zeitung*, April 29, 1907, 3.
[174] *Jüdische Mittag-Zeitung*, May 8, 1907, 2.

יודישע

מיטאג-צייטונג

ערשיינט טעגליך אום 12 אוהר מיטאגס.
(אויסער שבת און יאָבטאג.)

JÜDISCHE MITTAG-ZEITUNG	
Wychodzi codziennie w południe z wyjątkiem soboty i niedzieli.	
Redakcya i Administracya: Kraków ul. Grodzka l. 50.	

Kraków, 15 Maja 1907. | Nr. 16. | קראקא, מאנטאג ב' סיון תרס"ז.

יודישע וועהלער!

איבערמאָרגען פרייטאָג דען 17 מאי, זאָלט איהר וועהלען
ווי איין דעם איינציגען אמתן יודישען קאנדידאט פיר
דען וואהלקרייז קאָוומיערז. וויצעבירגערמייסטער ה׳

יאָזף סאַרע

Wiceprezydent Józef Sare

ער איז דער איינציגער מאַן. וועלכער וועט אייערע אינטע־
רעסען אם בעסטען פערטרעטען.

FIGURE 5.9. Front page of Józef Sare's *Jüdische Mittag-Zeitung* on May 15, 1907.

appeared through East Galicia, "where until now the majority of the Jews went hand-in-hand with the Polish authorities."[175]

Nevertheless, reflecting traditional hostilities that still separated the communities, the report concluded by decrying the history of the Jews as

[175] *Ruthenische Revue*, November 30, 1903, 327.

a tool of the Poles in oppressing the Ruthenians, which it complained still continued among the upper Jewish classes on the one hand, and among the Hasidim on the other. "There are only two classes of Jews," it concluded, "who have a mind and understanding for the strivings of the Ruthenian People: the students and the socialist workers."[176] But these groups, of course, constituted a small minority of the Jewish population.

Jewish-Ruthenian cooperation stepped up considerably in the aftermath of Romanczuk's famous parliamentary speech. In early 1906, for example, 5,000 people attended a cooperative meeting of Jews and Ruthenians in Zavalov on the subject of suffrage reform. The rally was chaired by the head of the Jewish community, Moshe Sonnenschein, with the Ruthenian leader Zochorko serving as vice chairman. Another Ruthenian speaker, Dr. Botshinski, spoke about how the *szlachta* (Polish nobility) exploited both Jews and non-Jews. According to the report, published in the Zionist Yiddish paper *Der Jud*, Botshinski "called upon Jews to hold fast to their nationality, because only in this way will they come to their rights." He closed by warning the Jews not to vote for such people as Byk and his friends, but only for "true Jews, who will represent Jewish interests."[177]

During the critical months before the election, Ruthenian and Jewish nationalist leaders often attended each other's rallies and even published in each other's papers. The content of these articles and speeches, however, often indicates the limits, rather than the heights, of Ruthenian-Jewish cooperation. Jewish nationalists writing in Ruthenian papers emphasized their common struggle against the Polish conservatives. David Malz, for example, a candidate in the Zydaczow-Bobrka urban district and a leading member of the Jewish National Party, wrote an editorial in the national-democratic Ruthenian daily *Dilo* that emphasized principally how the Zionists had abandoned the Jews' traditional alliance with the Poles and had thereby incurred their wrath. The relationship between the Poles and Jews in Galicia has been transformed by the election, Malz explained.

The representatives of the Jews in Galicia until now, the so-called Poles of the Mosaic confession, have sold out the entire Jewish People for their businesses bought from the Polish nobility. Together with the Ruthenians and the patriotic Polish elements, we want to end this oligarchy, which poisons and exploits the entire land through [their monopolies] on liquor trade and tavern-keeping.[178]

---

[176] *Ruthenische Revue*, November 30, 1903, 328.

[177] *Der Jud*, February 22, 1906.

[178] The original article, "V spravi ruso-zhydivs'kyi," appeared in *Dilo* on April 11, 1907. My thanks to Yohanan Petrovsky-Shtern for locating and translating this and the other relevant *Dilo* articles for me.

Malz's mention of alcohol touched on a very sensitive subject. It referred to the history of Ruthenian resentment against Jewish innkeepers who, as agents of the Polish nobility on whom their licenses and livelihoods depended, allegedly encouraged and exploited Ruthenian alcoholism. Malz, essentially admitting the grounds for Ruthenian anti-Semitism, thus tried to argue that Jewish nationalists had abandoned the Jewish-Polish alliance, and were now, together with the Ruthenians, at war with the Polish nobility. In fact, to win the hearts of his readers, Malz claimed that Polish chauvinists dubbed him a "Cossack" and a "Haidamak," identifying him, a national-minded and anti-assimilationist Jew, as the most rebellious representative of the Ukrainian people.[179] Those Jews who went against the Ruthenians, he wrote, did so under duress, forced by the *Kahal*, the gendarmes and the tax inspectors. Now he, the Zionist candidate, would lead the Jews to defend not only the Jewish but also the Ruthenian cause.[180] Meanwhile, to his Jewish readers, Malz hoped to reframe the story as evidence of an intractable Polish-Jewish national conflict. A translation of the *Dilo* article by the German-Zionist paper *Selbstwehr* also reprinted the following response of the conservative Polish organ *Slowo Polskie* to Malz's statement: "This is an unambiguous declaration of war in the name of the Jews on the address of the Poles. The Zionists are unmistakably calling the Jews to battle against the Poles. This will compel the Poles in Galicia to begin a ruthless and bitter struggle against Zionism across the board."[181]

Dilo itself seems to have accepted quite soberly, if bitterly, the difficulty faced by the Zionists in overcoming not only powerful Polish opposition to the Ruthenians, but also a deeply embedded mentality among traditional Jews that their natural allies in times of struggle were the Poles and not the Ruthenians.[182] The paper noted, for example, that "among

---

[179] The Haidamaks, who operated in Southern Ukraine during the eighteenth century, were runaway serfs who carried out guerilla attacks on travelers, towns, and Polish manors. They were usually a minor phenomenon but periodically grew more threatening, as in Uman in 1768 when they carried out a brutal massacre of Jews. Like the Chmielnicki uprising of the previous century, the Haidamaks symbolize Ukrainian resistance to Polish feudalization and its Jewish collaborators. Moshe Rosman, *Founder of Hasidism* (Berkeley, 1996), 54–5.

[180] *Dilo*, April 11, 1907.

[181] *Selbstwehr*, May 10, 1907.

[182] Responding the previous December to the first Jewish nationalist contributor to *Dilo* (Isaac Kohn, whose article "Jews and Ruthenians" was reprinted from Birnbaum's *Neue Zeitung*), the editors noted that Kohn was quite correct in highlighting the common interest of Jews and Ruthenians in overcoming Polish oppression. Nevertheless, they wrote, significant efforts were required to overcome the "historical traditions" that had

Jews in villages and townlets there reigned an obscurantism that makes them into the object of exploitation for the Polish-szlachta goals."[183] Still, it understood that the Zionists were different, and in the aftermath of Malz's piece *Dilo* began to prepare its readers for an alliance with the Jewish National Party by explaining how the Zionists differed from popular stereotypes (traditional innkeepers who oppressed the Ruthenians and acculturated Polish Jews who ignored their national strivings) and encouraging Ruthenians to vote for the Jewish candidate as long as he opposed the Polish Club.[184]

This encouragement clearly affected Ruthenians on the ground. Not only did almost 23,000 Ruthenians vote for the Zionist candidate over his Polish opponent in the minority seat elections, as we shall see, but the evidence indicates that Ruthenians were not simply following the directives of their national leaders. Rather they actually appreciated the overtures of nationalist Jews toward them. This was most obviously the case with Nathan Birnbaum, a long-time advocate of Jewish-Ruthenian cooperation. Ephraim Schreier recalled that during Birnbaum's visit to Tlumacz before the elections, "the Poles in the town conspired to attack him, whereupon the Ukrainians came out to meet him with cheers, and escorted him to the meeting hall, shouting **Mi za Bimboma** [*sic*]'We are for Birnbaum' (they could not pronounce the 'r')."[185] A similar incident was described at the time of the elections by *Dilo*, which reported how Ruthenians had to protect Heinrich Gabel during a visit to his electoral district because the police had incited local gangsters to murder him.[186]

To be sure, Ruthenian contributions to the Jewish press were far more skeptical and reserved. Just a month before the election, for example, the *Neue National-Zeitung* published a general appeal to Zionists from Romanczuk for an alliance between the two national camps, without any specific details about the upcoming election. Romanczuk explained

---

so far shaped Ruthenian-Jewish relations, namely, Jewish support for the dominant Poles, and the Ruthenians' association of Jews with the immediate cause of their social oppression. "Zhydy i rusyny" [Jews and Ruthenians], *Dilo*, December 7, 1906.

[183] "Vyborcha statystyka [Election Statistics]," *Dilo*, May 20, 1907.

[184] See, for example, "Zhydy i vybory" [Jews and Elections], *Dilo*, April 11, 1907, which concluded that Ruthenians and Jews would become good friends once they overcame the Polish *szlachta*'s domination of Galicia. Petrovsky-Shtern found that the language of the paper also began to reflect this new attitude. "Chauvinistic" Polish nationalists were consistently dubbed "Christian-socialist anti-semites," for example.

[185] Shlomo Bond, ed., *Tlumacz: Sefer Edut V'zikaron* (Tel-Aviv, 1976), 33.

[186] "Vyborchi rozboi [Election Violence]," *Dilo*, May 24, 1907.

at length how the Poles demanded total Jewish assimilation, whereas the Ruthenians, admittedly engaged in an economic struggle against the Jews as much as they were against the Poles, were in national and political regards totally different. They did not demand any assimilation whatsoever, he wrote, but merely Jewish neutrality. Romanczuk acknowledged a high degree of anti-Jewish feeling among the Ruthenian people (police reports from these years are in fact littered with incidents of Ruthenian attacks on Jews), but insisted this was only because Ruthenians were astounded to see Jews continuing to support Polish candidates. "The nationalist, Zionist, as well as social democratic Jews take an entirely different position," he admitted, "but they form only a small minority [of Galician Jews]." He concluded with hopes that the Jewish nationalists would increase their influence among Galician Jewry.[187]

Romanczuk's conciliatory tone was unusual; most Ruthenians expressed frustration bordering on exasperation at the lack of support from Jewish nationalist circles. A follow-up piece to Romanczuk's article, for example, sent by an unnamed Ruthenian nationalist, sharply attacked Jewish nationalists for failing to instruct the Jewish masses to support the Ruthenian national candidates in the rural districts where they had committed themselves to do so. "The practical Ruthenian politician must ask himself," he wrote, "what are the other parties offering for my support?" The author pointed out that Jewish nationalists hardly formed the entire opposition to the conservative Polish Club – the Social Democrats nominated their own candidates in most Galician districts – and that the Jews could not expect to receive one-sided support from the Ruthenians. "The Jewish-nationals must finally find the courage, despite all of the jostling and slander of the Polish press, to express themselves openly and clearly about their relationship to the Ruthenians, [and declare] what they can offer us. For now it might already be too late."[188]

To be fair, the strains on the relationship were not so one-sided. Although Straucher repeatedly appealed for the formation of Jewish national mandates in Parliament, at least for Galicia and Bukowina, Romanczuk did not ever again raise the issue.[189] He might have been constrained by his

[187] *Neue National-Zeitung*, April 12, 1907.
[188] *Neue National-Zeitung*, April 26, 1907.
[189] As far as this author could find. As no reference to the Jewish nationality was indexed in the parliamentary records, such a search had to be accomplished simply by reading every speech by Romanczuk on just about any subject. Even the December 1, 1905, bombshell was indexed only as one of the entries in the suffrage reform debate.

own camp. The Ruthenian nationalist leadership may have supported the Jewish national cause, hoping thereby to weaken the Polish position, but anti-Semitism remained extremely widespread among the Ruthenian people, and Romanczuk might have undercut his own support by pressing the Jewish issue too strongly. Still, this was hardly the full support one might expect from an electoral partner.

Moreover, during the campaign itself, Jewish nationalist leaders did make clear calls to support the Ruthenian candidates in the rural electoral districts of East Galicia. Landau's election booklet, for example, explicitly called for such action.

We want, yes we must do right by the 3 million Ruthenians among whom the largest portion of the Jewish population of Galicia lives. And this righteousness commands us to secure the Ruthenians the 28 mandates ... guaranteed by the Polish Club by only voting for Ruthenian candidates in these 19 electoral districts of East Galicia.[190]

Landau was at the same time careful to temper his rhetoric, however, that it should not be construed as anti-Polish. "This is certainly not anti-Polish," he added, because these were designed to be Ruthenian seats with the agreement of the Polish Club. Despite all of the vicious rhetoric against the Jewish lackeys of the Polish Club, Landau was clearly concerned about a Polish backlash against any Ruthenian-Jewish agreement that might be construed as unfairly anti-Polish. Thus his endorsement of Ruthenian candidates was limited to those rural districts alone. In mixed urban districts, seven of which contained a Jewish plurality, he recommended that Jews cautiously form local agreements with the Ruthenians.

Ultimately, Zionists did manage to forge an electoral agreement with the Ukrainophile Ruthenian national leadership, although it was not well publicized in either community. In fact, the only written evidence for this explicit agreement that I have located lies in the police report of the National Democrat's December 1906 conference.[191] Leila Everett has noted the following two provisions, which I have not been able to substantiate based on her references, although electoral results seem to confirm them.

[190] Landau, op. cit., 32. There were nineteen Ruthenian districts; nine were purely Ruthenian while ten were mixed. Each district elected two representatives; thus they expected to win all eighteen representatives from the purely Ruthenian districts and ten of the twenty representatives from the mixed districts.

[191] *OSA/AVA*, Innenmininisterium, Präsidiale, 22/Galizien 1906, Karton 2110.

1. In districts where populations were ethnically mixed, the Ruthenians were to vote for the Jewish nationalist candidate in final runoffs ... between a Polish and a Zionist candidate.

2. In predominantly Ruthenian districts the Jewish nationalist candidates were entered to attract Jewish votes away from the Polish opposition so that in the second voting the same voters could support the Ruthenian candidate who, with their help, had entered the second round.[192]

It was not at all clear how well either side would abide by the agreement. Nevertheless, the agreement itself certainly highlights the great strides which the Zionists had taken in one year.

THE RESULTS

By the time of the elections, the Jewish National Party had nominated candidates in twenty Galician districts (see Appendix B).[193] In addition, the party also nominated two candidates in Bukowina: Benno Straucher ran for reelection in Czernowitz (East) and Nathan Wender ran in Czernowitz (West). Finally, four other independent Jewish national candidates ran in Galicia without the official support of the party, none of whom won although two of whom fared reasonably well. Salomon Merz earned 728 votes (out of 4,427 cast) in urban district 16 (Tarnow), and none other than Joseph Bloch ran as an independent "national-Jewish and democratic" candidate in urban district 30 (Zolkiew, etc.).[194] Despite his vociferous protestations to the contrary, Bloch was listed as a Zionist

---

[192] Everett, op. cit., 173. She cites an article in *Dilo* as well as Edward Dubanowicz, *Stanowisko Ludności Żydowskiej w Galicyi Wobec Wyborów do Parlamentu Wiedeńskiego w r. 1907* (Lwów, 1907), but neither substantiates that specific agreement.

[193] See Dubanowicz, op. cit., and the *Jüdische Zeitung*, May 11, 1907. Dubanowicz lists as "Zionist" some candidates who were in fact independent, and both sources miss some candidates. The *Jüdische Zeitung* does not include Braun and Weissglas, for example, but its summary of election results later describes both as Jewish national candidates, in contradistinction to several "independent" nationalist candidates. For a list of Zionist results by district, see *Summarische Ergebnisse der Statistik der Reichsratwahlen von 1907*, op. cit., 44–9. Note that some candidates ran in multiple districts.

[194] The other two ran in rural district 58 (Mielnica, etc.), where an unknown candidate received just twenty-eight of the Ruthenian district's 48,421 votes cast, and rural district 66 (Brzezany, etc.), where an unknown candidate named Kornhäuser managed 156 votes out of 38,733 cast. *Summarische Ergebnisse*, op. cit., 48–9.

in the published electoral results.[195] He collected 639 votes, losing to the Polish candidate Ritter V. Starżyński in a landslide.[196]

Ultimately, their victory would not be so grand. When the dust settled, four candidates of the Jewish National Party had won seats in Parliament: Benno Straucher, Adolf Stand, Arthur Mahler (1871–1916), and Heinrich Gabel (1873–1910) (see Figure 5.10). Stand, who lost his Tarnopol bid, managed in Brody to edge out the Jewish assimilationist Szymon Wollerner by 300 votes (2,585 to 2,228) when the third-place social democrats supported him in the runoff as part of an agreement mandating Zionist support for the socialist candidate in the Tarnow runoff.[197] Mahler and Gabel both won minority mandates in rural East Galician districts with the help of the Ruthenians in runoff elections.[198] As promised, on June 18 the four constituted themselves as the first Jewish Club in Austrian parliamentary history. In addition, the independent Jewish candidate Adolf Gross, with 1,869 votes, won a sound victory in Cracow,[199]

---

[195] Bloch responded angrily to an article in the *Neue National-Zeitung* that described him as a Zionist candidate. "It is untrue," he wrote, "that I am a Zionist. It is far more true that I was never a Zionist [and] that I have never belonged to the Zionist party. It is further true that I did not run as a candidate on a "Zionist" platform but rather on a national-Jewish and democratic program." *Neue National-Zeitung*, July 5, 1907.

[196] Starżyński collected 4,841 of the district's 6,414 valid ballots (over 75%). The Ruthenian candidate received 928 votes. *Summarische Ergebnisse*, op. cit., 44–5. Bloch initially ran in Vienna's heavily Jewish Leopoldstadt district but withdrew from that race before the election. On his 1907 campaign, see Joseph Bloch, *Erinnerungen aus meinem Leben*, Vol. 3, 153–96. Note particularly his speech printed on page 186, where he promotes himself by arguing that no other district would elect an independent Jewish candidate, not even in Galicia where all Jewish deputies would be compelled to join the Polish Club.

[197] *Jüdische Zeitung*, June 5, 1907, 2, and *Summarische Ergebnisse*, op. cit., 44–5. The agreement seems to have been secret, however. The ZPS endorsed Stand on May 31, writing that while the party viewed both candidates as reactionary, it preferred Stand because as a member of a party with just four to five seats he would have less power to cause damage than Wollerner, the candidate of the Polish Club. *Der Sozial-Demokrat*, May 31, 1907, 1. Braude strangely recalled that election as one of the Zionists' most successful, writing incorrectly that Stand won on the first ballot. He completely ignored or hid the critical support of the Jewish socialists in Stand's election. Braude, op. cit., 210. In 1911, countless articles in the *Jüdische Zeitung* recalled incorrectly that the socialists had failed to keep their end of the agreement.

[198] Mahler initially received just 2,565 of the district's 30,000 votes but beat the Polish national candidate in the runoff with 12,948 votes to his 8,612. (The Polish candidate had initially received 5,730 votes.) Gabel initially received just 2,146 of the district's nearly 35,000 votes, but beat the Polish national candidate with 14,537 votes to his 9,212. (The Polish candidate had initially received 7,196.) *Summarische Ergebnisse*, op. cit., 48–9.

[199] *Summarische Ergebnisse*, op. cit., 44–5. The Jewish National candidate (Hilfstein) earned just 123 votes. As a result, the Zionists became known as the "1, 2, 3 party." Nella Rost Hollander, op. cit., 28.

Adolf Stand

Dr. Benno Straucher   Dr. Arthur Mahler

Jüdischnationale Reichsratsabgeordnete

FIGURE 5.10. Front page (left image) of *Jüdische Zeitung* on June 5, 1907. The paper could not yet confirm the victory of Gabel (right image).

267

while six other Jewish representatives were elected in Galicia: two Social Democrats (Diamand and Lieberman), and four Jews committed to joining the Polish Club (see Appendix A).

It is difficult to overestimate the enormous charge that the elections gave to the Jewish nationalist movement. Jewish nationalists officially garnered almost 25,000 votes in Galicia on the first ballot, almost all of which presumably came from Jews, at a time when the Zionist organization had fewer than 5,000 members in the whole province, including women and men too young to vote.[200] In addition, Jewish socialists and members of the Jewish Electoral Organization together received over 36,000 votes, although it is unclear how many of these came from non-Jews, or how many Jews voted for non-Jewish candidates. The source for Leila Everett's claim that 85 percent of eligible Jewish voters actually voted on election day is also unclear.[201] It is not certain how many eligible Jewish voters lived in Galicia, but in 1900 there were 199,661 employed Jewish men in the province.[202] Assuming the number remained stable until 1907, and that many working men were under the legal voting age of twenty-four, the Jewish national turnout seems quite good. In any case, a large majority of them at least showed up at the polls, or attempted to do so.

In addition to those elected, Jewish nationalists nearly won several other seats. While Stand only narrowly won his seat in Brody, other Jewish nationalists lost theirs by equally narrow margins of hundreds and even tens of votes. Moreover, they clearly would have won several more seats, perhaps tens of thousands of more votes, but for the outrageous corruption of the Galician elections. The abuse of power evident during the campaigning grew infamously worse during the election itself. In Kolomea, for example, where the Zionist Yehoshua Thon lost to the assimilationist Heinrich Kolischer 814 to 1,970 votes (the Jewish Social Democrat, Aaron Schorr, received 1,137), thousands of Jews were simply unable to vote. Voter registration in this majority Jewish city was held on a Saturday, and those Jews who refused to violate the Sabbath by signing their names remained unregistered. Moreover, thousands of Jews willing

---

[200] Henoch Halpern celebrated that the Zionist candidate from Gliniany received over 100 Jewish votes by noting both the youth of many Zionists as well as the temptation for selling one's vote by Jews who suffered great impoverishment. Motik Halpern (his father?) held a lecture in honor of the "great victory." Halpern, op. cit., 150.

[201] Everett, op. cit., 175.

[202] Jakob Thon, "Die Berufsgliederung der Juden in Galizien," *Zeitschrift für Demographie und Statistik der Juden*, August/September 1907, 116.

to sign their names failed to receive their voter cards on the eve of the election. Plus many election cards came with Kolischer's name already filled in, and ballots on which his name was crossed out and another written over it were disqualified. For this reason, 174 votes for Thon were invalidated. Besides all of this, "hooligans" were allegedly placed near all voting stations to rip the election cards out of the hands of known opponents to Kolischer, apparently under the eyes of the garrison forces stationed to prevent such abuse. And hundreds of Jews suspected of supporting Thon or Schorr were kept waiting for hours at the polls until they simply left and went home.[203] The authorities disqualified just enough votes to give Kolischer an absolute majority (by four votes) and thus avoid a runoff election in which Thon's and Schorr's supporters would probably have united against him.

The "terror tactics" used by the Polish candidate Wladyslaw Dulemba to defeat the Jewish National candidate Samuel Rappaport in the urban district based in Brzezany were so outrageous that the Jewish Nationalists and Ruthenians – including even the social democrats – jointly published a sixty-six-page protest book following the election.

Protest against the election of Dr. Wladyslaw Dulemba. A portrait of terror and crime, committed in favor of Dr. Wladyslaw Dulemba on the occasion of his election to the Austrian Parliament in the 29th Electoral District, the City District: Brzezany, Rohatyn, Chodorow, Erzozdowce, etc. (in Galicia). At the same time an Appeal to Civilized Europe.[204]

The book documents hundreds of cases of fraud throughout the 29th district whereby, for example, supporters of Rappaport were either denied the ability to vote on false grounds or threatened with dire consequences if they voted against Dulemba. The book also lists names of people who voted multiple times for Dulemba. Many of these charges are confirmed by a police complaint filed on May 31, 1907, above all the accusation that the local county prefect (*Bezirkshauptmann*) Count Dziedusycki [*sic*] frequently threatened Jewish voters with a massacre were Rappaport to win.[205]

---

[203] *Neue National-Zeitung*, May 31, 1907, 5, and Brawer, op. cit., 62–3.

[204] *Protest gegen die Wahl des Dr. Wladyslaw Dulemba* (Vienna, 1907). This was apparently written by Nathan Birnbaum; a manuscript copy lies in the Birnbaum archives in Toronto, Canada. My thanks to Jess Olson for bringing this information to my attention.

[205] See police reports in *OSA/AVA*, Innenmininisterium, Präsidiale, 22/Galizien 1907, Karton 2111.

The corruption involved in the defeat of Mordechai Braude and Nathan Birnbaum was equally egregious. Braude, whose best chances of victory lay in the Jewish "mandate" of Stanislau, lost in the runoff by just 123 votes. Among other abuses, 156 votes for the Zionist were disqualified because voters spelled his name "Marcus" with a "c" rather than with a "k" as he spelled it.[206] Birnbaum faced similar abuses. In Buczacz-Zaleszczyki, the Polish national candidate (Moysa) initially received just over 3,000 votes, while Birnbaum and the Ruthenian (Jarossewytsch) received just over 4,000 votes combined. Although Birnbaum, a long-time advocate of Ruthenian-Jewish cooperation, certainly received the full support of the local Ruthenians in the runoff (election posters for Birnbaum printed in Yiddish and Ukrainian attest to Jarossewytsch's endorsement), he was credited with only 2,434 votes while Moysa raked in 3,797.[207] As in the 29th district, Zionist supporters were denied suffrage on false grounds, false votes were registered for Moysa, Birnbaum supporters were arrested on no grounds, and garrison and municipal forces were used simply to keep Jews and Ruthenians out of the voting booths in the runoff. Birnbaum, who restarted his Viennese *Neue Zeitung* on June 12, published a massive four-page protest against Moysa's election, which included "barely one-hundredth" of the alleged irregularities. His full protest letter was over sixty pages.[208] Zvi Heller, recalling many of these same abuses, describes several men returning every five minutes to a voting station to submit the voting card of one of hundreds of dead men registered by the mayor. As they approached, someone called "*Kohanim*, get out, the dead are coming."[209] (The Polish Club rewarded Buczacz's Jewish mayor, Berish Shtern, for his services in that election by nominating him to serve as parliamentary representative in 1911.)[210]

---

[206] *Neue National-Zeitung*, May 31, 1907, 6.

[207] *Neue National-Zeitung*, June 14, 1907, 5. On the election posters, see Jess Olson, *Nation, Peoplehood and Religion in the Life and Thought of Nathan Birnbaum* (unpublished dissertation, Stanford University, 2006), 156.

[208] *Neue Zeitung*, June 28, 1907, 5–8. See also Olson, op. cit., 157–60, where he brings a variety of examples from Birnbaum's protest letter. See also *Neue National-Zeitung*, June 14, 1907, 5, where a detailed account of the electoral corruption in Cygany is published, including a list of how specific individuals were denied the right to vote. Moreover, the town registered just twenty-six votes for Birnbaum (versus 296 for Moysa), although 170 voters swore on oath that they cast their ballot for Birnbaum.

[209] Heller, "From My Memories" (Hebrew), in Israel Cohen, ed., *Sefer Buczacz* (Tel Aviv, 1956), 144. *Kohanim* are Jews of priestly ancestry who are forbidden to come into contact with corpses, other than those of their immediate family.

[210] Yehuda Mosner, "My Young Years in Buczacz" (Yiddish), in Nechemia Zucker, ed., *Pinkes Galitsye* (Buenos Aires, 1945), 478.

According to one activist, Polish authorities attempted similar tactics in Brody to prevent Stand's election there. However, local Zionists got wind of a telegram coming to the local mayor ordering him to use all means necessary to prevent Jewish voters from electing Stand and successfully intercepted the postman outside the mayor's villa. By the time military forces from Lemberg arrived at the voting station just after noon, most Jews had already voted and Stand made it to the runoff.[211]

To be sure, Zionists also seemed to have engaged in "terror tactics," although clearly on a scale far smaller than that of their opponents. Although they scarcely admitted it at the time, later Zionist sources themselves confirm their recourse to violence, particularly against those known to have collaborated with the authorities in exposing Zionist supporters among the Jews. Joachim Schoenfeld actually recalled with great pride the "justice" meted out to one such informer, an innkeeper who suddenly received a hard liquor license after years of unsuccessful applications. That fall, on the eve of Simchas Torah, a few young Zionists casually plied the man with stronger and stronger drinks until he passed out unconscious. They then placed him in a casket and left him on the doorsteps of his home with a note that read, "May the slanderers have no hope," a well-known prayer from the daily liturgy. Schoenfeld recalled this story proudly, adding, "The lesson was not forgotten, not by this individual, nor by any other *moshke* informer."[212] Gershon Bader similarly admitted that Zionists and their opponents *both* engaged in "terrorist means" during their campaign in Stryj.[213]

The police files from that period also confirm such abuses, including reports of less subtle attacks against Zionist opponents. The records include a series of complaints of Zionist intimidation against Jewish supporters of the Polish candidate. "Following the failing candidature of Dr. Braude, Zionists riot violently, attack peaceful citizens, threaten their lives," submitted a group of Jews in Stanislau. "We request immediate help and protection." The Polish electoral committee in Stanislau complained similarly: "Zionist excesses disturb citizens who hold differing opinions [*andersgesinnte*]. Attacks on the street, violent threats against supporters of the representative Stwiertnia calls for immediate intervention by the authorities. We request full protection, otherwise risk danger on life,

---

[211] David Klinghofer, "How Galicia Sent Its First Zionist Representative to the Austrian Parliament" (Yiddish), in *Galitsyaner Yidn Yoyvl Bukh* (Buenos Aires, 1966), 165–6.
[212] Schoenfeld, op. cit., 125.
[213] See Bader's unpublished biography of Tobias Aszkenaze, Salz's pro-Polish opponent in Stryj, in Bader, op. cit.

property and honor." Supporters of Joseph Bloch, who ran independently as a "national-Jew and Democrat," were charged with similar crimes. This from the Jewish community council of Rawaruska: "Supporters of Dr. Bloch attack his opponents in synagogues and on open streets and plazas. Many people are already severely injured, while the entire city is extremely alarmed. As the county prefect and garrison give us insufficient support, we request aid and military assistance." Apparently the violence did not even stop with the election, but continued for some time. "In revenge for us voting for Maysa [*sic*]," submitted three Jews in Tlumacz, "we were attacked by Zionists, pelted with stones and injured. We request assistance." Supporters of Moysa in Zaleszczyki charged in a similar telegram to Vienna, confirmed by separate police reports in Lemberg and Czernowitz, that Zionist students from Czernowitz attacked them both verbally and physically, pelting them with stinking eggs.[214] Such testimonies certainly offer a more balanced picture of election day events, although the evidence indicates that the abuses of the conservative Polish candidates were far more extensive.

Finally, Zionist success may be measured even beyond the votes they themselves received. Zionists demonstrated political power even in districts in which their own candidate did not win. In Lemberg, for example, where Braude represented the Jewish National Party, the Zionist veteran earned just 854 votes, while his uncle and candidate for the Polish Club, Samuel Horowitz, managed 1,676, apparently with the support of local Hasidim.[215] This roughly tied with Herman Diamand, the Social Democrat and one-time Zionist, who received 1,672 votes.[216] Zionists would decide the election in the runoff.

---

[214] See police reports in *OSA/AVA*, Innenministerium, Präsidiale, 22/Galizien 1907, Karton 2111. Naturally, in addition to Ruthenian complaints of violence, the file contains numerous Polish accusations of Ruthenian violence as well. One even charges the Ukrainian Radical Party with threatening both Poles and Jews with death if they dared to vote for the Polish candidate.

[215] Zevi Karl, "Lvov" (Hebrew), in Y. L. Fishman, ed., *Arim v'emahot b'Yisrael* (Jerusalem, 1946), 337. According to contemporary Zionist reports, Horowitz actively pursued local Hasidic leaders to secure their support. They allegedly demanded three things: general, equal, direct and secret election of the Jewish Community Board; that important matters like rabbinical appointments be decided by an elected community council with the board serving as advisor; and that he support the option of closing shop on Saturday rather than Sunday. Horowitz seemed willing to go along, one article concluded, but the Hasidim were allegedly divided about whether he would honor his word, some threatening to support the opposition. *Neue National-Zeitung*, May 3, 1907.

[216] *Summarische Ergebnisse*, op. cit., 44–5 and *Neue National-Zeitung*, May 24, 1907, 7.

The decision as to which candidate to support did not come easily. Both candidates, after all, presented themselves as assimilationist. Zionists recognized, however, that not all assimilationists were alike. Horowitz, despite his rhetoric of assimilationism, had ultimately maintained his connection with the Jewish community, while Diamand had cut himself off from his Jewishness entirely.[217] Recall Thon's support for Leon Horowitz in 1901 because of his outspoken Jewishness. Ironically, however, precisely for this reason they now decided to support Diamand. According to Braude, Zionists feared that Horowitz would be seen as a Jewish representative and that his ideology of "political submission to the authorities" would undermine "the awakening of the masses towards independent national awareness." Socialists, on the other hand, despite their assimilationism – which was far more pronounced than in the assimilationist camp itself – at least instilled political activism among the masses, which Zionists hoped could one day be turned in favor of the Jewish nationalist cause. The Jewish National Party therefore directed all of Braude's supporters to vote for Diamand in the runoff.[218]

In his memoirs, Braude recalled attempting to emphasize that the decision was based on the Zionists' ideological struggle against assimilationism and thereby to limit the personal attack on Horowitz, his uncle.[219] This is simply not plausible, however. Braude may have removed all personal attacks on Horowitz in the endorsement letter itself, but his entire campaign had been presented not as a struggle of nationalists against assimilationists, but as a populist struggle against corruption. At a rally just days before the election, for example, Braude spoke to thousands of Jewish *burger* and workers declaring,

I come to you without money and without corruption.... I come to you as a human being, whose entire possessions and assets are his Jewish heart and his genuine goodwill, to work for you and for all Jews! Here lies the main difference between the Jewish national candidate and opponents; I come with a program, with a genuine goodwill and they come – with corruption.[220]

---

[217] Local Jews recognized this as well. At a Zionist rally in April, for example, David Schreiber discussed Lemberg's "three Jewish candidates," to which the crowd shouted, "We have only two Jewish candidates – Diamand is no Jew!" *Togblat*, April 16, 1907, 1.

[218] Braude, op. cit., 218–21.

[219] Braude, op. cit., 206, 220. Neither Horowitz nor the rest of the family bought this argument. Braude's decision to sign the endorsement of Diamand, despite Horowitz's past personal support for Braude and his family, cost him many friends within his family, many of whom cut off all ties with him. Only his father defended him.

[220] *Neue National-Zeitung*, May 14, 1907, 2.

Moreover, the Zionist press, in announcing the endorsement, similarly focused overwhelmingly on Horowitz's corruption as the basis for the decision.[221] Despite Diamand's strong record of opposition to Jewish nationalism, stated the *Neue National-Zeitung*, Horowitz's reputation for corruption and "shameless" exploitation of his position on the *kahal* decided his fate. "The Jewish nationalists in Lemberg," wrote a local correspondent, "mobilized much greater forces for the election of Diamand [in the runoff], or rather, for the defeat of Horowitz, than they had for the election of Braude [in the first place]."[222]

Zionists did not give their support for free but rather used their leverage in Lemberg to secure socialist support elsewhere. After Braude's first-round Lemberg defeat, Jewish nationalists forged an agreement with the PPSD for both parties to support Diamand in Lemberg, but Braude and Stand in Stanislau and Tarnopol, respectively. In this event, Zionists respected the agreement and Diamand won with their support.[223] Jewish nationalists made a similar pact with the socialists in Brody and Tarnow. Zionists agreed to support the Jewish socialist candidate Josef Drobner in the Tarnow runoff after their candidate, Salomon Merz, came in third, in exchange for socialist support for Adolf Stand in the Brody runoff. In the runoffs, Stand narrowly defeated his assimilationist opponent while Drobner lost to the government-backed Baron Batalia, who also had the backing of Machsike Hadas.[224] Salo Baron, then a twelve-year-old gymnasium student in Tarnow, recalled a sudden and atypical spike in anti-Semitism during the election. A mass of peasants flooded the town just

[221] See, for example, *Neue National-Zeitung*, May 24, 1907, 4. The paper focused exclusively on Horowitz's corruption and the potential benefit of socialist support for Stand in Brody. Braude's argument about the threat Horowitz posed as an ostensibly "Jewish" leader does not appear at all.

[222] *Neue National-Zeitung*, May 31, 1907, 5. Poalei Zion, although ostensibly a socialist party, issued an especially lame endorsement of Diamand, writing that it would have preferred Daszyński, or indeed any other non-Jewish Social Democrat, to Diamand, who like all bourgeois Jews only approached his people (i.e., Jews) during election time. *Der Jüdischer Arbeiter*, May 24, 1907, 21 cited in Unger, op. cit., 136.

[223] *Neue National-Zeitung*, May 31, 1907, 5. The correspondent proudly boasted that the Lemberg Zionists, including the Orthodox *Mizrachi*, who would have opposed socialist anti-clericalism, all voted "like a disciplined army" for Diamand in the runoff. The Zionists lost both of the other races.

[224] *Machsike Hadas*, May 17, 1907, 3; Abraham Khomet, "Towards a History of Tarnow Jews" (Yiddish), in Khomet, ed., *Torne: kiem un hurbn fun a Yidisher shtat* (Tel-Aviv, 1954), 61. (Khomet incorrectly recalled the Zionist candidate being David Malz.) Khomet learned of the agreement from the *Togblat* but noted that the memoirs of Yehoshua Landau, one of the founders of the ŻPS, discussed an electoral compromise between Zionists and Drobner predating the first electoral round.

before the election, praying loudly in church for Batalia's victory and uttering threats were the Jewish socialist to win.[225]

Importantly, although the Ruthenians did rally behind Mahler, Gabel, and probably Birnbaum as they pledged in their agreement, elsewhere they may not have done so. The veteran Zionist Abraham Salz was soundly defeated in the runoff election when the Ruthenians allegedly backed the Polish social democratic candidate against him. Salz received 2,485 votes to Moraczewski's 3,380 in a district containing roughly 2,800 Jewish voters versus 3,600 Christians, proving to the Jewish nationalists that the Ruthenians failed to support Salz, although the numbers themselves are more ambiguous.[226] On the other hand, in Tarnopol, where Stand (with 1,056 votes) came in third place during the first round, both sides agreed that supporters of the Jewish nationalist candidate failed to rally behind the Ruthenian candidate (Gromnicki) in the runoff, despite a directive to do so by the Jewish National Party. In fact, they not only failed to support the Ruthenian, but a majority of them actually voted for the Jewish candidate of the Polish Club, Rudolf Gall, who had trailed behind his Ruthenian opponent in the first round 1,379 votes to Gromnicki's 1,529.[227]

It would be a mistake to call the agreement a failure, however. On the one hand, Leila Everett is correct in pointing out the cautiousness of the Zionist leadership in endorsing their Ruthenian allies.[228] Nevertheless, in light of Zionist fears of Polish reprisals, the Zionists' need to reach out to Polonized Jews, and especially their need to counter charges by Machsike Hadas that they threatened the Jewish community by opposing the Poles, Zionist declarations of political neutrality ought to be read by historians as a pro-Ruthenian position and not as a rebuff of the Ruthenians.

---

[225] Baron, op. cit., 4. Baron writes that his own teachers lowered his grades markedly during this exam period as a result of the anti-Semitic atmosphere during the election.

[226] *Summarische Ergebnisse*, op. cit., 44–5, and *Neue National-Zeitung*, June 7, 1907, 7. The *Neue National-Zeitung* cited Salz's defeat as proof that "the Ruthenians sooner vote for a social democrat than for a Jew." This may not be true, however. Salz initially came in second with 1,722 votes (compared to 2,015 for Moraczewski) and thus gained over 750 votes in the second round. The Ruthenian candidate initially received 482 votes, while the national democrat (Tobias Aszkenaze) received 1,331. In other words, the Ruthenians may have honored their agreement. The votes from Aszkenaze would have been sufficient to secure Moraczewski's victory. In fact, in his memoirs Salz blamed the assimilationists for his defeat, writing incorrectly that he received the most votes in the first round, but concluding possibly correctly that it was the assimilationists who threw their weight behind Moraczewski in the runoff and thereby elected him. A. Salz, "30 Years of Zionism (1884–1914)" (Polish), in Pięćdziesiąt Lat Sjonizmu (Tarnow, 1934), 20–1.

[227] *Summarische Ergebnisse*, op. cit., 44–5, and *Jüdische Zeitung*, June 5, 1907, 2.

[228] Everett, op. cit., 173–7.

Ultimately, even Everett admits, most Jews did heed Zionist directives to vote for the Ruthenians, while most Ruthenians supported Zionist bids where they were obliged to do so. Moreover, the evidence does not suggest a sense of mutual recriminations in the aftermath of the elections but rather that both sides recognized the efficacy of their alliance. They continued to support each other's resolutions in Parliament, for example, particularly regarding electoral corruption, and they continued to work together at popular rallies. Ruthenian leaders, speaking at the annual conference of the National Democratic Party in December 1907, praised the agreement as partially responsible for their electoral success and intended to repeat it during the forthcoming elections to the Galician Diet.[229] Moreover, throughout the post-election years, many impoverished Jewish gymnastics societies only managed to survive through the kindness of Ruthenian groups willing to rent their halls and equipment cheaply.[230] Jewish nationalists certainly remained supportive of the Ruthenian cause as well. When parliament rejected one of their joint resolutions to condemn the electoral corruption in Galicia, Stand, Mahler, and Gabel joined the Ruthenians in spontaneously rising up and singing "Ne pora, ne pora" [It's not time] and "Shche ne vmerla Ukraina" [Ukraine has not yet died], today the national anthem of Ukraine.[231]

Despite the historic achievement of a Jewish nationalist party in a European parliament, the election's broader significance was its role in the sudden politicization of the Jewish masses. As Braude wrote many years later, the principal purpose of the Jewish nationalists' decision to engage in parliamentary politics was never to win seats. If this had been their goal, they would not have wasted their scarce resources running candidates in over a dozen districts in which they had no chance of success and knew it. Rather, their purpose was to engage Galician Jews in the political process as much as possible, to educate them about the program of the Jewish nationalists, and to foster among them a sense of national community. And, to a great extent, they did achieve this goal. The cumulative effect of three months of nearly daily rallies meant that tens of thousands, probably hundreds of thousands of Jews who had never attended such rallies before now did so. Moreover, a large

---

[229] *OSA/AVA*, Innenministerium, Präsidiale, 22/Galizien 1908, Karton 2112.

[230] Josef Katz noted in a report at the fourth international Jewish tournament in Berlin, for example, that Betar in Tarnopol existed only out of Ruthenian generosity. Josef Katz, "Agitation in Galizien," *Jüdische Turnzeitung*, October/November 1908, 193.

[231] Taras Andrusiak, "The 1907 Ukrainian-Jewish Electoral Coalition," (Ukrainian) *I: nezalezhnyi kul'turolohichnyi chasopys* 8 (1996), 59.

majority of Galician Jewish men voted on election day, and of those who voted for Jews, over half of them went for the Jewish nationalists. "In Galicia," Everett correctly notes, "the Jewish mass vote became a political reality,"[232] and Jewish nationalists – somewhat exaggeratedly – took the lion's share of the credit. Leon Reich's comments at the Eighth Zionist Congress were entirely typical among the champions of Landespolitik in the Zionist organization.

We have taught the Jews for the first time to think politically independently. We have taught the Jew, a cowardly slave of the ruling authorities who crept away at the sight of a Polish magnate, for the first time to raise his head with pride. We have taught him for the first time to say proudly to the Polish *Szlachta* and the Jewish assimilationists: I am a Jew. I will only send a Jew to Parliament, [that] a Jew might speak there for me, might bring up Jewish issues, might call out loudly in the world that the Jewish People lives.[233]

Reich was celebrating not merely the politicization of Galician Jews but also their nationalization, their insistence that a Jew should represent them in Parliament just as Poles and Ruthenians insisted on their own representation. If not all politicized Jews voted for the Jewish nationalist candidate, Reich and the others felt certain that their newly realized Jewish pride would eventually go to work for them.

[232] Everett, op. cit., 175.
[233] *Stenographisches Protokoll der Verhandlungen des VIII Zionisten Congress* (Köln: Jüdischer Verlag, 1907), 63. Braude wrote similarly in his memoirs that the elections, "brought the masses of the people to a direct recognition in matters of state and the public. The masses felt themselves to be a part of the movement itself and to be responsible for its fate. In this way, the national movement was made into a real populist idea." Braude, op. cit., 212.

Conclusion

> Maybe history will recognize [Zionism's] mission as the fanfare that awakened their sleeping spirits and caused the Jews to be roused again and to fall in step with other peoples in doing their duty and claiming their rights. If so, Zionism will have fulfilled a great purpose, even if the founding of a Jewish state remains a utopia.
>
> Bertha Pappenheim, *On the Condition of the Jewish Population in Galicia* (1904)[1]

The historic formation of a Jewish Club in the Austrian Parliament did not result in any major legislative victories. The party did not succeed in achieving its major goal, the recognition of Yiddish as a legal *Umgangssprache* and the acquisition of national rights for Habsburg Jews. In fact, when Zionists in Bukowina succeeded in getting that province's diet to recognize the Jewish nationality, Jewish assimilationists in Vienna succeeded in persuading the national parliament to overturn that decision.[2] Moreover, the party lost all but one of its seats in the next election, held in 1911, when Benno Straucher alone won reelection. This was largely due to the failure of Zionists to repeat their historic agreement with the Ruthenians,[3] as well as to district gerrymandering and other

---

[1] Bertha Pappenheim, *Zur Lage der jüdischen Bevölkerung in Galizien* (Frankfurt am Main, 1904), 46. Pappenheim (1859–1936), a well-known German-Jewish feminist and Zionist, traveled to Galicia in 1902 to investigate the problem of the Jewish white slave trade.

[2] On the effort to recognize Yiddish in Bukowina, see Gerald Stourzh, "Max Diamant and Jewish Diaspora Nationalism in the Bukovina," in *From Vienna to Chicago and Back* (Chicago, 2007), 190–203. Diamant attempted to file the by-laws of a proposed Jewish theater association in Yiddish. When the local authorities refused to accept the paperwork, he sued, but the lawsuit was rejected by the Imperial Court in Vienna.

[3] According to Zvi Heller, a Zionist activist in Buczacz at the time, Polish authorities seeking to prevent a repeat of the 1907 elections guaranteed Zionists five parliamentary seats

forms of electoral corruption, rather than to a loss of Jewish votes. In fact, the Zionists received roughly the same number of votes in the 1911 elections as they had in 1907, about 30,000.[4]

Coverage of the election in the Jewish press was dominated by news of a massacre in Drohobycz. Jacob Feuerstein, vice mayor of the city and head of the local Jewish community, had been preventing supporters of the opposition candidates from voting out Nathan Löwenstein, with the help of two police units imported from Przemysl.[5] When a large group of Jews and Ruthenians gathered outside the district's one and only polling station demanding their right to vote, the troops' commander – allegedly with Feuerstein's permission – ordered his soldiers to fire. Twenty-six people were killed including women and one child, and dozens more were wounded. According to Shimon Lustig, who found his brother shot six times in the back just after the event, almost all of the victims were shot in the back. In other words, the soldiers fired even as the crowd was fleeing the scene. This account is confirmed by a witness correspondent to the *Neue Freie Presse*, who did however note that the troops had been extremely restrained that morning, despite the crowd's violent behavior (throwing stones, attacking police horses with broken chair legs, etc.).[6] Immediately after the massacre, Feuerstein fled the city to Vienna, where he twice narrowly escaped being lynched. Löwenstein renounced his victory but easily won the new election in October when Zionists decided – for unclear reasons – not to run again.[7]

Zionists, in print and rallies, focused their rage on Feuerstein and Löwenstein rather than on the commanding officer who gave the order to fire. They tried to use the moment to enflame popular passion against the assimilationist establishment. "The Jewish heroes from Drohobycz fell like Maccabees," declared the Viennese *Jüdische Zeitung*, which draped a stark, black-rimmed announcement of the massacre across its front

---

(Ringel, Stand, Reich, Zipper, and Thon) in exchange for their not repeating their agreement with the Ruthenians. The Poles simply ignored this obligation and defeated, with much chicanery, all five of those candidates. Heller, "From My Memories" (Hebrew), in Israel Cohen, ed., *Sefer Buczacz* (Tel Aviv, 1956), 146.

[4] For details on the 1911 elections, see Gaisbauer, *Davidstern und Doppeladler* (Vienna, 1988), 490–5, and *Summarische Ergebnisse der Statistik der Reichsratwahlen von 1911* (Brünn, 1911).

[5] For a partisan description of Feuerstein's tricks to rig the election, see Shimom Lustig, "The Zionist Movement in Drohobycz" (Hebrew), in Nathan Gelber, ed., *Sefer zikaron li-Drohobycz, Borislav veha-sevivah* (Tel-Aviv, 1959), 124. The author's brother was among those killed.

[6] *Neue Freie Presse*, June 23, 1911, 5.

[7] Lustig, op. cit., 125.

page on June 23. "Students, workers, shopkeepers, women and girls lay in their deathbeds. Jews – remember these victims always!" In this way, the paper linked the Zionists not only with the victims – whose names and occupations it listed – but with the broad Jewish masses. Notably, the *Jüdische Zeitung* did name the Ruthenian dead among the victims, but it otherwise packaged the massacre as a Jewish affair. The paper also organized a campaign to support the survivors and printed the names of every donor to the fund, suggesting the movement's paternal leadership of the Jewish people.[8]

In the years following the dramatic 1907 elections, Galician Zionists enjoyed a steady if not exponential period of growth. The number of Zionist organizations in Galicia doubled between 1907 and 1914, from about 250 to just over 500 different associations.[9] Membership (measured by the number of shekels collected) rose at a slightly better rate, from about 4,500 in 1908 to 6,116 in 1909, 6,499 in 1911, and 8,055 in 1912; it peaked at 13,745 shekel payers in 1913, the last full year before the outbreak of the First World War.[10] This was certainly not a period of ecstatic growth, although certain segments of the Jewish nationalist movement did grow more sharply. The Jewish gymnastics movement, for example, which struggled for its existence before 1907, experienced rapid growth in the period after that election, especially in the last years before the war. In 1909, the movement had active and stable organizations in at least four major cities (Lemberg, Tarnopol, Stanislau, and Cracow); by 1914, it had grown to twenty-seven associations in twenty cities, with a total membership of about 2,500.[11]

The elections also had a major impact on the Zionist organization itself. Emboldened by their electoral success, Galician Zionists voted at their "seventh Galician provincial conference" held in October 1907 to separate entirely from the Austrian Zionist organization.[12] Their

---

[8] *Jüdische Zeitung*, June 23, 1911, 1–4; *Jüdische Zeitung*, June 30, 1911, 1–3, *Jüdische Zeitung*, July 7, 1911, 2–4; *Jüdische Zeitung*, July 14, 1911, 4–5. See also *Die Welt*, June 23, 1911, 1–4, and *Die Welt*, June 30, 1911, 3–4.

[9] This is according to Gaisbauer's maximalist list of Zionist societies, which includes affiliated organizations such as gymnastics associations. Gaisbauer, op. cit., 239–44, 288–98. According to the report of the Galician Zionists' final conference in January 1914, the organization included just 173 societies at that time. *Die Welt*, January 16, 1914, 70.

[10] *Die Welt*, January 16, 1914, 70–1.

[11] See earlier, Chapter 4, as well as Joshua Shanes, "National Regeneration in the Ghetto: The Jewish *Turnbewegung* in Galicia," in Jack Kugelmass, ed., *Jews, Sports, and the Rites of Citizenship* (Urbana, 2007) 75–94.

[12] On the conference, see *Die Welt*, November 1, 1907, 13–14; November 8, 1907, 11–12; November 15, 1907, 12–13. In calling it the "seventh" *landeskonferenz*, a full six years

success at the polls, and especially their successful penetration into traditional Jewish communities, led most Galician Zionists to conclude that
Landespolitik was, in fact, the best means by which to advance their
cause. Most delegates at the conference still saw these goals as perfectly
compatible with their long-term objectives in Palestine, although this
position did have vocal opponents and the debate between the two sides
was a rancorous one.

The leading defender of Landespolitik was probably Braude, who had
directed the 1907 campaigns and argued persistently that it remained the
only means of reaching most Galician Jews. "Now that we have reached
another, better conception of Zionism," he declared at the Galician
conference,

we must together with the practical work in Palestine ... also get started with
Gegenwartsarbeit in the Diaspora, by which we can educate and organize our
People. We must summon up everything, in order to win the broad folk masses for
our idea, and this can only happen with a systematic, goal-oriented Jewish politics.
The small means, the Toynbee Halls and the credit unions [*Raiffeisenkassen*] do
not fulfill this goal.[13]

Besides, he concluded, Zionists did not have the slightest hope of improving the Jews' economic and cultural situation without working through
the state system.

Leon Reich, whose passionate celebration of the election results concluded the previous chapter, agreed that the successful politicization of
Galician Jews would eventually pay off for the Zionists. Reich regretted
that the Zionists did not work directly to win supporters for Palestine,
that is, for the Basel Program. Nevertheless, he expressed confidence
that the "true, good Zionists" would never turn away from Zionism as
a result of its domestic political program, as many feared, and that those
who were not yet Zionists would find their way to Zionism through the
process of politicization.[14]

Others disagreed. Mordechai Ehrenpreis, for example, argued at the
Eighth Zionist Congress that the recent political activity in Galicia, as
well as the newly won Jewish Club itself, weakened the "pure" Zionist
work. Despite its great moral significance, he insisted, domestic politics
damaged Zionist party objectives.

since their sixth conference (at which time they voted to join the Austrian federation),
Zionists were self-consciously returning to the period of autonomous Galician organization that began at their first conference in 1893.
[13] *Die Welt*, November 15, 1907, 12.
[14] *Stenographisches Protokoll der Verhandlungen des VIII. Zionisten Congress*, 1907, 63.

First, because it pushed a large portion of significant resources to another area. (Outcall: That is untrue!) That is your viewpoint. (Dr. Schalit: You apparently have a telephone connection between Galicia and Sofia that you know this so well.) Second, for another reason, which is of principal significance – domestic political activity won Zionism [many] embittered and fierce opponents, who without this activity they would not have had and would not [now] have.[15]

As to Braude's second point, that only through domestic politics could Zionists address the Jews' economic plight, Ehrenrpreis insisted that it was not the task of the Zionist Organization to alleviate Jewish hunger. "It is a movement for national rebirth," he insisted. "It has neither the will nor the program to end hunger."[16]

Braude's other childhood friend, Yehoshua Thon, also opposed him on this matter, despite having himself run in the election. Thon complained that the Zionists' contribution to Jewish politicization – which all Zionists admitted was the greatest accomplishment of the election – came at the expense of the Zionist movement itself, which he argued might have grown "ten-fold" to perhaps 60,000 members had they used that energy toward "pure Zionist" activities. The transformation of so many Galician Jews into Jewish nationalists was a great accomplishment, he admits, but "one conscious [*bewusster*] shekel payer is dearer to me than ten national Jews."

It is a great service of Dr. Braude that he has contributed so much towards the spreading of the national idea among Jews through the recent campaigns. But the claim that through this political work Zionism has grown in the land appears to me to be ungrounded.[17]

Israel Waldman expressed similar concerns about the effect of the elections on the Zionist movement. Waldman, who like Thon supported Zionist participation in domestic politics (he claimed to have spoken at eighty-six rallies during the campaign), decried the decision of the Galician leadership to forbid any reference to Zionism at the rallies of the Jewish National Party, arguing that this undermined the long-term interests of the Zionist movement. He recommended that the Jewish National Party be dissolved and the Zionist Organization itself take its place in directing domestic political campaigns.

---

[15] *Stenographisches Protokoll der Verhandlungen des VIII Zionisten Congress*, 1907, 65. Ehrenpreis was living in Sofia by then. His detractors noted this in their catcalls, to which Ehrenpreis responded that his residence in Bulgaria afforded him a critical distance with which to judge to the situation.

[16] *Stenographisches Protokoll der Verhandlungen des VIII Zionisten Congress*, 1907, 109.

[17] *Die Welt*, November 15, 1907, 12.

Ultimately, Waldman's suggestion won the day. The Jewish National Party was soon dissolved and delegates at the Galician Zionists' eighth conference in 1909 rejected proposals to split the domestic and Palestine activities back into separate organizations.[18] Delegates at that conference also voted to establish a Jewish People's Bank (again over the objections of Thon), a resolution that was realized with the help of the Zionist Viennese banker Lucian Brunner in April 1909. The bank was designed to service Jews denied credit by the assimilationist institutions because of their known anti-assimilationist politics.[19]

As Austria and Europe began to mobilize for war in the summer of 1914, Galician Zionists prepared as well. Most Galician Zionists shared the loyalty and patriotism of the overwhelming majority of Galician Jews, indeed of all Habsburg Jews, toward the empire generally and toward Franz Joseph in particular. Most Jews in the Habsburg Empire focused their attention squarely on Tsarist Russia and saw themselves and Austria-Hungary as liberators of Russian Jewry, thus uniting their Jewish and Habsburg loyalties.[20] Already in January 1914, Galician Zionists had issued a resolution calling Jews to arms against Tsarist Russia. Our great and beloved Kaiser was calling his peoples to the armed forces, it declared, and Jews were to be at the forefront of the response. "We have waited impatiently for this minute," it continued, finally to show our "unlimited love and deep gratitude towards [our] ruler." Detailing the terrible persecution that Jews suffered in Tsarist Russia, the resolution concluded by describing the war as "holy," adding that "all of us will go as Maccabeans and Bar Kochba."[21]

This view was also reiterated by the Zionist press. On August 28, for example, Saul Landau's *Neue National-Zeitung* affirmed in large front-page headlines that paper's commitment to the war effort, which promised the salvation of millions of Russian Jews by "the united forces of Germany and Austria-Hungary."[22] The following week, its headlines read in extra-large font, "For our Kaiser and our People [*Volk*]." The paper again united the goals of Austria-Hungary and world Jewry to defeat Tsarist Russia, and described the Jews' strong patriotism for the crown and willingness to sacrifice to achieve victory.[23]

[18] *Die Welt*, April 30, 1909, 385–7; May 5, 1909, 407–9.
[19] Gaisbauer, op. cit., 262.
[20] Manha Rozenblit, *Reconstructing a National Identity* (New York, 2001), 39–40.
[21] Gaisbauer, op. cit., 287–8.
[22] *Neue National-Zeitung*, August 28, 1914, 1.
[23] *Neue National-Zeitung*, September 4, 1914, 1.

Zionism generally remained a fringe political movement until 1917, when Britain issued the Balfour Declaration and seemed to fulfill Herzl's dream of an international charter for a Jewish home in Palestine. From one perspective, the Zionist movement in Galicia was no exception. Galician Zionism, despite its impressive mobilization in 1907, and despite its considerable organizational growth during the subsequent years, never became a mass movement before the First World War. At their final pre-war conference in early 1914, Galician Zionists could boast just 13,745 shekel payers, although the movement may have attracted many others who could not afford to pay their dues, and the number does not reflect spouses and children of shekel payers.[24] This was a significant jump from the roughly 4,500 members they counted in 1908, but it obviously still constituted only a tiny minority of the Galician Jewish population, nearly 900,000 strong in 1910. Moreover, few of the movement's most important domestic goals, not to speak of its long-term goal of a Jewish home in Palestine, were achieved. To this extent, Oscar Janowsky seems justified in classifying the period between 1907 and the First World War as one of "decline" for the Jewish nationalist movement, a period to which he devotes just two pages of his classic study of the struggle for Jewish national minority rights.[25]

Zionist success, however, ought to be measured more broadly than by its shekel count. If Zionism never became a mass movement before World War I, its contribution toward Jewish politicization was formidable nonetheless. Hundreds of thousands of Galician Jews attended Zionist lectures and rallies in the years before the First World War. Laibel Taubes alone could list over 132 towns in Galicia and Bukowina where he estimated speaking at thousands of rallies to over a quarter million Jews.[26] Moreover, Zionist campaigning not only brought out scores of thousands of Jews to rallies in 1906 and 1907, but it forced Zionist opponents to do the same. The triumph of the Jewish national idea, already visible by 1907, was largely a result of years of sustained Zionist agitation and pressure on its political opponents. The arguments toward Jewish national self-consciousness laid out by the Yiddish press in the 1890s had become standard fare across the Jewish political spectrum by the next decade. By 1907, no political party vying for Jewish votes could afford not to promote some sort of Jewish national program. Even

[24] *Die Welt*, January 16, 1914, 70–1.
[25] Oscar Janowsky, *The Jews and Minority Rights 1898–1919* (New York, 1933), 149–51.
[26] Laibel Taubes, *Zikhrones fun Laibel Taubes* (Vienna, 1920), 8–9.

when some of these alternative visions directly contradicted aspects of the Zionist ideology, such as its long-term goal of leaving Europe, it still represented a victory for the Jewish nationalist movement in that Galician Jews increasingly saw themselves as one of the empire's constituent nationalities and increasingly demanded the rights associated with this status. In short, by understanding Zionism not as a homogeneous ideology, single-mindedly focused on the attainment of a Jewish national home in Palestine, but rather as an umbrella term for a wide variety of Jewish national ideologies, it becomes far easier to reintegrate its history into the European framework in which it was born.

To what extent does the Jewish nationalist movement in Galicia confirm or conform to the nationalist typologies with which this study began? Gideon Shimoni's location of the genesis of Zionism in the collusion of modernizing Jewish "ethnicists" with "disappointed integrationists" is clearly borne out in the case of Galicia.[27] That Laibel Taubes and Adolf Stand could both be elected to the central committee at the Zionists' final prewar conference in January 1914 is perhaps symbolic of that relationship. That it was Stand, the consummate assimilationist-turned-Zionist, who was reelected as president of that organization is equally significant, for it highlights the essentially secular orientation of the Zionist movement, despite its ethnicist core.

To be sure, it did not generally present itself as a secular movement. Over the course of the 1890s and 1900s, while leadership of the movement remained vested in the secular intelligentsia, the movement as a whole moved increasingly to attract modernizing but still traditional Jews to the Jewish national idea, if not to the Zionist organization, through an activist politics in which it presented itself as the natural conclusion of religious Judaism. They made this argument from the time of their 1890–1 *Volksbibliothek* brochures, throughout the Yiddish-language periodicals of the 1890s, in synagogue rallies and lectures at the *fin-de-siècle*, and especially during the election campaigns in 1906 and 1907.

In truth, Zionism was a secular movement. Aside from the fact that Zionists clashed with most rabbinical authorities at the time in their arguably antinomian ideology of achieving national redemption through human agency, their fundamental understanding of themselves as Jews focused not on their relationship to God but on their relationship to other people. That is, nationalism replaced "Torah" as the central value of their lives. As Mordechai Ehrenpreis wrote of the founders of Zion in 1888,

[27] Shimoni, *The Zionist Ideology* (Hanover, 1995), 3–51, 389–92.

"religious observance was a personal matter."[28] This is why so many religious leaders opposed the movement, even those who came to support aspects of the Zionist project. (Recall the short-lived Yiddish paper *Der Emes'r Yid*, which made this argument explicitly.) Zionism in Galicia, as in Germany, was above all a movement that sought to create a positive, but secular Jewish identity. It sought to replace religion as the center of Jewish identity, or at least to portray nationalism as the natural conclusion of Judaism, even as it absorbed the myths and symbols of traditional Judaism.

Ultimately, then, Smith's emphasis on historical "preconditions" to modern nations does offer a compelling model with which to understand at least the building blocks of the Jewish nationalist movement in Galicia, despite its reifying weaknesses. Jewish intellectuals, influenced by the nationalist rhetoric that surrounded them but unable or unwilling to join other nationalist movements, increasingly turned inward to build a modern national identity, and they found ample material with which to do so. Galician Jews constituted a distinct ethnic group in the region: linguistically, religiously, economically and socially. Moreover, Judaism itself provided the linguistic and cultural building blocks with which Jewish nationalists could construct a modern nationalist consciousness: a collective understanding of Jewish peoplehood, reinforced by liturgy and ritual, a shared historical connection to a specific territory, and a unique common language.[29] As a result, the idea of Jewish nationhood influenced larger and larger numbers of Jews in Galicia, even as the Zionist movement itself remained quite small.

---

[28] Mordechai Ehrenpreis, *Bein Mizrach l'Maarav* (Tel-Aviv, 1986), 26.

[29] True, their veneration of Hebrew as the Jewish national language, critical because of its historical significance and existing high literature, was problematic for Zionists struggling to win recognition of the Jewish nation in Austria-Hungary, as it was clearly not a "language of daily use." This was partially overcome, however, by their development of a Yiddish-language press, an effort reinforced by the Jewish socialists (ŻPS) after 1905.

Appendix A

Jewish Parliamentary Representatives from Galicia, 1873–1911

1873–1879 Legislative Period

Name	Profession	District/Curia	Club
Nathan Ritter von Kallir	Banker	Brody Chamber of Commerce	Constitutional Party
Oswald Hönigsmann	Lawyer	Kolomea (City)	Constitutional Party
Joachim Landau (died 1878)	Lawyer	Brody (City)	Constitutional Party
Hermann Mises	Writer	Drohobycz (City)	Constitutional Party
Albert Mendelsburg	Banker	Cracow Chamber of Commerce	Polish Club

1879–1885 Legislative Period

Name	Profession	District/Curia	Club
Nathan Ritter von Kallir	Banker	Brody Chamber of Commerce	Liberal Club
Arnold Rapaport	Lawyer	Cracow Chamber of Commerce	Polish Club
Simon Schreiber (died 1883)	Rabbi	Kolomea (City)	Polish Club
Josef Samuel Bloch	Rabbi	Kolomea (City)	Polish Club (replaced Schreiber)

1885–1891 Legislative Period

Name	Profession	District/Curia	Club
Nathan Ritter von Kallir (died 1886)	Banker	Brody Chamber of Commerce	Liberal Club
Arnold Rapaport	Lawyer	Cracow Chamber of Commerce	Polish Club
Moritz Rosenstock	Merchant	Brody Chamber of Commerce	Polish Club (replaced Kallir)
Josef Samuel Bloch	Rabbi	Kolomea (City)	Polish Club

1891–1897 Legislative Period

Name	Profession	District/Curia	Club
Emil Byk	Lawyer	Brody (City)	Polish Club
Arnold Rapaport	Lawyer	Cracow Chamber of Commerce	Polish Club
Moritz Rosenstock	Merchant	Brody Chamber of Commerce	Polish Club
Josef Samuel Bloch (resigned 1895)	Rabbi	Kolomea (City)	Polish Club
Maximilian Trachtenberg	Lawyer	Kolomea (City)	Polish Club (replaced Bloch)

1897–1900 Legislative Period

Name	Profession	District/Curia	Club
Emil Byk	Lawyer	Brody (City)	Polish Club
Arnold Rapaport	Lawyer	Cracow Chamber of Commerce	Polish Club
Moritz Rosenstock	Merchant	Brody Chamber of Commerce	Polish Club
Maximilian Trachtenberg	Lawyer	Kolomea (City)	Polish Club
Heinrich Kolischer	Industrialist	Przemysl (City)	Polish Club
Jakob Piepes-Poratynski	Pharmacist	Lemberg Chamber of Commerce	Polish Club

1901–1906 Legislative Period

Name	Profession	District/Curia	Club
Emil Byk (died 1906)	Lawyer	Brody (City)	Polish Club
Josef Gold	Doctor	Brody (City)	Polish Club (replaced Byk)
Arnold Rapaport	Lawyer	Cracow Chamber of Commerce	Polish Club
Heinrich Kolischer	Industrialist	Brody Chamber of Commerce	Polish Club
Nathan Seinfeld	Asst. Railway Director	Kolomea (City)	Polish Club
Jakob Piepes-Poratynski (died 1905)	Pharmacist	Lemberg Chamber of Commerce	Polish Club (mandate given to Pole after 1905)

1907–1911 Legislative Period

Name	Profession	District/Curia	Club
Adolf Stand	Lawyer	Brody (City)	Jewish Club
Heinrich Gabel (died 1910)	Lawyer	Buczacz (Rural)	Jewish Club
Arthur Mahler	Visiting Professor	Trembowla (Rural)	Jewish Club
Adolf Gross	Lawyer	Cracow (City)	Independent
Herman Diamand	Businessman	Lemberg (City)	Social Democrat
Hermann Lieberman	Lawyer	Przemysl(City)	Social Democrat
Rudolf Gall	Industrialist	Tarnopol (City)	Polish Club
Josef Gold	Doctor	Złoczow (City)	Polish Club
Henryk Kolischer	Industrialist	Kolomea (City)	Polish Club
Nathan Loewenstein	Lawyer	Drohobycz (City)	Polish Club

Source: For 1873–1906: S. R. Landau, *Der Polenklub und Seine Hausjuden* (Vienna, 1907), 37–42; for 1907–1911: Harald Binder, *Galizien in Wien: Parteien, Wahlen, Fraktionen und Abgeordnete im Übergang zur Massenpolitik* (Vienna, 2005).

Appendix B

Party-Affiliated Jewish Candidates in Galician Districts in 1907 (winner in bold)

District	Jewish National Party and Independent Nationalists	Party of Independent Jews	Jewish Candidates of PPSD	Jewish Electoral Organization
3 (Lemberg III)	Markus Braude 854	–	**Herman Diamand** 1672, 2475	Samuel Horowitz 1676, 2448
9 (Cracow I)	–	–	Jan Englisch 854	–
12 (Cracow III)	Chaim Hilfstein 123	**Adolf Gross** 1869	–	Józef Sare 1589
13 (Przemysl)	–	–	**H. Lieberman** 3533	–
14 (Stanislau)	M. Braude 1204, 1853	–	Maks Seinfeld 222	Edmund Rauch 1119
15 (Tarnopol)	Adolf Stand 1056	–	–	**R. Gall** 1379, 2905 and M. Landau 477
16 (Tarnow)	S. Merz (Ind.) 728	–	Roman Drobner 1296, 1753	–
17 (Kolomea)	Osias Thon 824	–	Aaron Schorr 1137	**H. Kolischer** 1970
21 (Rzeszow, etc.)	–	–	M. Pelzling 703	–
22 (Jaroslaw, etc.)	–	–	Chaskel Peller 948	–
23 (Mielec, etc.)	G. Schmelkes 1200	–	–	–
25 (Sanok, etc.)	J. Gottlieb 62			

(*continued*)

District	Jewish National Party and Independent Nationalists	Party of Independent Jews	Jewish Candidates of PPSD	Jewish Electoral Organization
27 (Drohobycz, etc.)	Gershon Zipper 1231	–	Samuel Haecker 551	N. Loewenstein 3935
28 (Stryj, Kalusz)	A. Salz 1722, 2485	–	–	T. Aschkenase 1331
29 (Brzezany, etc.)	S. Rapaport 1141, 1579	–	–	–
30 (Zolkiew, etc.)	J.S. Bloch 639			
31 (Brody, etc.)	Adolf Stand 1493, 2585	–	Henrich Loewenherz 1244	S. Wollerner 1517, 2228
32 (Buczacz, etc.)	N. Birnbaum 2194, 2434	–	–	–
33 (Zloczow, etc.)	–	–	–	Josef Gold 3903
34 (Bobrka, etc.)	David Malz 1269	–	–	–
35 (Jaworzna, etc.)	Arthur Mahler 1041	–	–	–
36 (Biala, etc.)	–	–	D. Gross 2923, 3191, 490	–
56 (Peczenizyn, etc.)	S. Weissglas 1049	–	–	–
57 (Stryj, etc.)	Jakob Korkis 109	–	–	–
58 (Mielnica, etc.)	Unknown 28			
59 (Stanislau, etc.)	–	–	Maks Seinfeld 2396	–
60 (Podhajce, etc.)	H. Gabel 2146, 14537	–	–	–
63 (Przemyslany-Zloczow, etc.)	Laibel Taubes 308	–	–	–
66 (Brzezany, etc.)	A. Kornhäuser 156			
69 (Trembowla-Czortkow, etc.)	A. Mahler 2565, 12948	–	–	–
70 (Skalat, etc.)	Josef Braun 1590	–	–	–
Total First Round	25,381	1869	17,479	18,946

* The first number indicates total votes received. The second number, where applicable, indicates votes received in runoff election. PPSD is the Polish acronym for the Polish Social Democratic Party.

Bibliography

Primary Sources

1. Archives

Österreichisches Staatsarchiv, Allgemeine Verwaltungsarchiv Vienna (*OSA/AVA*)
    Ministerium des Innern, Präsidiale 22/Galizien 1903–1905, Karton 2109
    Ministerium des Innern, Präsidiale 22/Galizien 1906, Karton 2110
    Ministerium des Innern, Präsidiale 22/Galizien 1907, Karton 2111
    Ministerium des Innern, Präsidiale 22/Galizien 1908, Karton 2112
    Ministerium des Innern, Präsidiale 22/Galizien 1909, Karton 2113
    Ministerium des Innern, Präsidiale 22/Galizien 1910, Karton 2114
Central Archives for the History of the Jewish People, Jerusalem
    N. M. Gelber Papers
Central Zionist Archives, Jerusalem
    Ahron Marcus Papers
YIVO Institute for Jewish Research, New York
    Gershon Bader Papers
Leo Baeck Institute, New York
Nathan and Solomon Birnbaum Archives, Toronto, Canada

2. Newspapers and Journals

Newspapers/journals published outside of Galicia

Die Gerechtigkeit (Vienna, 1903–13)
Ha-Melitz (Odessa)
Jüdische Turnzeitung (Berlin, 1901–13)
Jüdisches Volksblatt (Vienna, 1899–1906)
    renamed *National Zeitung* (Vienna, 1906–7)
    renamed *Neue National-Zeitung* (Vienna, 1907–14)
Jüdische Zeitung (Vienna, 1907–14)
Neue Zeitung (Vienna, 1906–7)

Oesterreiche Wochenschrift (Vienna, 1884–1914)
Ruthenische Revue (Vienna, 1903–4)
renamed *Ukrainische Rundschau* (Vienna, 1905–7)
Selbst-Emanzipation (Vienna, 1885–93)
Selbstwehr (Prague, 1907–11)
Die Welt (Vienna, 1897–1914)

Newspapers/journals published inside Galicia by date of publication
(language noted)
Ivri Anochi/Ha'ivri (Hebrew, Brody: 1865–90)
Der Israelit (German, Lemberg: 1869–93)
Machsike Hadas-Kol Machsike Hadas (Hebrew, Lemberg: 1879–1913)
Drohobyczer Zeitung-Drohobyczer Handels-Zeitung (German, Drohobycz:
      1885–1913)
Hacharsu (Hebrew, Stanislau/Kolomea: 1888–9)
Yidishe folkstsaytung (Yiddish, Kolomea: 1890–1)
Izraelitishes folksblat (Yiddish, Kolomea: 1890–1)
Der folksfraynd (Yiddish, Kolomea: 1891–2)
Der Carmel-Der Wecker (Yiddish, Lemberg: 1893–4)
Yidishes familienblat (Yiddish, Tysmienica: 1893–4)
Yidishes folksblat (Yiddish, Tysmienica: 1894)
Jüdisches Wochenblatt (Yiddish, Lemberg: 1895)
Hamagid (Hebrew, Cracow: 1868–1903)
Ha-Am (Dos Folk) (Yiddish, Kolomea: 1895–7)
Mittheilungen des Vereines "Ahawath Zion" (German/Hebrew, Tarnow: 1898)
Krakauer Jüdische Zeitung (German, Cracow: 1898–1900)
Der Jud (Yiddish, Cracow-Warsaw: 1899–1903)
Jüdische Volksstimme (Yiddish, Cracow: 1899)
Jüdische Volks zeitung (Yiddish, Cracow: 1902–4)
Jüdische Gemeinde- und Vereins-Zeitung (Yiddish, Kolomea: 1903)
Der Emes'r Yid (Yiddish, Lemberg: 1904)
Togblat (from 1906, *Dos Lemberger Togblat*) (Yiddish, Lemberg: 1904–14)
Der Arbeiter (Yiddish, Cracow: 1905)
Freiheit (Yiddish, Cracow: 1905)
Der Sozial-Demokrat (Yiddish, Cracow: 1905–8)
Der Jud (Yiddish, Cracow: 1905–6)
Di Yidishe Folks Politik (Yiddish, Kolomea: 1906)
Hamicpe (Hebrew, Cracow: 1904–7)
Jüdische Mittag-Zeitung (Yiddish, Cracow: 1907)
Haeth (Hebrew, Lemberg: 1907)
Tygodnik (Dos Wochenblatt) (Yiddish, Cracow: 1907–11)
Die Jüdische Stimme (Yiddish, Tarnow: 1908)

3. Memoirs and Yizkor Books

Amitay, Mordekhai et al., eds., *Kehilat Rohatin veha-sevivah*. Tel-Aviv: Irgun
      yotse Roha'tin be-Yisra'el, 1962.

Austridan, Yeshayahu, *Sefer Yizkor le-hantsahat kedoshe Kehilat Ts'ortkov.* Haifa: Irgun yots'e Ts'ortkov be-Yisra'el, 1967.

Bader, Gershom, *Meine Zikhrones.* Buenos Aires: Tsentral-farband fun Poylishe Yidn in Argentine, 1953.

Bauminger, Arieh L., Meir Busak, and N. M. Gelber, eds., *Sefer Krako, `ir ve-em be-Yi´sra'el.* Jersualem: Mosad ha-Rav Kook, 1959.

Bergner, Hinde, *In di lange vinternekht: mishpoheh-zikhroynes fun a shtetl in Galitsye 1870–1900.* Montreal: M. Ravitch, 1946.

Bickel, Shlomo, ed., *Pinkas Kolomey.* New York: n.p., 1957.

Bloch, Joseph, *My Reminiscences.* New York: Arno Press, 1973 (orig. *Erinnerungen aus meinem Leben.* Vienna: R. Löwit, 1922).

Erinnerungen aus meinem Leben, Vol. 3. Vienna: R. Löwit, 1933.

Blond, Shlomo, *Tismenits: a matseyveh oyf di hurves fun a farnikhteter Yidisher kehila.* Tel-Aviv: ha-Menorah, 1974.

ed., *Tlumacz: Sefer Edut V'zikaron.* Tel-Aviv: Tlumacz Societies in Israel and the U.S.A., 1976.

Blumental, Nachman, *Sefer Borszczow.* Tel Aviv: Irgun yotse Borshts'ov be-Yisrael, 1960.

ed., *Sefer-yizkor Baranov (Barniv).* Jerusalem: Yad va-shem, 1964.

Braude, Mordechai Ze'ev, "Memoirs of Rabbi Dr. Mordechai Ze'ev Braude (1870–1908)," (Hebrew) in Dov Sadan, ed., *Zikaron Mordechai Ze'ev Braude.* Jerusalem: Ha-Sifriyah ha-Tsiyonit, 1960: 15–230.

Cohen, Israel, ed., *Sefer Buczacz.* Tel-Aviv: Am Oved, 1956.

Ehrenpreis, Mordechai, *Bein Mizrach l'Maarav.* Tel-Aviv: Sigalit, 1986.

Eshel, Yonah and Moshe Hanina, eds., *Sefer ha-zikaron li-kedoshe Bolihov.* Haifa: Hotsaat Irgun yotse Bolihov be-Yisrael, 1957.

Fenster, Israel, *Sefer Burshtin.* Jerusalem: Herrat Entsiklopedyah shel galuyot, 1960.

Fishman, Y.L., ed., *Arim v'emahot b'Yisrael.* Jerusalem: Mosad Harav Kook, 1946.

Gelber, N. M., ed., *Sefer zikaron li-Drohobycz, Borislav veha-sevivah.* Tel-Aviv: Irgun Yotse Drohobits, Borislav veha-sevivah, 1959.

ed., *Entsiklopedych shel Galuyot,* Vol. 4 (L'vov). Jerusalem: Hevrat Entsiklopedyah shel galuyot, 1956.

and Israel Ben-Shem, eds., *Sefer Z'olkiv.* Jerusalem: Hevrat Entsiklopedyah shel galuyot, 1969.

Gelbart, Mendl, *Sefer zikaron le-zekher kehilat Dobromil.* Tel-Aviv: Dobromiler farayn in Yisroel un Amerike, 1964.

Gertner, Yehoshua, *Megiles Kosov.* Tel-Aviv: Amcha, 1981.

Halpern, Henoch., *Megiles Gline.* New York: Glinaner Emergency Relief Committee, 1950.

Karu, Baruch, ed., *Sefer Kehilat Zloczow.* Tel-Aviv: Irgun 'ole Zlots'ov, 1967.

Khomet, Avraham, *Torne* (Tarnow): *kiem un hurbn fun a Yidisher shtat.* Tel-Aviv: Landsmanshaftn fun Torner Yidn, 1954.

Korekh, Asher, *Kehilat Gelina.* Jerusalem: Asher Korekh, 1950.

Bagola uva-moledet. Jerusalem: Hotsa'at Gazit, 1941.

Korngruen, Philip, *Entsiklopedych shel Galuyot,* Vol. 3. (Tarnopol). Jerusalem: Hevrat Entsiklopedyah shel galuyot, 1955.

Kressel, Getzel, ed., *Sefer Kosov (Galitsyah ha-mizrahit)*. Tel-Aviv: ha-Menorah, 1964.

Kudish, Natan, Shimon Rozenberg, and Avigdor Rotfeld, eds., *Sefer Stryj*. Tel-Aviv: Irgun Yotzej Stryj, 1962,

Landau, Saul, *Sturm und Drang im Zionismus*. Vienna: Neue National-Zeitung, 1937.

Lindman, Nahum and Mordechai Koyfman, eds., *Galitsyaner Yidn Yoyvl bulek*. Buenos Aires: Tsentral farband fun Galitsyaner Yidn in Argentine, 1966.

Mahler, Rafael, *Sefer Sanz*. Tel-Aviv: Irgun yotzei Sanz b'New York, 1970.

Malz, David, "Revolutionary Zionism (1880–1895)" (Polish) in *Pięćdziesiąt Lat Sjonizmu* (Tarnow, 1934): 63–70

Margoshes, Joseph, *A World Apart: A Memoir of Jewish Life in Nineteenth Century Galicia*. Boston: Academic Studies Press, 2008.

Mencher, Aryeh, *Sefer Przemysl*. Tel-Aviv: Irgun yotzei Przemysl b'yisrael, 1964.

Miller, Saul, *Dobromil: Life in a Galician Shtetl 1890–1907*. New York: Loewenthal Press, 1980.

Miron, Elijahu, *Bielitz-Biala*. Tel-Aviv: E. Meron, 1973.

Noy, Dov and Mark Schutzman, eds., *Sefer zikaron li-kehilat Kolomeyah veha-sevivah*. Tel-Aviv: Irgun yots'e Kolomyah veha-sevivah ba-arets uva-tefutsot, 1972.

Nussenblatt, Tulo, ed., *Theodor Herzl Jahrbuch*. Vienna: H. Glanz, 1937.

Okrutony, Joseph, *Pinkas Hakehillot: Encyclopaedia of Jewish Communities, Vol. 3: Western Galicia and Silesia* (Hebrew). Jerusalem: Yad Vashem, 1984.

Pinkas Hakehillot: Encyclopaedia of Jewish Communities, Vol. 2: Eastern Galicia (Hebrew). Jerusalem: Yad Vashem, 1980.

Sefer Galitzia. Galician Society of Buenos Aires, 1968.

Salz, Abraham, "30 Years of Zionism (1884–1914)" (Polish) in *Pięćdziesiąt Lat Sjonizmu* (Tarnow, 1934): 7–21

"Cooperation and Conflict with Herzl" (Polish) in *Pięćdziesiąt Lat Sjonizmu* (Tarnow, 1934): 51–59

Schoenfeld, Joachim, *Jewish Life in Galicia under the Austro-Hungarian Empire and in the Reborn Poland 1898–1939*. Hoboken, N.J.: Ktav, 1990.

Schusheim, A. Y., "Jewish Politics and Jewish Parties in Galicia" (Yiddish) in Nechemia Zucker, ed., *Pinkes Galitsye*. Buenos Aires: Galitsyaner farband, 1945: 29–83.

Silberbusch, David, *Mi-pinkas zikronotai*. Tel-Aviv: Va'ad Yovel ha-shemonim, 1935.

Menschen und Geschehenisse. Vienna: Literatur Freunde, 1931.

Siegelman, Isaac, *Budzamower Yizkor-Buch*. Haifa: Yotse Budzanov be-Yisrael uve-Artsot-ha-Berit, 1968.

Taubes, Laibel, *Zikhrones fun Laibel Taubes*. Vienna: Adria, 1920.

Tenenbaum, Josef, *Galicie: Main Alte Haim*. Buenos Aires: Tsentral-farband fun Poylishe Yidn in Argentine, 1952.

Thon, Yehoshua, "Images from L'vov" (Hebrew), in Yisrael Cohen and Dov Sadan, eds., *Pirkey Galitsye*. Tel-Aviv: Am Oved, 1957. (Originally published in Yiddish in *Heint*, 1922.)

Wald, Moshe Yaari, ed., *Kehilat Resha: sefer zikaron*. Tel-Aviv: Irgune bene Resha be-Yisra'el uve-Artsot ha-Berit, 1967.

Walzer, Michael and Natan Kudish, eds., *Lantsut: hayeha ve-hurbanah shel kehilah Yehudit*. Tel-Aviv: Irgune yots'e Lantsut be-Yisra'el uve-Artsot ha-Berit, 1963.

Weichart, Michael, *Zikhrones*. Tel-Aviv: Menora, 1960.

Zucker, Nechemia, ed., *Gedenkbukh Galitsye*. Buenos Aires: Zikhroynes, 1964.

——— ed., *Pinkes Galitsye*. Buenos Aires: Galitsyaner farband, 1945.

4. *Other Primary Sources*

Acher, Mathias (N. Birnbaum), "Die jüdisch-nationale Bewegung," *Ruthenische Revue* (August 1904): 371–6.

——— "Die Sprachen des jüdischen Volkes," *Jüdische Abende: Vortrage aus der Literatur des ostjüdischen Volkssprache ("Jargon")*, No. 1 (December 18, 1904).

Agnon, S. Y., *A Simple Story*, translated by Hillel Halkin. New York: Schocken Books, 1985.

——— "Bi-na'arenu u-vi-zqenenu," in *Kol sipurav shel Shmuel Yosef Agnon*, Vol. 3. Tel-Aviv: Schocken, 1960: 273–350.

Bericht des Curatoriums der Baron Hirsch Stiftung zur Beförderung des Volksschulunterrichtes im Königreich Galizien und Lodomerien mit dem Grossherzogthume Krakau und Herzogthume Bukowina. Vienna, 1894–1913.

Bader, Gershom (Gustav), ed., *Jüdischer Volkskalender*. Lemberg, 1895–1912.

——— "Jewish-National or Zionist" (Yiddish), in *Jüdischer Volkskalender*, Vol. 8. 1902.

——— "Machanayim: The Galician Colony" (Yiddish), in *Jüdischer Volkskalender*, Vol. 8. 1902.

——— "The National Movement among Our Jewish Brothers in Galicia" (Hebrew), *Achi'asaf* (1894–5): 171–186.

Birnbaum, Nathan, *Die jüdische Moderne: Frühe zionistische Schriften*. Augsburg: Ölbaum, 1989.

——— *Protest gegen die Wahl des Dr. Wladyslaw Dulemba*. Vienna, 1907.

——— *Ausgewählte Schriften zur jüdischen Frage*. Czernowitz: Birnbaum & Kohut, 1910.

Bloch, Joseph, *Der nationale Zwist und die Juden in Oesterreich*. Vienna: M. Gottlieb, 1886.

Borochov, Ber, *Ketavim*, Vol. 3. Tel-Aviv: ha-Kibuts ha-me'uhad, 1955–66.

Die Reichsrathswahlen in Ostgalizien im Jahre 1897, edited by Ausschusse des ruthenischen Landeswahlcomités. Vienna, 1898.

Die Debatten über die Judenfrage in der Session des galizischen Landtages vom J. 1868. Lemberg: Stauropigianischen Instituts-Buchdruckerei, 1868.

Dubanowicz, Edward, *Stanowisko Ludności Żydowskiej w Galicyi Wobec Wyborów do Parlamentu Wiedeńskiego w r. 1907*. Lwów: Polonia, 1907.

Ehrenpreis, Mordechai, *Der Kantchik, oder Kinos noch Tisha B'av* (Yiddish). Lemberg, 1890.

"The Zionist Movement in Galicia" (Hebrew), *Hamagid*, November–December 1894.

Le'an?: masot sifrutiyot, edited with an introduction and notes by Avner Holzman. Jerusalem: Mosad Bialik, 1998.

"Vor Herzl und mit Herzl, zur Vorgeschichte des Baseler Kongresses," in *Theodor Herzl Jahrbuch*. Vienna: H. Glanz, 1937.

Engelmann, Richard, "Österreich's städtische Wohnplätze mit mehr als 25,000 Einwohnern Ende 1910, ihr Wachstum seit 1869 und die konfessionelle und sprachliche Zusammensetzung ihrer Bevölkerung 1880–1910," *Statistiche Monatsschrift* 40 (1914): 413–510.

Farn Kongress: Oisgabe fun di yidishe Soz.-Dem Partei in Galizien (n.a.), June 2, 1905.

Fleischer, Siegfried, "Enquête über die Lage der jüdischen Bevölkerung Galiziens," in Alfred Nossig, ed., *Jüdische Statistik*. Berlin: Jüdischer Verlag, 1903.

Freund, Fritz, *Das österreichische Abgeordnetenhaus: Ein biographisch-statistisches Handbuch*. Vienna: Wiener Verlag, 1907.

Glaser, Eliyahu, *Rede*. Cracow, 1903.

Goldberg, Shmuel, *Vas iz Zionismus?*. *Folks-bikhlech*, no. 2 (1904).

Grossman, Henryk, *Der Bundizm in Galizien*. Cracow: Ferlag der Sotsial-democrat, 1907.

Gutman, Samuel, *Der Wecker*. Lemberg, 1891.

Hecke, Wilhelm, *Volksvermehrung, Binnenwanderung und Umgangssprache in Österreich*. Brünn: Irrgang, 1914.

"Die Städte Österreichs nach der Volkszählung vom 31. December 1910," *Statistiche Monatsschrift* 39 (1913): 177–221.

"Die Methode und Technik der österreichischen Volkszählungen," *Statistiche Monatsschrift* 38 (1912): 466–74.

Henes, M., "Chanukah," *Folks-bikhlech*, no. 1. (1903).

Herzl, Theodor, *Der Judenstaat*. Leibzig and Vienna: Breitenstein, 1896.

Hickman, A. L., *G. Freytag's Reichsrats Wahlkarte (1873–1901)*. Vienna, 1901.

Inama-Sternegg, Karl Theodor von, *Handbuch der Vereine für die im Reichsrathe Vertreteten Königreiche und Länder*. Vienna: Manz, 1892.

Kamelhar, Moshe, *Rabi Dov Ber Maizlish: gadol ba-Torah medinai ve-lohem*. Jerusalem: Mosad ha-Rav Kook, 1970.

Korkis, Abraham, "Zur Bewegung der jüdischen Bevölkerung in Galizien," in Alfred Nossig, ed., *Jüdische Statistik*. Berlin, 1903.

"Die Wirtschaftliche Lage der Juden in Galizien," *Der Jude* (1917): 464–71, 532–9, 608–15.

Landau, Saul, *Der Polenklub und seine Hausjuden*. Vienna: C.W. Stern, 1907.

Unter jüdischen Proletariern. Vienna: Rosner, 1898.

Syonizm. Cracow, 1897.

"Die jüdisch-nationale Bewegung und die Ruthenen in Galizien," *Ukrainische Rundschau* (May 1907): 147–51.

Leisner, Judah, *Sefer Milhamot Bloch*. Lemberg: Chaim Rohatyn, 1891.

Lewicky, Eugen, *Galizien: Informativer Ueberblick über nationale, wirtschaftliche, soziale und kulturelle Zustände des Landes*. Vienna: Verlag des Bundes zur Befreiung der Ukraina, 1916.

Locker, Berl, "Ostgalizien," *Der Jude* (1923), 146–157.

Lozynskyj, Mychajlo, "Die jüdische Frage in Galizien und die österreichische Sozialdemokratie," *Ukrainische Rundschau* (May 1906): 168–74; (June 1906): 208–14.

Marcus, Ahron, *Dr. Theodor Herzl's "Judenstaat" besprochen in der Generalversammlung der "Chowewe Erez Israel" in Krakau am 10. Januar 1897*. Cracow: J. Fischer, 1897.

Nossig, Alfred, *Materialien zur Statistik des Jüdischen Stammes*. Vienna: C. Konegen, 1887.

Pinson, Koppel, ed., *Nationalism and History: Letters on Old and New Judaism by Simon Dubnow*. Philadelphia: Jewish Publication Society of America, 1958.

Rauchberg, Heinrich, *Die Statistischen Unterlagen der Österreichischen Wahlreform*. Brünn: F. Irrgang, 1907.

Bevölkerung Österreichs auf Grund der Ergebnisse der Volkszählung vom 31. December 1890. Vienna: A. Hölder, 1895.

Reichenberg, Christian, *Wie kann das Elend eines Theiles der Juden in Galizien und der Bukowina durch die Baron Hirsch'sche Zwölfmillionen-Stiftung gemildert werden? Eine Studie*. Vienna: n.p., 1891.

Rosenfeld, Max, *Die polnische Judenfrage: Problem und Lösung*. Vienna: R. Löwit, 1918.

"Nationale Autonomie der Juden in Oesterreich," in *Heimkehr: Essays Juedischer Denker*. Czernowitz: L. Lamm, 1912.

"Für eine Nationale Autonomie der Juden in Österreich," *Der Jude* (1916/17): 290–97.

Rosenhek, Ludwig, *Festscrift zur Feier des 100. Semesters der Akademischen Verbindung Kadimah*. Vienna: Glanz, 1933.

Salz, Abraham, *Makkabäer-Rede*, Drohobycz: Zionistische Jugend, 1899.

Schimmer, G. A., *Die Juden in Oesterreich nach der Zählung vom 31.December 1880*. Vienna: A. Hölder, 1881.

Die Reichsraths-Wahlen vom Jahre 1879 in Oesterreich. Stuttgart: Julius Maier, 1880.

Statistik des Judenthums in den im Reichsrathe Vertretenen Königreichen und Ländern, Vienna: Druck der Kaiserlich-Königlichen Hof- und Staatsdruckerei, 1873.

Stand, Adolf, *Kitve Stand*. Tel-Aviv, 1942.

Starkel, Juliusz, *Fundacya Hirscha i Sprawa Zydowska w Galicyi*. Lwow, 1890.

Summarische Ergebnisse der Statistik der Reichsratswahlen Von 1911. K.K. Statistiche Zentralkommission, Brünn, 1911.

Summarische Ergebnisse der Statistik der Reichsratswahlen Von 1907. K.K. Statistiche Zentralkommission, Brünn, 1907.

Statuten des Vereines für Colonisation Palästinas "Ahawath Zion" in Tarnow. 1899.

Stenographische Protokolle der Verhandlungen des I-VIII Zionisten Congress. 1897–1907.

Stenographische Protokolle des Österreichisches Abgeordnetenhauses. Vienna, 1897–1911.

Tenenbaum, Josef, "Wirtschaftspolitische Postulate der Juden in Ostgalizien," *Der Jude* (1919): 5–11.

Thon, Jacob, *Die Juden in Österreich.* Berlin: Bureau für Statistik der Juden, 1908.

Twain, Mark, "Concerning the Jews," *Harpers Magazine* (Summer, 1898). Reprinted in *The Man that Corrupted Hadleyburg and Other Stories and Essays.* New York: Harper and Bartal, 1900.

Yehoshua (Osias), Thon, *Essays zur Zionistischen Ideologie.* Berlin: Kedem, 1930.

Ketavim. Warsaw: Ahiasaf, 1923.

Waschitz, Osias, "Jüdische Politik in Galizien," *Ukrainische Rundschau* (October 1906): 377–88.

Wilhelm, Arthur, ed., *Die Reichsrats-Abgeordneten des allgemeinen Wahlrechtes.* Vienna, 1907.

Secondary Sources

Almog, Shmuel, "Was Herzl a Jewish Nationalist?" in Gideon Shimoni and Robert S. Wistrich, eds., *Theodor Herzl: Visionary of the Jewish State.* Jerusalem: Magnes Press, 1999: 65–181.

Zionism and History: The Rise of a New Jewish Consciousness. Jerusalem: Magnes Press, 1987.

"Alfred Nossig: A Reappraisal," *Studies in Zionism* 7 (Spring 1983): 1–29.

Anderson, Benedict, *Imagined Communities: Reflections on the Origin and Spread of Nationalism.* London: Verso, 1983.

Andlauer, Teresa, *Die jüdische Bevölkerung im Modernisierungsprozess Galiziens (1867–1914).* Frankfurt am Main: Peter Lang, 2001.

Andrusiak, Taras, "The 1907 Ukrainian-Jewish Electoral Coalition" (Ukrainian), *Ï: nezalezhnyi kul'turolohichnyi chasopys* 8 (1996): 57–9.

Armstrong, John A., *Nations before Nationalism.* Chapel Hill: University of North Carolina Press, 1982.

Aron, Willy, "Herzl and Aron Marcus," in Raphael Patai, ed., *Herzl Year Book*, Vol. 1. New York: Herzl Press, 1958:183–93.

Aronson, I. Michael, *Troubled Waters: The Origins of the 1881 Anti-Jewish Pogroms in Russia.* Pittsburgh: University of Pittsburgh Press, 1990.

Avineri, Shlomo, "Zionism and the Jewish Religious Tradition: The Dialectics of Redemption and Secularization," in Shmuel Almog, Jehuda Reinharz, and Anita Shapira, eds., *Zionism and Religion.* Hanover: Brandeis University Press, 1998: 1–12.

The Making of Modern Zionism: The Intellectual Origins of the Jewish State. New York: Basic Books, 1981.

Bacon, Gershon, *The Politics of Tradition: Agudat Yisrael in Poland, 1916–1939.* Jerusalem: Magnes Press, 1996.

Bader, Gershom, *Medinah va-ḥakhameha*. New York: National Booksellers, 1934.

Balaban, Mayer, "Herz Homberg in Galizien," *Jahrbuch für Jüdische Geschichte und Literatur* 19 (1916): 189–221.

Baron, Salo, *Under Two Civilizations: Tarnow, 1895–1914*. Palo Alto, Calif.: Stanford University Press, 1990.

"The Revolution of 1848 and Jewish Scholarship, II," *Proceedings of the American Academy for Jewish Research* 20 (1951): 62–83.

Bartal, Israel and Antony Polonsky, "The Jews of Galicia under the Habsburgs," *Polin* 12 (1999): 3–24.

Bartal, Israel, *The Jews of Eastern Europe, 1772–1881*. Philadelphia: University of Pennsylvania Press, 2005.

"Responses to Modernity: Haskalah, Orthodoxy, and Nationalism in Eastern Europe," in Shmuel Almog, Jehuda Reinharz, and Anita Shapira, eds., *Zionism and Religion*. Hanover: Brandeis University Press, 1998: 13–24.

"From Traditional Bilingualism to National Monolingualism" in Lewis Glinert, ed., *Hebrew in Ashkenaz*. Oxford University Press, 1993: 141–50.

"'The Heavenly City of Germany' and Absolutism a la Mode d'Autriche: The Rise of the Haskalah in Galicia," in Jacob Katz, ed., *Towards Modernity: The European Jewish Model*. New Brunswick: Transaction Books, 1987: 33–42.

"The Image of Germany and German Jewry in East European Jewish Society during the 19th Century," in Isadore Twersky, ed., *Danzig, between East and West: Aspects of Modern Jewish History*. Cambridge, Mass.: Harvard University Press, 1985.

"From Corporation to Nation: Jewish Autonomy in Eastern Europe, 1772–1881," *Jahrbuch des Simon-Dubnow-Instituts* 5 (2006): 17–31.

Bein, Alex, "The Origin of the Term and Concept "Zionism," *Herzl Year Book* 2. New York: Herzl Press, 1959: 1–27.

Beller, Steven, *Herzl*. New York: Grove Weidenfeld, 1991.

"Patriotism and the National Identity of Habsburg Jewry, 1860–1914," *Leo Baeck Institute Yearbook* 46 (1996): 215–38.

Berkowitz, Michael, *Zionist Culture and West European Jewry before the First World War*. Cambridge: Cambridge University Press, 1993.

Biale, David, *Power and Powerlessness in Jewish History*. New York: Schocken Books, 1986.

Biderman, Israel, *Mayer Balaban: Historian of Polish Jewry*. New York: Biderman Book Committee, 1976.

Bihl, Wolfdieter, "Die Juden," in Adam Wandruszka and Peter Urbanitsch, eds., *Die Habsburgermonarchie 1848–1918*, III/2 ("Die Völker des Reiches"). Vienna: Verlag der österreichischen Akademie der Wissenschaften, 1980: 880–948.

Binder, Harold, *Galizien in Wien: Parteien, Wahlen, Fraktionen und Abgeordnete im Übergang zur Massenpolitik*. Vienna: Verlag der Österreichischen Akademie der Wissenschaften, 2005.

"Making and Defending a Polish Town: "Lwów" (Lemberg), 1848–1914," *Austrian History Yearbook* 34 (2003): 57–81.

"Die Wahlreform von 1907 und der polnisch-ruthenische Konflikt in Ostgalizien," *Österreichische Osthefte* 38 (1996): 293–321.

Birnbaum, S. A., "Nathan Birnbaum and National Autonomy," in Josef Fraenkel, ed., *The Jews of Austria*. London: Valentine and Mitchell, 1967.

Blanning, T.C.W., *Joseph II and Enlightened Despotism*. London: Longman Group, 1970.

Bloch, Chaim, "Theodor Herzl and Joseph S. Bloch," in Raphael Patai, ed., *Herzl Year Book*, Vol. 1. New York: Herzl Press, 1958: 154–64.

Blum, Richard, *Geschichte der jüdische Turn- und Sportbewegung 1895–1914*. Unpublished master's thesis, Maccabi World Union Archives, Ramat Gan.

Blum, S., "The Jewish Worker and the Polish Social-Democratic Party in Galicia" (Yiddish), in F. Kursky et al., eds., *Di Yidishe sotsyalistishe bavegung biz der grindung fun "Bund."* Vilna: YIVO, 1939: 520–6.

Bohachevsky-Chomiak, Martha, *Feminists Despite Themselves: Women in Ukrainian Community Life, 1884–1939*. Edmonton: Canadian Institute of Ukrainian Studies Press, 1988.

Brawer, A. W., *Galitzia v'yehudeha. Studies in Galician Jewry in the 18th Century* (Hebrew). Jerusalem: Mosad Byalik, 1965.

Brix, Emil, *Die Umgangsspachen in Altösterreich zwischen Agitation und Assimilation*. Vienna: Böhlau, 1982.

Bross, Jacob, "The Beginning of the Jewish Labor Movement in Galicia" (Yiddish), in F. Kursky et al., eds., *Di Yidishe sotsyalistishe bavegung biz der grindung fun "Bund."* Vilna: YIVO, 1939: 482–519. (Abridged English translation in YIVO *Annual* [1950]: 55–84.)

"Towards a History of the J.S.D.P. in Galicia" (Yiddish), in *Royter pinkes; tsu der geshikhte fun der Yidisher arbeter-bavegung un sotsyalistishe shtremungen bay Yidn*, Vol. 2. Warsaw: Kultur-Lige, 1921: 22–48.

Broszat, Martin, "Von der Kulturnation zur Volksgruppe: Die national Stellung der Juden in der Bukowina im 19. und 20. Jahrhundert," *Historische Zeitschrifte*, Band 200, Heft 3, June 1965: 572–605.

Brubaker, Rogers, *Ethnicity without Groups*. Cambridge, Mass.: Harvard University Press, 2004.

Nationalism Reframed: Nationhood and the National Question in the New Europe. New York: Cambridge University Press, 1996.

"Myths and Misconceptions in the Study of Nationalism," in John Hall, ed., *The State of the Nation*. New York: Cambridge University Press, 1998: 272–306.

Bussgang, Julian J., "The Progressive Synagogue in Lwów," *Polin* 11 (1998): 127–53.

Buszko, Jozef, "The Consequences of Galician Autonomy after 1867," *Polin* 12 (1999): 86–99.

"Die Stellung der Polen und Ukrainer zur jüdischen Frage im autonomen Galizien," *Österreichische Osthefte* 38 (1996): 275–91.

Cahnman, Werner J., "Scholar and Visionary: The Correspondence between Herzl and Ludwig Gumplowicz," in Raphael Patai, ed., *Herzl Year Book*, Vol. 1. New York: Herzl Press, 1958.

Ciuciura, Theodore, "Provincial Politics in the Habsburg Empire: The Case of Galicia and Bukovina," *Nationalities Papers* 13, no. 2 (Fall 1985): 247–73.

Cohen, Mitchel, "A Preface to the Study of Jewish Nationalism," *Jewish Social Studies* 1 (1994): 3–83.

Davies, Norman, *God's Playground: A History of Poland*. New York: Columbia University Press, 1982.

Doron, Joachim, "Jüdischer Nationalismus bei Nathan Birnbaum," in Walter Grab, ed., *Jüdische Integration und Identität in Deutschland und Österreich 1848–1918*. Tel-Aviv: Tel-Aviv University, 1984: 199–230.

Dynner, Glenn, *Men of Silk: The Hasidic Conquest of Polish Jewry*. New York: Oxford University Press, 2006.

Einäugler, Karol, "The First Yiddish May-Call in Galicia and the May Issue of "Arbeter" (1894)" (Yiddish), in F. Kursky et al., eds., *Di Yidishe sotsyalistishe bavegung biz der grindung fun "Bund."* Vilna: YIVO, 1939: 512–19.

Eisen, Georg, "Zionism, Nationalism and the Emergence of the Jüdische Turnerschaft," *Leo Baeck Institute Yearbook* (1983): 247–62.

Eisenbach, Artur, *The Emancipation of the Jews in Poland, 1780–1870*, edited by Antony Polansky, translated by Janina Dorosz. Oxford: Basil Blackwell, 1991.

"Das galizische Judentum während des Völkerfrühlings und in der Zeit des Kampfes um seine Gleichberechtigung," in *Studia Judaica Austriaca* 8 (1980): 75–92.

Elon, Amos, *Herzl*. New York: Holt, Rinehart and Winston, 1975.

Etkes, Immanuel, ed., *HaDat vehaHayim: Tenuat haHaskalah ha-Yehudit beMizrah Europa*. Jerusalem: Zalman Shazar Center for Jewish History, 1993.

"Immanent Factors and External Influences in the Development of the Haskalah Movement in Russia," in Jacob Katz, ed., *Towards Modernity: The European Jewish Model*. New Brunswick: Transaction Books, 1987: 13–32.

Everett, Leila P., "The Rise of Jewish National Politics in Galicia, 1905–1907," in Andrei S. Markovits and Frank E. Sysyn, eds., *Nationbuilding and the Politics of Nationalism: Essays on Austrian Galicia*. Cambridge, Mass.: Harvard University Press, 1982: 149–177.

Feiner, Shmuel, *Haskalah and History: The Emergence of a Modern Jewish Historical Consciousness*. London: Littman Library, 2002.

"Towards a Historical Definition of the Haskalah," in Shmuel Feiner and David Sorkin, eds., *New Perspectives on the Haskalah*. London: Littman Library, 2001: 184–219.

Fishman, Joshua, *Ideology, Society, and Language: The Odyssey of Nathan Birnbaum*. Ann Arbor: Karom Publishers, 1987.

Language and Nationalism: Two Integrative Essays. Rowley, Mass.: Newbury House Publishers, 1972.

Fraenkel, Josef, "The Chief Rabbi and the Visionary," in *The Jews of Austria*. London: Valentine and Mitchell, 1967: 111–29.

Frank, Alison, *Oil Empire*. Cambridge, Mass.: Harvard University Press, 2005.

Frankel, Jonathan, *Prophecy and Politics: Socialism, Nationalism, and the Russian Jews 1862–1917*. Cambridge: Cambridge University Press, 1981.

"Assimilation and the Jews in Nineteenth-Century Europe: Towards a New Historiography?" in Jonathan Frankel and Steven Zipperstein, eds.,

Assimilation and Community: The Jews in Nineteenth-Century Europe. Cambridge: Cambridge University Press, 1992.

"The Dilemmas of Jewish National Autonomism: The Case of Ukraine 1917–1920," in Howard Aster and Peter J. Potichnyj, eds., *Ukrainian-Jewish Relations in Historical Perspective.* Alberta: Canadian Institute of Ukrainian Studies Press, 1988.

"Crisis as a Factor in Modern Jewish Politics, 1840 and 1881–82," in Jehuda Reinharz, ed., *Living with Antisemitism.* Hanover: Brandeis University Press, 1987.

Friedmann, Filip, *Die Galizischen Juden im Kampfe um ihre Gleichberechtigung (1848–1868).* Frankfurt am Main: J. Kauffmann Verlag, 1929.

"Die Judenfrage im galizischen Landtag," *Monatsschrift für Geschichte und Wissenschaft des Judentums* (1928): 379–90, 457–77.

Gaisbauer, Adolf, *Davidstern und Doppeladler.* Vienna: Böhlau, 1988.

Gasowski, Tomasz, "Jewish Communities in Autonomous Galicia: Their Size and Distribution," in Andrzej Paluch, ed., *The Jews in Poland*, Vol. 1. Cracow: Jagiellonian University, 1992: 205–22.

"From *Austeria* to the Manor: Jewish Landowners in Autonomous Galicia," *Polin* 12, 1999: 120–36.

Gelbard, Arye, "Cracow and the Beginning of the Jewish Labor Movement in Poland," (Hebrew), in Elchanan Reiner, ed., *Krako-Kaz'imyez'-Krakov: mehkarim be-toldot Yehude Krakov.* Tel Aviv: Tel-Aviv University, 2001:191–204.

Gelber, N. M., *Busk: Toldot Yehudeha.* Tel-Aviv: Olamenu, 1962.

Toldot ha-tenva ha-tsiyonit be-Galitsyah 1875–1918. Jerusalem: Rubin Mass, 1958.

Toldot Yehude Brody (1584–1943). Jerusalem: Mosad ha-Rav Kook, 1955.

Aus zwei Jahrhunderten: Beiträge zur neueren Geschichte der Juden. Vienna: R. Löwit, 1924.

The National Autonomy of Eastern-Galician Jewry in the West-Ukrainian Republic 1918–1919, in Isaac Lewin, ed., *A History of Polish Jewry during the Revival of Poland.* New York: Shengold, 1990.

"History of the Jews in Kolomea" (Yiddish), in Shlomo Bickel, ed., *Pinkas Kolomey.* New York, 1957: 13–95.

Gellner, Ernest, *Nations and Nationalism.* Oxford: Blackwell, 1983.

Golczewski, Frank, *Polnisch-Jüdische Beziehungen 1881–1922.* Wiesbaden: Steiner, 1981.

"Rural Anti-Semitism in Galicia before World War I," in Chimen Abramsky, Macej Jachimczyk, and Antony Polonsky, eds., *The Jews in Poland.* Oxford: Basil Blackwell, 1986.

Gold, Hugo, *Geschichte der Juden in der Bukowina.* Tel-Aviv: Olamenu, 1958.

Goldscheider, Calvin and Alan Zuckerman, *The Transformation of the Jews.* Chicago: University of Chicago Press, 1984.

Goldsmith, Emanuel S., *Architects of Yiddishism at the Beginning of the Twentieth Century.* London: Associated University Presses, 1976.

Grodziski, Stanislaw, "The Jewish Question in Galicia: The Reforms of Maria Theresa and Joseph II, 1772–1790," *Polin* 12 (1999): 61–72.

Grunwald, Kurt, "A Note on the Baron Hirsch Stiftung Vienna 1888–1914," *Leo Baeck Institute Yearbook* 17 (1972): 227–236.

Guesnet, Francois, "Hanuka and Its Function in the Invention of a Jewish-Heroic Tradition in Early Zionism, 1880–1900," in Michael Berkowitz, ed., *Nationalism, Zionism, and Ethnic Mobilisation.* Leiden: Brill, 2004: 227–45.

Hann, Chris and Paul Robert Magocsi, *Galicia: A Multicultured Land.* Toronto: University of Toronto, 2005.

Hart, Mitchell B., "Moses the Microbiologist: Judaism and Social Hygiene in the Work of Alfred Nossig," *Jewish Social Studies* 2, no. 1 (1995): 72–97.

Haumann, Heiko, "Nationale Gegenwartsarbeit im Schtetl: Anfange des Zionismus in Galizien," in *Der Erste Zionistenkongress von 1897.* Vienna: Karger, 1997.

Häusler, Wolfgang, *Das galizische Judentum in der Habsburgermonarchie im Lichte der zeitgenössischen Publizistik und Reiseliteratur von 1772–1848.* Munich: R. Oldenbourg, 1979.

"Das Österreichische Judentum zwischen Beharrung und Fortschritt," in Adam Wandruszka and Peter Urbanitsch, eds., *Die Habsburgermonarchie 1848–1918,* Vol. 4 *Die Konfession.* Vienna: Verlag der Österreichischen Akademie der Wissenschaften, 1995: 633–69.

Hertz, Jacob S. "The Bund's Nationality Program and Its Critics in the Russian, Polish and Austrian Socialist Movements," *YIVO Annual of Jewish Social Science* 14 (1969): 53–68.

Hertzberg, Arthur, *The Zionist Idea: A Historical Analysis and Reader.* Philadelphia: Jewish Publication Society, 1997.

Hever, Hannan, "The Struggle over the Canon of Early-Twentieth-Century Hebrew Literature: The Case of Galicia," in Steven Kepnes, ed., *Interpreting Judaism in a Postmodern Age.* New York: New York University Press, 1996: 243–77.

Himka, John-Paul, *Religion and Nationality in Western Ukraine: The Greek Catholic Church and the Ruthenian National Movement in Galicia, 1867–1900.* Montreal: McGill-Queen's University Press, 1999.

Galicia and Bukowina: A Research Handbook about Western Ukraine: Late 19th and 20th Centuries. Alberta: Alberta Culture and Multiculturalism, Historical Resources Division, 1990.

Galician Villagers and the Ukrainian National Movement in the Nineteenth Century. London: Macmillan Press in association with University of Alberta, 1988.

Socialism in Galicia: The Emergence of Polish Social Democracy and Ukrainian Radicalism (1860–1890). Cambridge, Mass.: Harvard Ukrainian Research Institute, 1983.

"The Construction of Nationality in Galician Rus': Icarian Flights in Almost All Directions," in Ronald Suny and Michael Kennedy, eds., *Intellectuals and the Articulation of the Nation.* Ann Arbor: University of Michigan Press, 1999: 109–64.

"Ukrainian-Jewish Antagonism in the Galician Countryside during the Late Nineteenth Century," in Howard Aster and Peter J. Potichnyj, eds., *Ukrainian-Jewish Relations in Historical Perspective.* Alberta: Canadian Institute of Ukrainian Studies Press, 1988.

"Dimensions of a Triangle: Polish-Ukrainian-Jewish Relations in Austrian Galicia," *Polin* 12 (1999): 25–48.

Hirshaut, Julian, *In Gang Fun Der Geshichte*. Tel-Aviv: I. L. Peretz Publishing, 1984.

Hobsbawm, Eric, *Nations and Nationalism since 1780*. Cambridge: Cambridge University Press, 1990.

and Terence Ranger, eds., *The Invention of Tradition*. Cambridge: Cambridge University Press, 1983.

Hödl, Klaus, *Als Bettler in die Leopoldstadt: Galizische Juden auf dem Weg nach Wien*. Vienna: Böhlau, 1994.

"Galician Jewish Migration to Vienna," *Polin* 12 (1999): 147–63.

Holzer, Jerzy, "Jüdisches Leben und Akkulturation im Lemberg des 19. und 20. Jahrhunderts," in Peter Fässler, Thomas Held, and Dirk Sawitzki, eds., *Lemberg-Lwow-Lviv: Eine Stadt im Schnittpunkt europäischer Kulturen*. Vienna: Böhlau, 1995.

"Enlightenment, Assimilation, and Modern Identity: The Jewish Elite in Galicia," *Polin* 12 (1999): 79–85.

"Zur Frage der Akkulturation der Juden in Galizien im 19. und 20. Jahrhundert," *Jahrbücher für Geschichte Osteuropas* 37 (1989): 217–27.

Hroch, Miroslav, *Social Preconditions of National Revival im Europe*. New York: Columbia University Press, 2000.

"Zionismus als eine europäische Nationalbewegung," *Judentum und Christentum* 1 (2000): 33–40.

"Real and Constructed: The Nature of the Nation," in John Hall, ed., *The State of the Nation: Ernest Gellner and the Theory of Nationalism*. New York: Cambridge University Press, 1998: 91–106.

"Language and National Identity," in Richard Rudolph and David Good, eds., *Nationalism and Empire: The Habsburg Empire and the Soviet Union*. New York: St. Martin's Press, 1992: 65–78.

"From National Movements to the Fully-formed Nation: The Nation-building Process in Europe." Reprinted in Gopal Balakrishnan, ed., *Mapping the Nation*. London: Verso, 1996.

"The Social Interpretation of Linguistic Demands in European National Movements." San Domenico (Florence): European University Institute Working Papers 94/1, 1994.

Hryniuk, Stella, *Peasants with Promise: Ukrainians in Southeastern Galicia 1880–1900*. Edmonton: University of Alberta, 1991.

Hrytsak, Yaroslav, "A Ukrainian Answer to the Galician Ethnic Triangle: The Case of Ivan Franko," *Polin* 12 (1999): 137–46.

Hundert, Gershon, *The Jews in a Polish Private Town*. Baltimore: Johns Hopkins University Press, 1992.

Isaievych, Iaroslav, "Galicia and Problems of National Identity," in Ritchie Robertson and Edward Timms, eds., *The Habsburg Legacy*. Edinburgh: Edinburgh University Press, 1994: 37–45.

Jacobs, Jack, *On Socialists and "The Jewish Question" after Marx*. New York: New York University Press, 1992.

Janowsky, Oscar, *The Jews and Minority Rights*. New York: Columbia University Press, 1933.

Jenks, William Alexander, *The Austrian Electoral Reform of 1907*. New York: Columbia University Press, 1950.

Jensen, Angelika, *Sei stark und mutig! Chasak we'emaz! 40 Jahre jüdische Jugend in Österreich am Beispiel der Bewegung "Haschomer Hazair" 1903 bis 1943*. Vienna: Picus Verlag, 1995.

John, Michael and Albert Lichtblau, "Mythos 'deutsche Kultur.' Jüdische Gemeinden in Galizien und der Bukowina," in Martha Keil and Eleonore Lappin, eds., *Studien zur Geschichte der Juden in Österreich*. Vienna: Philo, 1997.

Judson, Pieter, *Guardians of the Nation: Activists on the Language Frontiers of Imperial Austria*. Boston, Mass.: Harvard, 2006

Exclusive Revolutionaries: Liberal Politics, Social Experience, and National Identity in the Austrian Empire, 1848–1914. Ann Arbor: University of Michigan Press, 1996.

Judson, Pieter and Marsha Rozenblit, eds., *Constructing Nationalities in East Central Europe*. New York: Berghahn Books, 2005.

Kahane, Abraham, *Divrei Zikaron LeToldot Harav Gedelia Schmelkes*. Przemysl: Torah va-'avodah, 1933.

Kann, Robert A., *The Multinational Empire: Nationalism and National Reform in the Habsburg Monarchy, 1848–1918*. New York: Columbia University Press, 1950.

Karniel, Josef, *Die Toleranzpolitik Kaiser Josephs II*. Gerlingen: Bleicher Verlag, 1986.

"Das Toleranzpatent Kaiser Josephs II. für die Juden Galiziens und Lodomeriens," *Tel-Aviv Jahrbuch* 11 (1982): 55–89.

Katz, Jacob, *Tradition and Crisis: Jewish Society at the End of the Middle Ages*, translated by Bernard Dov Cooperman. New York: New York University Press, 1993.

Jewish Emancipation and Self-emancipation. Philadelphia: Jewish Publication Society, 1986.

ed., *Towards Modernity: The European Jewish Model*. New Brunswick: Transaction Books, 1987.

"From Ghetto to Zionism, Mutual Influences of East and West," in Isadore Twersky, ed., *Danzig, between East and West: Aspects of Modern Jewish History*. Cambridge, Mass.: Harvard University Press, 1985.

Kedouri, Elie, *Nationalism*, 4th, expanded ed. Oxford: Blackwell, 1993.

Kieniewicz, Stefan, *The Emancipation of the Polish Peasantry*. Chicago: University of Chicago Press, 1969.

Kieval, Hillel, *The Making of Czech Jewry: National Conflict and Jewish Society in Bohemia, 1870–1918*. New York: Oxford University Press, 1988.

King, Jeremy, *Budweisers into Czechs and Germans*. Princeton: Princeton University Press, 2002.

"The Nationalization of East Central Europe: Ethnicism, Ethnicity, and Beyond," in Maria Bucur and Nancy Wingfield, eds., *Staging the Past: The Politics of Commemoration in Habsburg Central Europe, 1848 to the Present*. West Lafayette, IN: Purdue University Press, 2001: 112–52.

Kisman, Joseph, "The Jewish Social-Democratic Movement in Galicia and Bukowina" (Yiddish), in G. Aronson et al., eds., *Di Geshikhte fun Bund*, Vol. 3. New York: Farlag Unzer Tsayt, 1960: 337–482.

Klanska, Maria, *Problemfeld Galizien: zur Thematisierung eines nationalen und politisch-sozialen Phänomens in deutschsprachige Prosa 1846–1914*. Vienna: Böhlau, 1991.

"Galizien und Bukowina," in Anrei Corbea and Michael Astner, eds., *Kulturlandschaft Bukowina*, Iasi: Editura Universitatii, 1990.

Klier, John, "The Myth of Zion among East European Jewry," in Geoffrey Hosking and George Schöpflin, eds., *Myths and Nationhood*. New York: Routledge, 1997: 170–81.

Kohlbauer-Fritz, Gabriele, "Yiddish as an Expression of Jewish Cultural Identity in Galicia and Vienna," *Polin* 12 (1999): 164–76.

Kornberg, Jacques, *Theodor Herzl: From Assimilation to Zionism*. Bloomington: Indiana University Press, 1993.

Kozińska-Witt, Hanna, *Die Krakauer Jüdische Reformgemeinde 1864–74*. Frankfurt am Main: Peter Lang, 1999.

"The Association of Progressive Jews in Kraków, 1864–1874," *Polin* 23 (2010): 119–34.

"Ludwig Gumplowicz's Programme for the Improvement of the Jewish Situation," *Polin* 12 (1999): 73–8.

Kraft, Claudia, "Die jüdische Frage im Spiegel der Presseorgane und Parteiprogramme der galizischen Bauernbewegung im letzten Viertel des 19. Jahrhunderts," *Zeitschrift für Ostmitteleuropa-Forschung* 45 (1996): 381–410.

Kressel, G., "*Selbst-Emancipation*" (Hebrew), *Shivat Zion* 4 (1956): 55–99.

Kuhn, Rick, *Henryk Grossman and the Recovery of Marxism*. Urbana: University of Illinois, 2007.

"The Jewish Social Democratic Party of Galicia and the Bund," in Jack Jacobs, ed., *Jewish Politics in Eastern Europe: The Bund at 100*. New York: New York University Press, 2001.

"Organizing Yiddish Speaking Workers in Pre-World War One Galicia: The Jewish Social Democratic Party," in Leonard Jay Greenspoon, ed., *Yiddish Language and Culture Then and Now*. Omaha: Creighton University Press, 1996.

Kühntopf-Gentz, Michael, *Nathan Birnbaum Biographie*. Unpublished dissertation, Eberhard-Karls-Universität zu Tübingen, 1990.

Kuzmany, Börries, "Center and Periphery at the Austrian-Russian Border: The Galician Border Town of Brody in the Long Nineteenth Century," *Austrian History Yearbook* 42 (2011): 67–88.

Landau, Moses, *Geschichte des Zionismus in Oesterreich und Ungarn*. Unpublished dissertation, University of Vienna, 1925.

Lederhendler, Eli, *Jewish Responses to Modernity: New Voices in America and Eastern Europe*. New York: New York University Press, 1994.

Lehmann, Rosa, *Symbiosis and Ambivalence: Poles and Jews in a Small Galician Town*. New York: Berghahn Books, 2001.

Lestchinsky, Jacob, "The Mother-Tongue of the Jews in Independent Poland" (Yiddish), *YIVO Bleter* 22, no. 2 (November–December 1943): 147–62.

Lichtblau, Albert, ed., *Als hätten wir dazugehört: Österreichisch-Jüdisch Lebensgeschichten aus der Habsburgermonarchie*. Vienna: Böhlau, 1999.

Lukowski, Jerzy, *The Partitions of Poland: 1772, 1793, 1795*. London: Longman, 1999.

Luz, Ehud, *Parallels Meet: Religion and Nationalism in the Early Zionism Movement (1882–1904)*. Philadelphia: Jewish Publication Society, 1988.

"The Limits of Toleration: The Challenge of Cooperation inbetween the Observant and the Nonobservant during the Hibbat Zion Period, 1822–1895," in Shmuel Almog, Jehuda Reinharz, and Anita Shapira, eds., *Zionism and Religion*. Hanover: Brandeis University Press, 1998: 44–54.

Macartney, C. A., *The Habsburg Empire 1790–1918*. New York: Macmillan, 1969

Magocsi, Paul Robert, *The Roots of Ukrainian Nationalism: Galicia as Ukraine's Piedmont*. Toronto: University of Toronto Press, 2002.

Historical Atlas of East Central Europe. Seattle: University of Washington Press, 2002.

Galicia: A Historical Survey and Bibliographic Guide. Toronto: University of Toronto Press, 1983.

"The Language Question as a Factor in the National Movement," in Andrei Markovits and Frank Sysyn, eds., *Nationbuilding and the Politics of Nationalism: Essays on Austrian Galicia*. Cambridge, Mass.: Harvard University Press, 1982: 220–38.

Mahler, Rafael, *Hasidism and the Jewish Enlightenment: Their Confrontation in Galicia and Poland in the First Half of the Nineteenth Century*. Philadelphia: Jewish Publication Society of America, 1985.

A History of Modern Jewry: 1780–1815. New York: Schocken Books, 1971.

"The Economic Background of Jewish Emigration from Galicia to the United States," *YIVO Annual of Jewish Social Science* 7 (1952): 255–67.

"The Social and Political Aspects of the Haskalah in Galicia," *YIVO Annual* (1949): 64–85.

Marschall von Bieberstein, Christoph Freiherr, *Freiheit in der Unfreiheit: Die nationale Autonomie der Polen in Galizien nach dem österreichisch-ungarischen Ausgleich von 1867*. Wiesbaden: Harrassowitz, 1993.

Mayer, Sigmud, *Die Wiener Juden: Kommerz, Kultur, Politik 1700–1900*. Vienna: R. Löwit Verlag, 1918.

Malecki, Jan M., "Cracow Jews in the 19th Century: Leaving the Ghetto," *Acta Poloniae Historica* 76 (1997): 85–96.

Manekin, Rachel, "The Debate over Assimilation in Late Nineteenth-Century Lwów," in *Insiders and Outsiders: Dilemmas of East European Jewry*. London: Littman Library, 2010: 120–30.

"Orthodox Jewry in Cracow at the Turn of the Twentieth Century," (Hebrew), in Elchanan Reiner, ed., *Krako-Kaz'imyez'-Krakov: mehkarim be-toldot Yehude Krakov*. Tel Aviv: Tel-Aviv University, 2001: 155–90.

"Orthodox Jewry in Kraków at the Turn of the Twentieth Century," *Polin* 23 (2010): 165–98.

"Taking It to the Streets: Polish-Jewish Print Discourse in 1848 Lemberg," *Simon Dubnow Institute Yearbook* 7 (2008): 215–27.

"Rules for the Behavior of Jewish Teachers in the Schools of Galicia and Ludomeria" (Hebrew), *Gal Ed: On the History and Culture of Polish Jewry* 20 (2006): 113–24.

"'*Deitschn*,' 'Poles' or 'Austrians'?" (Hebrew), *Zion* 68 (2003): 223–62.

"Politics, Religion, and National Identity: The Galician Jewish Vote in the 1873 Parliamentary Elections," *Polin* 12 (1999): 100–19.

"The New Covenant: Orthodox Jews and Polish Catholics (1879–1883)" (Hebrew), *Zion* 64 (1999): 157–86.

Tzmichta v'Gibusha shel Haortodoxia HaYehudit B'Galitsia 1867–1883. Unpublished dissertation, Hebrew University, Jerusalem, 2000.

McCagg, William O. Jr., *A History of Habsburg Jewry 1670–1918.* Bloomington: Indiana University Press, 1989.

Melzer, Emanuel, "Between Politics and Spirituality: The Case of Dr Ozjasz Thon, Reform Rabbi of Kraków," *Polin* 23 (2010): 261–8.

Mendelsohn, Ezra, *Painting a People: Maurycy Gottlieb and Jewish Art.* Hanover: Brandeis University Press, 2002.

Zionism in Poland: The Formative Years, 1915–1926. New Haven, Conn.: Yale University Press, 1981.

"Jewish Assimilation in L'viv: The Case of Wilhelm Feldman," in Andrei Markovits and Frank Sysyn, eds., *Nationbuilding and the Politics of Nationalism: Essays on Austrian Galicia.* Cambridge, Mass.: Harvard University Press, 1982: 94–110.

"Wilhelm Feldman and Alfred Nossig: Assimilation and Zionism in Lvov" (Hebrew), *Gal Ed* 9 (1975): 89–111.

"From Assimilation to Zionism in Lvov: The Case of Alfred Nossig," *Slavonic and East European Review* 49 (1971): 521–34.

Meyer, Michael, "The German Model of Religious Reform and Russian Jewry," in Isadore Twersky, ed. *Danzig, between East and West: Aspects of Modern Jewish History.* Cambridge, Mass.: Harvard University Press, 1985: 67–91.

Miron, Dan, *A Traveler Disguised.* New York: Schocken Books, 1973.

Mishkinsky, Moshe, "The Attitudes of the Ukrainian Socialists to Jewish Problems in the 1870s," in Howard Aster and Peter J. Potichnyj, eds., *Ukrainian-Jewish Relations in Historical Perspective.* Alberta: Canadian Institute of Ukrainian Studies Press, 1988: 57–68.

Mosse, George, *Confronting the Nation: Jewish and Western Nationalism.* Hanover: Brandeis University Press, 1993.

Myovich, Samuel T., *Josephism at Its Boundaries: Nobles, Peasants, Priests, and Jews in Galicia, 1772–1790.* Unpublished dissertation, Indiana University, 1994.

Myslinski, Jerzy, "Issues of the socio-political press in Galicia during the years 1881–1913" (Polish), *Rocznik historii czasopiśmiennictwo polskiego* 4, no. 1 (1965): 115–33, and 4, no. 4 (1965): 80–98.

Nathans, Benjamin, *Beyond the Pale: The Jewish Encounter with Late Imperial Russia.* Berkeley: University of California Press, 2002.

Naygreshl, Mendel, "Modern Yiddish Literature in Galicia" (Yiddish), in *Fun noentn ovar.* New York: Cyco Bicher Farlag, 1955: 265–398.

Niger, Samuel, "Yiddish Literature in the Past Two Hundred Years," in *The Jewish People Past and Present*, Vol. 3. New York, 1952: 105–205.

Olson, Jess, *Nation, Peoplehood and Religion in the Life and Thought of Nathan Birnbaum.* Unpublished dissertation, Stanford University, 2006.

"A Tale of Two Photographs," in Kalman Weiser and Joshua Fogel, eds., *Czernowitz at 100*. Lanham: Rowman and Littlefield, 2010: 23–44.

Opalski, Magdalena and Israel Bartal, *Poles and Jews: A Failed Brotherhood*. Hanover: Brandeis University Press, 1992.

Orbach, Alexander, *New Voices of Russian Jewry: A Study of the Russian-Jewish Press of Odessa in the Era of the Great Reforms 1860–71*. Leiden: E. J. Brill, 1980.

Pearson, Raymond, *National Minorities in Eastern Europe 1848–1945*. London: Macmillan Press, 1983.

Piasecki, Henryk, *Sekcja Żydowska PPSD i Żydowska Partia Socjalno-Demokratyczna 1892–1919/20*. Wrocław, 1983.

"Herman Diamand w Latach 1890–1918," *Biuletyn Żydowskiego Instytutu Historycznego*, 106 (1978): 33–49.

Poppel, Stephen M., *Zionism in Germany 1897–1933: The Shaping of a Jewish Identity*. Philadelphia: Jewish Publication Society, 1977.

Porter, Brian, *When Nationalism Began to Hate: Imagining Modern Politics in Nineteenth-Century Poland*. New York: Oxford University Press, 2000.

Prokop-Janiec, Eugenia, "Jewish *Moderna* in Galicia," *Gal-Ed* 14 (1995): 27–38.

Rabin, Chaim, "The National Idea and the Revival of Hebrew," in Jehuda Reinharz and Anita Shapira, eds., *Essential Papers on Zionism*. New York: New York University Press, 1996: 745–62.

Rechter, David, "A Nationalism of Small Things: Jewish Autonomy in Late Habsburg Austria," *Leo Baeck Institute Yearbook* (2007): 87–109.

Reifowitz, Ian, *Imagining an Austrian Nation: Joseph Samuel Bloch and the Search for a Multiethnic Austrian Identity, 1846–1919*. Boulder: East European Monographs, 2003.

Reiss, Anshel, *Breishit Tenuat Hapoalim Hayehudim B'Galitsia*. Tel-Aviv: Arzi, 1973.

Rosenfeld, Gavriel, "Defining "Jewish Art" in Ost and West, 1901–1908. A Study in the Nationalisation of Jewish Culture," *Leo Baeck Institute Yearbook* 39 (1994): 83–110.

Rosenfeld, Max, "Die jüdische Bevölkerung Galiziens 1867–1910," *Zeitschrift für Demographie und Statistik der Juden* (October–November–December 1915): 96–105, and (January–February–March): 1916: 16–21.

"Die jüdische Bevölkerung Galiziens von 1772–1867," *Zeitschrift für Demographie und Statistik der Juden* (September–October 1914): 138–45.

Rosman, Moshe, *Founder of Hasidism: A Quest for the Historical Ba'al Shem Tov*. Berkeley: University of California Press, 1996.

The Lords' Jews: Magnate-Jewish Relations in the Polish-Lithuanian Commonwealth during the Eighteenth Century. Cambridge, Mass.: Harvard Ukrainian Research Institute, 1990.

Rost Hollander, Nella, *Jehoshua Thon: Preacher, Thinker, Politician*. Montevideo, Uruguay: Beit Galizia, 1966.

Rozenblit, Marsha, *Reconstructing a National Identity: The Jews of Habsburg Austria during World War I*. Studies in Jewish History. New York: Oxford University Press, 2001.

The Jews of Vienna: 1867–1914. Albany: State University of New York Press, 1983.

"The Jews of the Dual Monarchy," *Austrian History Yearbook* 23 (1992): 160–80.

"A Note on Galician Jewish Migration to Vienna," *Austrian History Yearbook* 19–20 (1983–84): 143–52.

"The Assertion of Identity: Jewish Student Nationalism at the University of Vienna before the First World War," *Leo Baeck Institute Yearbook* 27 (1982): 171–86.

Rubstein, Ben-Zion, *Galizia un ihr Bevölkerung* (Yiddish). Warsaw, 1923.

Rudnytsky, Ivan L., "Ukrainian-Jewish Relations in Nineteenth-Century Ukrainian Political Thought," in Howard Aster and Peter J. Potichnyj, eds., *Ukrainian-Jewish Relations in Historical Perspective*. Alberta: Canadian Institute of Ukrainian Studies Press, 1988: 69–83.

"The Ukrainians in Galicia Under Austrian Rule," in Andrei S. Markovits and Frank E. Sysyn, eds., *Nationbuilding and the Politics of Nationalism: Essays on Austrian Galicia*. Cambridge, Mass.: Harvard University Press, 1982: 23–67.

Salmon, Yosef, *Religion and Zionism: First Encounters*. Jerusalem: Magnes Press, 2002.

"Herzl and Orthodox Jewry," in Gideon Shimoni and Robert S. Wistrich, eds., *Theodor Herzl: Visionary of the Jewish State*. Jerusalem: Magnes Press, 1999: 294–307.

"The Book *Shivat Zion* and Its Historical Background" (Hebrew), in Avraham Slucki, *Shivat Zion*. Jerusalem: Ben-Gurion University of the Negev Press, 1998: 7–60.

"Zionism and Anti-Zionism in Traditional Judaism in Eastern Europe," in Shmuel Almog, Jehuda Reinharz, and Anita Shapira, eds., *Zionism and Religion*. Hanover: Brandeis University Press, 1998.

"The Rise of Jewish Nationalism on the Border of Eastern and Western Europe: Rabbi Z. H. Kalischer, David Gordon, Peretz Smolenskin," in Isadore Twersky, ed., *Danzig, between East and West: Aspects of Modern Jewish History*. Cambridge, Mass.: Harvard University Press, 1985.

"The Controversy over Etrogim from Corfu and Palestine, 1875–1891" (Hebrew), *Zion* 65 (1990): 75–106.

Schmidl, Erwin A., "Jews in the Habsburg Armed Forces," *Studia Judaica Austriaca* 11 (1989): 95–151.

Schoeps, Julius H., "Modern Heirs of the Maccabees – The Beginnings of the Vienna Kadimah, 1882–1897," *Leo Baeck Institute Yearbook* 27 (1982): 155–70.

Shanes, Joshua, "National Regeneration in the Ghetto: The Jewish *Turnbewegung* in Galicia," in Jack Kugelmass, ed., *Jews, Sports, and the Rites of Citizenship*. Urbana: University of Illinois, 2007: 75–94.

"Ahron Marcus: Portrait of a Zionist Hasid," *Jewish Social Studies* 16, no. 3 (Spring/Summer, 2010): 116–61.

"An Unlikely Alliance: The 1907 Ukrainian-Jewish Electoral Coalition," *Nations and Nationalism* 15, no. 3 (2009): 483–505.

"The Transformation of Zionist Religious Rhetoric as Seen through Its Yiddish-Language Propaganda: The Case of Galicia," *Studies in Jewish Civilization* 16 (2005): 285–96.

"Fort mit den Hausjuden!" Jewish Nationalists Engage Mass Politics," in Michael Berkowitz, ed., *Nationalism, Zionism and Ethnic Mobilization of the Jews in 1900 and Beyond* (Brill, 2004): 153–78.

"Neither Germans nor Poles: Jewish Nationalism in Galicia before Herzl, 1883–1897," *Austrian History Yearbook* 34 (2003): 191–213.

"Papers for the "Folk": Jewish Nationalism and the Birth of the Yiddish Press in Galicia," *Polin* 16 (2003): 167–87.

Shedel, James, "Austria and Its Polish Subjects, 1866–1914: A Relationship of Interests," *Austrian History Yearbook*, 19–20, Part 2 (1983–84): 23–42.

Sherman, C., "Bund, Galuth Nationalism, Yiddishism," *Herzl Institute Pamphlet*, No. 6. New York, 1958.

Shimoni, Gideon, *The Zionist Ideology.* Hanover: Brandeis University Press, 1995.

Shumsky, Dimitry and Yfaat Weiss, "Jews in a Multi-Ethnic Network: Introduction," in *Jahrbuch des Simon-Dubnow-Instituts* 5 (2006): 101–15.

"On Ethno-Centrism and Its Limits," in *Jahrbuch des Simon-Dubnow-Instituts* 5 (2006): 173–88.

Silber, Michael, "From Tolerated Aliens to Citizen-Soliders: Jewish Military Service in the Era of Joseph II," in Pieter Judson and Marsha Rozenblit, eds., *Constructing Nationalities in East Central Europe.* New York: Berghahn Books, 2005: 19–36.

"The Beating Jewish Heart in a Foreign Land" (Hebrew), *Cathedra* (1995): 84–105.

Sinkoff, Nancy, *Out of the Shtetl: Making Jews Modern in the Polish Borderlands.* Providence: Brown University Press, 2004.

"Strategy and Ruse in the Haskalah of Mendel Lefin of Satanow," in Shmuel Feiner and David Sorkin, eds. *New Perspectives on the Haskalah.* London: Littman Library, 2001: 86–102.

Sirka, Ann, *The Nationality Question in Austrian Education: The Case of Ukrainians in Galicia 1867–1914.* European University Studies, Publications, Series 3, History and Allied Sciences, 12. Frankfurt-am-Main: Peter D. Lang, 1980.

Smith, Anthony, *The Nation in History: Historiographical Debates about Ethnicity and Nationalism.* Hanover: Brandeis University Press, 2000.

Myths and Memories of the Nation. Oxford: Oxford University Press, 1999.

Nationalism and Modernism: A Critical Survey of Recent Theories of Nations and Nationalism. London: Routledge, 1998.

The Ethnic Origins of Nations. Oxford: Blackwell, 1986.

"The 'Golden Age' and National Renewal," in Geoffrey Hosking and George Schöpflin, eds., *Myths and Nationhood.* New York: Routledge, 1997: 36–59.

"Nationalism and the Historians." Reprinted in Gopal Balakrishnan, ed., *Mapping the Nation.* London: Verso, 1996.

"Zionism and Diaspora Nationalism," *Israel Affairs* 2, no. 2 (Winter 1995): 1–19.

"The Question of Jewish Identity," *Studies in Contemporary Jewry* 8 (1992): 219–33.

Snyder, Timothy, "Kazimierz Kelles-Krauz, 1872–1905: A Polish Socialist for Jewish Nationality," *Nations and Nationalism* 3, no. 2 (1997): 201–29.

Sorkin, David, *The Transformation of German Jewry, 1780–1840.* New York: Oxford University Press, 1987.

"The Impact of Emancipation on German Jewry: A Reconsideration," in Jonathan Frankel and Steven Zipperstein, eds., *Assimilation and Community: The Jews in Nineteenth-Century Europe.* Cambridge: Cambridge University Press, 1992.

"Port Jews and the Three Regions of Emancipation," *Jewish Culture and History* 4, no. 2 (Winter 2001): 31–46.

Sroka, Łukasz Tomasz, "Changes in the Jewish Community of Kraków in Autonomous Galicia," *Polin* 23 (2010): 73–4.

Stanislawski, Michael, *A Murder in Lemberg: Politics, Religion, and Violence in Modern Jewish History.* Princeton: Princeton University Press, 2007.

Zionism and the Fin de Siècle: Cosmopolitanism and Nationalism from Nordau to Jabotinsky. Berkeley: University of California Press, 2001.

"Haskalah and Zionism: A Reexamination," in Ruth Kozodoy, David Sidorsky, and Kalman Sultanik, eds., *Vision Confronts Reality.* New York: Herzl Press, 1989.

Stauter-Halsted, Keely, *The Nation in the Village: The Genesis of Peasant National Identity in Austrian Poland, 1848–1914.* Ithaca: Cornell University Press, 2001.

"Jews as Middleman Minorities in Rural Poland: Understanding the Galician Pogroms of 1898," in Robert Blobaum, ed., *Antisemitism and Its Opponents in Modern Poland.* Ithaca: Cornell University Press, 2005: 39–59.

Stein, Shimshon, *Machanayim.* Jerusalem: Achva, 1978.

Stillschweig, Kurt, "Nationalism and Autonomism among East European Jewry," *Historica Judaica,* 6 (1944): 27–68.

"Die nationalitätenrechtliche Stellung der Juden im alten Österreich," *Monatsschrift für Geschichte und Wissenschaft des Judentums* 81 (July–August 1937): 321–40.

Stöger, Michael, *Darstellung der gesetzlichen Verfassung der galizischen Judenschaft.* Lemberg: Kuhn u. Millikowski, 1833.

Stone, Daniel, "Knowledge of Foreign Languages among Eighteenth-Century Polish Jews," *Polin* 10 (1997): 200–18.

Stourzh, Gerald, *From Vienna to Chicago and Back.* Chicago: University of Chicago Press, 2007.

Die Gleichberechtigung der Nationalitäten in der Verfassung und Verwaltung Österreichs 1848–1918. Vienna: Verlag der Österreichischen Akademie der Wissenschaften, 1985.

"Galten die Juden als Nationalität Altösterreichs?" *Studia Judaica Austriaca* 10 (1984): 73–98.

Struve, Kai, *Bauern und Nation in Galizien: über Zugehörigkeit und soziale Emanzipation im 19. Jahrhundert.* Göttingen: Vandenhoeck and Ruprecht, 2005.

"Gentry, Jews, and Peasants: Jews as Others in the Formation of the Modern Polish Nation in Rural Galicia during the Second Half of the Nineteenth Century," in Nancy Wingfield, ed., *Creating the Other: Ethnic Conflict and Nationalism in Habsburg Central Europe*. New York: Berghahn, 2003.

Szabo, Franz A. J., "Austrian First Impressions of Ethnic Relations in Galicia: The Case of Governor Anton von Pergen," *Polin* 12 (1999): 49–60.

Taylor, A.J.P., *The Habsburg Monarchy 1809–1918*. Reprinted New York: Harper and Row, 1965.

Tokarski, Sławomir, *Ethnic Conflict and Economic Development: Jews in Galician Agriculture 1868–1914*. Warsaw: Wydanwnictwo TRIO, 2003.

Toury, Jacob, *Die Jüdische Presse im Österreichischen Kaiserreich*. Tübingen: Mohr, 1983.

"Josef Samuel Bloch und die jüdische Identität im österreichischen Kaiserreich," in Walter Grab, ed., *Jüdische Integration und Identität in Deutschland und Österreich 1848–1918*. Tel-Aviv: Tel-Aviv University, 1984: 41–64.

"Troubled Beginnings: The Emergence of the Österreichisch-Israelitische Union," *Leo Baeck Institute Yearbook* 30 (1985): 457–75.

"Jewish Townships in the German-Speaking Parts of the Austrian Empire – Before and After the Revolution of 1848/1849," *Leo Baeck Institute Yearbook* 26 (1981): 55–72.

"Herzl's Newspaper: The Creation of *Die Welt*," *Zionism* 1, no. 2 (Autumn 1980): 159–72.

Unger, Shabtai, *Po`ale-Tsiyon ba-kesarut ha-Ostrit, 1904–1914*. Tel-Aviv: Ben-Gurion Research Center, 2001.

The Zionist Labour Movement in Galicia from Its Beginning to the Year 1908 (Hebrew). Unpublished master's thesis, Tel-Aviv University, 1976.

Unowsky, Daniel, *The Pomp and Politics of Patriotism: Imperial Celebrations in Habsburg Austria, 1848–1916*. West Lafayette, Ind.: Purdue University Press, 2005.

"Peasant Political Mobilization and the 1898 Anti-Jewish Riots in Western Galicia," *European History Quarterly* (July 2010): 412–35.

Vital, David, *Zionism: The Formative Years*. Oxford: Clarendon Press, 1982.

The Origins of Zionism. Oxford: Clarendon Press, 1975.

"Nationalism, Political Action, and the Hostile Environment," in Jehuda Reinharz, ed. *Living with Antisemitism*. Hanover: Brandeis University Press, 1987.

Walz, Stefan, *Staat, Nationalität und jüdische Identität in Österreich vom 18. Jahrhundert bis 1914*. Frankfurt: Peter Lang, 1996.

Wandycz, Piotr, *The Lands of Partitioned Poland 1795–1918*. Seattle: University of Washington Press, 1974.

Wigoder, Geoffrey, ed., *New Encyclopedia of Zionism and Israel*. New York: Herzl Press, 1994.

Wingfield, Nancy, ed., *Creating the Other: Ethnic Conflict and Nationalism in Habsburg Central Europe*. New York: Berghahn, 2003.

Wistrich, Robert S., *The Jews of Vienna in the Age of Franz Joseph*. Oxford: Oxford University Press, 1989.

Socialism and the Jews: The Dilemmas of Assimilation in Germany and Austria-Hungary. London: Associated University Presses, 1982.

"The Clash of Ideologies in Jewish Vienna (1880–1918). The Strange Odyssey of Nathan Birnbaum," *Leo Baeck Institute Yearbook* 33 (1988): 201–30.

"Austrian Social Democracy and the Problem of Galician Jewry 1890–1914," *Leo Baeck Institute Yearbook* 26 (1981): 89–124.

Marcin Wodzinski, *Haskalah, Hasidism in the Kingdom of Poland: A History of Conflict.* London: Littman Library, 2005.

Wolff, Larry, *The Idea of Galicia: History and Fantasy in Habsburg Political Culture.* Stanford: Stanford University Press, 2010.

Wrobel, Piotr, "The Jews of Galicia under Austrian-Polish Rule 1869–1918," *Austrian History Yearbook* 25 (1994): 97–138.

Wunder, Meir, *Meorei Galitsye: Encyclopedia L'Chachmei Galitsye.* Jerusalem, 1978.

Zahra, Tara, *Kidnapped Souls: National Indifference and the Battle for Children in the Bohemian Lands, 1900–1948.* Ithaca: Cornell University Press, 2008.

Żbikowski, Andrzej, "The Impact of New Ideologies: The Transformation of Kraków Jewry between 1895 and 1914," *Polin* 23 (2010): 135–63.

Index